THE ARROW Scrapbook

REBUILDING A DREAM AND A NATION

Peter Zuuring

Arrow Alliance PRESS

Dalkeith, Ontario - 1999

June 23/99

Hello Jim

It's has been a long journey but all is finally happening. Thank for your confidence.

[signature]

The Arrow Scrapbook
Rebuilding a Dream and a Nation

Canadian Cataloging in Publication Data

ISBN 1-55056-690-3

Main entry under title:

The Arrow Scrapbook:
Rebuilding a Dream and a Nation

      Includes index.
      ISBN 1-55056-690-3
      1. Arrow...Aviation
      2. Rebuilding...History, Canada

First Printing, May 1999

Design by Peter Zuuring & Jozef VanVeenen
Typesetting and Layout by Jozef VanVeenen
Cover Design - Jozef VanVeenen
Photo Editing/Retouching - Jozef VanVeenen
Editing - Dane Lanken
Printed and Bound in Canada by Friesens

The Arrow Alliance has strived to ensure content accuracy and validity. All photo and document credits have been verified. In many instances photos and/or documents were only provided and not taken or produced by the accredited individual or institution. Given the size, breadth and sheer volume of material presented, should the reader discover any inadvertent errors and/or omissions, please contact The Arrow Alliance with corrections so that subsequent printings can be updated.

Contact Us

Phone/Fax: (613) 874-2838

E-mail: director@arrow-alliance.com

Website: www.arrow-alliance.com

Address: 21570, The Laggan Road

R.R. #1, Dalkeith, Ontario K0B 1E0

Dedication

In honour of the men and women
who put their energy, creativity and trust
into a major national defence project.
The Arrow was meant to protect
us from an enemy outside
our borders, yet was destroyed
by our friends within.

25201

RL 201

The Arrow Scrapbook

Contents

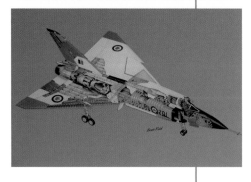

Preface

Paul Hellyer

A Day to Remember

Hellyer Says Whole Industry *Arrow* Placed In Peril

FEB 23 1959

Opposition Begins Attack Over Cancellation of Arrow

OTTAWA, Feb. 23—*Canadian Press* The Commons today embarked on an emergency debate on what Paul Hellyer, former associate defence minister, called a "crisis" in the Canadian aircraft industry.

Prime Minister Diefenbaker, replying to Mr. Hellyer's demand for such a debate, said the Government "welcomes the fullest discussion of the matter today."

The debate came on the heels of the Government's announcement Friday of the cancellation of the Arrow jet interceptor program, and the action of A. V. Roe (Canada) Limited in laying off some 14,000 workers in its two subsidiaries at Malton, Ont., Avro Aircraft Limited and Orenda Engines Limited.

Liberal's Charge

Mr. Hellyer, Liberal MP for Toronto Trinity, in presenting a motion calling for suspension of the day's normal business to permit the debate, said the crisis in the aircraft industry was "caused by delay and confusion" in Government defence policy...

At the request of Speaker Roland Michener, he deleted the phrase referring to "delay and confusion." Mr. Michener said it might lead to too wide a debate.

His motion said the crisis threatened "the disintegration of this important sector of our national economy."

After Speaker Michener indicated he was prepared to agree to the emergency debate, Prime Minister Diefenbaker said the opportunity for debate "will be welcome on the part of my colleagues and myself."

"After all, none of us has any monopoly on our feelings to our fellow men," Mr. Diefenbaker said.

Mr. Hellyer, opening the debate, recalled that just 50 years ago today the first flight of a heavier-than-air aircraft was made in Canada—the Silver Dart at Baddeck, N.S.

Montreal Star, Feb. 23, 1959
Courtesy, Montreal Gazette.

"It should be a day of applause; it should be a day when Canada could sing her gratitude for the growth and development which has taken place in the last 50 years. The sun rose in the East 50 years ago for the Canadian aircraft industry. But it went down Friday."

Paul Hellyer, in the Parliament of Canada, February 22, 1959, commenting on the fiftieth anniversary of flight in Canada and the death of the Avro Arrow

Peter Zuuring,
Author

"Knowledge Grows Like a Tree"

University
of Toronto slogan

Foreword
The Arrow is addictive

*W*hen you get involved with the Arrow, start to dig into its saga, you get frustrated, disturbed and intrigued. You just cannot get it out of your mind. You wonder, how could this have happened? How could a whole industry just evaporate overnight? How could Canada's military give up the fastest jet in the world? How could a government and a prestigious aircraft company get to such a sorry state that a major industrial venture vanished and the lives of thousands of working Canadians were turned upside down?

The simple truth is that the technology and physical assets of the Arrow program belonged to the Canadian government. It had the power to do what it wanted with them, and it did. After Black Friday, when the Arrow program was cancelled, the physical pieces were destroyed or scattered to other government agencies, scrap yards — or the basements (via pockets and lunch pails) of unhappy former employees. By the fall of 1959, all vestiges of an innovative decade had been destroyed.

Why did this happen? How did it happen? Who was responsible?

Some answers have been provided. Authors Palmira Campagna and Greig Stewart pointed to players who had major roles in shaping and executing the policy of the day. But details on these roles are still being unearthed today as new documents are declassified. From a technological point of view, the book *Arrow* covers the conception, development, construction and destruction of the aircraft. I was completely fascinated by the story, actually sat in a Tim Horton's for three hours taking in every page and photo. But still I wanted more! The CBC television mini-series, *Shutting Down the National Dream: The Avro Arrow Story*, attracted a record two and a half million viewers, acquainted some with the whole tragic saga, rekindled the interest of many others.

So, what has been learned?

Could we prevent an episode like this from happening again? What could be done today to bring closure to these bad memories and, at the same time, provide an opportunity and a lesson for renewal? I have an idea for an exciting national project that I explore in the latter part of this book. If the idea interests you, please let me have your comments and suggestions.

In preparing this manuscript, I spoke to many former Avro/Orenda employees and all ranks of RCAF personnel. I spent more than fourteen months in the archives of the National Aviation Museum, the National Research Council, the Department of Defence Directorate of Heritage and History, the National Archives, the Defence Department Photo Unit and the basements of many Arrow enthusiasts. I looked at hundreds of documents, drawings and reports. I read reams of correspondence. Still, the opinions and conclusions I have drawn are my own. I hope I have provided a credible, meaningful and entertaining work.

Peter F. Zuuring
Dalkeith, Ontario
April 1999

Arrow art: looking into the afterburner of an Iroquois Mk II

Photo: Peter Zuuring

1038CN-180(CAS)

MEMORANDUM

13 Mar 59

MAR 13 1959

File: 1038CN-

The Minister

Arrow Cancellation - Disposal of Materiel

1   The termination proceedings for the Arrow Weapon System contract, as a result of the Government's decision to cancel the project, will involve the disposal of a considerable amount of materiel. The major items on which disposal decisions are required are:

    (a) 5 Arrow Mk 1 aircraft with their 19 Pratt and Whitney J75 engines.

    (b) 3 Arrow Mk 2 airframes and 10 Iroquois engines. These items are in various stages of assembly since the first complete Arrow/Iroquois aircraft was not scheduled to fly until early May;

    (c) 2 Hughes MA-1 electronic systems.

2   The 5 Arrow 1 aircraft are strictly development prototypes that have flown only 65 hours total. It has been estimated that 1000 flying hours are required to clear these aeroplanes for airworthiness and reliability. Consequently, there is considerable development left to be done before they could be used by the RCAF. We have explored the possible use of these aircraft by the National Aeronautical Establishment as research vehicles. However since spare parts are in short supply, the aircraft would have to be maintained by AVRO at Malton. Considering the development left to be done, the difficulties in supporting the aircraft and the cost of doing the research flying from AVRO, it has been concluded that this approach is not practical. In summary, then, it can be said that there is no use in the RCAF or NAE for these aircraft.

DIRECTOR ... CANCELLED

.../2

3   The Mark 2 airframes and the Iroquois engines have not reached the stage in production, assembly or test where they could be put together and flown as proven vehicles in any reasonable time. Consequently, these are nothing more than components of an unfinished project. The MA-1 electronic system is at least two months away from a prototype installation in a Mark 1 aircraft. Thus, this system is in the category of unassembled components.

4   Since there is no practical use for the Arrow or its major components, the RCAF intends with your approval to:

    (a) negotiate with the USAF for the return of the 19 J75 engines (original cost: $6.9M) and the 2 MA-1 electronic systems (original cost: $1.7M);

    (b) make the necessary arrangements to dispose of the Arrow airframes and Iroquois engines.

(Hugh Campbell)
Air Marshal
Chief of the Air Staff

I concur in H.(a) but would wish to be informed of the proposed method of disposal of the airframes + engines in 4(b) before final action is taken

George Pearkes

MAR 18 1959

Hugh Campbell, Chief of the Air Staff, recommends disposing of the Arrows.

Per ardua ad astra

"Through Adversity to the Stars"
-slogan of the RCAF (inherited from the RAF)

O n August 25, 1958, the Canadian military's chiefs of staff and its chairman, General Charles Foulkes, unofficially cancelled the CF-105 Arrow program. A further six months was to pass before the Right Honourable John G. Diefenbaker, Prime Minister of Canada, stood up in the House of Commons and did it officially. Ironically, on that day, February 20, 1959, J.L. Plant, president and general manager of Avro Aircraft Limited, received a letter from Air Commodore G. G. Truscott stating that "we are finally getting communications in line."

About three weeks later, chief of the air staff, Air Marshal Hugh Campbell, concluded that there was no practical use for the Arrow or its major components. He suggested to George Pearkes, Minister of Defence, that the RCAF negotiate with the United States Air Force for the return of nineteen J-75 engines and electronic instruments, and that the necessary arrangements be made to dispose of the Arrow airframes and Iroquois engines.

By May 12, 1959, all tooling, jigs, parts-in-process and four Mk II Arrows in various states of completion were being reduced to scrap by Avro under the watchful eyes of the Department of Defence Production. Four operational Mk I Arrows were on hold pending a possible deal with the United Kingdom. A fifth Mk I Arrow, RL-202, had not been repaired after its November 7, 1958 accident. An aerial photo taken by Russell on May 8, 1959, clearly shows the stricken Arrow at the Avro plant in Malton, Ontario, with nose assembly, access panels, flight-control surfaces and control boxes removed. After inquiries by Britain's Royal Aeronautical Establishment for the use of the Mk I fell by the wayside, the remaining Mk I Arrows were put to the torch. A scrap yard at Ancaster, Ontario, was busy

from May 15 to July 17, 1959, working under cover, hurriedly, until the deed was irrevocably done.

The Orenda Iroquois engines' fate was more protracted. Neither the loan of an operational engine and expertise to the British Bristol-Siddeley nor a U.S. Curtis-Wright licensing deal did anything to stave off the demise of this exceptional product. The Department of Defence Production passed the engines and parts to the Crown Assets Disposal Corporation on November 30, 1960. Rumour has it that a scrap dealer in Buffalo, New York, bought the lot after the engines had been rendered inoperable. But the trail stops dead and the mystery of who really bought the engines remains.

Air Marshal Hugh Campbell at the Avro CF-105 rollout ceremonies. What a change of heart just a year and a half can bring!

Avro Newsletter, Spring 1958

Foulkes' Testimony
Liberals Planned To Cancel Arrow

OTTAWA — Gen. Charles Foulkes, chairman of the chiefs of staff committee from 1951 to 1960, testified yesterday that the Liberal Government of Prime Minister St. Laurent decided in 1957 it would cancel the Arrow interceptor program as soon as it was returned to power in that year's election.

As it turned out, a Conservative Government under Prime Minister Diefenbaker was elected and the "unfortunate" Defence Minister George Pearkes was faced with the awkward decision.

Gen. Foulkes told the Commons defence committee that in the summer of 1957 the chiefs of staff "stampeded" the new Government into the NORAD agreement with the United States.

The Government had run into trouble with the NORAD agreement in the Commons and as a result it was hesitant about making early decisions on the Arrow and the CF-104 low-level jet bomber program.

The Arrow was finally cancelled in February, 1959.

Gen. Foulkes said the chiefs concluded it didn't make sense to produce an $8,000,000 interceptor in Canada when one could be obtained in the U.S. for $2,000,000. They couldn't see where the money would come from.

He said the decision to proceed with the CF-104 program was delayed more than two years because of the delay in the decision of the Arrow.

Gen. Foulkes said the first loyalty of a chief of staff is to his service. This loyalty often came in conflict with a viable defence policy.

"But you can't expect the chiefs to cut their own throats," he said. Decisions on defence policy must be imposed by Government.

GEN. FOULKES

Gen. Foulkes confirmed the 1959 statement of Mr. Diefenbaker that the chiefs of staff had recommended cancellation of the Arrow.

Montreal Star, Oct. 23, 1963
Courtesy, *Montreal Gazette*

It never ceases to amaze me that a project of this magnitude, started in 1953 and worked on diligently by thousands of people for six years, could be so utterly destroyed by a handful of determined officials in a matter of days. Wrecking is always easier than building! Still, nothing should be taken away from the creativity, ingenuity, perseverance and skill of the people that made up A.V. Roe Canada Limited. The organizational strength and foresight of its management made it Canada's third largest corporation in just twelve years and produced incredible leading-edge products.

Photo: Nam, Molson collection

Herb Nott's celebrated 1959 aerial photo, above, is eclipsed by Russell's photo to the right showing 202 being dismantled. I believe this to be the start of the Mk I series cut-up.

Photo: May 8, 1959 Russel, Fednews.

The Arrow Scrapbook - *Per ardua ad astra*

Then and Now
The Arrow faced adversity and became a fallen star

Important pieces of the Arrow program are still with us!

Arrow wind tunnel model, mounted on a sting, testing for pitch-up. Part of the extensive testing Avro undertook to ensure a functional and safe interceptor.

Photo, P. Brennan

Taxi trials are progressing. Another successful day for Jan Zurakowski. The Arrow was starting to show promise, beauty and power.

Photo, P. Brennan

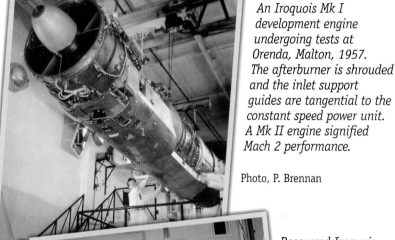

An Iroquois Mk I development engine undergoing tests at Orenda, Malton, 1957. The afterburner is shrouded and the inlet support guides are tangential to the constant speed power unit. A Mk II engine signified Mach 2 performance.

Photo, P. Brennan

Same wind tunnel model in an Etobicoke basement today.

Photo, Peter Zuuring

Recovered intact air conditioning unit found behind and under the observer's seat in RL-206. Now at the National Aviation Museum, Ottawa.

Photo, Peter Zuuring

Recovered Iroquois development engine from the Hamilton War Plane Heritage Museum. The engine is being received by National Research Council personnel who have agreed to refurbish the motor on their own time. The afterburner will be discovered later in a Hamilton airport dump.

Photo, Peter Zuuring

The Arrow Scrapbook

It all started...

Avro's plant at Malton.
Looking South-West
from Airport Road and
Derry Road West.
The lancaster test-bed,
Jetliner and first
CF-100 prototypes
are visible.

Photo, P. Brennan

Chapter Two

Back in the 'fifties

"Nobody told us we couldn't do it!" Jim Floyd, speaking about his days at Avro.

Even though the CF-100 problems were resolved with time, lingering seeds of doubt were sown with respect to engineering design, manufacturing & program management.

By the early 1950s, A.V. Roe Canada Limited had several successes behind it. The first North American passenger Jetliner had flown, and the pre-production models of the first all-weather subsonic fighter-interceptor, the CF-100 Canuck, were complete. Full production was being sorted out, although not without some major problems. The management team that was to oversee the Arrow program was in place, while government work provided an ever-increasing cash surplus.

Even before the CF-100 was proven and in service, a supersonic replacement was being discussed to meet the ever-changing Soviet threat. Avro, as a forward-thinking company, would not lose the opportunity to make its interests known. In 1951, it submitted a brochure detailing three possible solutions. The Royal Canadian Air Force responded in 1952 with a requirements document that led to Avro winning a design-study contract the following year.

While these "blue sky" discussions were going on, disturbing events were unfolding for the military and the company. CF-100 design flaws and production delays occupied the minds of the RCAF and its political masters. The outbreak of the Korean War did not make things any easier. The Jetliner was sitting unsold because of war production restrictions in the United States, while in Canada an unimaginative Trans-Canada Airlines and a preoccupied military bought foreign equipment (the Viscount and the ill-fated Comet both from the United Kingdom). C.D. Howe, the federal "Minister of Everything," told Avro that as long as the government was paying the bills, fixing the CF-100 was the first priority and forget about anything else. In one stroke, any potential commercial airline business was left in the dust.

It took thousands of engineering changes over two years, from June 1950 when the first production orders were given, to July 1952 for the first CF-100 (#18108) to be delivered to the RCAF. Returned aircraft in the interval had suffered from bent wings, popped rivets and shoddy workmanship. Cockpit pressurization problems may have caused the first Canuck crash on April 5, 1951, which killed both pilot and observer. Understandably, the company cancelled its plan to show the CF-100 at the Farnborough air show that year.

In the House of Commons, politicians berated Howe by saying that the CF-100 project, if not a fiasco, was at least an excessively costly experiment ($100 million to date). It was so behind schedule that there was real danger of obsolescence before delivery – something like the "being taken over by events" that the company would hear in years to come. Even though the CF-100 problems were resolved with time, lingering seeds of doubt were sown with respect to the company's engineering, design, manufacturing and program management.

CF-100 over Malton, looking North, with the Avro plant in view.

Photo, P. Brennan

"It flew through the air with the greatest of ease..."

- Paul Hellyer speaking about the Arrow after cancellation

The Arrow is born

A.V. Roe Canada Limited was presented in the mid-1950s with the gigantic task of building a new supersonic interceptor aircraft and a new engine at the same time. This was not the usual marginal improvement over existing systems, but the creation of an airframe and an engine that were to operate at twice the speed of existing models. The many problems in engineering design, manufacturing technology, manpower, flight testing, finance and the delicate job of maintaining relations with a single client, the government of Canada, were challenges faced on a daily basis.

The critical specifications: pull a 2-G turn at 50,000 feet doing Mach 1.5 while maintaining speed and altitude.

Excerpt: Arrow Mk II specification brochure.

Basic design parameters of the CF-105, issued by the RCAF, yet conceived with Avro's help.

National Archives

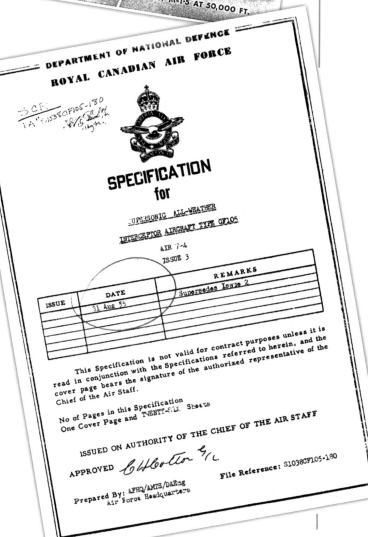

The often-seen photo of the Arrow design team. Many man-years of experience gave confidence the the job could be done.

Clipping, Avro Newsmagazine, special issue Spring 1958.

*RCAF Group Captain
Ray Foottit acknowledges that
the CF-105 looks like the
USAF's F-102.*

Letter, National Archives

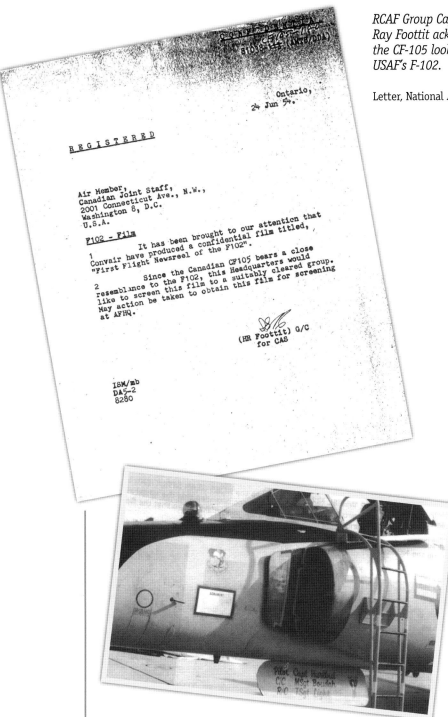

*Ken Barnes holding the
original master area rule
model used to streamline
the Arrow's design.*

Photo, Peter Zuuring

In all engineering aspects, the aircraft was technically noteworthy both for the time of its design in Canada and for the considerable advancements made in the fields of aerodynamics, aeroelasticity, structures, systems, avionics and armaments, to name a few. The delta wing design was a compromise between performance, stiffness, fuel capacity and fire-control stability. Extensive "area rule" calculations to reduce supersonic drag were carried out. New manufacturing techniques were implemented and new materials refined. Structural calculations were simulated using stress matrix calculations supported by empirical testing. The use of computers to reduce the tedious arithmetic calculations was extensive and new for the time.

The air forces of Britain and the U.S. shared information freely with the RCAF. Key suppliers also helped in informing and putting into practice data, techniques and applications which made it seem that Avro was indeed working on the cutting edge – some would say ahead of its time.

Ken Barnes was a senior designer working with Jim Chamberlin, Avro's chief aerodynamicist. He recalls how, on one of Sir Roy Dobson's visits, he was asked to take one of the swept wing proposal drawings, resketch it as a delta, skip lunch, and make it look original.

*USAF F-102. Note air intakes, supersonic
shock wave initiator, boundary layer
diverter and V-shaped canopy.*

Photo, Revell model handbook.

The CF-105 Arrow

14

Cutaway
drawing of the
MK I Arrow
in *Flight*
magazine,
October 1957

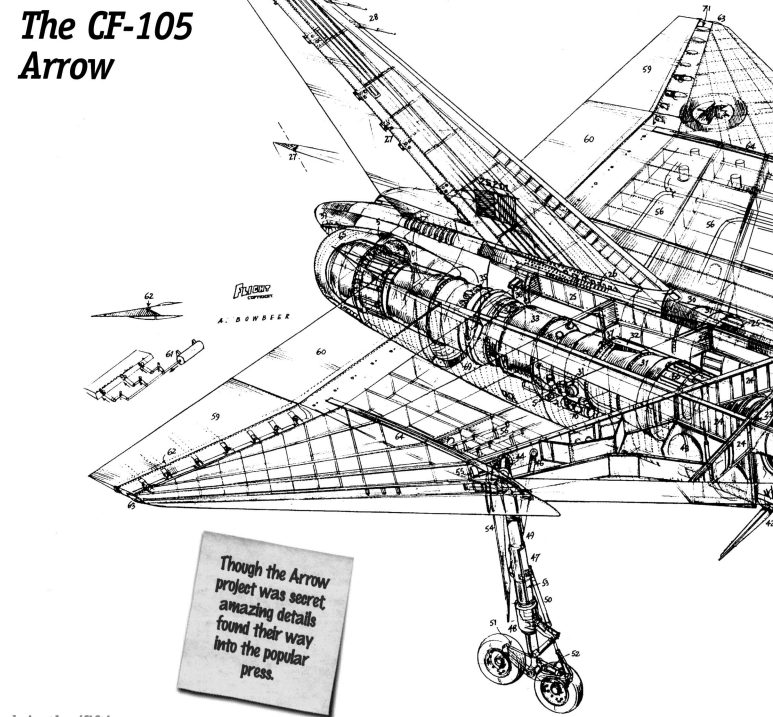

(1) Dielectric nose-cap
(2) Scanner mountings
(3) Ice-detection unit
(4) Electronics bay doors
(5) Production break-lines
(6) Cockpit floor line
(7) Martin-Baker Mk 4 seats
(8) Tempered glass 1in thick
(9) Forged magnesium canopies
(10) Radar scope viewing hood
(11) Boundary-layer bleed air
(12) Perforated intake wedge
(13) Tie-bar stabilizers
(14) Nose undercarriage leg door
(15) Door over nosewheel bay
(16) Landing and taxi lamps
(17) Steering cylinder
(18) Scissor link (diagrammatic)

(19) Air-conditioning discharge
(20) Frames assembled on ducting
(21) Weapons bay bracing tubes
(22) Integral fuel tank
(23) Wing/centre fuselage joint
(24) Forged and machined spars
(25) Wing central torsion box
(26) Multiple fin anchorages
(27) Rudder hinges on starboard side
(28) Dual pressure heads
(29) Dielectric fin tip
(30) Dielectric spine skinning
(31) Blow-off valve through shroud
(32) Saddle oil tank under shroud
(33) Engine combustion section
(34) Engine turbine section
(35) Afterburner fuel gallery
(36) Nozzle actuators

Though the Arrow project was secret, amazing details found their way into the popular press.

AVRO CF-105 ARROW Mk 1 (Two Pratt and Whitney J75 turbojets with afterburners)

Basic data: Span, 50ft; overall length, 77ft 9.65in without nose probe, approximately 83ft 2in with probe; height on ground (mean values, dependent upon loading), 21ft 3in to tip of fin, 14ft 6in to top of pilot's canopy; main undercarriage track, 25ft 5.66in; wheelbase, 30ft 1in. Estimated areas: gross wing area, 1,550 sq ft; net wing area, 1,085 sq ft; elevators, 146 sq ft; ailerons, 88 sq ft; fin, 145 sq ft; rudder, 48 sq ft. Gross weight, over 65,000 lb. **Performance** (estimated): Design Mach number, more than 2. (A clue to this value is provided by the intake design. Each of the vertical intake wedges appears to have an included angle of some 11 deg, while the Mach line back to the intake lip, upon which the inclined shock may be expected to be focused, has an angle of 35 deg. When these angles are inserted in standard curves the resulting free-stream Mach number for a perfect gas works out to 2.35. At the tropopause Mach 2.35 is approximately 1,555 m.p.h.) The service ceiling may be expected to be at least 70,000ft; a figure of "13 miles" has been mentioned. This height should be reached in little more than four minutes. The Arrow is designed to operate from existing R.C.A.F. airfields.

Engine data: Pratt and Whitney J75. Two-spool (split-compressor) turbojet, the compressor having nine low-pressure stages and seven high-pressure stages, respectively driven by two-stage and single-stage turbines. There are multiple annular flame tubes in a common combustion space. The accessories are grouped under the compressor and the saddle-type oil tank, housing some 8 U.S. gal, is mounted on top. The afterburner has multiple spray bars and flame-holders, and the propulsive nozzle is of variable area, there being 12 individually operated segments in the Arrow unit. Installation diameter, about 58in; basic diameter, about 45in; overall length, about 290in; dry weight, about 7,000lb; mass flow, about 250 lb/sec; pressure ratio, 12.5:1; maximum rating, 16,500 lb dry, or 24,000 lb with reheat.

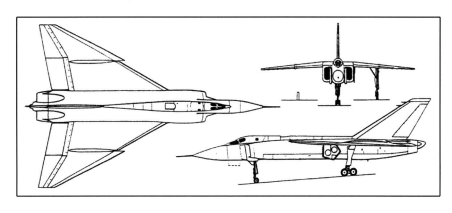

Drawing, Avro Arrow MK I brochure, 1957

Understandably, such disclosures would bother the RCAF more and more.

(37) Engine front mounting
(38) Engine rear mounting
(39) Braking parachute box
(40) Weapons bay limits
(41) Armament-pack hinges
(42) Air brakes (2)
(43) Wheel-well door
(44) Skewed hinge
(45) Back-stay
(46) Telescopic side-stay
(47) "Liquid Spring" units
(48) Sliding lower leg
(49) Ultra-high-strength steel
(50) Collapsible tie (see p. 652)
(51) Anti-pitch brake links
(52) Shock-absorber recuperator
(53) Rigid brake piping
(54) Leg doors parallel to hinge

(55) Main retraction jack
(56) Integral fuel tanks
(57) Machined skin panels
(58) Conical camber and "dog-tooth"
(59) Ailerons
(60) Elevators
(61) Schematic control system
(62) Full-span piano hinge
(63) Navigation lights
(64) Fairing over wing-break
(65) Titanium skinning
(66) Floating duct
(67) Duct rises over weapons bay
(68) Wedge contains air outlets
(69) Ovality of frames for (70)
(70) Powerplant accessories
(71) Upper linkage fairings
(72) "Saw-cut" channel

Detailed mock-ups were built to show the RCAF Arrow Mk I and Mk II concepts before committing to hard tooling.

Equipment and armament layout of the Arrow.

AVIONICS
ARMAMENT
EQUIPMENT
FUEL
ENGINE

Schematic on the left shows placement of main systems.

The Arrow Mk I wooden mock-up is being converted to a MK II type. Note the Iroquois engine mock-up and entry gantry in place. The port wing is suspended by a wire from the ceiling. Dorsal farings and weapons pack have been removed.

The large pipe on top carried engine bleed air to the heat exchanger unit behind the observer's cockpit.

Photo, L. Wilkinson

Some of the differences between the Mk I and Mk II Arrows, as listed at an Avro engineering conference in September 1957.

(extract) Arrow Mk II Engineering Conference at Avro, Sept. 1957

NRC Parkin Library

1. Installation of the Astra I integrated elctronics system

2. Fitting of the Sparrow 2D missiles

3. The replacement of the P/W J-75 engines with Orenda Iroquois 2 models

4. A redesigned radar nose and modified electrical system

5. Engine changes affected the intake geometry, inner wing structure, duct and engine bay structure, rear fuselage structure, engine controls, air conditioning and pressure systems, as well as the addition of an external fuel tank attachment.

6. RCAF comments and test results from the **Arrow 1** program deleted the rain repellent system, enlarged the navigator's cockpit window and replaced the proportionator fuel system with an absolute pressure transfer arrangement.

Engineering conferences were held to inspect Arrow models, the Mk I (above) in the spring of 1956 and the Mk II (left) in the fall of 1957. The cherry picker was part of the ground equipment needed to service the Arrow.

Photos, L. Wilkinson

Visibility mock-ups

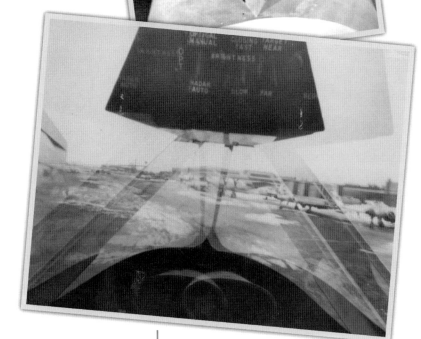

Test pilot Mike Cooper-Slipper looks a bit bug-eyed in the mock-up Arrow cockpit. The view was equally distorted looking out.

Photo, W. Farrence

Both these letters indicate the RCAF was far from happy with the Arrow's cockpit design. The forward "V" was one thing, general visibility was another. The problems also included the observer's cockpit. The tone of the letters speak for themselves.

National Archives

A wooden cockpit mock-up placed on a truck at various angles within the Arrow pitch attitude showed the effect of the slanted glass plates. A thin black separator, courtesy of the USAF, solved the problem.

Photo, W . Farrance

Weapons, fire and flight control systems for the Arrow Mk II

Big CF-105 Contract Let to U.S. Company

SEP 28 1956

By JAMES A. OASTLER
Of The Star's Ottawa Bureau

OTTAWA, Sept. 28—An American firm has been granted a multi-million dollar contract to provide a complete electronics weapon and navigation system for the still-secret, 1,500-mph jet fighter, the RCAF's CF-105.

The Department of Defence Production told THE MONTREAL STAR today the contract had been given the Radio Corporation of America, but that it was still listed as "classified" or secret, and that its value and extent would not be disclosed.

The contract was let through the United States Air Force, for "a complete electronic system for fire control, navigation and communication, and an integrated automatic flight control system."

The aeronautical division of the Minneapolis-Honeywell Regulator Company will work with RCA on an associate basis, with responsibility for development of the automatic flight controls.

A spokesman for the RCAF also confirmed that the contract had been let. He said that "arrange-

ments have been made through the Department of Defence Production and the United States Air Force for the development by two United States firms, of an integrated electronics system for the CF-105.

"It is being developed to RCAF specifications.

"Some of the development work will be farmed out to Canadian firms.

"The multi-million dollar development includes the building of a limited number of systems to go into some of the prototype models of the CF-105, to be used for testing purposes.

"It is planned that any production which will flow from this development, will be done in Canada," the spokesman said.

Asked why the contract was let through the United States Air Force, the spokesman here said this procedure was normal when the Canadian Government sought the services of an American company for a classified job.

Similarly, when the United

See CF-105—Page 4, Col. 1

Montreal Star story noting that the RCAF had granted a weapons and flight control systems contract to RCA via the USAF.

Clipping, *Montreal Star* 1956

The USAF used the Falcon guided missile and Aim-1 fire control system to such a degree that an alternative needed to be developed. Douglas was working on the Sparrow for the U.S. Navy. The RCAF was convinced of the Sparrows' potential superiority and was encouraged by the USAF to join in its development. When the U.S.Navy dropped the program, the RCAF elected to continue on its own. Avro was forced to go along. Now Avro had to deliver a so called "Weapon System" i.e. airframe, engine, missile and fire control system.

Components and placement of the Sparrow II and Astra fire control systems.

Diagram, Arrow Mk II Brochure

At Avro, major test facilities are built

Avro's main office is still standing in Malton, ready to be reoccupied by a new generation of aviation engineers.

Photo, Peter Zuuring

Specially built fuel rig tests ability to feed engines at any attitude. Fuel transfer, to maintain flight balance, was simulated.

The Iroquois engine's flying test bed was a converted B-47, lent from the USAF, for "Project North-Wind."

Photo, P. Brennan

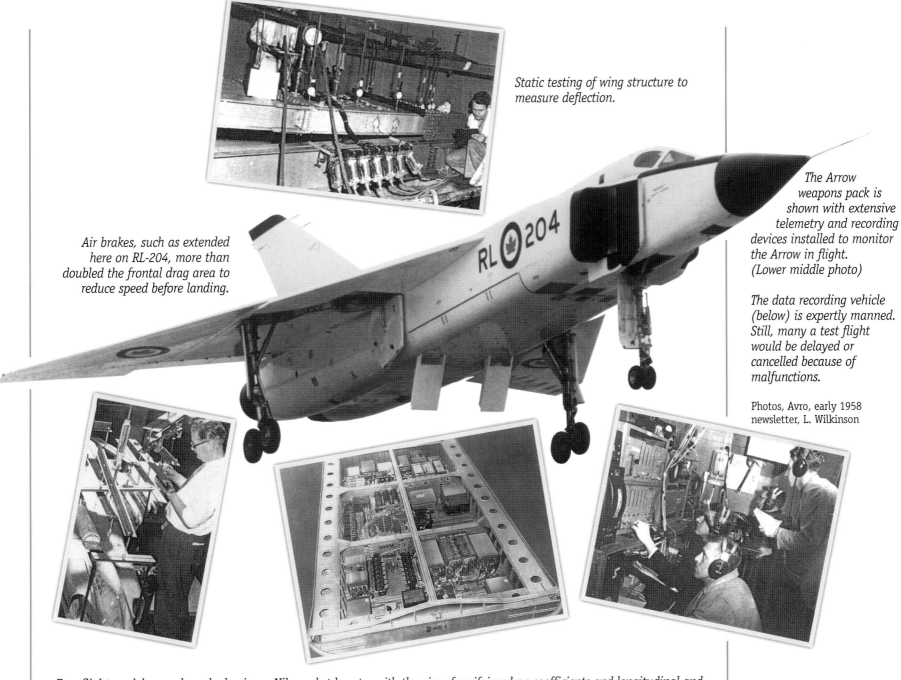

Static testing of wing structure to measure deflection.

Air brakes, such as extended here on RL-204, more than doubled the frontal drag area to reduce speed before landing.

RL●204

The Arrow weapons pack is shown with extensive telemetry and recording devices installed to monitor the Arrow in flight. (Lower middle photo)

The data recording vehicle (below) is expertly manned. Still, many a test flight would be delayed or cancelled because of malfunctions.

Photos, Avro, early 1958 newsletter, L. Wilkinson

Free-flight models were launched using a Nike rocket booster with the aim of verifying drag coefficients and longitudinal and lateral stability, and otherwise detecting design problems. Nine models were shot into Lake Ontario. The solubility of their magnesium construction makes recovery doubtful.

Photos, Avro, early 1958 Newsletter

Hundreds of tons of steel were used to manufacture hard tooling, jigs and fixtures

Cook-Craigie Plan

To avoid the logjam that occurs when large quantities of new military aircraft must undergo extensive "debugging" before they are combat-ready, USAF last year adopted the Cook-Craigie procurement plan (AW Apr. 12, 1954, p. 13).

Known formally as the Initial Low Rate of Aircraft Production Plan, it provides for holding output to a relatively low level for 18-24 months while the delivered aircraft are "wrung out" in an extensive test program. During this period, major airframe, engine and component problems are worked out and necessary modifications cranked into the plane's production pattern.

This plan eliminates experimental tooling, prototypes and drawings. First aircraft are built with production-type tooling and from production drawings.

The plan gets its informal name from Gens. Laurence Craigie and Orval Cook, who, together with Gen. Donald Putt, are given principal credit for putting it into operation.

Traditional development programs of the day involved the manufacture of a small number of prototypes, built on experimental tooling. Test flying would wring out the problem areas, finally leading to a solid redesign. Production tooling could then be built in confidence, with relatively lower initial costs.

The "Cook-Craigie Plan" adopted by Avro and accepted by the RCAF, was copied from USAF experience. The real problem was getting finished aircraft delivered to squadrons in as short a time as possible. This method was supposed to save significant time, not necessarily money. By the early 1960s, only vestiges of the plan were in use. More sophisticated critical path planning techniques, using computer technology, had arrived.

This skin-stretching machine improved the shape-stability of parts after die-forming. A 2 percent elongation required thousands of pounds of pull.

Photo, Avro, early 1958 Newsletter

Large, very rigid jigs were used throughout the Arrow program. This one assembled the air tunnel dividers that formed a portion of the aircraft's centre section. Note the solid floor anchors.

Photo, P. Brennan

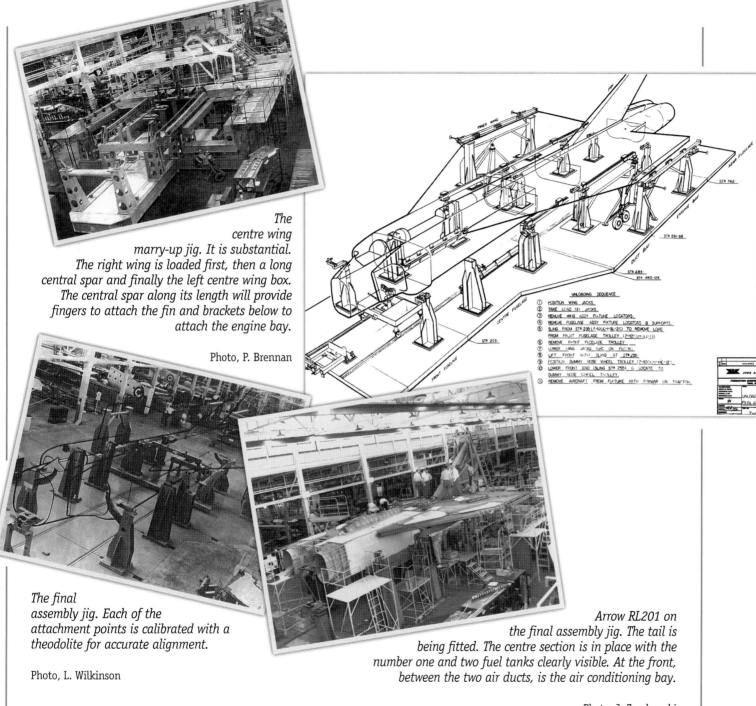

The centre wing marry-up jig. It is substantial. The right wing is loaded first, then a long central spar and finally the left centre wing box. The central spar along its length will provide fingers to attach the fin and brackets below to attach the engine bay.

Photo, P. Brennan

Artist's rendering of an Arrow on the final assembly jig, with the unloading sequence clearly spelled out. Most of the major components of the Arrow, including the nose and centre sections, duct bay and engine bay, had their own assembly jig.

Drawing, Arrow engineering brochure, Ken Barnes

The final assembly jig. Each of the attachment points is calibrated with a theodolite for accurate alignment.

Photo, L. Wilkinson

Arrow RL201 on the final assembly jig. The tail is being fitted. The centre section is in place with the number one and two fuel tanks clearly visible. At the front, between the two air ducts, is the air conditioning bay.

Photo, J. Zurakowski

RL-201 out of the final assembly jig,
being positioned for finishing.

Photo, L. Wilkinson

RL-201 from the back, being positioned. Is that Jan Zurakowski walking briskly away from the Arrow?

25

Photo, J Zurakowski

Back in the 'fifties - The Arrow Scrapbook

Large capital and manpower commitments were made

A bell-crank is being installed in the elevator control box. Because there were more than 400 screws attaching the box to the wing, interchangeability was a problem.

Photo, P. Brennan

Large-scale hot-air heat treating equipment, including a quick water-quench bath, were needed to maintain strength and minimal weight for the special aluminum alloys used in the supersonic airframe.

Photo, Avro Newsletter

With more than 7500 people working at Avro alone you can imagine numerous people on the shop floor. These men are working on the front nose section of RL-201. The scale is impressive. Clecos were used then as they are today. In fact, many of the manufacturing techniques haven't changed today.

Photo, P. Brennan

The Arrow program required extensive bonding of dissimilar metals. This giant autoclave produced the required heat and pressure for optimal bonding.

Photo, Avro Newsletter

Large pantograph-type milling machines, the biggest to date, were installed for the integrally stiffened inner wing skins and large-scale spars, formers, ribs etc.

Photo, Avro Newsletter

This request for information and subsequent estimates of manpower and industrial effort from April 1958 is representative of the whole Arrow program. The initial thirty-seven aircraft were to be expanded to some 600. The tables indicate that thousands of people and millions of dollars were at stake.

Documents, National Archives

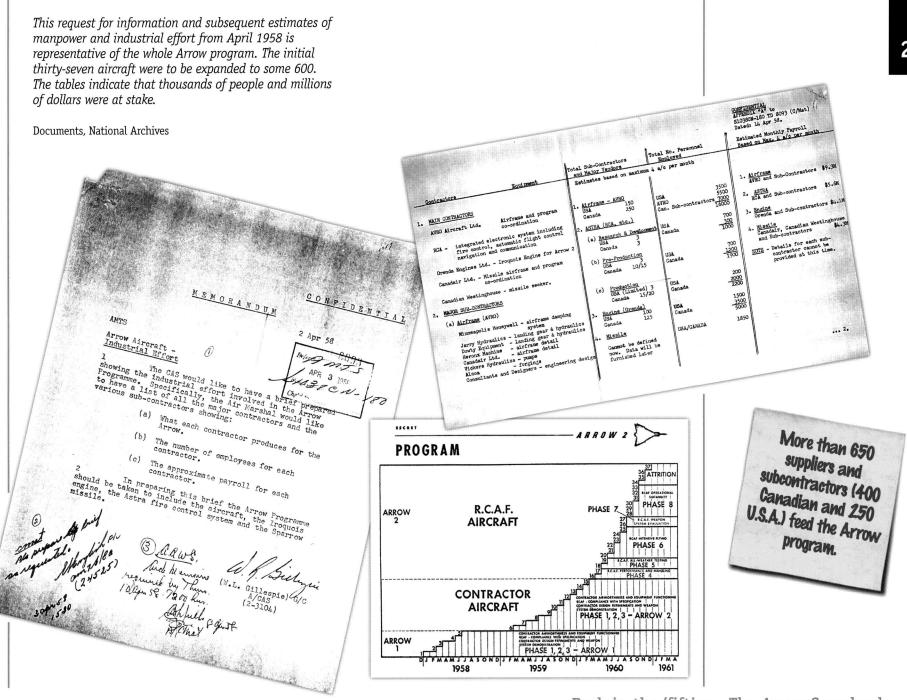

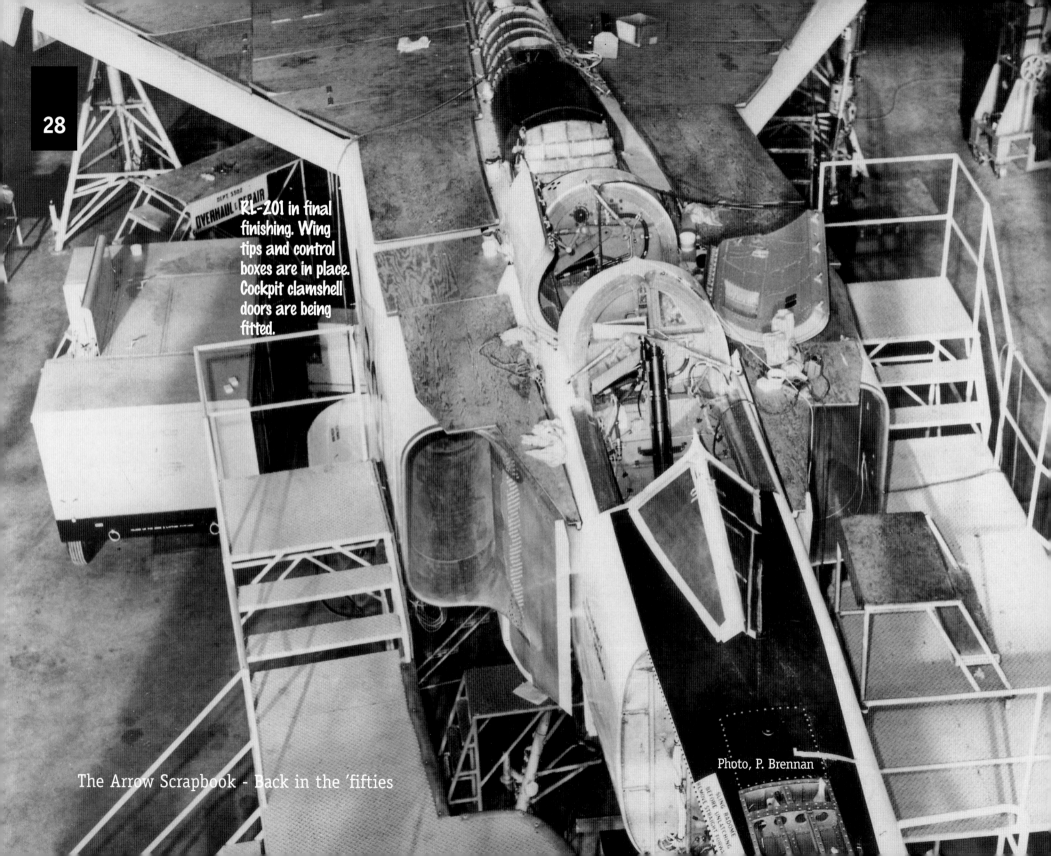

RL-201 in final finishing. Wing tips and control boxes are in place. Cockpit clamshell doors are being fitted.

The Arrow Scrapbook - Back in the 'fifties

Photo, P. Brennan

The scale of the Arrow
is particularly striking.
Note the size of the
landing gear.

Engine bay
blow-in doors on
fuselage side.

No safety
shoes
required.

Photo, L Wilkinson

Back in the 'fifties - The Arrow Scrapbook

Orenda,
a mythical
force in
Native lore.
The Iroquois
engine carried
on the tradition.

Orenda experienced the same growth

The designers of the Iroquois were in the main the same people who worked on the successful Orenda series. That is to say, there was an important buildup of expertise that formed the basis of Project Study Group PS-13.

Because the Avro CF-100 replacement interceptor would be supersonic, a completely new generation of engine would be needed. Other manufacturers were working in the field with the usual 15-20 percent incremental changes. To fit the Arrow, the Iroquois design requirements meant skipping a complete generation of engine. You will recall that the original Arrow Mk I design called for engines first from Rolls-Royce, then Curtis-Wright, Pratt and Whitney and, finally, Orenda, - four changes in all.

The booming Orenda plant in Malton in the 1950s, looking South.

Photo, P. Brennan

In just twenty days, after receiving approval from the Hawker-Siddeley Group's Design Council (fall 1953), the Orenda team, headed by Harry Keast, came up with the basic engine layout:

- A twin spool (shaft within a shaft) axial flow turbine
- An air mass flow rate of 280 - 300 lb./sec. or 20,000 lb. dry thrust at sea level
- An engine weighing about 4500 lbs.
- Two air compressors and two turbines for operational efficiency connected by a high-velocity, annular combustion chamber, and
- An integrated afterburner with convergent, variable area nozzle to maximize thrust through the full range of throttle settings.

The successful Orenda engine powered the CF-100 and F-86 Sabres. Close to 4000 were built. A.V. Roe proved it could produce an engine and an airframe at the same time, contrary to popular opinion.

The engine that started it all for Orenda Engines Limited, the Chinook (right). Only four were produced. Note the similarities with the Orenda engine (above).

Photos, P. Brennan

Although these specifications appear straightforward, achieving any one of them and then putting them together in an efficient way, was no mean feat.

The use of; titanium, magnesium and special nickel-alloy steels, new fabricating techniques for hollow blades and stators, new design parameters for transonic blades, longitudinally balanced front and rear single bearing mounts, internally mounted utilities, thermodynamically optimized flows and exit temperatures, an oxygen-injected high-altitude re-light system, a variable thrust fuel-injected afterburner ignited by a hot streak from the combustion chamber, variable pitch stators between the low and high-pressure compressors, and more.

Orenda engineers knew what they were doing!

At cancellation, the Iroquois MK II, already a second generation, was ready for first flight in the Arrow. The Iroquois MK I was a development and preproduction model. Airborne trials in the B-47, on loan from the USAF, were still in progress. The demise of the Iroquois engine was more tragic then that of of the Arrow itself.

An Iroquois MK III was already on the drawing board, and a tuned-down, even lighter civilian version was planned as a potential first-class power plant for airline use.

There was a very bright future for Orenda's Iroquois.

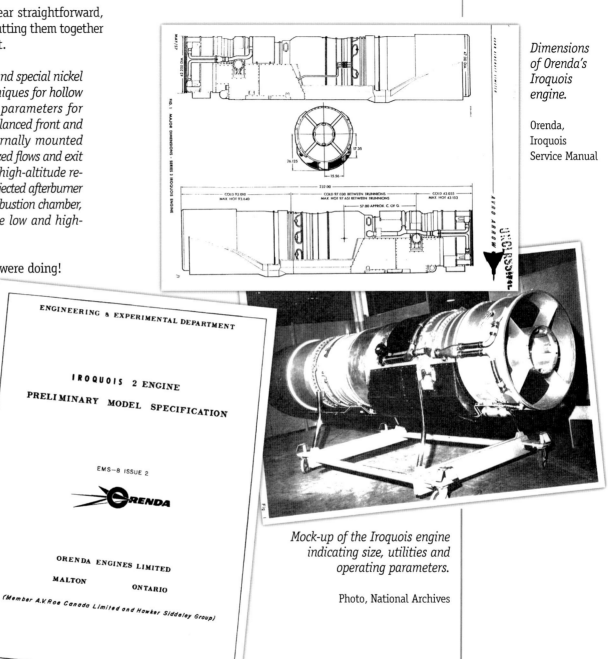

Dimensions of Orenda's Iroquois engine.

Orenda, Iroquois Service Manual

Mock-up of the Iroquois engine indicating size, utilities and operating parameters.

Photo, National Archives

The Iroquois Mk II engine

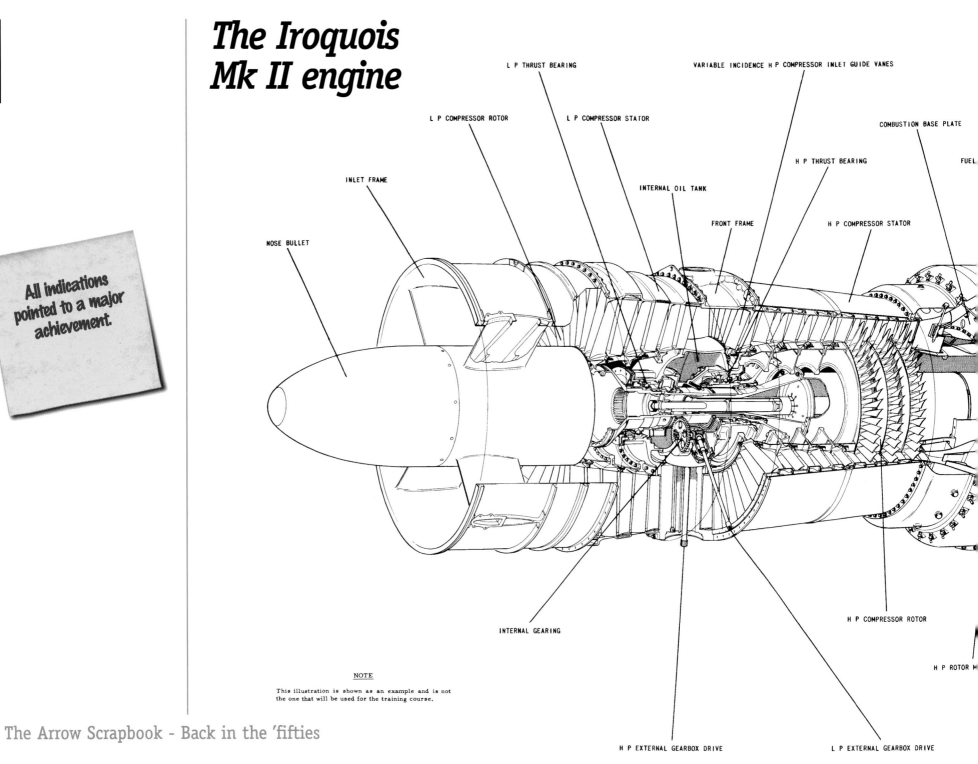

All indications pointed to a major achievement.

L P THRUST BEARING

VARIABLE INCIDENCE H P COMPRESSOR INLET GUIDE VANES

L P COMPRESSOR ROTOR

L P COMPRESSOR STATOR

COMBUSTION BASE PLATE

INLET FRAME

INTERNAL OIL TANK

H P THRUST BEARING

FUEL

NOSE BULLET

FRONT FRAME

H P COMPRESSOR STATOR

INTERNAL GEARING

H P COMPRESSOR ROTOR

H P ROTOR M

NOTE

This illustration is shown as an example and is not
the one that will be used for the training course.

H P EXTERNAL GEARBOX DRIVE

L P EXTERNAL GEARBOX DRIVE

FIGURE 1 SECTION THROUGH IROQUOIS ENGINE

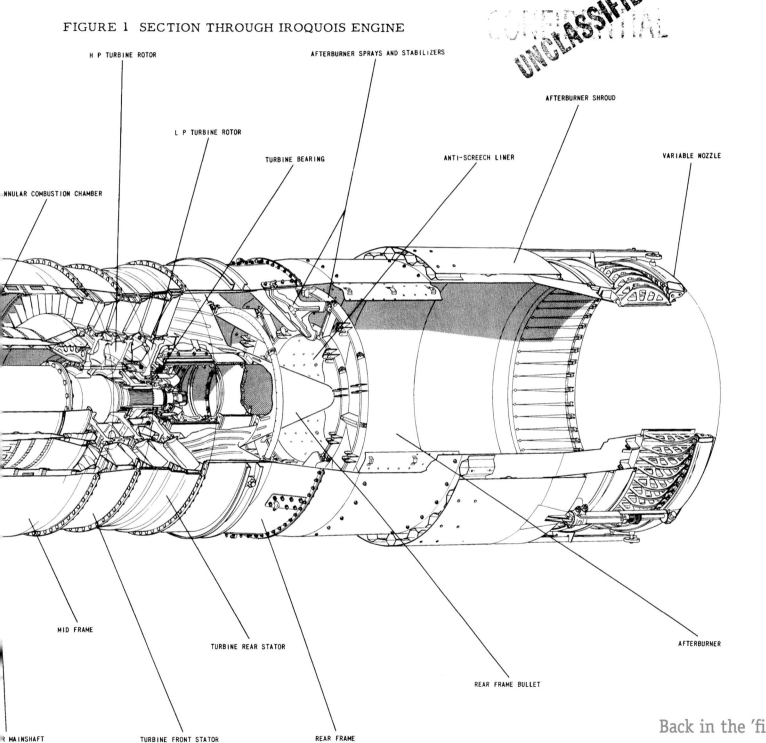

H P TURBINE ROTOR

AFTERBURNER SPRAYS AND STABILIZERS

CONFIDENTIAL
UNCLASSIFIED

L P TURBINE ROTOR

AFTERBURNER SHROUD

TURBINE BEARING

ANTI-SCREECH LINER

VARIABLE NOZZLE

NNULAR COMBUSTION CHAMBER

MID FRAME

TURBINE REAR STATOR

AFTERBURNER

REAR FRAME BULLET

R MAINSHAFT

TURBINE FRONT STATOR

REAR FRAME

The Orenda Engines Ltd. team had honed its expertise on the very successful Orenda engine and its variants. The Iroquois engine was truly a masterful design - it weighed about 4500 pounds and produced 26,000 pounds of thrust with afterburners. Unfortunately, it was never tested in the Arrow.

Orenda Iroquois
Design Specifications, 1957

Contracts let to third parties

Test cell number four at the National Research Council's laboratory in Ottawa. Engine X-105 is being tested under icing conditions. Heating the bullet nose, inlet farings and first stage low pressure compressor stator housing prevented build up of ice.

Photo, NRC Report, Ottawa

Test cell number four today. Jim Macleod of the NRC engine lab stands in the foreground.

Photo, Peter Zuuring

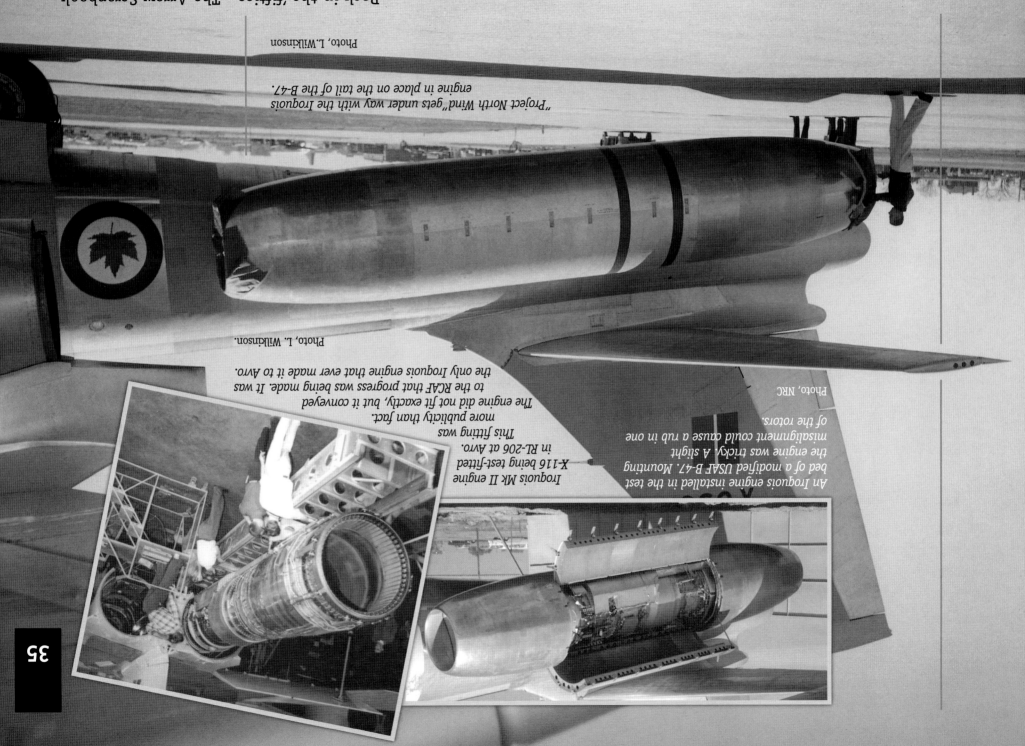

Photo, L. Wilkinson.

"Project North Wind" gets under way with the Iroquois engine in place on the tail of the B-47.

Photo, L. Wilkinson.

Iroquois Mk II engine X-116 being test-fitted in RL-206 at Avro.

This fitting was more publicity than fact.

The engine did not fit exactly, but it conveyed to the RCAF that progress was being made. It was the only Iroquois engine that ever made it to Avro.

Photo, NRC.

An Iroquois engine installed in the test bed of a modified USAF B-47. Mounting the engine was tricky. A slight misalignment could cause a rub in one of the rotors.

35

Engine test facilities were built...

Artist's rendering of the Orenda High-Altitude Test Facility, Malton, Ont.

Drawing, A.V. Roe Ltd..

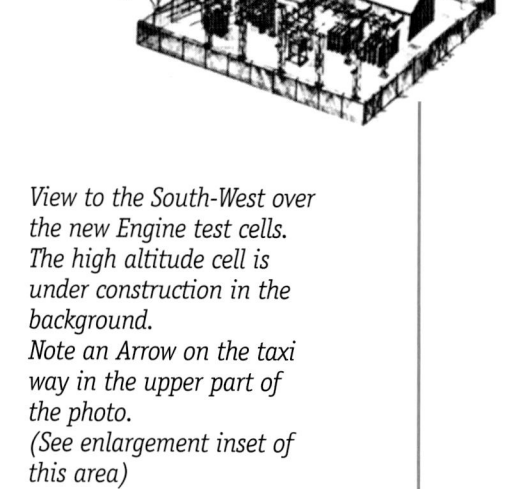

View to the South-West over the new Engine test cells. The high altitude cell is under construction in the background.
Note an Arrow on the taxi way in the upper part of the photo.
(See enlargement inset of this area)

Photo, L. Wilkinson

at Malton

and at Nobel.
(Near Parry Sound, Ontario)

Standing in this photo is Peter Brennan, 1958.

Photo, P. Brennan

These extensive test facilities were owned by the Canadian government. Orenda leased them on a long-term basis as part of the takeover of Turbo Research in the late 1940s. Full-up engines, such as the Orenda series that powered the CF-100 and the Iroquois under development for the Arrow program were tested at Orenda in Malton.

At Nobel, only partial engines were evaluated. Whole compressor or turbine sections were tested to destruction. Much fundamental work was completed. Materials were evaluated. Improved blade design, such as the air-cooled rig for the Iroquois turbine section above were developed.

The large steam power plant on the left dominated the Nobel site.

Photo, P. Brennan

In the spring of 1958, everyone at OEL was confident that the success of the Orenda would be repeated with the Iroquois program.

A Mk I, Iroquois development engine is being prepared for a test run in the new Orenda Cells. A number of changes were made to the first stage of the high pressure compressor in the Mk II version. Variable guide vanes improved recovery from rotary stalls. Inlets and afterburners were simplified.

Photo, NAM

Supersonic Motor Deal

Canadians Sell to U.S. Top Jet Engine Rights

Canadian Press

SEP 30 1957

TORONTO, Sept. 30—Orenda Engines Limited has sold for an undisclosed sum manufacturing rights for Canada's latest jet engine to a United States firm, the Curtiss-Wright Corp.

The deal was disclosed yesterday in a joint statement by Crawford Gordon, president of A. V. Roe Canada Limited and Orenda board chairman; and Roy T. Hurley, president of Curtiss-Wright.

The engine is the Iroquois, which will power the 34-ton Delta-winged Arrow, Canada's new supersonic jet interceptor to be unveiled at suburban Malton next Wednesday.

The agreement also gives Curtiss-Wright permission to sell and develop further the engine.

Lastly, the seven-year pact provides for an exchange of technical information between Orenda and Curtiss-Wright.

Mr. Gordon said Canada and Orenda would achieve three principal advantages from the agreement:

"First, it represents tangible evidence of the extent of the collaboration and co-ordination that exists between our two countries on defence projects.

"Second, in the long run, it means a saving of cost to both Canada and the United States through elimination of duplication of effort.

"Third: By sharing costs and through technical liaison between the two companies, it will be possible for Canada and the U.S. to obtain higher performance engines in a shorter period of time."

speed in relation to the speed of sound; "Mach 1" equals the speed of sound.

The top speed of the arrow has been estimated at 1,600 miles an hour, more than twice the speed of sound at sea level.

The Arrow was built by Avro Aircraft Limited, a sister firm of Orenda engines. Both are members of the A. V. Roe Canada group.

There was no indication as to what specific types of aircraft would get the Iroquois in the U.S. however, W. R. McLachlan, Orenda president, said, "it is anticipated that the two companies will collaborate in the development of further variants of the Iroquois, suitable for the very high-speed, high-altitude interceptions and bombers now on the drawing board and for commercial applications."

Costs Reduced

Mr. Hurley, said, "we estimate this mutual arrangement has re-

Final inspection...

Photo, A.V. Roe Annual Report

Iroquois Mk II in the Orenda Test Cell. Getting closer to a production engine.

Photo, L. Wilkinson

The Iroquois Mk II, the lightest most powerful engine in the western arsenal...had we had a chance to complete it.

The polishing and buffing section of the Orenda Engines Ltd.. plant. Housekeeping is excellent.

Photo, M. Barber

Back in the 'fifties - The Arrow Scrapbook

Another grand view of the Orenda Engines Ltd.. plant. Hundreds of machine tools were needed to produce the engines. Shop cleanliness seemed to be a priority at Orenda.

Photo, M. Barber

The Iroquois engine promised to be a real winner for A.V. Roe and for Canada. The USAF was interested in it for the F-106. The French indicated they would like several hundred for their Mirage program. A Curtis-Wright licensing deal waited for the 150 hour test to kick in the agreement signed a year and a half earlier. When cancellation came, why did Hawker-Siddeley not continue the program, complete it and take advantage of the licensing options provided for such an occasion? The British group started the project under its own steam. Why was it that, two years after cancellation, Iroquois engines were still to be found in the Rheem Container storage area behind the Orenda Plant? Bristol Siddeley, the British engine manufacturer, got the loan of one of the last engines produced. What happened to it? The USAF was testing several engines in Tullahoma in late 1958. Did it return them? The paper trail goes cold after 1962.

Dignitaries visiting the control room of the nearly completed high-altitude test facility.

Photo: Orenda News magazine, 1958

GAS TURBINE ENGINES

CANADA – Orenda Engines Iroquois

179

Model and type	...Iroquois 2. Turbojet, 10-stage 2-spool axial compressor, annular combustor, 3-stage turbine, afterburner. Military engine.
Intake	Annular magnesium alloy air intake casing. 4 radial struts support electric generator in nose. Hot bleed air anti-icing system.
Compressor (low-pressure)	3-stage axial flow type. Drum type magnesium alloy casing, with fabricated steel stator blades. Disc-type titanium alloy rotor, with titanium alloy blades, mounted on small diameter shaft supported in 1 ball thrust bearing at front end and in 1 ball steady bearing at rear end where connected to inner drive shaft from low-pressure 2nd and 3rd-stage turbine wheels.
Compressor (high-pressure)	7-stage axial flow type. Drum type steel rotor, with steel blades. Disc type steel casing, with steel stator blades, mounted on large diameter tubular shaft supported in 1 ball thrust bearing at front end and in 1 roller bearing at rear end where connected at high-pressure 1st-stage turbine wheel. Pressure ratio 8.0:1, and air mass flow 350 lb (159 kg)/sec/static.
Combustor	Annular type. 2-piece steel outer shell. Flame chamber of Nimonic 75 alloy. 32 vaporizing type burners. Upstream injection.
Turbine	3-stage axial flow type. Drum type steel casing, with hollow nozzle vanes and solid stator blades. 1st-stage turbine wheel, with cast Inco alloy blades, mounted on rear end of large diameter tubular shaft supported in 1 roller bearing ahead of wheel. 2nd and 3rd-stage turbine wheels mounted on small diameter tubular shaft supported in 1 roller bearing behind wheels.
Afterburner	Integral type. 12-spray bar fuel injector, and additional injectors, with 2 flame holders downstream. Fully variable convergent nozzle, with 60 segments mounted on rollers on cam tracks, operated by 4 hydraulic actuators through unison ring.
Control system	Hydro-mechanical type. Automatic starting and acceleration controls. Turbine inlet temperature control. Single-lever master control. each compressor rotor system. Overspeed governor for Lucas-Rotax Proportional Flow Control system, comprising 2 Lucas-Rotax air turbine driven centrifugal type fuel pumps, 1.000 psi (70 kg/cm²), with automatic pressure regulators; and range temperature flow control unit, with altitude control, acceleration control, range temperature trim, and throttle valve.
Fuel system	Emergency fuel control, range temperature trim, and throttle valve. Air vented enclosure for pumps and controls. turbine driven fuel transfer pump. 32 Orenda burner-vaporizers. Return system. Pressure pump, 90 psi (6.3 kg/cm²). United Aircraft Products Hi-D fuel-cooled heat exchanger. Bendix-Utica air gearbox. Bendix-Scintilla TGLN-19 high-energy ignition, and 2
Lubrication	AiResearch ATS 140 air turbine starter mounted on external
Accessories	igniter plugs, for main engine. Hotstreak ignition for afterburner.
Diameter and length	......42.0 in and 231.0 in	1 067 mm and 5 865 mm
Frontal area	......9.6 ft²	0.89 m²
Weight	......4,650 lb	2 100 kg
Power/weight ratio (reheat)	..6.45 lbt/lb	6,45 kgp/kg
Fuel specification	......MIL-F-5624	3-GP-22b (JP-4)
Fuel consumption (reheat)	..1.8 lb/lbt/hr	1 800 g/kgp/hr
Oil specification	......MIL-L-7808 (synthetic)	3.0 vs vis (Turbo 15)
Oil consumption	......2.5 lb/hr	1 134 g/hr
Rating (take-off)	..30,000 lbt (13 600 kgp)/static, reheat	
Rating (take-off)	..23,000 lbt (10 100 kgp)/static, normal	

Note: The normal fuel consumption of this engine without afterburner is 0.85 lb/lbt/hr (850 g/kgp/hr). The power/weight ratio without afterburner is 5.25 lbt/lb (5,25 kgp/kg).

Reprinted from *Gas Turbine Engines*, 1959. It was rated the best.

Unexpectedly, Sputnik got the Headlines.

Rollout, October 4, 1957

Photo, Avro Newsletter, 1958

FRED T. SMYE, Executive Vice President, Aeronautical Division, A. V. Roe Canada Ltd., addresses the 12,000 people gathered for the ceremony. With him on the platform can be seen left to right: Dr. Adam Zimmerman, Chairman, Defence Research Board; Gen. Charles Foulkes, Chief of Staff, Canadian Army; Sir Roy Dobson, Chairman of the Board, A. V. Roe Canada Ltd.; Gen. Leon W. Johnson, USAF, U.S. Representative, NATO Standing Committee; Hon. G. R. Pearkes, VC, Minister of National Defence; A/V/M L. E. Wray, AOC, Air Defence Command, RCAF; Hon. J. A. D. McCurdy, first Canadian pilot; A/M H. L. Campbell, Chief of Air Staff, RCAF; W. R. McLachlan, Executive Vice President, Administration and Co-ordination, A. V. Roe Canada, Ltd.; Crawford Gordon, President and General Manager, A. V. Roe Canada Ltd.; Frank R. Miller, Deputy Minister of National Defence; W. H. Huck, Assistant Deputy Minister, DDP; A/V/M M. M. Hendricks, Air Member for Technical Services, RCAF; and A/M W. A. Curtis, Vice-Chairman of the Board, A. V. Roe Canada Ltd. Most Avro employees saw ceremony.

The Avro CF-105: To Be Or Not To Be?

SOME time around the end of next month, Canada's costliest experiment in national security will take off on its first test flight. This is the Avro CF-105 or Arrow. It is designed to fly at 60,000 feet and close to 1,500 miles per hour. The Arrow was designed to intercept enemy bombers, and it is to be armed with guided missiles to hit them. It will also be able to carry a hydrogen bomb. If it is eventually approved to replace the CF-100 in squadron service, the cost will run to $1,000,000,000 or more over a period of years.

NOV 13 1957

The appalling cost of this aircraft is enough to stagger government ministers and serious people everywhere. We are a middle power, with a budget and an industry to match. If this alone were not enough to give us pause, there is

Clipping, *Montreal Star, Gazette*

Photo, *Avro Horizons Magazine*, Fall/Winter 1957-1958

Many of the hounorable guests were not so hounorable when it came to standing up for the Arrow a little more than a year after the aircraft was first rolled out on October 4, 1957. Bizarrely, it was on the same day that the Soviets launched their first Sputnik, an event that grabbed more headlines than the

Arrow. John Diefenbaker's minority government extended the Arrow program, fearing the effects of a large layoff, though uncertainty continued to plague the project. Contrary to the clipping, first flight was still almost six months away.

RL ● 201

25201

A great shot of rollout. After the main ceremony common employees were invited to see their Arrow.

Photo, P. Brennan

Back in the 'fifties - The Arrow Scrapbook

First flight of the Arrow took place on March 25, 1958, 172 days after rollout. Many problems surfaced and were fixed. Was Jan nervous for that first flight? You bet...but not in the way you might think.

Test pilot Jan Zurakowski, heart and soul of the Arrow

Original flight certificate for RL-201, Spring 1958.

Certificate, National Archives

"The unpleasant part of my first flight was the feeling of responsibility combined with the realization that the success of this aircraft depends on thousands of components, especially electronic and hydraulic, with only a small percentage under my direct control. Yet total responsibility for first flight was mine."

Jan Zurakowski after a Meteor test flight.

Photo, National Archives

SECRET
Report 71/PROJ 7/1-2

AVRO AIRCRAFT LIMITED

DESIGN CERTIFICATE

FOR FLIGHT TRIALS OF ARROW 1 AIRCRAFT

SERIAL NO. 25201

Aircraft .... Arrow (CF-105) Mk. 1 ....

Serial No. .... 25201 .... Contractor .. Avro Aircraft Limited ....

Spec. No. ..... AAMS-105/1 Iss. 1 Dec. 1956 .... Appendix ....

Contract, I.T.P. or Loan Agreement No. ....

Engine Type ..... Two Pratt & Whitney J.75 Model JT4A23 ....

Arrow 1 Aircraft, Serial No. 25201, is hereby certified for the purpose of carrying out flight trials.

The aircraft is to be operated in accordance with the following:-

1. The recommendations and limitations of Part 4 of the Arrow 1 Pilot's Operating Instructions dated April 1958.

2. The limitations specified in Model Specification AAMS-105/1 Issue 1 December 1956 up to and including amendment No. 2 (Preliminary).

3. Operating restrictions listed in Section C of this document.

4. Special limitations listed in Section B of this Certificate. These over-rule the recommendations and/or requirements of 1,2 and 3 above where applicable.

DATED .... 20th May 1958 .... SIGNED ....

If anyone is identified with the Avro Arrow project it surely would be Jan Zurakowski. From flight instruction in Poland at the onset of WW II, to a Spitfire ace with the Polish Air Force (RAF), to Gloster test pilot and finally to Avro, he has earned the respect of many. Even today he gets a standing ovation when asked to appear. He has been articulate and forthright in his assessment of the Arrow fiasco. He speaks out with authority. He was there!

Jan does not believe the accepted myths that the plane was too expensive, it would fall apart in time, no one wanted to buy it, the Americans scuttled it and that it was obsolete before it could be delivered, etc., etc.. He acknowledges that there were problems to sort out and that the management structure to identify and fix those problems often became political. One of these turf problems involved the preparation and reporting of flight tests. If the flight envelope did not push the edge, potential problem areas could be suppressed. If pilots reported to the design office, management might not even find out. Jan told me that this type of thing was going on at Gloster as well as Avro.

The Gloster Meteor was quite unstable in certain parts of the flight envelope. Jan explored and reported on these limitations. Final reports on this issue neglected to tell the whole story. Apparently this happened on numerous occasions and convinced Jan to get out.

Testing the CF-100

Photo, National Archives

At Avro, a similar organizational structure between flight test, engineering design and management would lead to similar problems. In fact, Jim Floyd had to fire one of the aerodynamicists who refused to supply reports on the grounds that "there could be a wrong interpretation by pilots." There was a directional stability problem with the Arrow at high subsonic air speeds. The test pilot's role was to explore these difficult areas to make it functional and safer for those who had to follow.

Jan Zurakowski getting ready for another test flight...it looks like a serious conversation is in progress.

Photo, L. Wilkinson

2520

RL 201

Back in the 'fifties - The Arrow Scrapbook

1958
Arrows on the ground

RL-202 taxis by the west of the Avro plant. Because the Mk II program was under way, jigs and fixtures of the Mk I program were stored outside.

Photo, L. Wilkinson

The Arrow program was under the magnifying glass from the beginning. In his diary, Air Marshal M. M. Hendrick cites the importance of a test flight, using RCAF personnel, before another program review is undertaken. There were marked differences in reported test flight results between Avro and the RCAF.

Diary Extract, DHIS/HER

> **DIARY FOR 28th MAR 58**
>
> Discussed the policy for the flying of the aircraft by Air Force pilots. We agreed that they should be flown as soon as practicable by the Air Force to confirm the statements made by the company's pilots with which Johnny Plant agrees. It is also essential that the Air Force fly the aeroplane prior to our approaching the Government for re-assessment of the programme, which being this fall means that the flying by the Air Force should be done early this summer, with which Mr. Plant also agrees. At the same time he points out the need to get five flights in with not more than eight or ten hours of engine time left before engine changes are required with the hold-up that this involves. I stated also that we preferred the programme not to be held up, nor to allow us to fly it, if the two things were in conflict, but one handling flight at least should be done before we have to re-assess the programme.

Arrow RL-201 taxis out to the flight line. By the way, "RL" stands for Roe Limited. Group Captain Ray Foottit assures me it's not Robert Lindley.

Photo, P. Brennan

RL-203 taxis back, looking very much the sentinel, stationed in the far north for the defence of Canada.

Photo, P. Brennan

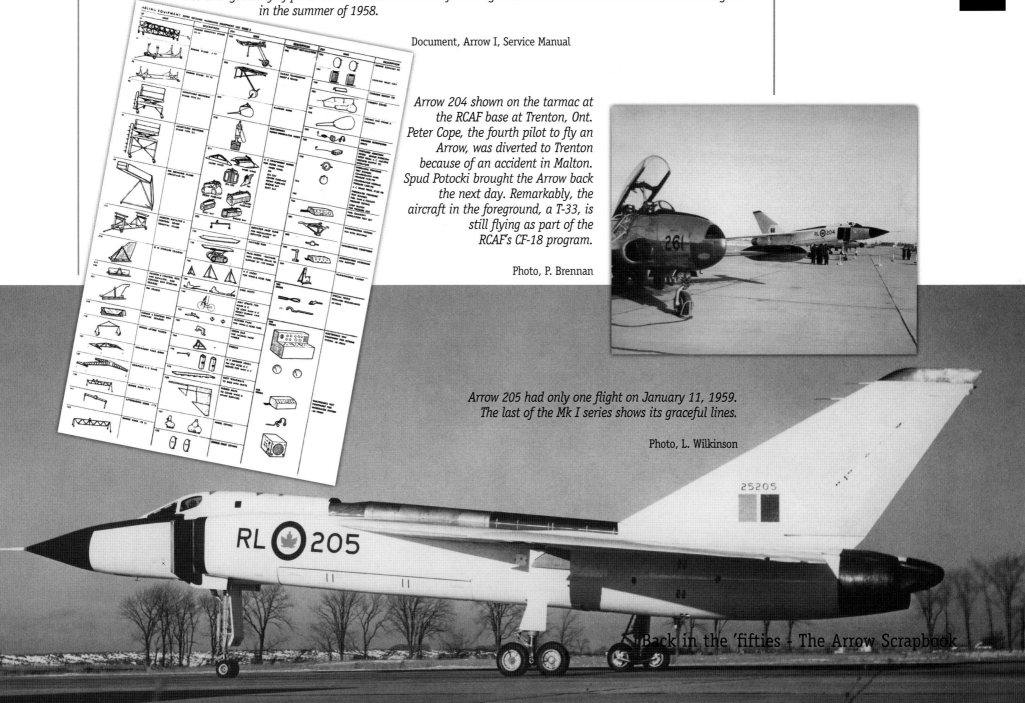

It was not only Avro that required extensive new equipment for the Arrow program. The RCAF was called upon to purchase ground-handling equipment, some of which is illustrated in this diagram. Large cranes and access platforms were suggested to service damaged Arrows. Hangar facilities, special crew-stations and communications equipment were required to ensure that an Arrow could be up and prepared for interception at 50,000 feet in about 15 minutes. Difficulties in maintainability and the interchangeability of parts were to become an issue favouring cancellation when the Arrow was reviewed again in the summer of 1958.

Document, Arrow I, Service Manual

Arrow 204 shown on the tarmac at the RCAF base at Trenton, Ont. Peter Cope, the fourth pilot to fly an Arrow, was diverted to Trenton because of an accident in Malton. Spud Potocki brought the Arrow back the next day. Remarkably, the aircraft in the foreground, a T-33, is still flying as part of the RCAF's CF-18 program.

Photo, P. Brennan

Arrow 205 had only one flight on January 11, 1959. The last of the Mk I series shows its graceful lines.

Photo, L. Wilkinson

Flying Arrows

The Arrow looked beautiful in flight, but clouds were forming on the horizon. The RCAF and its CEPE (Central Experimental and Proving Establishment) tried to impress upon Avro the need for a comprehensive testing timetable. According to Flight Lieutenant Jack Woodman, "They did not have a written test plan. I didn't understand it then, nor do I today." With nearly a year (beginning in March 1958) and five aircraft, only seventy hours of test flying were completed. Why wasn't more accomplished? The USAF's F-106 did a hundred hours of test flying in its first month.

Photo, L. Wilkinson

The chart shows the Arrow's flight envelope. Measuring high-speed flight at low altitude was a problem, as supersonic ground speeds might only register as 400 to 500 knots on the instruments. (Lower density air reduced drag, IAS (indicated air speed) was only a measure of air pressure on a static boom). Over the ground speed was only measurable with radar. There was no reliable Mach meter in the Arrow's cockpit.

Chart, Arrow Service Manual

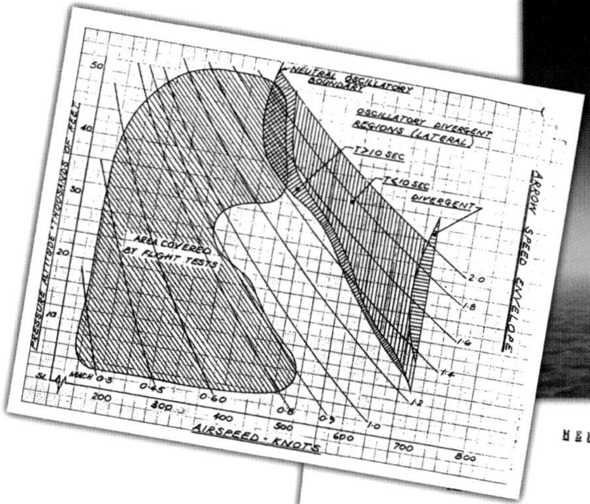

Arrow RL-203 in "mushing" first flight with a Sabre and the Clunk looking on. Note the small pipes sticking out the bottom rear. These tested take-off and touch-down runway contact.

Photo, P. Brennan

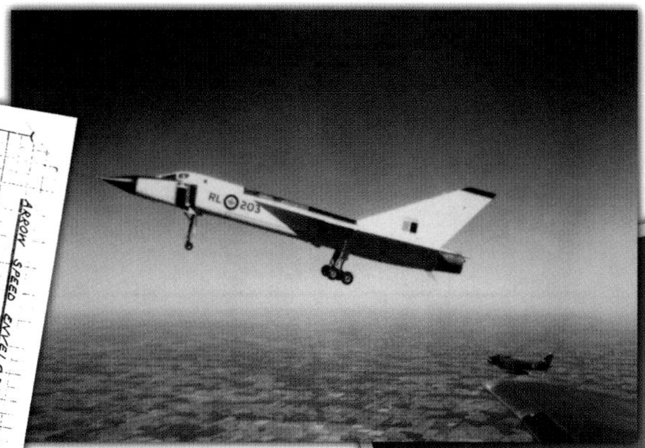

The Arrow's great expanse of wings, 1250 square feet, is dramatically shown in this underside photo.

Photo, L. Wilkinson

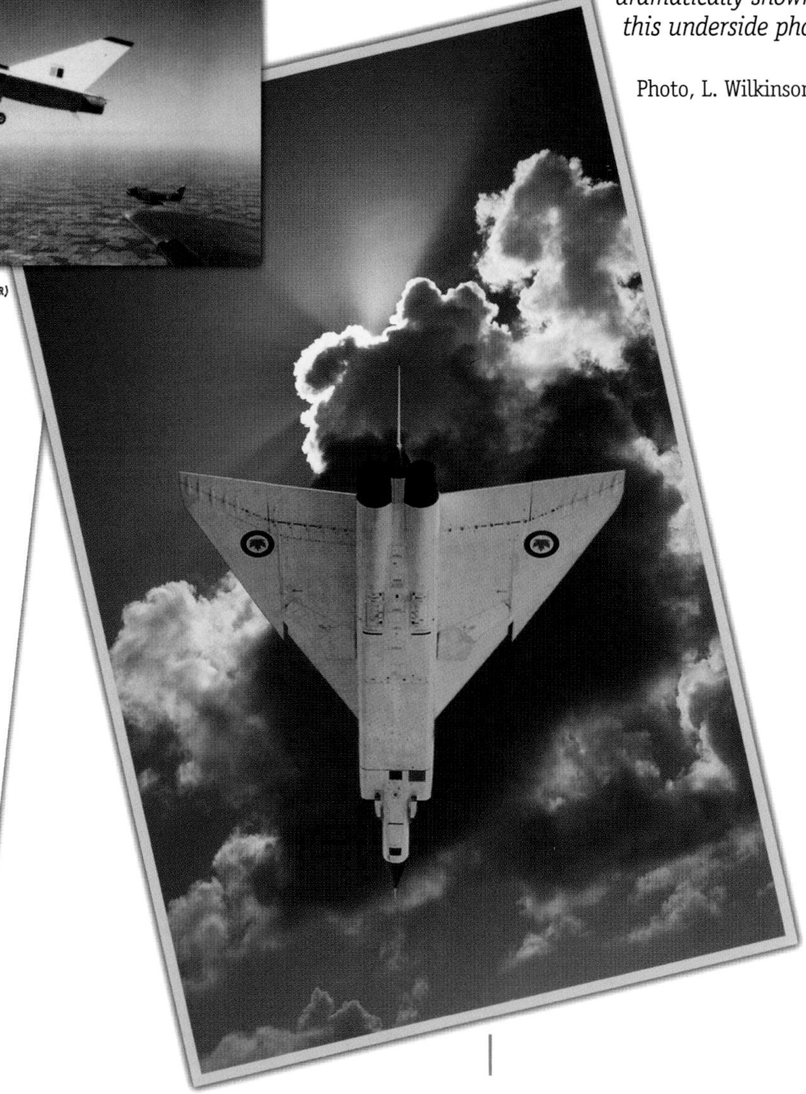

The name for the CF-105 was chosen by the RCAF as indicated in this letter. Slemon, Chief of the Air Staff, and the Defence Minister liked the name. Wing Commander Gervais brings forth the Arrow and comments on its appropriateness. "I shot an arrow into the air, it fell to earth, I know not where." A very prophetic statement as time would show.

Letter, National Archives

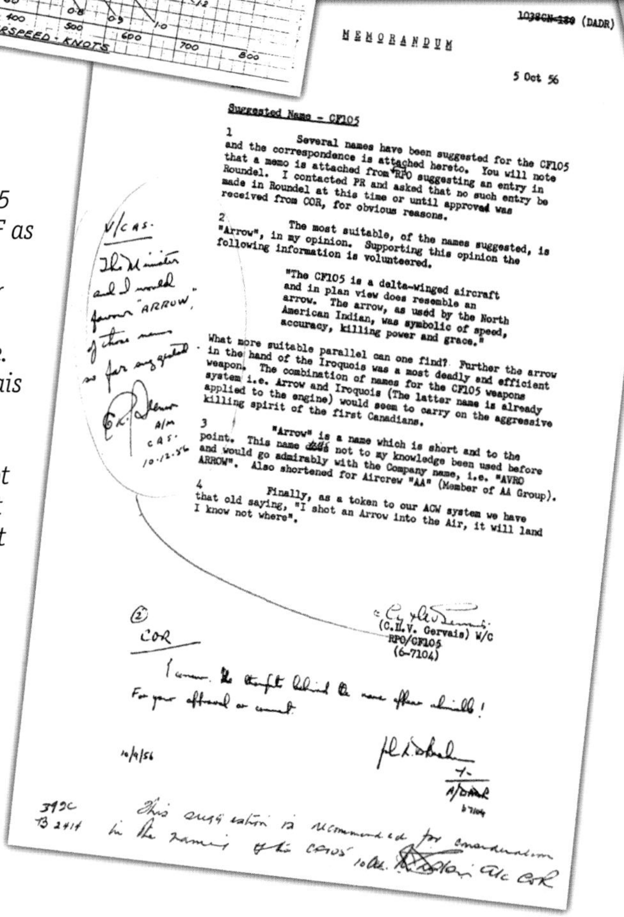

Foottit warns Avro... No Accident!

Wing Commander Ray Foottit warned Avro through the Technical Services Detachment in Malton that first flight better be a safe one. The tone of the letter does not suggest much confidence in Avro's assurances. The summer of 1958 involved yet another review of the Arrow program. Did the accident contribute to negative deliberations?

Letters, National Archives

On approach, the port landing gear did not complete its cycle and hung up slightly askew, with landing wheels turned outward. Jan Zurakowski did not have any indication that this had happened. Note the landing track on the runway. He would have landed on the east side to give more time for the plane to slow down without going off the tarmac. However, on leaving the concrete, all landing gear collapsed and the plane came to an abrupt halt. There were no injuries, although damage was more extensive than thought.

Jan recalls when he was first talking to a Dowty engineer about the main gear he was amazed to hear that "this was the most complicated landing gear ever." Jan's thoughts were..."too bad it wasn't the simplest." Apparently, landing gear are often troublesome during development – in the Arrow's case it was no exception. Braking, nose steering, para-brake operation all gave problems. Because the plane was heavy and the amount of space for efficient brake placement was limited, the edge was walked. Magnesium hubs got so hot that they burned. Because of the heat, tires also failed. So what happened? A link in the gear shortening mechanism jammed, perhaps from dirt, with the effect that it did not extend fully. Voila!

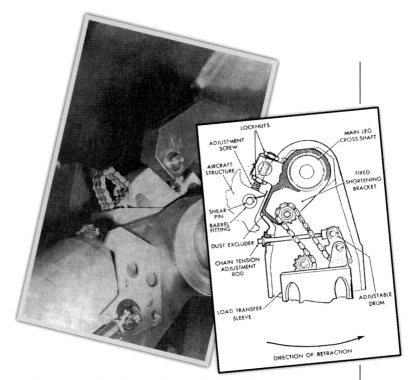

A close-up of the fouled chain, with the linkage clearly out of its track. As the hydraulic cylinder rotated the shaft, the chain stayed put and pulled up the rotating gear. This should have reversed itself, by gravity, on lowering.

Photo, Avro Report

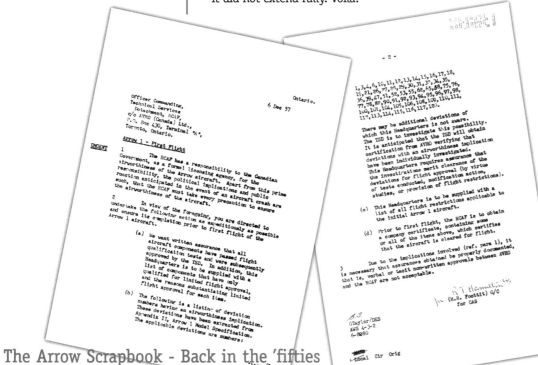

The track of RL-201 as it yawed its way off the runway, coming to rest just in the dirt at the edge.

Photo, P. Brennan

A beached RL-201 lies on the edge of the runway, the landing gear collapsed. Zurakowski walked away unhurt. There was extensive damage to the nose wheel well and the underside engine bay area. Holes had to be cut in the upper fuselage and wings to attach lift cables..

Photo, L.Wilkinson

Second accident, November 11, 1958

It appeared that heavy breaking had been applied when RL-202 landed. The main gear wheels locked, and the magnesium hubs began to burn. Smoke billowed out behind. Test pilot Bud Potocki said later the plane appeared light on landing and that full brake pressure was not applied. However, he lost directional control and the Arrow skidded off the runway to the East. The right landing gear collapsed, the others were damaged, and the plane ended up on its right side. Potocki climbed out on to the nose of the plane and lowered himself to the ground from the air data boom. Again there were no injuries.

Photos, L. Wilkinson & P. Brennan

The Arrow Scrapbook - Back in the 'fifties

MEMORANDUM

9 Dec 58

Ref Our C1038CN-180 (DFS) 23 Sep 58

Referred to AAWS
DEC 10 1958
1C38CN-80

AAWS

Aircraft Accident - Arrow 25202
AVRO Flight Test Methods - Flight Safety Considerations

1   The primary cause of the subject accident has been
assessed "Pilot Error", with "Briefing" and "Materiel"
annotated as contributing factors. The D14 is attached for
your perusal.

2   The qualifications and abilities of the personnel
who direct and participate in this type of development programme should be of the highest order. Accordingly, both the
pilot error and briefing errors committed in this instance
are inexcusable. In this regard your attention is invited to
our referenced correspondence which included a report
containing several comments on the flight safety aspects of
AVRO's flight test programme. It is pointed out that a
thorough briefing for the test in question should have indicated that a measured landing, under the existing wind
conditions, would achieve no useful purpose. Further, in this
particular test the landing was to be measured to determine if
a safe landing could be conducted on runway 28-10 (length
7,200 feet) on occasions when the wind favoured that runway.
The runway that was used for the test, 14-32, is 11,050 feet
in length. However, 2,300 feet was used before the aircraft
touched down, thus only 7,750 feet was available for the
landing roll. Consequently, because of the pilot error
involved the test landing was attempted with only 500 feet
more runway than is available on runway 28-10. The implications are obvious and should have been apparent to the test
pilot.

3   In para 13 of the attached D14 the AOC of AMC has
stated:

         "I feel the removal from further test flying duties
         on the Arrow aircraft of the pilot in question,
         whose judgement induced him so to hazard his air-
         craft in the still early stages of its flight
         testing, should be considered seriously".

Further comments in this respect by DFS are not considered
necessary. However, it is now apparent that unless AVRO adopts
a professional approach to their flight testing of the Arrow,
the complete loss of an aircraft for avoidable causes should
not be surprising.

(JJ Jordan) G/C
DFS
25779

The RCAF concluded that the pilot was at fault and that there was significant evidence that Avro had been negligent. It warned that a major accident appeared inevitable.

Letter, National Archives

The RCAF conclusion, indicating pilot error as the cause of the RL-202 accident seems well thought out. However, Avro's investigation is definitely at odds. Apparently, the AFCS (automatic flight control system) may have malfunctioned in that on landing full down elevator was indicated. If true, the plane would have ballooned from ground effect and feeling light, less than full pressure on the brakes could have locked the wheels. Fortunately, some teenagers had sneaked up beside the airport runway to take pictures. They were caught and upon learning they had taken pictures, Avro quickly developed them and found indeed, the elevators were in a full down position. So Spud Potocki's explanation of the landing now made sense and Avro blamed a malfunction of the AFCS as the probable cause.

Jan Zurakowski, too, was blamed for a CF-100 accident in which the landing gear retracted while landing. The plane was checked out on jacks and the gear seemed to respond perfectly, thus pointing the finger at Zura. When this checking was complete a mechanic went up to the plane and slapped it hard saying, "You see, that's really a good old aircraft." At which point the gear retracted all by itself, much to everyone's surprise. It was later established that a short was created through landing vibrations. At first everyone thought pilot error was the cause.

The tone of the RCAF letter is strong and doesn't pull any punches. By this time the cancellation of the program was only a matter of time. You can see that, in the minds of some of the RCAF, Avro was not doing good work. When the program was terminated RCAF personnel just went on about their business.

Not many raised a public voice of protest. Were they disillusioned?

One of the intruder photos. RL-202 elevators do not appear to be in the down position... does this strengthen the RCAF position?

Photo, Ross Richardson, Nick Wolochatiuk, one of the teenagers.

A.V. Roe became Canada's third largest company in twelve years, a remarkable feat by any measure. But Avro was building an empire whereas the RCAF wanted an airplane. These different goals were bound to collide.

GROWTH AND ACHIEVEMENT

THE YEAR ending July 31, 1958 was one of significant development in the corporate life of your company.

A measure of the growth that occurred in the year is the increase in consolidated assets from $145,754,527 to $310,400,714; the increase in consolidated sales from $234,811,024, to $370,751,856 for 1958 and the doubling of employment to 41,000.

Another yardstick of growth is the increase in capital stock. The number of common shares issued and outstanding at the year end was 8,111,941 compared with 4,763,500 the year before together with 140,000 5¾% Preferred Shares. About 43% of the outstanding common is held by the public; the balance by the Hawker Siddeley Group which took up 200,000 out of an issue of 240,000 of the preferred shares and during the year converted 100,000 of them into common shares. There were 16,088 registered holders of preferred and common shares at July 31, 1958 (of which 96% were Canadian residents) against a total of 2,716 shareholders the year before.

In terms of growth, the outstanding event of the year was the acquisition of 77% interest in Dosco. Immediately after assuming control last October a program of reorganization was started to strengthen management and re-align the various units into a more cohesive and effective operation. This program is proceeding satisfactorily. While reduced demand for coal and steel had a substantial effect on Dosco operations, the steps that have and are being taken, augur well for the long-range profitability of Dosco, within the framework of an expanding Canadian economy.

In the matter of technical achievement, the notable events were the success of the initial test flight program of the Avro Arrow; the progress made with the Orenda Iroquois jet engine and the development of an armoured tracked carrier for the Canadian Army. These projects represent tangible evidence of a high level of technical and productive capability.

As a result of events of the year, your company has achieved its aim of broadening its industrial base. The scope of activities now extends from mining basic materials such as coal and iron ore, to the manufacture of products ranging from screws, wire and nails to intricate electro-mechanical devices, advanced aircraft, jet engines, railway rolling stock and equipment, highway trailers, buses, naval and merchant ships.

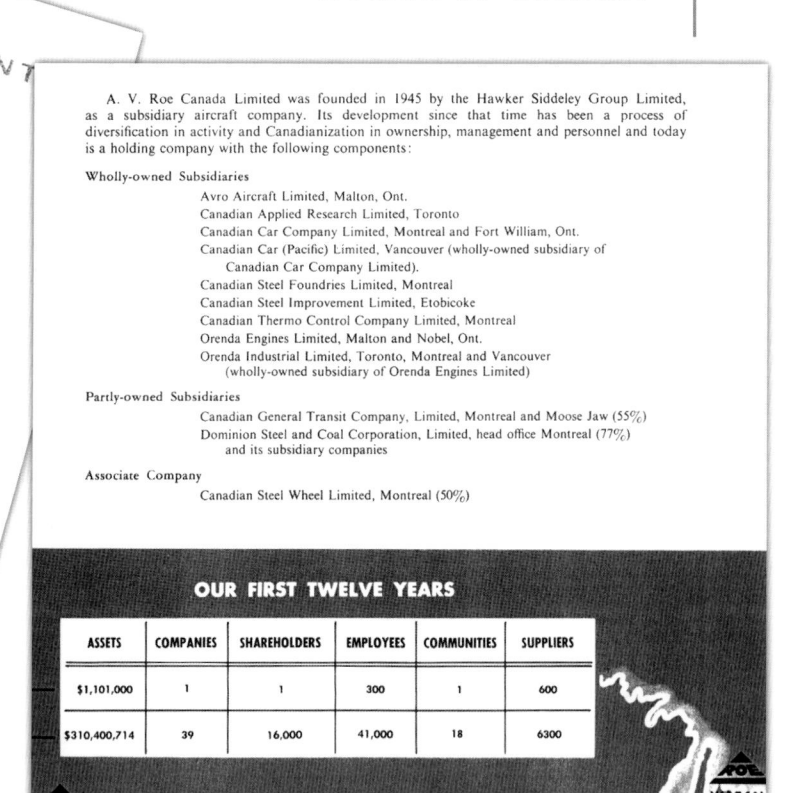

A. V. Roe Canada Limited was founded in 1945 by the Hawker Siddeley Group Limited, as a subsidiary aircraft company. Its development since that time has been a process of diversification in activity and Canadianization in ownership, management and personnel and today is a holding company with the following components:

Wholly-owned Subsidiaries

Avro Aircraft Limited, Malton, Ont.
Canadian Applied Research Limited, Toronto
Canadian Car Company Limited, Montreal and Fort William, Ont.
Canadian Car (Pacific) Limited, Vancouver (wholly-owned subsidiary of Canadian Car Company Limited).
Canadian Steel Foundries Limited, Montreal
Canadian Steel Improvement Limited, Etobicoke
Canadian Thermo Control Company Limited, Montreal
Orenda Engines Limited, Malton and Nobel, Ont.
Orenda Industrial Limited, Toronto, Montreal and Vancouver (wholly-owned subsidiary of Orenda Engines Limited)

Partly-owned Subsidiaries

Canadian General Transit Company, Limited, Montreal and Moose Jaw (55%)
Dominion Steel and Coal Corporation, Limited, head office Montreal (77%) and its subsidiary companies

Associate Company

Canadian Steel Wheel Limited, Montreal (50%)

OUR FIRST TWELVE YEARS

ASSETS	COMPANIES	SHAREHOLDERS	EMPLOYEES	COMMUNITIES	SUPPLIERS
$1,101,000	1	1	300	1	600
$310,400,714	39	16,000	41,000	18	6300

Extract from, A.V.Roe Canada Ltd.. 1958 Annual Report

Avro Aircraft Limited

Fred T. Smye
Vice-President
and General Manager

Jim C. Floyd
V.P. Engineering

Harvey R. Smith
V.P. Manufacturing

Joseph A. Morley
V.P. Sales and Service

Orenda Engines Limited

Walter R. McLachlan
Vice-President
and General Manager

Charles A. Grinyer
V.P. Engineering

Earle K. Brownridge
V.P. Manufacturing

Frank L. Trethewey
V.P. Sales and Service

As Avro Canada Limited grew, resentment increased over the company's cost-plus profits and its success in using taxpayers' money to take over a strategic sector of the Canadian economy. Though it was 46 percent owned and operated by Canadians, Avro was still a British company. For the 14,000 people working for Avro and Orenda, however, the important thing remained the creation of beautiful aircraft to grace – and defend – Canadian skies.

The Arrow Scrapbook - Back in the 'fifties

Photo, Mcdonnell Douglas Photo unit

The management of
A.V. Roe Canada Ltd..
was building a large,
vertically integrated,
enterprise.

*Crawford Gordon,
Viscount Montgomery,
Air Marshal Curtis and
Sir Roy Dobson –
entertaining important
guests. Later, they would
enjoy a private dinner at
Avro's elegant retreat,
"Briarcrest" – sill in
existence at the corner of
Islington and Dixon in
Etobicoke, Ont.*

Photo, National Archives,
Peter Zuuring

Profits from Canadian
government
cost-plus contracts
helped fund the
takeovers.

A.V. Roe Canada Limited employees going home after another day at work. Just doing their job.

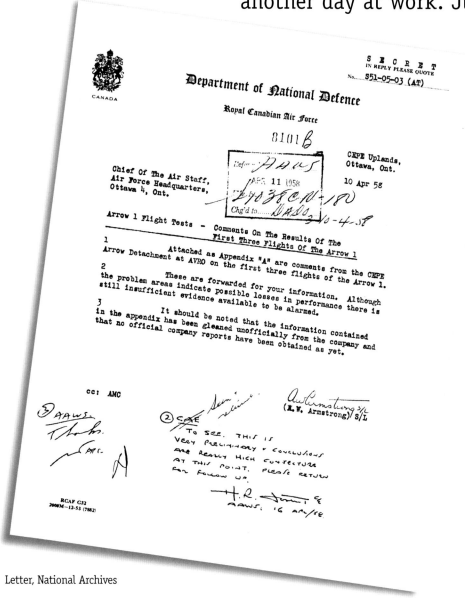

Letter, National Archives

Meanwhile at the RCAF, storm clouds were gathering.

Back in the 'fifties - The Arrow Scrapbook

S- 1038CN-180 VOL.

ROYAL CANADIAN AIR FORCE

SUBJECT

EQUIPMENT AND SUPPLIES
- SECTION 38CN EQUIPMENT
- CF105 AIRCRAFT - GENERALLY

FOR CROSS REFERENCES SEE INSIDE COVER

REFERRED	NEW VOL CR MA JUN 5 - 1957	DATE OF PASS	INITIALS	DATE OF P.A.	INITIALS	DATE OF S.F.	CENTRAL REGISTRY	INSERTED IN C.R. BY
DIE Enott	WITH PAPERS CR JUN 6 1957			14/6/57	JCC			
DAI/Eng 6	WITH PAPERS CR JUN 18 1957						JUN 14 1957	S
DAI Ens	②							
AMD Bomb BF	15-7-57		Jul			JUL - 8 1957	S
CAE/Cook	REQUISITION CR JUL 23 1957		24 Jul			JUL 22 1957	S
			28 July			JUL 25 1957	

Meantime in the RCAF

So what's up?

The RCAF's record of the Arrow program consists mostly of files. I spent months looking into hundreds of boxes at the National Archives in Ottawa. Less than fifty Arrow-related pictures are available, and these from the Department of National Defence Photo Unit at the National Research Council in Ottawa.

With regard to the files, we know that letters and documents are often edited and may not represent the real views behind the words. The files are full of examples of this. Still, it is clear that there was an erosion of RCAF confidence in A.V. Roe Canada Limited and its ability to deliver the Arrow on time and within budget and specifications. The changing threat seen in the advent of Sputnik and the ICBM further created doubt as to the usefulness of a jet interceptor, especially given its dramatic costs. Once the military chiefs lost faith, it was not long before a cost-cutting government got wind of it and cancelled the Arrow program for them.

Doubts took flight at the RCAF

*Air Vice-Marshal
M.M. Hendrick*

Photo, DND

The RCAF's mood was not so buoyant

*Extracts from Air Vice Marshal
Hendrick's Diary.*

In fact, feelings were becoming downright ugly. When reading the record you sense a build up of tension. The RCAF is anxious to have the Arrow. It wants it to be the best. 1958 will become a showdown year.

It has invested heavily in many ways. The Chiefs of Staff see Avro expanding, going public, hiring ex-RCAF officers like Wilf Curtis and John Plant in a sort of payoff scheme. They have waited patiently through the delays, cost increases and compromises. They have deflected inter-service rivalries. The army and the navy want their toys, too. Internal strife between the missile faction and the manned flyers was legion.

Diary for 29th Oct 57

The Cabinet this morning approved one year further development of the 105, and the Sparrow which meant to initiate procurement of 29 pre-production aircraft, and to continue the preproduction programme for the Sparrow. Total amount of $176,000,000 for 58-59 with commitment author-ity for the programme in future years is understood to have been author-ized. This approval went on at the same time as the Chiefs of Staff Committee were solemnly debating whether or not they should recommend the programme.

The facts which lead to this unusual circumstance are as follows:

The Air Force recommended the cancellation of the CF100 Mark 6 when under direction from the Minister to reduce their budget to $850,000,000 in 58-59. They did this reluctantly pointing out the operational risk, and the affect on AVRO's production. The reaction from AVRO and Orenda was immediate that this would cause unemployment after the 1st of Nov and personal representations were made to the Ministers. This lead to an extra ordinary unofficial Cabinet Meeting on Saturday, the 25 Oct attended by McLaughlin of Orenda, and Smye of AVRO, the Deputy Minister, and five Ministers including Mr. Green and Mr. Pearkes and Mr. Flemming. A great many half-baked ideas were tossed around to try and improve, and relieve the unemployment situation. Mr. Green stated that the critical time was between now and April during which no announced layoffs could possibly be allowed to take place, AVRO recommended our ordering of 20 additional Mark 5's as a stop gap over and above the 35 additional Mark 5's which we asked for on the cancellation of the Mark 6. The companies were promised an answer by Tues. 29th of Oct.

In the meantime during the week of the 21st a briefing to the Chiefs of Staff was presented by the CAS, outlining the reasons why the Arrow Prog-ramme should continue (at the Army's request) this was followed by an additional briefing by DRB purporting to show the relative cost per kill of various alternative systems. This briefing was most inadequate, and gave the Chiefs of Staff very little to go on. The Chiefs of Staff had tacitly agreed to the 105 Programme, although the Army felt that it was improper and we should cancel the aeroplane forthwith launch on a missile defence programme. The Army did not specify what kind of missile partic-ularly, but merely had the feeling that the development had been so rapid in the last few years that we were backing an obsolete system. The Air Force contended in rebuttle that we were not turning our backs on missiles and in the meantime we had to cover ourselves with the manned fighter. Furthermore, both fighter and missile were complementary, neither one could do the whole task by itself. On the Tuesday the Chiefs of Staff assembled to hear the CAS briefing once more, with a view to approving it for presen-tation to the Cabinet Defence Committee. On the previous evening the Minister became impatient, realizing his undertaking to give an answer on the following day, and accordingly held a long interview with the CAS that evening, wrote his own paper, and agreed to put to Cabinet the proposal for one year continuation of the programme. He would not go along with an accelerated programme, costing an additional $27,000,000 in 58-59 although this alternative had been put before Chiefs of Staff at the request of Gen. Folkes to meet the criticism that the Arrow wuld be late. This accelerated programme could advance the matter by 6 months.

Mr. Pearkes went before the Cabinet with his own paper, got the approval for the programme and in addition 20 extra Mark 5 aeroplanes and announced the fact in answer to questions that afternoon in the house.

The presentation of this whole programme was fraught with great confusion during the 10 day period prior to this decision. Part of this was due to continuing adjustments of figures and drafts against a deadline. A Commit-tee A/C's Cornblat, Hodgson, were made the focal points to do the writing chiefly because Chief of Plans was ill. Four papers were finally made available as optional for the presentation to the Chiefs, one the Arrow by itself, two the Sparrow by itself, three, a combined programme of both on original timing and four a combined programme of both accelerated by 6 months. In addition to these four papers, it was necessary to table the general costs of Air Defence, including, Arrow, Sparrow, BOMARC, ground environment between, over the next ten years in broad terms for the informat-ion of the Chiefs of Staff.

Not only did the RCAF have to deal with the forces, it had to deal with its political taskmasters too. It was bad enough to have to go to C.D. Howe every six months and ask for more money without having much to show for it. Now, it had a change of government which did not have the ownership or the knowledge to deal adroitly with the issues. To make matters even worse, the definition of the threat facing Canada and North America was changing by the day. The age of the ICBM was dawning. Red fever and the Red's diabolical intentions fueled the fires of weapons development. Goaded on by zealous suppliers, it is no wonder that tensions were running high. One former high-ranking RCAF officer likened dealing with A.V. Roe Canada Ltd., as being the virgin in the whorehouse.

Air Vice Marshal M.M. Hendrick, (AMTS), was responsible to the Chief of the Air Staff, Hugh Campbell. He kept a daily diary which is part of the Raymont Collection in DND's Directorate of Heritage. It makes fascinating reading. Just after the Conservatives were elected in June 1957, the Arrow was once again up for its six months review. George Pearkes, the new minister of defence, was an ex-military man himself. He knew the players and got things done – to the amazement of the Chiefs of Staff. For example, he walked down to Diefenbaker's Office and had the NORAD agreement signed in a few hours. He took matters into his own hands when

the chiefs could not come to some consensus about the CF-100, MK-VI program or the Arrow budget for the coming year.

I have reproduced Hendrick's views of the matter. I find them lucid, practical and to the point.

Air Vice-Marshal J. Easton, missile man

Photo, DND

Interceptor, Missile or both?

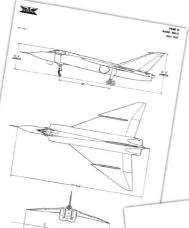

The Canadian government's budget in 1957 was about $6 billion. Defence took a quarter of this or about $1.5 billion, with the RCAF taking half of that. In turn, the Arrow program took about $200 million of the RCAF's share.

How did the RCAF get involved in the Arrow Program?

In the beginning...

Letter, National Archives

Even before the CF-100 was in production, Avro was looking for the next step. Every arms manufacturer knows that the Father, Son and Holy Ghost of survival when dealing with a single customer is to have a project in development, one in design and one in production. The world was going supersonic. Canada was not going to be left out. As Fred Smye, Vice President and General Manager of Avro said, "The company was not going to stand idly by and let the design, research and development staff and facilities, built up successfully over a decade, go down the drain." Canada had built up a winning reputation by having manufactured more than 16,000 aircraft, from scratch, during the war years. A.V. Roe Canada did finally get the CF-100 and Orenda engine program on track. Avro and the RCAF were ready for bigger things.

Jogged by the company, supported by design studies, the RCAF issued AIR-7-3, "Design Studies of Prototype Supersonic, All-weather, Interceptor Aircraft." In April 1953, Avro was issued a design, mock-up and wind tunnel contract for $200,000. By June of the same year, a family of delta wing aircraft included a high-wing version that was the right weight and allowed for easy engine installation...the CF-105. By August 1953 , a further $300,000 had been authorized to complete the design study. The Rolls-Royce RB-106 was chosen to power the 1225 square foot delta.

During October 1953, a ministerial directive stopped all work on the project - *first cancellation*.

By the Spring of 1954 the program was re-instated with a firm contract to produce two prototypes and one airframe for static test purposes. Funds increased from $500,000 to $1,325,000. The company reviewed the engine availability and included the Curtis Wright J-67, Pratt & Whitney J-57 and possibly the J-75. Avro evaluated

the use of the Cooke-Craigie method of slow manufacture, directly with hard production tooling to speed up eventual deployment. Area rule studies to streamline the fuselage were undertaken.

Up until this time frame, 1954, the National Aeronautical Establishment, mirrored on the RAE, had carried out key design work for the RCAF. The Defence research Board, a part of DND, used to advise the forces on technical matters. As Avro was now doing what it thought was its work, a rivalry of sorts was developing. In fact, John Parkin of the NAE was warning the RCAF that Avro was too optimistic in its drag estimations and that essentially the design was flawed.

The RCAF was already uneasy with Avro's capabilities because of the difficulties with the CF-100. Having to deal with the NAE and DRB criticisms did not help. It got to such a state that a so-called neutral third party, NACA of the U.S.A. was brought in to arbitrate the issue. A preliminary meeting first without Avro and then including Avro, settled the issue diplomatically. In the end, NACA leaned

favourably toward Avro's findings. Its summaries are included for interest on the next page. Clouds gathered and were dispersed - the NAE never forgot its loss of influence. Members of that delegation remember the issues even today.

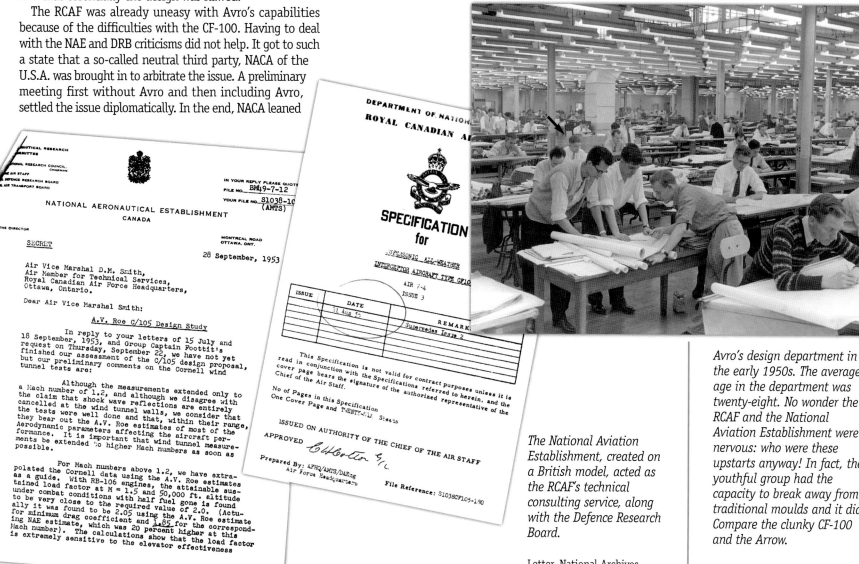

Avro's design department in the early 1950s. The average age in the department was twenty-eight. No wonder the RCAF and the National Aviation Establishment were nervous: who were these upstarts anyway! In fact, the youthful group had the capacity to break away from traditional moulds and it did. Compare the clunky CF-100 and the Arrow.

The National Aviation Establishment, created on a British model, acted as the RCAF's technical consulting service, along with the Defence Research Board.

Letter, National Archives

Photo, Ross Richardson
(See arrow highlight)

UNCLASSIFIED

JOINT REPORT ON AN RCAF-DRB-NAE VISIT
TO N.A.C.A. LANGLEY LABORATORIES TO DISCUSS AERODYNAMIC
PROBLEMS OF AVRO CF-105 AIRCRAFT - 19 NOVEMBER 1954

SUMMARY

N.A.C.A. comments on CF-105 design problems are
summarized as follows:

(a) The Company's estimate of zero lift drag at subsonic and supersonic speeds should be increased by 50 percent
or more.

(b) Substantial reductions in drag throughout the
supersonic speed range should be possible by proper application
of the area rule.

(c) Present intake lip design is likely to result in
prohibitive drag penalties at supersonic speeds.

(d) The high drag due to lift associated with low
aspect ratio delta wings makes them poor planforms for high
endurance and long range.

(e) The high drag due to lift is not improved by the
negative camber proposed by the firm. Correctly designed
positive camber should be used to reduce substantially both
drag due to lift and trim drag.

(f) A wind tunnel programme would be required to
develop the means proposed by A.V. Roe to ensure intake
stability.

(g) The CF-105 wing planform is of the type which gives
serious pitch-up tendencies. Cures developed in wind tunnels
do not always work out in flight.

(h) The directional stability characteristics of the
CF-105 are poorer than had been experienced in the United
States. A wind tunnel programme should be pursued.

(i) All steps should be taken to ensure aerodynamic
stability before resorting to electronic means.

(j) It is possible that the use of elevons rather than
separate elevators and ailerons would result in lower trim
drag and higher reversal speed.

PLEASE RETURN
DSIS
LOAN COPY

UNCLASSIFIED
Copy No: 4
UNLIMITE

JOINT REPORT ON AN RCAF-DRB-NAE VISIT
TO N.A.C.A. LANGLEY LABORATORIES TO DISCUSS AERODYNAMIC
PROBLEMS OF AVRO CF-105 AIRCRAFT - 19 NOVEMBER 1954.

Date 25.4.56

MAR 22 1956

These RCAF documents were found at the National Archives. The first meeting excluded Avro. To this day, former Avro employees as high up as Jim Floyd did not know this meeting had taken place. It is clear that the tone of the minutes from the second meeting was more conciliatory, favouring Avro's findings. Strategically the RCAF, in cooperation with the DRB and the NAE, wanted to stake its ground before Avro got involved. Was the NAE trying to set up Avro to assert its position?

The CF-100 development program involved only two prototypes and used older techniques and longer time frames than the Arrow. It was also dwarfed by the size of the Arrow program. Because air speeds doubled with the Arrow, breaking the sound barrier for the first time in Canada, everyone was a little nervous. Some argued for inherent stability while Avro's chief aerodynamicist, Jim Chamberlin, stated that instability augmented by controlled surfaces with more and more refinements is what made flight possible. The photo at left shows a CF-100 ready for a test flight with Waterton and Rogers at the controls. The Arrow program never got beyond this point.

Photo, Ross Richardson

More opinions!

NACA, National Advisory Committee for Aeronautics

Document 1 (page 1):

UNCLASSIFIED
UNLIMITED

SECRET
UNCLASSIFIED

This document consists of _3_ pages
No. _1_ of _27_ Copies, Series _A_

Meeting to Discuss CF-105 Problems
Held December 20 and 21, 1954
at
National Advisory Committee For Aeronautics
1512 H Street, Northwest, Washington, D. C.

Introduction

A meeting was held at NACA Headquarters on December 20 and 21, 1954, between Canadian officials, representatives of A. V. Roe (Canada) Ltd., and NACA staff members to discuss technical problems in connection with the CF-105 airplane design. The following were in attendance:

Abbott, Ira H. - Headquarters, National Advisory Committee for Aeronautics (Chairman)
Ames, M. B., Jr. - Headquarters, National Advisory Committee for Aeronautics (part time)
Armstrong, A. W. - Squadron Leader, Royal Canadian Air Force
Chamberlin, J. A. - A. V. Roe (Canada) Ltd.
Crowley, John W. - Headquarters, National Advisory Committee for Aeronautics (part time)
Dobranski, J. Stalony - A. V. Roe (Canada) Ltd.
Dryden, Hugh L. - Headquarters, National Advisory Committee for Aeronautics (part time)
Floyd, J. C. - A. V. Roe (Canada) Ltd.
Foottit, H. R. - Group Captain, Royal Canadian Air Force
Frick, Charles W. - Ames Aeronautical Laboratory, NACA
Gilchrist, A. W. R. - Defence Research Board
Green, J. J. - Defence Research Board
Lindley, R. N. - A. V. Roe (Canada) Ltd.
Lucas, J. H. - A. V. Roe (Canada) Ltd.
MacPhail, D. C. - National Aeronautical Establishment, Canada
Morris, J. - A. V. Roe (Canada) Ltd.
Pearson, E. O. - Headquarters, National Advisory Committee for Aeronautics (part time)
Plant, J. L. - Vice Marshal, Royal Canadian Air Force
Smye, F. T. - A. V. Roe (Canada) Ltd.
Templin, R. J. - National Aeronautical Establishment, Canada
Toll, Thomas A. - Langley Aeronautical Laboratory, NACA
Whitcomb, Richard - Langley Aeronautical Laboratory, NACA
Woodward, F. A. - A. V. Roe (Canada) Ltd.
Wyatt, D. D. - Lewis Flight Propulsion Laboratory, NACA

#F 126599

Classification cancelled / changed
by authority of _U.S. DoD HQ CDN_
SOATI
Date _13 Dec 91_
Signature _Lindsay_
Unit / Rank / Appointment _DSIS_

SECRET
UNCLASSIFIED

Document 2 (page 2):

UNCLASSIFIED
SECRET

2

The following paragraphs summarize the discussion.

Drag

It was basically agreed that, in line with the area distribution curves at Mach 1.5 submitted by AVRO, and provided that (a) the intake and ramp bleed area is investigated and cleaned up where necessary, and (b) the afterbody is well faired in after the nozzles, the zero lift drag at Mach 1.5 may be as low as .020. This value may be approached by further model investigations. The AVRO estimate from area distribution and skin friction considerations was .0184. The configuration is considered to be generally reasonable with regard to drag.

Wing

Positive Camber

It was agreed that there is little to be gained by conical positive camber for the particular mission of this aircraft, i.e. Mach 1.5 at 50,000 feet, and there might be some loss of maximum supersonic speed. It was agreed, however, that to get the maximum flexibility in the aircraft, it would be a good thing to provide structurally for the possible future application of positive camber at the leading edge in case the emphasis shifted from the supersonic mission to a long-range type of mission, provided that the structural penalties are not too severe. AVRO's reasons for going to negative camber were also understood and appeared reasonable.

Pitch-up

It was agreed that the notch or leading edge extension proposed by AVRO should alleviate pitch-up, and that there would be a drag increment of between .001 and .002 at supersonic speeds to be added to the above estimate.

Intakes

It was generally agreed that the amount of diffusion and the diffusion angle involved at the intake were not excessive. AVRO pointed out that if tests later showed that a parallel section of duct was necessary to provide stabilization, this could be done without extensive structural modification.

UNCLASSIFIED
SECRET

Document 3 (page 3):

UNCLASSIFIED
SECRET

3

The problem of intake instability was agreed to be difficult and even vicious, and this required extensive test work prior to flight since it could have catastrophic effects in flight.

Stability

It was generally agreed that while artificial lateral stabilization is undesirable in itself, the obvious aerodynamic cures such as a large increase in fin area could be unacceptable so far as performance of the aircraft is concerned. A concentrated test program was recommended to explore aerodynamic means of providing lateral stability, particularly fin and rudder effectiveness.

It was particularly suggested that AVRO examine the effect of low directional stability. AVRO is doing a dynamic analysis. It was recommended that five degrees of freedom should be examined since the state of the art has now reached a point where the dynamic behavior of aircraft cannot be predicted from a cursory examination of the configuration and derivatives. AVRO agreed and is checking those areas of the flight envelope which are considered to be critical. It was noted that problems of this type are not peculiar to the CF-105 configuration but appear to be associated with the mass distributions of modern high performance fighters.

PLEASE RETURN
THIS
LOAN COPY

12/22/54

Ira H. Abbott
Assistant Director for Research
National Advisory Committee for Aeronautics

UNCLASSIFIED
SECRET

To develop the new supersonic interceptor required a shift in procedure. It takes a certain number of flying hours to test, prove and evaluate an aircraft or a weapon system before it goes into operational use. As aircraft became more complex, the number of flying hours increased. Thus, before World War II sufficient development flying time was achieved by ordering two prototype airplanes, testing them for a year, and then putting the aircraft into production. If this practice was followed now, because of increased complexity, it would take years to complete the test program – hence the notion of being obsolete before it ever went into production. The Arrow was not excluded from this type of criticism.

So, to get in the increased flying hours a greater number of aircraft must be produced as rapidly as possible on the first order. This scheme is called the Cooke-Craigie method in the U.S.A. and the Batch Method in the U.K. It was adopted for use in the Arrow program. In addition "ABC" groups, American, British and Canadian, were formed to make technology transfer easier among these allies. If war was to come, we would have gone with what we had. There would have been no time to rebuild. With similar cockpit layouts, transition time from one type to another would be minimized.

The U.K. used about twenty-five aircraft in the Batch Method, while the U.S.A. used about fifty or sixty. An approximate mean of thirty-seven airplanes was considered adequate to put in the 1700 hours of development flying prior to squadron use. Nothing must be overlooked so the development program was divided into eight phases.

Phase	Type	No. of Aircraft	Flying Hours
1	Contractor tests	5 Mk I, 3 Mk II	535
2	RCAF initial tests	5 Mk I, 3 Mk II	254
3	Cont. improvement	10 Mk II	283
4	RCAF handling	2 Mk II	112
5	RCAF, all-weather	2 Mk II	80
6	RCAF intensive Trls.	2 Mk II	54
7	RCAF weapons Trls.	9 Mk II	375
8	Operational/Attrition	4 Mk II	0
Total		37 Aircraft	1693

The flying hours estimated accrue from the various flight test programs required to prove the airframe, engine, electronics and missile systems separately and together as a single weapons system. Each of these involve the probing of areas that have not been explored previously. Probing these progressively and safely at incremental altitudes, speeds and manoeuvres, is the heart of the flight test program. The ultimate objective of the program is to enter squadron service with a weapon of known performance.

At cancellation, you will recall that only some seventy hours of test flying was completed using the first five Mk I airframes and J-75 engines. A lot of hours remained before the so-called "weapon system" was ready for use.

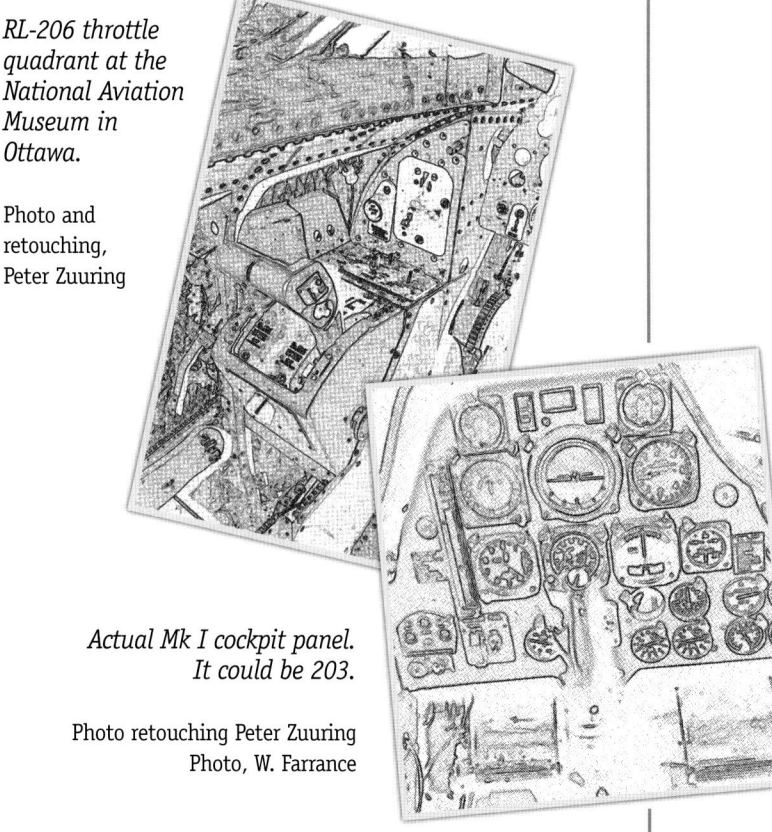

RL-206 throttle quadrant at the National Aviation Museum in Ottawa.

Photo and retouching, Peter Zuuring

Actual Mk I cockpit panel. It could be 203.

Photo retouching Peter Zuuring
Photo, W. Farrance

In 1955, the program began to heat up

RCAF rational for getting involved in the PS 13, Iroquois engine .

Letter, RCAF National Archives

With regards to the engine, Orenda had not been standing still either. Seeing an opportunity developing in the CF-105, building on its acquired expertise, OEL started a supersonic engine project of its own. After investing about $9 million in the project, the RCAF was impressed with the effort and agreed to take over the development cost and program. A further CF-105 engine crisis with non-availability and out-of-country timetables helped gel the idea that Orenda had a winner in our own backyard...a world beater if it lived up to expectations. Orenda had a good track record of design and manufacture. The Orenda series of engines for the Sabre F-86 and CF-100 programs was a success by any standard.

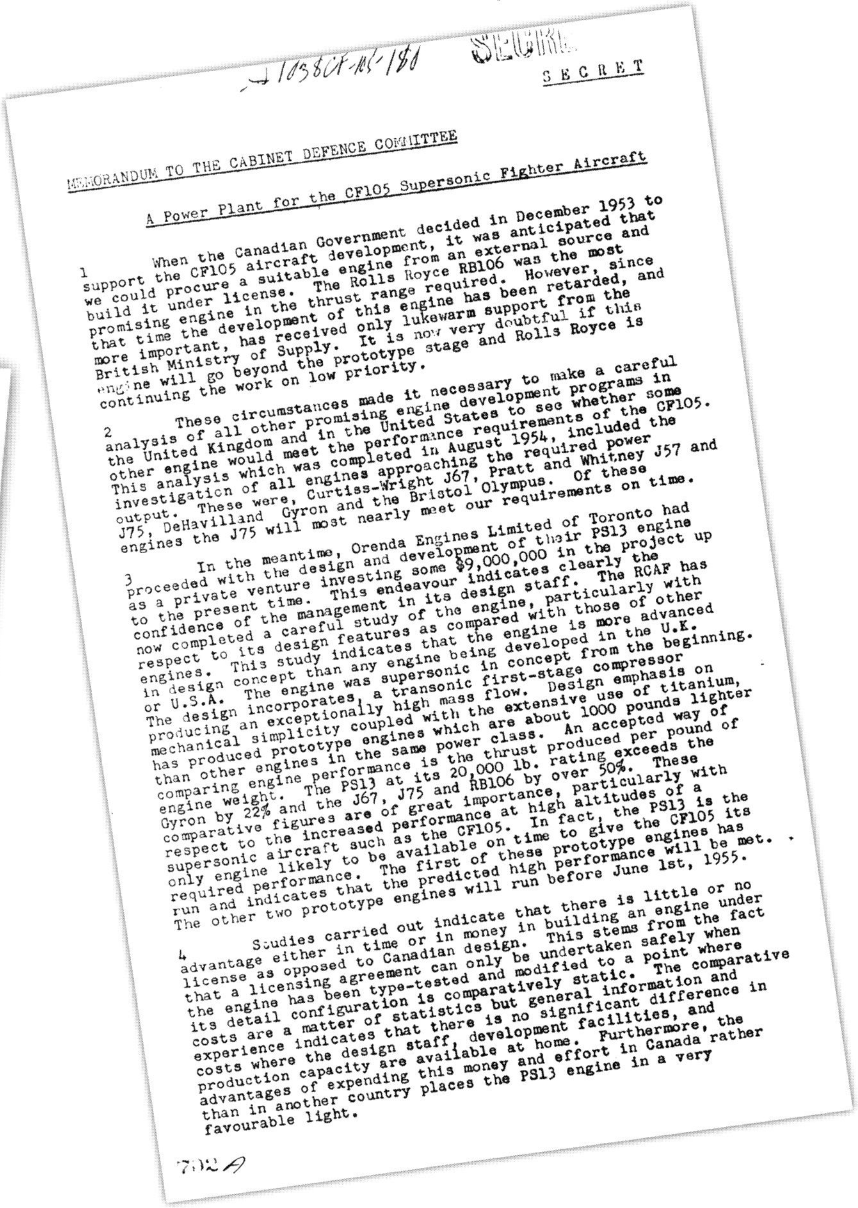

SECRET

MEMORANDUM TO THE CABINET DEFENCE COMMITTEE

A Power Plant for the CF105 Supersonic Fighter Aircraft

1 When the Canadian Government decided in December 1953 to support the CF105 aircraft development, it was anticipated that we could procure a suitable engine from an external source and build it under license. The Rolls Royce RB106 was the most promising engine in the thrust range required. However, since that time the development of this engine has been retarded, and more important, has received only lukewarm support from the British Ministry of Supply. It is now very doubtful if this engine will go beyond the prototype stage and Rolls Royce is continuing the work on low priority.

2 These circumstances made it necessary to make a careful analysis of all other promising engine development programs in the United Kingdom and in the United States to see whether some other engine would meet the performance requirements of the CF105. This analysis which was completed in August 1954, included the investigation of all engines approaching the required power output. These were, Curtiss-Wright J67, Pratt and Whitney J57 and J75, DeHavilland Gyron and the Bristol Olympus. Of these engines the J75 will most nearly meet our requirements on time.

3 In the meantime, Orenda Engines Limited of Toronto had proceeded with the design and development of their PS13 engine as a private venture investing some $9,000,000 in the project up to the present time. This endeavour indicates clearly the confidence of the management in its design staff. The RCAF has now completed a careful study of the engine, particularly with respect to its design features as compared with those of other engines. This study indicates that the engine is more advanced in design concept than any engine being developed in the U.K. or U.S.A. The engine was supersonic in concept from the beginning. The design incorporates a transonic first-stage compressor producing an exceptionally high mass flow. Design emphasis on mechanical simplicity coupled with the extensive use of titanium, has produced prototype engines which are about 1000 pounds lighter than other engines in the same power class. An accepted way of comparing engine performance is the thrust produced per pound of engine weight. The PS13 at its 20,000 lb. rating exceeds the Gyron by 22% and the J67, J75 and RB106 by over 50%. These comparative figures are of great importance, particularly with respect to the increased performance at high altitudes of a supersonic aircraft such as the CF105. In fact, the PS13 is the only engine likely to be available on time to give the CF105 its required performance. The first of these prototype engines has run and indicates that the predicted high performance will be met. The other two prototype engines will run before June 1st, 1955.

4 Studies carried out indicate that there is little or no advantage either in time or in money in building an engine under license as opposed to Canadian design. This stems from the fact that a licensing agreement can only be undertaken safely when the engine has been type-tested and modified to a point where its detail configuration is comparatively static. The comparative costs are a matter of statistics but general information and experience indicates that there is no significant difference in costs where the design staff, development facilities, and production capacity are available at home. Furthermore, the advantages of expending this money and effort in Canada rather than in another country places the PS13 engine in a very favourable light.

IROQUOIS MOCK-UP PHOTOGRAPHS

ORENDA

JULY 1956

ORENDA ENGINES LIMITED

ENGINEERING and EXPERIMENTAL DEPARTMENT

MALTON ONTARIO

(Member A.V. Roe Canada Limited and Hawker Siddeley Group)

UNCLASSIFIED

As in the case of the airframe, Orenda also produced mockups of their product prior to committing to hard tooling.

Letter, RCAF National Archives

Cost escalation...

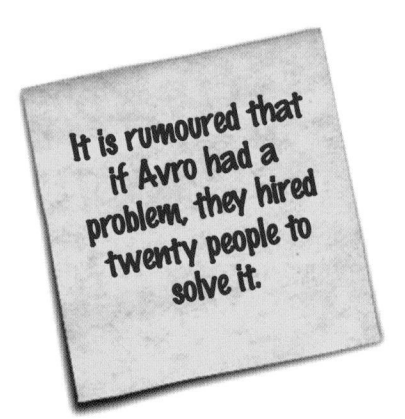

It is rumoured that if Avro had a problem, they hired twenty people to solve it.

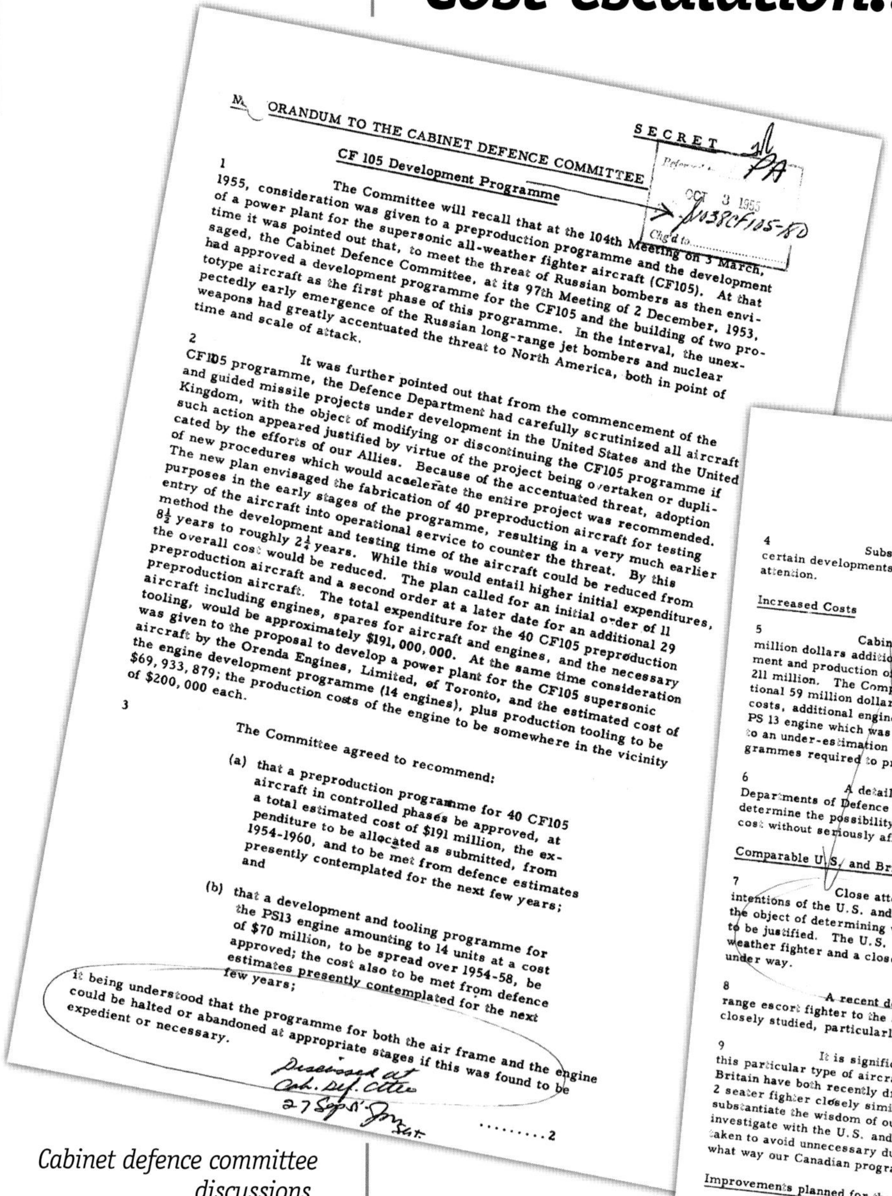

MEMORANDUM TO THE CABINET DEFENCE COMMITTEE

SECRET

CF 105 Development Programme

1

The Committee will recall that at the 104th Meeting on 3 March, 1955, consideration was given to a preproduction programme and the development of a power plant for the supersonic all-weather fighter aircraft (CF105). At that time it was pointed out that, to meet the threat of Russian bombers as then envisaged, the Cabinet Defence Committee, at its 97th Meeting of 2 December, 1953, had approved a development programme for the CF105 and the building of two prototype aircraft as the first phase of this programme. In the interval, the unexpectedly early emergence of the Russian long-range jet bombers and nuclear weapons had greatly accentuated the threat to North America, both in point of time and scale of attack.

2

It was further pointed out that from the commencement of the CF105 programme, the Defence Department had carefully scrutinized all aircraft and guided missile projects under development in the United States and the United Kingdom, with the object of modifying or discontinuing the CF105 programme if such action appeared justified by virtue of the project being overtaken or duplicated by the efforts of our Allies. Because of the accentuated threat, adoption of new procedures which would accelerate the entire project was recommended. The new plan envisaged the fabrication of 40 preproduction aircraft for testing purposes in the early stages of the programme, resulting in a very much earlier entry of the aircraft into operational service to counter the threat. By this method the development and testing time of the aircraft could be reduced from 8¼ years to roughly 2¼ years. While this would entail higher initial expenditures, the overall cost would be reduced. The plan called for an initial order of 11 preproduction aircraft and a second order at a later date for an additional 29 preproduction aircraft. The total expenditure for the 40 CF105 preproduction aircraft including engines, spares for aircraft and engines, and the necessary tooling, would be approximately $191,000,000. At the same time consideration was given to the proposal to develop a power plant for the CF105 supersonic aircraft by the Orenda Engines, Limited, of Toronto, and the estimated cost of the engine development programme (14 engines), plus production tooling to be $69,933,879; the production costs of the engine to be somewhere in the vicinity of $200,000 each.

3

The Committee agreed to recommend:

(a) that a preproduction programme for 40 CF105 aircraft in controlled phases be approved, at a total estimated cost of $191 million, the expenditure to be allocated as submitted, from 1954-1960, and to be met from defence estimates presently contemplated for the next few years; and

(b) that a development and tooling programme for the PS13 engine amounting to 14 units at a cost of $70 million, to be spread over 1954-58, be approved; the cost also to be met from defence estimates presently contemplated for the next few years;

it being understood that the programme for both the air frame and the engine could be halted or abandoned at appropriate stages if this was found to be expedient or necessary.

Discussed at Cab. Def. Ctte 27 Sept '55

.........2

Cabinet defence committee discussions.

File, National Archives, RCAF files

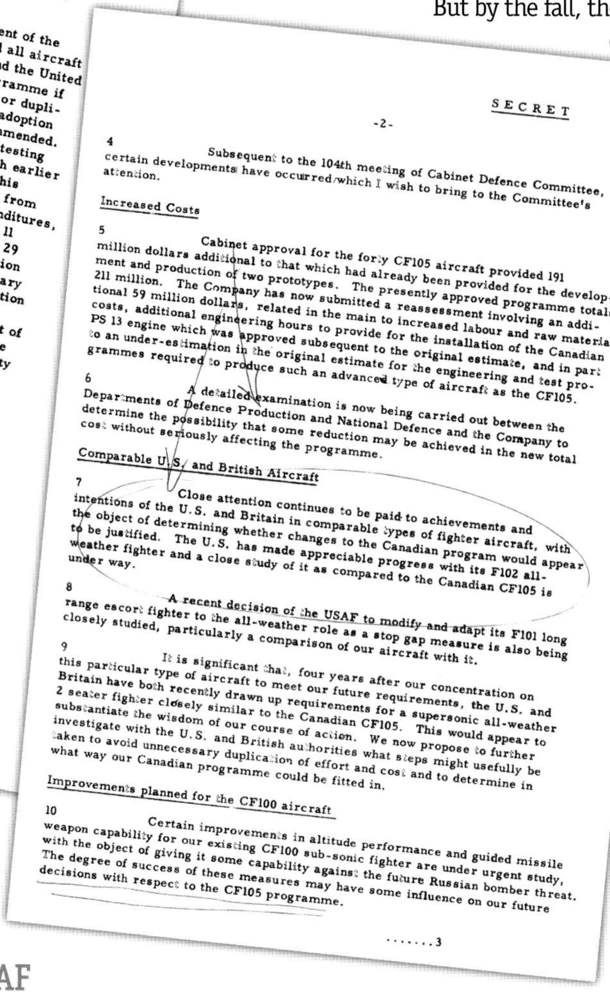

SECRET

-2-

4

Subsequent to the 104th meeting of Cabinet Defence Committee, certain developments have occurred which I wish to bring to the Committee's attention.

Increased Costs

5

Cabinet approval for the forty CF105 aircraft provided 191 million dollars additional to that which had already been provided for the development and production of two prototypes. The presently approved programme totals 211 million. The Company has now submitted a reassessment involving an additional 59 million dollars, related in the main to increased labour and raw material costs, additional engineering hours to provide for the installation of the Canadian PS 13 engine which was approved subsequent to the original estimate, and in part to an under-estimation in the original estimate for the engineering and test programmes required to produce such an advanced type of aircraft as the CF105.

6

A detailed examination is now being carried out between the Departments of Defence Production and National Defence and the Company to determine the possibility that some reduction may be achieved in the new total cost without seriously affecting the programme.

Comparable U.S. and British Aircraft

7

Close attention continues to be paid to achievements and intentions of the U.S. and Britain in comparable types of fighter aircraft, with the object of determining whether changes to the Canadian program would appear to be justified. The U.S. has made appreciable progress with its F102 all-weather fighter and a close study of it as compared to the Canadian CF105 is under way.

8

A recent decision of the USAF to modify and adapt its F101 long-range escort fighter to the all-weather role as a stop gap measure is also being closely studied, particularly a comparison of our aircraft with it.

9

It is significant that, four years after our concentration on this particular type of aircraft to meet our future requirements, the U.S. and Britain have both recently drawn up requirements for a supersonic all-weather 2 seater fighter closely similar to the Canadian CF105. This would appear to substantiate the wisdom of our course of action. We now propose to further investigate with the U.S. and British authorities what steps might usefully be taken to avoid unnecessary duplication of effort and cost and to determine in what way our Canadian programme could be fitted in.

Improvements planned for the CF100 aircraft

10

Certain improvements in altitude performance and guided missile weapon capability for our existing CF100 sub-sonic fighter are under urgent study, with the object of giving it some capability against the future Russian bomber threat. The degree of success of these measures may have some influence on our future decisions with respect to the CF105 programme.

.......3

In early 1955, Avro and Orenda obtained contracts to build forty Arrow preproduction aircraft and engines at a cost of $191 million and $70 million respectively, spread over three years. But by the fall, there was already confusion within the federal cabinet's defence committee over the cost of the Arrow program as shown by minutes of the October 3, 1955 meeting.

The program had slipped in time and increased in costs. The program now called for thirty seven airframes (three preproduction models were deleted to save costs during 1955) for $211 million and an engine development program delivering fourteen prototypes for a further $70 million. Each additional engine was to cost about $200,000. General program costs would escalate some further $59 million because of changes in material / labour costs, design modifications, and the finalizing of the whole aircraft design enabling more complete and more accurate estimates.

Understandably, Avro had a cost-plus contract. No supplier, with so many uncertainties, would enter into a fixed price at this stage. (Only when the writing was on the wall with respect to the whole program in late 1958 did Avro commit to a fixed delivery price.) In late 1956 Avro again re-evaluated the program... the fourth iteration.

Avro's program number four, issued in December 1956, indicated an increase in Arrow costs of about 20 percent, substantial but dwarfed by later dramatic increases.

Report, Avro files

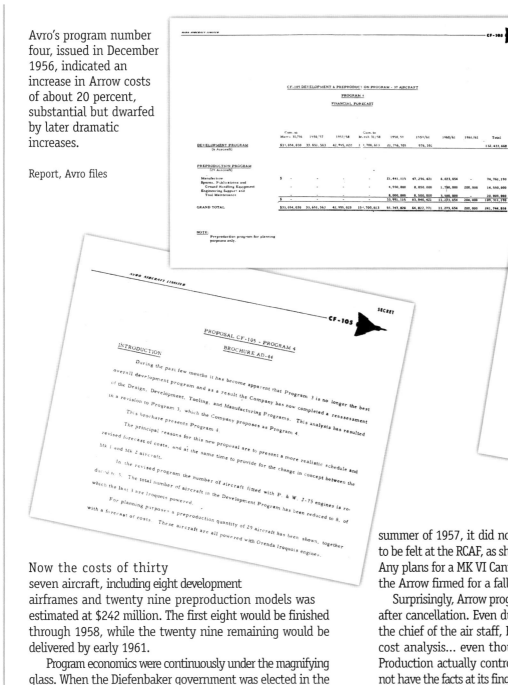

Now the costs of thirty
seven aircraft, including eight development airframes and twenty nine preproduction models was estimated at $242 million. The first eight would be finished through 1958, while the twenty nine remaining would be delivered by early 1961.

Program economics were continuously under the magnifying glass. When the Diefenbaker government was elected in the summer of 1957, it did not take long for election promises to be felt at the RCAF, as shown by the above review meeting. Any plans for a MK VI Canuck were dropped and options for the Arrow firmed for a fall review.

Surprisingly, Arrow program costs were only pinned down after cancellation. Even during that critical spring of 1958, the chief of the air staff, Hugh Campbell, again asked for a cost analysis... even though the Department of Defence Production actually controlled the cost. Why did the RCAF not have the facts at its finger tips...after all it was its program?

Interesting discussions took place among senior RCAF officers following John Diefenbaker's election as Prime Minister in 1957.

File, National Archives, RCAF files

The U.S. and Britain review Canada's Arrow program

[Document facsimile — NOTES OF A MEETING TO REVIEW A USAF APPRAISAL OF THE CF105 HELD AT AVRO AIRCRAFT, MALTON]

[Document facsimile — EVALUATION OF THE CANADIAN CF.105 ... FIGHTER FOR THE RAF]

Both the Americans and the British made numerous visits to A.V. Roe Canada Limited and toured the Malton facilities. The Americans came in November 1955 and the British in late December of the same year to evaluate the Arrow program.

The Americans said, "There are always unforeseen difficulties in any new project of an advanced nature; however, there did not appear to be any requirements beyond the state of existing knowledge, and the whole project was considered only a normal development risk."

The British reaction was more detailed covering a fifty-plus page report. They highly praised the effort yet cautioned on delivery times, manpower needs and slightly optimistic aerodynamic forecasts. They concluded that the engineering effort appeared about twice what the effort would be in the U.K. Drag coefficients were thought to be somewhat optimistic by about 10-15 percent. Delays of one to one and a half years to squadron service might be expected.

Generally upbeat reports gave confidence both to Avro and the RCAF.

Reports, NRC

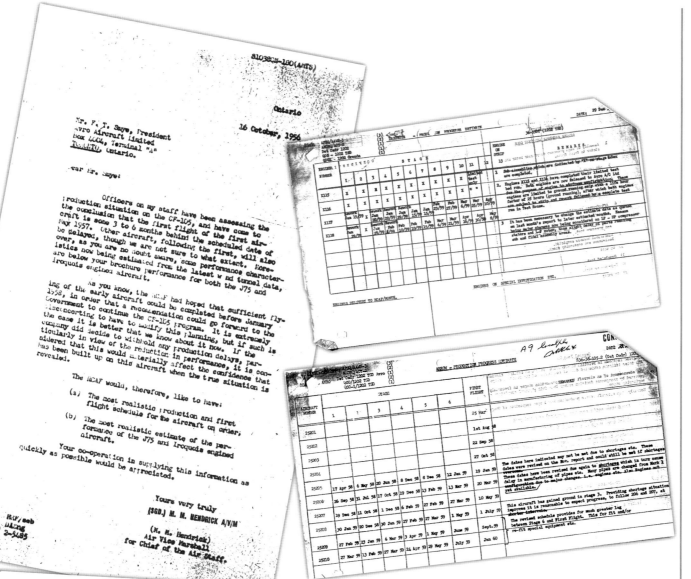

S1038CM-180(ANTS)

Ontario

16 October, 1956

Mr. F. T. Smye, President
Avro Aircraft Limited
Box 6006, Terminal "A"
TORONTO, Ontario.

Dear Mr. Smye:

Officers on my staff have been assessing the production situation on the CF-105, and have come to the conclusion that the first flight of the first aircraft is some 3 to 6 months behind the scheduled date of May 1957. Other aircraft, following the first, will also be delayed, though we are not sure to what extent. Moreover, as you are no doubt aware, some performance characteristics now being estimated from the latest wind tunnel data, are below your brochure performance for both the J75 and Iroquois engined aircraft.

As you know, the RCAF had hoped that sufficient flying of the early aircraft could be completed before January 1958, in order that a recommendation could go forward to the Government to continue the CF-105 program. It is extremely disconcerting to have to modify this planning, but if such is the case it is better that we know about it now. If the company did decide to withhold any production delays, particularly in view of the reduction in performance, it is considered that this would materially affect the confidence that has been built up on this aircraft when the true situation is revealed.

The RCAF would, therefore, like to have:

(a) The most realistic production and first flight schedule for the aircraft on order;

(b) The most realistic estimate of the performance of the J75 and Iroquois engined aircraft.

Your co-operation in supplying this information as quickly as possible would be appreciated.

Yours very truly
(SGD.) M. M. HENDRICK A/V/M

(M. M. Hendrick)
Air Vice Marshall
for Chief of the Air Staff.

MMH/seb
DING
2-5485

15. **General Foulkes** stated that he was gravely concerned with the delay in the CF105 programme and suggested that every effort must be made to accelerate it. Unless this were done, it might well appear that a great deal of money was being spent on an aircraft and its associated missile and ground environment which would be outmoded before it became fully operational.

Every level of the RCAF expressed concern about delays in the Arrow program, beginning in early 1956 and continuing through 1957 and 1958. Both Air Vice Marshal M.M. Hendrick in this letter and chief of the defence staff General Charles Foulkes, in a late-1957 cabinet defence committee meeting, worried about delays in deliveries and last minute changes for the Iroquois engine and the Arrow airframe. The delays were probably normal for a project of that magnitude, but the problem was that Avro raised expectations and then delayed delivery not once, but on numerous occasions. The RCAF learned the real state of progress through a process it called "backing and filling," that is, from the guys on the floor.

Letter, minute and charts,
National Archives, RCAF files

From specifications to rollout...

Avro and the RCAF did not square off all the time. The photo on the right shows Wing Commander Ray Foottit presenting the 1956 McCurdy award for aeronautical excellence on behalf of the Canadian Aeronautical Institute to Jim Floyd, vice-president of engineering at Avro. Both men had (and have today) vast experience in project management and leadership. Foottit served under Air Vice Marshal Hendrick, and Floyd worked at Avro for Fred Smye and later Jim Plant, a former RCAF officer. Confrontation was, perhaps, inevitable, but these two men made things work.

Photo, A.V. Roe Canada
1958 Annual report

With specification books in hand, RCAF personnel attended a Mk I "mock-up conference" at the Avro plant in Malton in the spring of 1956 and another for the Mk II in the fall of 1957. Extensive arrangements were made to funnel the commentary and suggestions gathered over the three-day events. Comments ranged from "how do you lock the observer's canopy when there is no observer?" (a small door was installed in the bulkhead behind the pilot's seat) to the serviceability of the aileron and the elevator control boxes. All comments were categorized into various levels of "musts" and "wants" and most were acted on. Note that the

specifications were revised to January 1959, as current as they got.

RCAF acceptance of an aircraft was based on first flight. The plane was then loaned back to the company on an indefinite basis for further development. The first flight of RL-202 was premature according to the RCAF, just to gain acceptance and perhaps to meet some milestone.

The Arrow Mk II specifications book ran to 270 pages.

NRC, Parkin Lib.

Wooden mockup CF-206 ready for the conference. Note weapons pack in the foreground.

ARROW 2 MOCK-UP

ENGINEERING EVALUATION

CONFERENCE

SEPTEMBER 1957

AVRO AIRCRAFT LIMITED

MALTON — ONTARIO

Wooden mockup showing cockpit access and nose electronics.

Once the wooden mockup was approved a full metal version was built to test tooling.

About 200 people attended these mockup conferences. Maps of the Avro facility were handed out so that members could find their way to the washroom and luncheon areas.

RCAF personnel confer with Avro engineers about the large radar dish that would give the Arrow sufficient look ahead to have time to prepare their missile attack.

On the left a less spectacular roll-out for RL 203. In fact it was walked over to the fueling area and then the engines were started up.

Photos left and right, Aviation Videos Ltd.

As was the case when we reviewed Avro and Orenda the RCAF was right there when RL 201 came out of the main jig.

Weight and performance problems

MEMORANDUM

CAE

Arrow 2 - Aircraft Performance
17 Jan 58

1. Reference is made to your S1038CN-180 (CAE) 7 Jan 58 and Periodic Performance Report No 12 on the Arrow 2 which was attached.

2. A review of previous periodic performance reports shows a steady decline in aircraft performance particularly in the sustained load factor at 50,000 ft M 1.5. It is realized that the weapon and fire control system changes added considerable weight and drag penalty and a subsequent reduction in performance could be expected. However, few changes have been made in the equipment specified by the RCAF since periodic performance report No 10. DSE and CARDE studies indicate that a sustained load factor of 2 at 50,000 feet is not as critical a characteristic as it was considered to be when initially specified (1952). A load factor minimum of 1.5 at 50,000 feet M 1.5 may well be an acceptable compromise in the light of present developments.

3. The range and radius of action reductions in performance are more disturbing. Regarding radius of action it is noted that the present figures are above but are approaching the required minimums. It is not intended at this stage to change the minimums. However, any improvement in radius of action, as indicated in report No 10, is an operational advantage. Combat ceiling and time-to-height are both verging on minimum specifications also. The ferry range, as indicated in paras 2 and 4 of your memo, is the most obvious deterioration in performance and worthy of the most serious consideration.

4. The CAS specified in his memo to ANTS, VCAS, reference S1038-CF105-180 (CAS) dated 29 Mar 55, that the Arrow was to be capable of operation in any theatre. With the range offered (by dropping the external tank when empty) in report No 12, it would be hazardous if not an impossible task to ferry the aircraft to Europe via Goose Bay, Keflavik and Prestwick involving distances of 1312 nm and 740 nm respectively. (Present CF100 and F100 route) The southern route from Newfoundland via Azores to the UK also involves prohibitive distances of 1235 nm and 1175 nm respectively.

5. The change in the Arrow performance may, it is understood, be partially as a result of optimizing the engines at M 2, rather than M 1.5. The advantages of optimizing at M 2, would appear questionable from the results shown in report No 12. COR's memo to CAE accepted the fact that a M 1.5 aircraft/missile combination was acceptable initially with

---

- 2 -   SECRET
S1038CN-1

plans to go forward for later improved versions of the missile/aircraft combination. All proposed mission profiles have used M 1.5 as the speed parameter. The decision to optimize the engines at M 2, would therefore appear to have been unnecessary.

6. In summary:

(a) The mission radii of 200 nm high speed and 300 nm maximum range are still valid as minimum requirements. Increasing these radii should be considered in later marks of the aircraft.

(b) Combat ceiling and time to height are acceptable but will stand little further degradation.

(c) A possible reduction in load factor to a minimum of 1.5 g at 50,000 feet M 1.5 could be considered (subject to further DSE study).

(d) A reduction in ferry range to 1254 nm is not acceptable.

7. It would be appreciated if you could advise:

(a) the implications in reverting to a M 1.5 engine contracturally, time-wise and in design, and

(b) the possible advantages in range and radius of action if the engines are optimized at M 1.5 which could lead to a compromise on the ferry range minimum.

(W.W. Bean) A/C
COR
2-2843

The time is spring 1958. Remember this is the critical summer when the chiefs gave up on the Arrow program. I am told that all aircraft gain weight as they evolve. Unfortunately, the accompanying performance losses showing up at this time did not help.

Document, National Archives, RCAF Files

You will recall that one of the hardest specifications to meet was the 2-G turn at Mach 1.5 at 50,000 feet without loss in altitude or speed. The RCAF admitted that changes to the weapon and fire control parts of the program had added weight and drag. Perhaps the "G" load factor could be reduced to 1.5 without compromising the intercept mission. The weight increase and reduction in performance indicated by the reports put mission stats in question, especially *time to height and combat range*. Of even more importance was the compromise of the ferry range of the Arrow. Even with a drop tank it was questionable if it could make it to Europe. Remember if war came we would have gone with what we had. There would be no time to rebuild, especially if the conflict went nuclear. The question was raised that the unauthorized decision to optimize the airframe and engine for Mach 2 could have had the effect of reduced performance in the Mach 1.5 zone.

Unfortunately, information about weight gains apparently was again suppressed, much to the consternation of the RCAF. Communications continued to be a problem with *backing and filling* being the one sure way of learning what was up. Group Captain Ray Foottit, the RCAF chief man on the job, in his January 1958 *Aircraft* magazine article, "The Search For Management" talked about faulty communication and its effect.

He said, "Sometime ago the USAF projects office suffered from lack of information due to negligence on the part of many contractors. It was pointed out that a company will run into a difficult technical problem that is going to take some time to solve. Instead of notifying the projects office immediately, the company holds back. Then the project slips and the project office is caught short in its planning. The RCAF has had some problems like this with Canadian contractors." Could he have been referring to the Arrow program?

As the Chiefs of Staff deliberated, Avro was being formally informed again of the seriousness of the weight gain and subsequent deterioration of performance. The first accident happened in June 1958. Cost increases were being scrutinized. Communication and open dealing was being questioned. A.V. Roe Canada Limited was acquiring other companies to become Canada's third largest with 40,000 employees. We can understand the government's concerns...yet were they managing what was after all, its business?

During the spring of 1958 events are unfolding which would contribute to the RCAF's insecurity.

CONFIDENTIAL S1038CN-180 (AMTS/AAWS)

MEMORANDUM

21 Jul 58

Ref S1038CN-180 (AMTS/AAWS) 16 Jul 58, AWS 4-2 to AWS 4
Re: Weight Growth

AAWS

Arrow 2 - Weight Control

1   We have been aware of a steady weight growth of Arrow 2 from the monthly AVRO weight reports. In both Arrow 1 and Arrow 2 this has been almost linear from 1954 to the present.

2   At the present time there is no contractual obligation on the part of the contractors to institute a weight control program. To offset this, we have included such a program in WSC 1-2 para 3.7 and the contractual responsibility in the Statement of Responsibility, which is not yet contractually binding. This latter is designed to have each associate embark on a program and the co-ordinating contractor to monitor and advise AAWS where weight can be saved, etc. All we can do at the present time is complain and point up marginality of the weapon system.

3   With regard to the specific item of trapped fuel, we did voice our concern and, as you are aware, for the Arrow 2, the 220 pounds or so of trapped fuel presently envisaged is much less than the 438 pounds observed in the above reference, and is considered to be somewhat less than established originally - whether this will all be substantiated is, of course, speculative.

4   At the same time, other areas are growing; the initial engine will be overweight; the RCA system grew 80 or so pounds; the hydraulics 56 or so pounds. AVRO has taken the lead in the electrics with a weight penalty clause in the G.E. contract but has little control over other associates' products.

5   Recommendations:

(a) Sharply worded letter to all associates pointing out marginality (AWS 3 will co-ordinate).

(b) Establish contractually, the policy described briefly in para 2 above (AWS/DDP et al).

(c) Demand programs from:

   (i) Associates, including substitution of materials;

   (ii) Co-ordinating Contractor, including monitoring and advising on deletion of equipment (several thousands of pounds were eliminated this way in a later Mark of CF100).

(DW Goss) W/C
AWS 3
2-4943

The problem of weight control and changing performance is common to most aircraft development. The difficulty with communications as a contributing factor to a souring of relations was not new then nor is it today!

Letters, National Archives, RCAF Files

COPY
SECRET

S36-38-105-15 (Det Cmdr)

PA B-2

AAWS
AWS 2
AWS 4
AWS/DDP

TO NOTE & RETURN AWS3, PLEASE.

Malton Ontario
25 July 1958

Mr. J.A. Morley,
Vice-President Sales & Service,
Avro Aircraft Limited,
Malton, Ontario.

Dear Sir: Re: Increase of Arrow Weight and
                Deterioration of Performance

As you are undoubtedly aware, AFHQ has become extremely alarmed about the steady increase in weight of the Arrow Aircraft, an increase which to date has shown no signs of levelling off. This concern has been accentuated because Avro has suppressed the latest weight report which apparently indicates another large jump in the OWE of the Arrow Aircraft.

Attached to this letter is a very rough graph prepared by the TSD to indicate the trends in Arrow OWE, range and fuel requirements. Although the accuracy of this graph may be questioned, there can be no doubt that the trends exist. If the deterioration shown were to continue unabated, it would not be very long before the Arrow could not meet specification requirements for both the high speed and maximum range missions. It would then, of course, be operationally unacceptable to the RCAF. Although it can be argued that such deterioration is not likely to occur, the RCAF requires proof that this is indeed not going to happen.

Para 2.1(j) of the Statement of Responsibilities, included as Appendix 20 of the Arrow Aircraft Statement of Work, points out that each associate contractor must maintain adequate weight control and reduction measures. Para 3.7 of Specification WSC 1-2 also specifically requires a weight control program to be carried out by the airframe manufacturer. Para 3.1 (g) of the Statement of Responsibilities define the responsibility of the co-ordinating contractor to advise AAWS of the adequacy of all associated contractors' programs, which are not only a requirement of the Statement of Responsibilities, but also presently being included in revisions to their particular WSC specification.

It is apparent that Avro's responsibilities, both as a co-ordinating contractor and as an associate contractor, are not at the moment being properly fulfilled. It must be understood that AFHQ emphatically desires that the Statement of Responsibilities' provisions be enforced and expects that your company will provide, at an early date, the complete details of an all-inclusive weight control and reduction program. Because of your double responsibilities, this submission should advise how you expect to monitor the programs being carried out by the other contractors.

Because of this continuing weight increase, and particularly because of the concern over the suppressed weight report, AFHQ has directed the undersigned to be at all times aware of the current performance and weight status of the Arrow aircraft. The TSD will be expected to be able to supply, at periodic intervals, figures and/or graphs which illustrate improvement or deterioration of the aircraft's important characteristics as well as explanations for these changes whenever they occur. So that this information can

..../2

- 2 -
SECRET

be supplied, it is essential that Avro make the TSD aware of all changes in the aircraft as soon as these changes are discovered by the design group. Notification of formal changes are not await the approval or publication of periodic weight change reports. With your assistance, the TSD will devise a means of informing AFHQ of any change in the aircraft which adversely affects or which improves its physical characteristics or performance.

It is requested that you reply to this letter as soon as possible, advising:

(a) Means by which your company intends to carry out the comprehensive airframe weight reduction program,

(b) The means by which you will monitor and advise AAWS on the weight programs of the other associate contractors, and

(c) Some means whereby the TSD can be continually aware of the operational characteristics of the Arrow aircraft.

An interim reply before the holidays would be appreciated.

Yours very truly,

(G.B. Waterman)
Wing Commander,
1202 Technical Services Detachment,
Avro Aircraft Limited,

Maintainability and interchangeability.

From the beginning of the Arrow program, it was clear that quick turn-arounds were going to be required. When an upper-wing design was chosen, it was based on the idea that the engines could be easily accessible and dropped down for change-over. As the design of the fuselage proceeded, it became apparent that cooling of the engine bay could best be achieved by placing the engines in a ram-air-pressurized tunnel. Now the engines had to be removed from the rear...not a happy story for the RCAF (as one of the designers told me). While ease of maintenance became a major issue, no other problem was to linger as long as the

National Archives
RCAF Files

CONFIDENTIAL
IN REPLY PLEASE QUOTE
S1038CN-101 (AOC)

Department of National Defence 0035

OTTAWA, Ontario,
31 Jan 58

Chief of the Air Staff,
Air Force Headquarters,
Ottawa, Ontario.

Arrow II Control Box and
Control Surface Interchangeability

1   Reference is made to your letter S1038CN-180(AMTS) 25 Oct 57 and to letters written by various AOsC of AMC, appealing for a great improvement in the interchangeability and maintainability of the control box area of the Arrow II aircraft. The AMC letters are C1035N-101(AOC) 23 Jul 56, S1038CN-101(AOC) 2 Nov 56, and S1038CN-101 (A/AOC) 23 Aug 57, and copies are attached for your ready reference. In spite of all this, the following situation remains:

   (a) Bearings in the control box have only limited flying approval and the initial bearing inspection period will be not more than 50 hours.

   (b) The elevator hinge pin cannot be removed without removal of aileron control box or removal of elevator hinge from its control box. The elevator hinge is held on by 102 close tolerance bolts over a length of some 11 ft. It is very doubtful that this hinge is interchangeable or that it can be made so.

   (c) Access to elevator control box is by a removable panel held on by 500 close tolerance stressed bolts. It is very doubtful that this panel could be made interchangeable, and in any case it does not provide the ready access required for maintainability.

   (d) Access to aileron and rudder actuating mechanism can only be obtained by removal of the control boxes. These are held on by 400 close tolerance bolts for the aileron and 372 for the rudder. The Maintenance Appraisal Team estimates (based on tests) that removal and replacement of any one control box would take at least 70 man hours.

   (e) The aileron hinge members are integral parts of the aileron control box and the aileron, so that hinge wear or damage can only be rectified by replacement of the major component. In the case of the box with its 400 close tolerance bolts, the component cannot, in our opinion, be interchangeable.

2   The lack of ready access to a vital part of the flying control system could seriously prejudice the maintainability (and therefore the ultimate success) of the aircraft in service. The situation has not changed significantly since the first of the attached letters in July 1956, and I would appreciate the opportunity of discussing this subject personally at an early date.

(C. L. Annis) A/V/M
AOC AMC

attach.

c.c. OC TSDs AVro

-2-

5   The whole problem will be closely followed by this HQ through the medium of the Interchangeability Committee and your staff will be kept fully informed. It is urgently recommended that the stand taken by our Interchangeability Committee be strongly supported by letter from your office.

(J.L. Plant) A/V/M
AOC AMC

cc: OC TSDs
A.V.Roe (Canada) Ltd.,
Malton, Ont.

Attach: App "A".

CONFIDENTIAL
S1038CN-180 (AMTS)

VRo Canada Limited
P.O. Box 130, Terminal "A"
Toronto, Ontario.

Ontario
31 July, 1956

Attention: MR. NYE

Re: CF105 Interchangeability
Specification MIL-I-8500

Dear MR. Nye:

      Questions regarding interchangeability have been raised at various committee meetings to which your representatives have been replying, in effect, that VRo has by no means been neglecting this requirement. While this is undoubtedly true, information received from our Air Material Command indicates instances of insufficient interchangeability. This information is contained in the attached papers.

      It is requested that your reply to the criticism in these papers, as we also love that elevators and ailerons must be interchangeable and that elev tors and ailerons must be provided for. Further, we believe that without at least this amount of interchangeability, your cost flying program will be jeopardized. It is requested that you reassure us on this point also.

Yours sincerely

(Signed) G. G. Truscott

(M.M. Hendrick)
Air Vice Marshal
for Chief of the Air Staff.

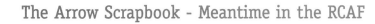

Control boxes at NAM,

Photo, Peter Zuuring, NAM

interchangeability and maintainability of control surface linkage boxes.

Control boxes were most likely to be damaged through ground accidents, sudden "G" forces, combat or just plain use. The main problem was the manner in which they were fastened to the central fuselage. Hundreds of high tensile screws needed to be undone. Because holes did not line up from one box to the next, oversize holes had to be re-drilled and tapped, limiting the life of the surface and wing structure. Furthermore the elevator box could not be removed without taking the aileron box off first. Needless to say, this created quite some concern. Avro's solution was to extend bearing life, split control surface to minimize buckling and basically stay the course.

Though production tooling was used from the beginning, it wasn't good enough for this part of the aircraft. Most attachments were drilled in situ and fastened right there. For example, on the fin, the structure was placed on the upright protruding fingers, clamped in place, drilled and fastened. This method ensured a tight, strong and permanent joint. If the fin had to be replaced it was unlikely that the holes could be drilled in exactly the same spot with the result that not all fasteners carried their loads evenly. The correspondence presented is representative. Many trials were conducted to evaluate the problems involved. Make no mistake, keeping the Arrow in the air and mission-ready was not resolved. The specification called for a thirty-minute turn-around on the flight line.

One of Avro's responses to the control box problems.

Letter, National Archives

The above letter is testimony to the fact that the problem was around for a long time and was not resolved.

Avro and Orenda accused of mismanaging the Arrow program

Group Captain Ray Foottit, the RCAF project manager on the Arrow program, spelled out the second major breakdown in communications within a year (the first being the optimization of the airframe and engine for Mach 2 when the specification called for Mach 1.5 without approval from the RCAF). The second was the drop in performance and changes in scheduling as noted in this letter. Foottit has said that this letter was designed to jolt A.V. Roe into more appropriate action. Apparently, it was deliberately kept at his level so that a rescuable position was possible.

The Arrow had not flown yet but tensions were high. The time from rollout to first flight was to take nearly six months...everybody was nervous!

Letters, the National Archives, RCAF files

*(a three number suffix means the file is **top secret**, two numbers means it is **secret**)*

C O P Y

S E C R E T

8103ECN-180(AMTS/AAWS)

4 Dec 57. Ontario.

Mr. F.T. Smye, President,
Avro Aircraft Limited,
P.O. Box 400, Terminal "A",
Toronto, Ontario.

Dear Sir:

Re: Arrow - Project Management

Reference is made to the discussion between yourself, Mr. Floyd and G/C Foottit on 22 Nov 57, at which time the RCAF accused Avro and Orenda of mismanaging the Arrow program since:

(a) There was a sudden, unexpected reduction of the aircraft's performance, which the RCAF contended Avro should have been aware of, and should have reported to the RCAF, as early as last spring.

(b) There was a change in aircraft scheduling, that was not reported properly to the RCAF in spite of the fact that the RCAF presented a schedule to all contractors on the Arrow program at two meetings last May, with Senior Avro personnel in attendance, which did not agree with the schedule Avro were working to at that date.

As a result of our meeting on 22 Nov it was agreed that Avro would investigate both these accusations and supply briefs to the RCAF on both points. These briefs have now been received and we have reviewed them.

The following are the conclusions reached from our review:

(a) **Performance Brief: Avro Report Dated 28 Nov 57**
RCAF Conclusions:

(1) The brief confirms our contention that the performance reduction could have been assessed in a preliminary manner in the Spring/57 (possibly as early as Feb-Mar 57).

(11) Consequently the brief confirms our contention that there has been mismanagement of the engineering aspects of the program. This is verified by Mr. Morley's letter dated 5 Nov 57, saying "No significant performance change" and Mr. Lindleys verbal statement 13 Nov saying there was a possible change, later confirmed by Mr. Floyd in telecon 20 Nov 57 to G/C Foottit.

S E C R E T

- 2 -

(b) **Schedule Brief: Avro Letter Dated 29 Nov 57**
RCAF Conclusions:

(1) The brief is a history of the scheduling situation which tacitly admits there was confusion though it finished up with the note that "we are not forming any comments on the above analysis as the position is self evident".

(11) The part that is "self evident" from our analysis is that this, too, has been mismanaged by the Company.

We have further questions and comments on both these will be the subject of separate discussions and correspondence, since they are only sidelights to the project management accusations which precipitated this review.

The seriousness of this project management situation cannot be over emphasized since this is the second major breakdown in RCAF-Company communications during 1957. As you know, the first occurred when both companies proceeded with the "Mach 2" version without providing the RCAF with unambiguous advice as Mr. Morley has admitted in his letter to the TSD dated 5 Nov 57.

We will discuss the situation with you at Avro on 5th Dec. and in accordance with our meeting on 22 Nov, referred to in Para 1, we will expect you to advise on how the situation can be remedied so that I can make my recommendations to the RCAF Chief Aeronautical Engineer on the future of the Arrow program.

Yours truly,

Sgd. H.R. Foottit,
Group Captain,
for Chief of the Air Staff.

8103A

JAN 9 1958
1038CN-180
A/AWS
3/1/58

S E C R E T

M E M O R A N D U M   8 Jan 58

AMTS

Conduct of Correspondence

1   Attached hereto is a letter which was forwarded from your Division to Avro Aircraft Limited. The CAS has asked me to draw this letter to your attention and requests that any such letters - particularly dealing with policy, programmes or service-company relations - be signed by at least an Air Member, or preferably the CAS himself.

2   Air Marshal Campbell asks if you would be good enough to draw this matter to the attention of your staff for future guidance.

(W.L. Gillespie) G/C
A/CAS
2-3104

Attach.   A/CAS

The reasons for the particular letter was explained to CAS. The matter was deliberately kept at this level to disconnect Mr. Smye & to avoid embarassing the Company at too high an official level.   JAN 10 1958

In January 1958, the Avro engineering section was re-organized. Was this coincidental with the mismanagement accusation? Avro's statement indicated that Mr. J.A. Chamberlin was appointed chief of design - a staff position in which he would advise the chief engineer. Mr. F. Brame took over as chief of technical design. Guest Hake left the engineering group to become quality control manager and chief inspector for the company, replacing Fairbairn who retired.

Both Hendrick, AMTS and Foottit knew what was happening. The Hendrick diaries provide a look at the man who seems to have it all together. He stepped back from the problem and counselled restraint and discussion. John Plant, the former RCAF officer, was now president and general manager of Avro Aircraft...he was one of the RCAF's own, who will understand its position and be able to deal with it.

Diary extract from the Raymond Collection,
DND, DHIS/HER

Since last November, the Avro CF-105 Arrow weapon system has been under the management of a Project Office.

THE SEARCH FOR MANAGEMENT

By GROUP CAPTAIN H. R. FOOTTIT

"The military needs and demands the highest calibre of management."
—*General C. S. Irvine, USAF*

THE HOUSE was in an uproar. On all sides the Prime Minister was being blasted with a barrage of harsh and bitter words. This was May 7, 1940, and the British forces had just been thrown back into the Norwegian seas by the victorious German Army.

Prime Minister Neville Chamberlain —whose appearance and rolled umbrella had become the very symbol of

---

AVRO Problems

retired & now
C/VRoe to G.Menger

Tech Service
Detachment

DIARY FOR 6 DEC 57

Discussed with Foottit his report on his discussions with Mr. Smye, concerning the management problems of AVRO, as covered in his memorandum of the 6th December, file S1038CN-180.

We agreed that we would ask A/V/M Plant to take the sales and service organization out of the channel of communication between the company and the Air Force, and ask that our Engineering Weapons System Group would work directly with the engineering cells on any given subject in the company itself. We agreed that we would examine the TSD to be sure that there were sufficient number of qualified engineers each to deal with a special phase of the project. The breadth of which would be within his capabilities, both in knowledge and in time. Each such officer would have full access to everybody in the company dealing with that particular subject, and would have a primary job of intelligence keeping us informed of what is going on in the subject from day-to-day. They would have a second role of solving minor engineering problems in this field on behalf of the Air Force.

If this number of new specialist officers is large it will require an additional Wing Commander to co-ordinate their activities and to be a Deputy TSD Commander.

Channels of official communication will still go through the TSD files so that they can all be in one place.

It was agreed that I would discuss with John Plant these two moves as a first step in view of the fact that company changes of organization are likely to take some time to affect.

The essence of this problem is that if the company is having difficulty keeping track of its own work, but if the work itself in detail is adequate then we must set up an intelligence system which keeps us fully advised of what they are doing anyway regardless of how they co-ordinate. On problems of finance, which previously affected Sales and Service, this can be a side line which the company can deal with by separate department, divorced from engineering and working with Department of Defence Production and with CMat.

AVM

Having lived with A.V. Roe for years, being aware of the problems first hand, Foottit gathered more experience from the USAF. It had lived the program delays and compromises. The establishment of an on-site project office in conjunction with the Technical Service Detachments makes sense...getting it going is something else as you will see in Jack Woodman's early experiences.

Arrow Project Office

FOLLOWING this USAF procedure the RCAF last November instituted a project office for the CF-105 "Arrow", the supersonic interceptor now in Avro Aircraft's flight test hangar. This Arrow office brings together all the various engineering functions of the RCAF and has, or will have, personnel from the Department of Defence Production, the Defence Research Board, the RCAF's Air Materiel Command, and technical talent, working for the group, from the various contractors associated with the Arrow program. It also includes officers drawn from the financial and logistics directorates of RCAF Headquarters.

For some time the RCAF, DRB, and DDP have recognized that it takes more than a government group to manage such a complex weapon system as the Arrow. As the USAF's General Clarence S. Irvine put it recently, "The infinite complexity of modern aircraft or weapon systems precludes detail supervision from the military." Consequently plans are going forward for establishing a "Co-ordinating Contractor" for the Arrow. This contractor will be responsible for knitting together the detailed efforts of the other companies that hold government contracts for major portions of the Arrow system—such as Orenda Engines Ltd., with the Iroquois engine, and the Radio Corporation of America with the integrated electronic system. In this way the coordinating contractor, with all the associate contractors, can demonstrate and deliver to the RCAF an operationally functional Arrow weapon system, with all the direct support equipment that is vital to keeping the airplane flying.

Slow Starter: With this Arrow Weapon System Project Office just

(Continued on page 64)

AIRCRAFT

Article extracted from January, 1958 *Aircraft* magazine.

Privately, the USAF told the RCAF that it was concerned with the concentration of missile and fire control technology in virtually one company, namely Hughes. It was interested in developing a second source. When it found out that the RCAF wanted a more ambitious product than the Hughes Falcon, it suggested RCA because it had capacity and would be recommended by the USAF. The RCAF believed that the US Navy's Sparrow missile development was superior - the RCAF could piggyback on the program. Everybody was happy with this choice except A.V. Roe which had great confidence in the Hughes product as it was already developed and deployed. When a bidding process eliminated Hughes, the "pie in the sky" RCA proposal was accepted by the RCAF, at bargain basement prices.

Sparrow and Astra...

RCA was notoriously late with its work. Cockpit outfitting was being held up, electronic installations and testing delayed. W. Farrance told me when the programs were cancelled everybody scrambled to outfit RL-206 so that it would be ready to fly.

RCA Newsletter, showing Camden progress of radar electronics.

When the Sparrow program was dropped by the US Navy, Canadair, along with Westinghouse Canada, took over the development. RCA, Camden N.J., continued the fire control and instrumentation package, designated as ASTRA.

Photo, 1958 *Aircraft* magazine

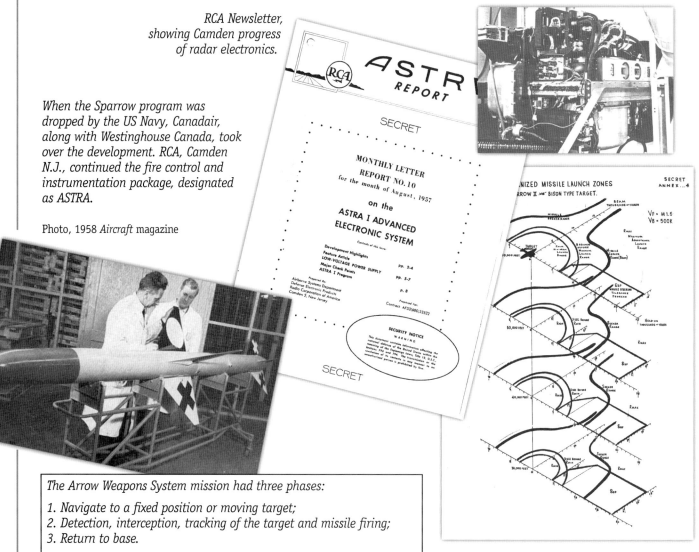

The Arrow Weapons System mission had three phases:

1. *Navigate to a fixed position or moving target;*
2. *Detection, interception, tracking of the target and missile firing;*
3. *Return to base.*

ASTRA could detect a target some twenty-five miles out and get as close as three or four miles before firing. It all happened in seconds.

Chart above, National Archives

Achilles heel of the Arrow program?

"The decision to adopt the Sparrow missile and the Astra Fire Control System was supported by those officers in the RCAF and the Department of Defence Production who were anxious to put Canada into the age of advanced electronics and missilery. This in itself was a desirable objective but should not have been put on the back of the Arrow project, which was taking Canada into the very exacting realm of supersonic flight." (Fred Smye commenting on Canada's choice of missile and fire control.) Earlier in the summer of 1956, when this choice was formalized and Avro took on the management of a so-called "weapons system," Fred

Smye predicted that, because of the uncertainty of this development, the whole Arrow program might be threatened and even the very independence of the RCAF if, indeed, it would not kill both. Prophetically, Sparrow/Astra came into the program last and were first to go, pulling the Arrow and Orenda projects down with them - just as Fred Smye had predicted.

Excerpt, *Canadian Aviation and the Avro Arrow*, F. Smye

Photos show the Astra radar assembly and spline communication electronics being worked on for the mockup.

Photos, Aviation Videos

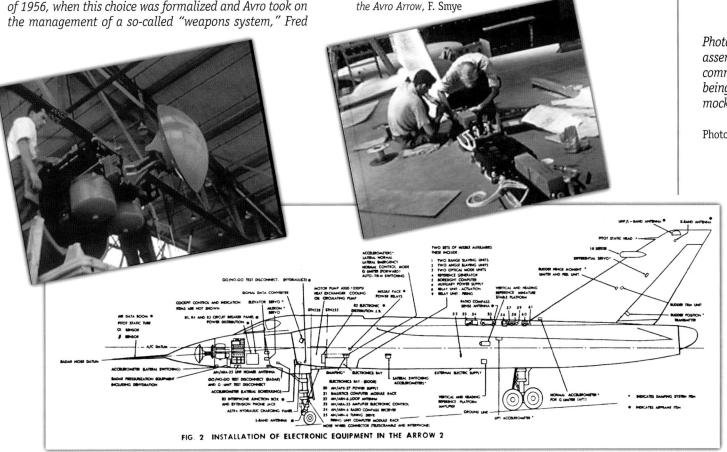

FIG. 2 INSTALLATION OF ELECTRONIC EQUIPMENT IN THE ARROW 2

Electronic systems of the Arrow Mk II

Schematic,
NRC, MK II Manual

Getting ready for first flight

Flight Lieutenant Woodman was pleased with his first flight - see appendices for details of second flight.

Photo, *Avro Newsmagazine*

S36-33-105-14-1 (Arrow Det.)

PAB-3

Malton, Ont. 10 Jan 58.

Commanding Officer,
Central Experimental & Proving Establishment,
RCAF Station, Uplands,
Ottawa, Ontario.

Attention: S/L A.W.Armstrong

Progress Report - Period Ending 31 Dec 57
- P5 Arrow Detachment - Avro

Administration - General

1   The company have provided a telephone for this office:
Local 2417 under Avro's Bell Telephone Exchange Butler 6-4411.

2   Recent action has been taken through the DDP representative
at Avro to provide a Secretary for this office, and it is hoped that one
will be available within the coming month.

Monitoring

3   With the completion of the ground tests on the first Arrow,
an appreciation can be made of the problems associated with monitoring
the company's activities. It would appear that the information
desired by this office is available, but according to the company's
interpretation, we are not officially entitled to it. Therefore, any
information obtained by this detachment has been provided by the
company purely on a personal basis. This is not a problem within
itself, but it creates the problem of having to locate the correct
source of information and maintaining that something important has not
been overlooked. There is no assurance that information eventually reaches this
office but in many cases, the problems, etc., are history by that time
and no longer current.

4   We are still awaiting direction on what our recognized role
is at this company. Discussions with the TSD have indicated their
willingness (?) and the desirability of a split in responsibility,
when covering the flight trials. It has been suggested through the TSD
to AFHQ that CEPE become the authority on handling, stability and
control, performance, and instrumentation, while the TSD handle the
balance. Astra was discussed but it seems to be an involved
situation, but one which should be decided upon at an early date.
The whole problem of who is the authority on flight testing must be
resolved at the earliest possible date, not only to clarify our
position here at the company but to ensure that the RCAF and company
realise who is who.

Phase I Program

5   A Phase I program was prepared by the company but lacked
sufficient detail to ensure that the company are in possession of a
firm set of requirements during Phase I of the flight trials. The
company are now attempting a re-draft of the program to achieve same.

Contd......

6   The necessity of such a plan was evidenced during the
ground tests. A very obvious fact has shown itself during these
initial trials. There is a reasonably large amount of confusion,
dis-organization and inexperienced direction in this company when
it comes to carrying out an organized preliminary program. This
could possibly be caused by the production group, who have been
placed in charge of these initial tests. Flight test personnel
have no control of the situation, and very often are unaware of the play
by play program. The company certainly has not shown any valid
reason why their whole program should not be watched very closely,
and at times directed. There was an obvious lack of a firm set of
requirements to which they could have worked, because nobody
besides the one man (Fred Mitchell, who detailed the day-to-day
tests) appeared to know what was taking place or what further
tests had to be done.

Flying and Aircraft Handling:

Chase Aircraft

7   One CF-100 Mark 5 (18513) and one Sabre Mark 6 (23744)
have been made available to the company for chase purposes. It
has been decided by the company and this office that both aircraft
will be used on the first flight of the CF-105, and the Company
wish to fly one of the aircraft themselves.

Advance Test Results

8   Engine runs were completed during this period, however
behind schedule. The difficulties causing delays have been covered
by the Advance Test results which have been forwarded to you under
separate cover as they became available.

9   Low speed taxi trials commenced on 24 Dec 57. A total of
6 runs were carried out to complete the program. Attempts were made
on 5 of the runs to stream the drag chute, and successful operation
was realised on 2 of the 5 runs. In the three cases of failure, the
parabrake doors or mechanism failed to operate properly. With the
present design, the chute requires approximately 1½ hours to pack
plus a further ½ hour to install in the aircraft.

10   With proper drag chute operation the brake temperatures
do not exceed limits. Without drag chute operation, the brake
temperatures readily exceed limits to the extent that the wheels become
cherry red with heat. On one such run, after parking the aircraft,
the right rear tire blew under excessive heat and pressure. A complete
new set of wheels, brakes and tires were required.

11   The low speed taxi trials have been terminated and the
aircraft is now being prepared for high speed taxi trials and the flying
first flight. Considerable work is required to clear the flying
control system prior to the first flight and it appears that the
delay will involve at least 3 weeks.

Aerodynamics

12   There has been no well defined progress during the month
of December. The flying control and damping system has been studied,
taxi trials have been monitored, and the company's written Phase I
test program has received some attention. Discussions with the
company on the stability and control aspects of the Arrow have
broadened our knowledge of the problems, the full realisation
of which will depend on flight results.

Contd......

- 3 -

13   The taxi trials provided no real aerodynamics data. As
discussed previously, the taxi trials have indicated the calculated
limited energy absorption capability of the brakes, a factor which
dictates a very high reliability requirement on the para-brake. Of
course, the para-brake hasn't shown this reliability as yet, but the
company are aware of the requirement and are probably more concerned
than the RCAF, since they must face the problem first.

Instrumentation

14   Instrumentation Pack for Arrow A/c No. 25201 - Installation
of hardware and equipment in the first pack is essentially complete,
even though one or two small items are not yet available. A checkout
of the installed equipment has indicated several snags that are still
being cleared. In due time, however, it is expected that the pack
will be available for calibration.

15   Calibration Trolley - The calibration trolley to be used
for the c/n purpose still requires further work for completion, but
the equipment is now installed. Further detail on this (DATAKON)
is attached hereto. The equipment in question is of custom design
by Avro and it is felt that with slight modification, it would serve
a similar purpose for the RCAF during phase 4 testing of the Arrow.

16   Damping System Instrumentation - Attached hereto is an
interdepartmental memorandum received unofficially from the company.
The list has just recently been completed and involves 45 parameters
of the Damping System to be measured on Arrow A/c No.25201. As
noted in the memorandum, similar details for Arrow A/c 25202 and
25203 will be available at a later date. The measurements will be
recorded on a 50 trace CEC oscillograph. Each pack will contain
one such oscillograph.

N. Sugimoto F/L
for (JF Woodman) F/L
OC Arrow Detachment,
Avro Aircraft Ltd.

Jack Woodman, CEPE pilot stationed at Malton, showed his frustrations in getting settled there.

Memo, National Archives, RCAF files

The schedule was so tight and the pressures so intense that daily progress reports were implemented, leading to first flight.

Progress Report, National Archives, RCAF Files

Summary of first RCAF flight April, 1958

"From 1 hour 10 minutes flying time the initial impression is favourable. The aircraft was flown from 180 knots IAS at 15,000 feet to Mach 1.4 at 45,000 feet. It was flown in three different modes of control and assessed at low and high indicated airspeeds. The envelope thus far flown by the contractor was not entirely investigated, however generally, the results of the tests carried out are better than originally expected. The problem areas of the aircraft, at this time, are assessed as serious and difficult to control, but not as dangerous, and it is felt that with an improvement of the artificial feel and the completion of the stability augmentation, the aircraft should be very pleasant to fly."

As can be seen by the included documents, a lot of effort went into first flight. The RCAF insisted that all components be cleared for flight worthiness and that only written assurances would be accepted. See Foottit's letter in the corporate section, "Back in the Fifties."

Problem areas of the aircraft are assessed as serious and difficult to control.

Security concerns

The amount of information that found its way into the popular press and the hands of everyday people continues to amaze me. For a secret national defence project how was this possible? We have the impression that the U.S.A. is much more guarded and serious about security. A.V. Roe did get permission for most of its public relations, but you get a sense that the RCAF did so reluctantly. There is the view that your enemy needs to know what you are capable of, especially if deterrence and mutual destruction is the strategy.

The "4 X 4" pocket guide to the Arrow was allowed but discouraged. The second printing of the Standard Aircraft Characteristics was preceded with a stern warning about security and content the summer before.

Brochure, P. Brennan

Avro described the future of the Arrow program, i.e. the Mk IIA and Mk III, Mach 3 interceptor and its mission capabilities.

SECRET
UNCLASSIFIED

The
AVRO ARROW

THE ROYAL CANADIAN AIR FORCE

E.L. POULSEN AAWS/PWS-2

ARROW 2A AND ARROW 3 PERFORMANCE PREDICTIONS

The figures on ARROW 2A and ARROW 3 performance presented herewith were prepared on very short notice and consequently the basic data used in the calculations could not receive sufficient analysis to make it possible to give definitive figures. For this reason, they are believed to be only sufficiently accurate to give a qualitative and comparative impression of the possibilities of developing the ARROW 2 into improved versions.

In these calculations it has been assumed that full advantage is taken of the various features that distinguish the ARROW 2A and ARROW 3 from the ARROW 2. In practice, and on further study, it may not be entirely possible to realise the full gain assumed. Hence, it cannot be guaranteed that some degradation will not take place as the result of further studies.

AVRO AIRCRAFT LIMITED

December 5, 1957.

SECURITY WARNING

This document is classified "SECRET" and is intended solely for the use of the recipient and such persons as have been delegated to use it in the course of their duty and may only be used in connection with work performed for or on behalf of Her Majesty's Canadian Government.

The unauthorized retention or destruction of this document or disclosure of its contents to any unauthorized person is forbidden.

Failure to comply with any of the above instructions is an infraction of the Official Secrets Act.

Any unauthorized person obtaining possession of this document, by finding or otherwise, must forward it, together with his name and address, in a registered envelope, to the Engineering Division, AVRO Aircraft Ltd., Malton, Ontario, Canada.

This is copy number ......9....

Issued to ....

Date ....

DEPARTMENT OF DEFENCE PRODUCTION

OATH OF SECRECY
BY TENDERERS, CONTRACTORS, THEIR EMPLOYEES AND OTHERS

In the Province of **ONTARIO**   In the matter of Defence Contracts

County of **PEEL**

I, **SIDNEY YOUNG**   of **109 Whitburn Crescent, De**

Date of birth **December 12th, 1926**   Place of birth **Mount Albert, O**

do solemnly declare

that I am an officer or employee of **DE HAVILLAND AIRCRAFT OF CANADA LIM**

and may have occasion to have access to or knowledge of contracts, specifications, plans, draw information, equipment, materials or articles (hereinafter referred to as "documents, material disclosed in connection with defence contracts or work.

2. That I have read the excerpts from the Official Secrets Act printed on the reverse side hereof.

3. That I will observe all precautions and security measures required by the Official Secrets Act and such further instructions as the Minister may from time to time give in respect of such documents, material or information (whether classified or not) and will not during the course of my employment or thereafter divulge, disclose or communicate any knowledge or information in respect thereof to any person not entitled thereto nor will I permit any such person to inspect or have access to such documents, material or information.

And I make this solemn declaration conscientiously believing it to be true, and knowing that it is of the same force and effect as if made under oath, and by virtue of The Canada Evidence Act.

Declared before me at **MALTON** Ontario *Sydney Young*

this **16th** day of **April** 196**4**

James H. ... Commissioner, etc.

NOTE: This form is to be completed in duplicate. One copy is to be retained by Declarer and one to be forwarded to Director of Industrial Security, Department of Defence Production, Ottawa. See excerpts from the Official Secrets Act on the reverse side hereof.

AVRO AIRCRAFT LIMITED

ARROW 2

TWIN ENGINE SUPERSONIC ALL-WEATHER

FIGHTER

STANDARD AIRCRAFT CHARACTERISTICS

MARCH 1958

ISSUE 2

Documents, National Archives, RCAF files

A new batch of Avro employees take and sign an oath of secrecy. All documents were security rated and labelled. The company issued product brochures that not only reported specification that were at odds with what the military understood, but they were presented in a format that permitted easy removal from the plant.

The brochure on the right described, in detail, the capabilities of the Mk II Arrow. It doesn't take too long to agree with the RCAF that this is sensitive material and should be disallowed or curtailed severely. The information must be accurate for those who are in a position to get the data...apparently it wasn't. Remember that A.V. Roe was building an enterprise, not just another aircraft. Company newsletters, supplier advertisements and industry association publications all revealed Arrow information. As Jim Floyd said," The Arrow Program was in the shop window." No wonder the Arrow became a symbol of competence and national pride – it was promoted as such.

Letters, National Archives, RCAF files

In preparation for first flight, Avro got together with the photo section and test pilots to review coverage. First responsibility was "engineering coverage," second responsibility, "publicity coverage." Furthermore, the minutes of the meeting indicated, "Providing the Arrow flight characteristics are satisfactory the CF-100 will then devote approx. 5 minutes to obtaining photographs for publicity purposes... and...upon returning to base, the CF-100 will take additional pictures for publicity purposes during the early phase of joining the circuit providing the Arrow is not in trouble." The letter above discusses the breaches of security with respect to the flight test program as it got under way - open channel communications? No encryption of flight data? Note the letter's date May 1958, that crucial period when the *real* fate of the Arrow was being decided!

Runaway costs

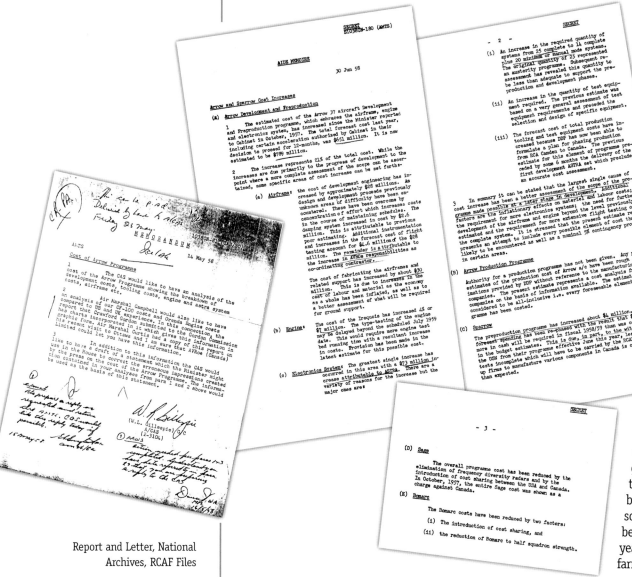

Report and Letter, National
Archives, RCAF Files

Once again, the CAS, Air Marshal Hugh Campbell, requested up-to-date costing information on the Arrow program, not only to satisfy himself but to help the Defence Minister, George Pearkes, answer questions and set the record straight.

As these reports show, The Arrow Weapons System, as it was now called in 1958 has escalated enormously. As is admitted, the main cause was the adoption of the Sparrow missile and Astra fire control development program, as well as increases in material and labour at Avro and a small increase from Orenda for the Iroquois.

These revised estimates played, I believe, a significant role in forming the opinion that the Arrow program was too rich for the day. Timing could not have been worse. The Diefenbaker government was in place with a majority and felt that election promises of reduced spending had to be taken seriously. The degree of technical sophistication of the parliamentarians may have been limited, given the fact that 1958 was the first year that tractors outnumbered horses on Canadian farms.

Avro's assessment was up as well

MAY 1958

SECRET

FIGURES SHOWN INCLUDE FEE, AND SALES TAX WHERE APPLICABLE	CUMULATIVE TO MARCH 31 1958	1958 - 1959	1959 - 1960	1960 - 1961	1961 - 1962	TOTAL
1. BASIC DEVELOPMENT	$52,402,975					$52,402,975
2. PRODUCT IMPROVEMENT AND FLIGHT TEST - INCLUDING ADDITIONAL ENGINEERING FOR SUCH PROJECTS AS: SLED TEST, SUPPORT TO RCA, CANADAIR, ORENDA, ETC.						
3. TOOLING - (INCLUDING TOOL IMPROVEMENT)	$25,058,519	4,840,799	20,166,822	14,112,426		54,013,803
4. 8 AIRCRAFT MANUFACTURING PROGRAM- (INCLUDING TOOL MAINTENANCE)						
a. AIRCRAFT	$31,011,863	21,164,261	1,030,568			30,929,886
b. SPARE PARTS	317,346	5,215,000	2,002,195			54,178,319
c. PUBLICATIONS	440,738	1,660,141	976,297			6,508,643
d. GROUND SUPPORT EQUIPMENT	689,654	1,216,096	94,248			2,100,879
TOTAL	$32,459,601	29,255,498	3,072,740			1,999,998
5. 29 AIRCRAFT MANUFACTURING PROGRAM- (INCLUDING TOOL MAINTENANCE)						
a. AIRCRAFT	$1,593,170	33,078,237	66,008,877	13,985,002		64,787,839
b. ENGINEERING SUPPORT TO PRODUCTION		2,760,369	4,099,278	3,620,599		
c. SPARE PARTS		288,750	5,775,000	9,160,988		
d. PUBLICATIONS			2,203,740	1,697,273		114,665,286
e. GROUND SUPPORT EQUIPMENT		1,501,500	2,249,940	250,067		10,480,246
TOTAL	$1,593,170	1,501,500				15,224,738
GRAND TOTAL	$111,514,265	37,628,856	80,336,835	28,713,929		3,901,013
	91,459,708	104,606,965	42,826,355			4,001,507
						148,272,790
						350,407,293

ARROW PROGRAM COST ESTIMATES - SUMMARY

The RCAF was not the only one assessing what the Arrow program was going to cost. The above table extracted from an Avro financial summary of manpower and work for the Malton facility, dated May 1958, clearly shows significant increases in the Arrow preproduction program from just a year and a half earlier...from $242 million to $350 million or 45%. The data for the Iroquois program has not been located. The RCAF and previous Orenda figures show much less escalation. There is no mention of the "weapons system" concept nor any increases in cost because of the extended management responsibility.

File, private collection

The USAF and RAF not interested?

In the spring of 1958 the Chief of the Air Staff wanted a summary of the U.S.A and U.K. interest in the Arrow. This document makes interesting reading, especially the last entry describing the lack of interest by the USAF.

If I had not come across a telex from the Washington embassy air attaché describing a meeting between the Canadian Ambassador and the Secretary of the USAF, and if I hadn't been lucky in coming across the minutes of the same meeting written up by the Department of Defence Production, I would just have taken this summary at face value. You will see that there is a lot more to the tale and I might add...an opportunity missed!

See the next section.

Jan Zurakowski told me that the normal time to consider selling a military jet is when it is operational. Anything earlier is quite hopeless. Why would anyone want a product that is incomplete? Can you imagine, " We're having a bit of a problem with our program, delays and such, not sure when it will be done or how much it will cost, but, you'd be interested to buy some, wouldn't you?" The ridiculousness of the situation is beyond me. Obviously, the cartoonist from *Legionary* thought so, too! Pearkes was out in the cold!

The documents comes from the
National Archives, RCAF files.

The pictures are:
Charles Foulkes, Chief of the Defence Staff and Chairman of the Chiefs of Staff Committee, Hugh Campbell, Chief of the Air Staff, and the Honourable George Pearkes, Minister of National Defence.

SECRET
APPENDIX G

UNITED KINGDOM AND UNITED STATES INTEREST
IN THE CF 105

DATE	USA	UK
Jun 54	General Twining advised the CAS that the USAF had initiated a design competition for a long range interceptor and was interested in the CF 105. He requested approval for the Air Research & Development Command to evaluate the CF 105 against the USAF long range interceptor specifications at the same time as the proposals from industry were evaluated.	
Jul 54	In reply to General Twining's letter, the CAS forwarded a copy of the design study of the supersonic All-Weather Interceptor Aircraft - May 1953. The CAS stated that he was pleased to exchange information and views on a project of such importance to the two countries as it was in keeping with an objective discussed between the Air Force Chiefs of Great Britain, the United States and Canada "to require the enemy to compete in the technological field with the combined brains and resources of the English speaking Allies rather than the three components thereof, and that such collaboration would be superior to the individual and in some cases overlapping efforts". The CAS also pointed out that Canadian Government approval to proceed with the prototype production of the CF 105 was given on the clear understanding that the US and UK had not embarked nor were planning to embark on a similar aircraft.	
Aug 54	As the result of the exchange of letters between Gen. Twining and the CAS, a briefing team of RCAF officers and AVRO officials visited ARDC HQ on 26 Aug 54 to give a presentation on the CF 105 operational requirement, the concept of operations and how the CF 105 design meets the RCAF requirement.	

- 2 -

DATE	USA	UK
Sep 54	The Commander ADC, USAF, requested a copy of the brochure on the CF 105. A copy of AV Roe brochure "Twin-Engine All-Weather Fighter CF 105" was forwarded to ADC, USAF.	
Oct 54		The RCAF were asked to comment on the operational requirement for an integrated control system. The RAF operational requirements personnel considered the RCAF requirement sound.
Jan 55	In Dec 54 it was decided that special wind tunnel tests should be carried out but facilities were not available for such tests in Canada. USAF assistance was requested to arrange the trials and in Feb 55 General Putt DCS/Development wrote to the Director of the National Advisory Committee for Aeronautics on the urgency and significance of the CF 105 to the joint defence of North America. A meeting was held subsequently to arrange the wind tunnel tests.	
Nov 55	At the request of the CAS and Chairman DRB, a USAF team headed by General G.E. Price, Director of Requirements and Deputy Chief of Staff (Development) was invited to visit AV Roe to study the CF 105 programme and to form an independent opinion on the technical and operational soundness of the project. In addition the team was requested to answer the question "should the RCAF proceed with development and production of the CF 105 in the face of firm US Air Force programme for development and production of the F102B medium range interceptor; the F101B long range interceptor; and the LRIXI which is being developed to replace the F101B?	

DATE	USA	- 4 -	UK
Apr 56			The question of charges for a license to permit the CF 105 to be manufactured in the UK was the subject of a letter from the Deputy Minister DDP to Sir Roy Dobson. This letter covered royalty payments, provision of components from Malton and the use of drawings, tools, etc., as the basis for a possible licensing agreement.
May 56			In reply to a letter from the CAS on comparative studies on all weather aircraft carried out in Canada, Air Marshal Pike stated that there is no doubt that the CF 105 is a very attractive proposition to the RAF except that it is rather late to meet their requirement date of early 1961, and even this date could only be achieved by using a British fire control system. This would reduce the capability of the aircraft and is therefore less attractive. He expresses the opinion that the chances of obtaining the CF 105 for the RAF are rather small.
Feb 57	The Advanced Interceptor Committee, chaired by General Boyd USAF, met in Toronto to discuss with the RCAF, AVRoe officials and Orenda officials the general question of an advanced interceptor in the time period 1960-70. The Committee agreed with the major points of Canadian thinking in relation to the operational requirement, design characteristics and armament.		
Apr 57	The RCAF were informed informally that the USAF ADC were most interested in keeping fully abreast of the development of the CF 105 because development of follow on interceptors to the F106 appeared to be slipping badly and the CF 105, as it is further developed, might fill this need.		

DATE	USA	- 5 -	UK
Jan 58	The Canadian Ambassador in Washington met on 30 Jan 58 with the US Secretary of the Air Force, who confirmed that there was no place for the Arrow weapon system in the US Air Force. A copy of the report by the DDP representative in Washington on this discussion by the Canadian Ambassador is attached as Annex 1.		

DATE	US	- 3 -	UK
Nov 55 (Cont'd)	A reply dated 9 Nov 55 was received from Mr. Donald A. Quarles, Secretary for the Air Force to the Minister of National Defence which stated that as a result of the evaluation the USAF recommends that development and production of the CF 105 proceed as now planned.		
Dec 55			The Minister of Supply (UK) requested from the Minister of Trade & Commerce permission for the Director, Royal Aeronautical Establishment and the Deputy Chief of Staff RAF to visit AVRoe to examine the CF 105 aircraft. The team visited AVRoe in Jan 56. The highlights of their report were, general agreement with the aerodynamic calculations; that the electronics system will still be superior to the best British equipment available in the same time period; and included comparative costs for buying 100 aircraft in Canada, manufacturing 100 aircraft in the UK with a UK engine and US fire control system and manufacturing 100 aircraft in UK using a British engine and fire control system. The report stated that the use of a British fire control system would downgrade the performance of the aircraft very materially. The best course of action would have been to buy 100 CF 105s from Canada but this was discarded as being financially impossible.
Jan 56	Orenda Engines Ltd received informal word that "the USAF are interested in the aircraft but not interested if it is fitted with the J75 propulsion. The PS13 (Iroquois) is what is wanted." It was also disclosed that the USAF were interested in the PS13 for several other aircraft projects including primarily the B52.		

Who else was misled by the incomplete reference?

Cartoon, *Legionary* February, 1959

Perhaps more room for optimism than the RCAF summary of interest would indicate!

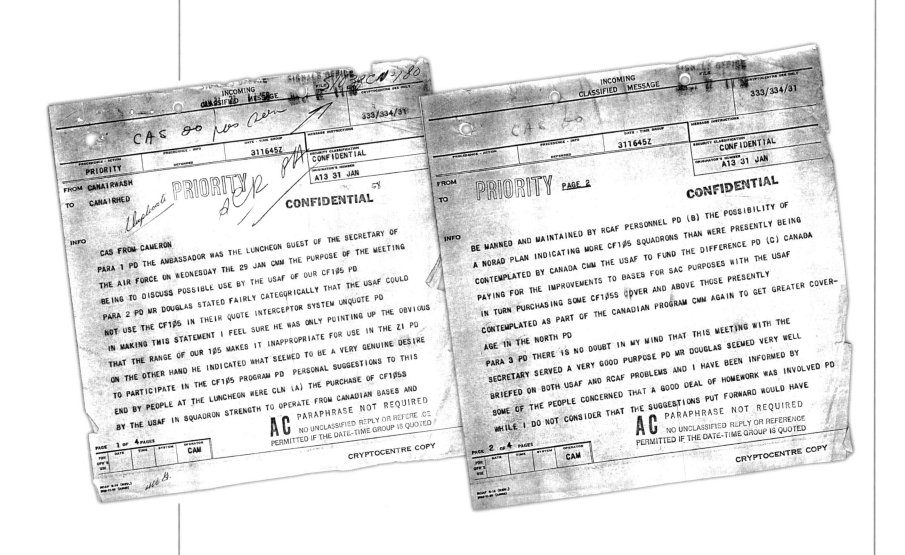

INCOMING CLASSIFIED MESSAGE
333/334/31

DATE - TIME GROUP 311645Z

SECURITY CLASSIFICATION: CONFIDENTIAL
ORIGINATOR'S NUMBER: A13 31 JAN

PRIORITY

FROM: CANAIRWASH
TO: CANAIRHED

CONFIDENTIAL

CAS FROM CAMERON

PARA 1 PD THE AMBASSADOR WAS THE LUNCHEON GUEST OF THE SECRETARY OF THE AIR FORCE ON WEDNESDAY THE 29 JAN CMM THE PURPOSE OF THE MEETING BEING TO DISCUSS POSSIBLE USE BY THE USAF OF OUR CF105 PD

PARA 2 PD MR DOUGLAS STATED FAIRLY CATEGORICALLY THAT THE USAF COULD NOT USE THE CF105 IN THEIR QUOTE INTERCEPTOR SYSTEM UNQUOTE PD IN MAKING THIS STATEMENT I FEEL SURE HE WAS ONLY POINTING UP THE OBVIOUS THAT THE RANGE OF OUR 105 MAKES IT INAPPROPRIATE FOR USE IN THE ZI PD ON THE OTHER HAND HE INDICATED WHAT SEEMED TO BE A VERY GENUINE DESIRE TO PARTICIPATE IN THE CF105 PROGRAM PD PERSONAL SUGGESTIONS TO THIS END BY PEOPLE AT THE LUNCHEON WERE CLN (A) THE PURCHASE OF CF105S BY THE USAF IN SQUADRON STRENGTH TO OPERATE FROM CANADIAN BASES AND

PARAPHRASE NOT REQUIRED
AC NO UNCLASSIFIED REPLY OR REFERENCE PERMITTED IF THE DATE-TIME GROUP IS QUOTED

PAGE 1 OF 4 PAGES
OPERATOR: CAM

CRYPTOCENTRE COPY

INCOMING CLASSIFIED MESSAGE
333/334/31

DATE - TIME GROUP 311645Z

SECURITY CLASSIFICATION: CONFIDENTIAL
ORIGINATOR'S NUMBER: A13 31 JAN

PRIORITY PAGE 2

FROM
TO

CONFIDENTIAL

BE MANNED AND MAINTAINED BY RCAF PERSONNEL PD (B) THE POSSIBILITY OF A NORAD PLAN INDICATING MORE CF105 SQUADRONS THAN WERE PRESENTLY BEING CONTEMPLATED BY CANADA CMM THE USAF TO FUND THE DIFFERENCE PD (C) CANADA PAYING FOR THE IMPROVEMENTS TO BASES FOR SAC PURPOSES WITH THE USAF IN TURN PURCHASING SOME CF105S OVER AND ABOVE THOSE PRESENTLY CONTEMPLATED AS PART OF THE CANADIAN PROGRAM CMM AGAIN TO GET GREATER COVERAGE IN THE NORTH PD

PARA 3 PD THERE IS NO DOUBT IN MY MIND THAT THIS MEETING WITH THE SECRETARY SERVED A VERY GOOD PURPOSE PD MR DOUGLAS SEEMED VERY WELL BRIEFED ON BOTH USAF AND RCAF PROBLEMS AND I HAVE BEEN INFORMED BY SOME OF THE PEOPLE CONCERNED THAT A GOOD DEAL OF HOMEWORK WAS INVOLVED PD WHILE I DO NOT CONSIDER THAT THE SUGGESTIONS PUT FORWARD WOULD HAVE

PARAPHRASE NOT REQUIRED
AC NO UNCLASSIFIED REPLY OR REFERENCE PERMITTED IF THE DATE-TIME GROUP IS QUOTED

PAGE 2 OF 4 PAGES
OPERATOR: CAM

CRYPTOCENTRE COPY

This copy of the telex from the Washington based RCAF attaché to the Canadian Department of National Defence headquarters clearly indicated that the USAF would like to assist the CF-105 financially, not for its own use, but as a quid pro quo to have access to Canada's far North for mutual defence. Read the Department of Defence Production's same meeting minutes on the next page.

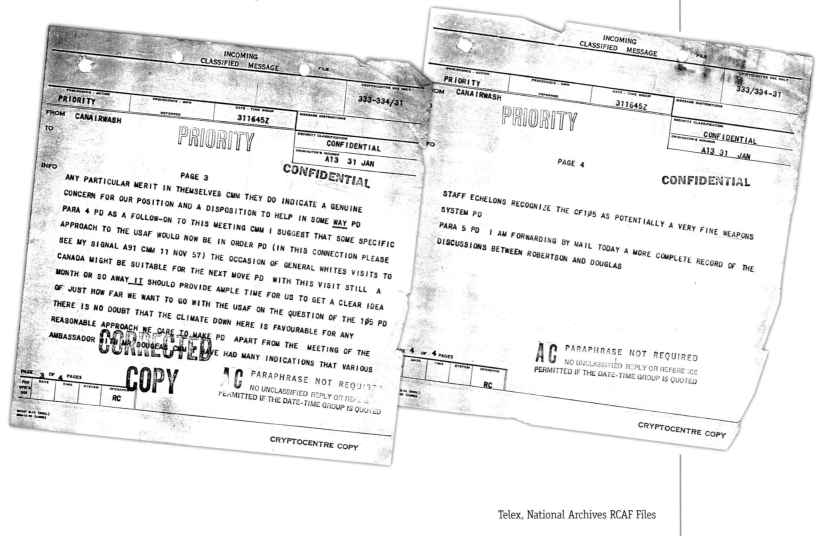

INCOMING CLASSIFIED MESSAGE

PRIORITY

FROM CANAIRWASH

DATE - TIME GROUP
311645Z

333-334/31

SECURITY CLASSIFICATION
CONFIDENTIAL
ORIGINATOR'S NUMBER
A13 31 JAN

CONFIDENTIAL

PAGE 3

ANY PARTICULAR MERIT IN THEMSELVES CMM THEY DO INDICATE A GENUINE CONCERN FOR OUR POSITION AND A DISPOSITION TO HELP IN SOME WAY PD PARA 4 PD AS A FOLLOW-ON TO THIS MEETING CMM I SUGGEST THAT SOME SPECIFIC APPROACH TO THE USAF WOULD NOW BE IN ORDER PD (IN THIS CONNECTION PLEASE SEE MY SIGNAL A91 CMM 11 NOV 57) THE OCCASION OF GENERAL WHITES VISITS TO CANADA MIGHT BE SUITABLE FOR THE NEXT MOVE PD WITH THIS VISIT STILL A MONTH OR SO AWAY IT SHOULD PROVIDE AMPLE TIME FOR US TO GET A CLEAR IDEA OF JUST HOW FAR WE WANT TO GO WITH THE USAF ON THE QUESTION OF THE 105 PD THERE IS NO DOUBT THAT THE CLIMATE DOWN HERE IS FAVOURABLE FOR ANY REASONABLE APPROACH WE CARE TO MAKE PD APART FROM THE MEETING OF THE AMBASSADOR ... DOUGLAS ... VE HAD MANY INDICATIONS THAT VARIOUS

CORRECTED COPY

AC PARAPHRASE NOT REQUIRED
NO UNCLASSIFIED REPLY OR REFERENCE
PERMITTED IF THE DATE-TIME GROUP IS QUOTED

PAGE 3 OF 4 PAGES

RC

CRYPTOCENTRE COPY

INCOMING CLASSIFIED MESSAGE

PRIORITY

FROM CANAIRWASH

DATE - TIME GROUP
311645Z

333/334-31

SECURITY CLASSIFICATION
CONFIDENTIAL
ORIGINATOR'S NUMBER
A13 31 JAN

CONFIDENTIAL

PAGE 4

STAFF ECHELONS RECOGNIZE THE CF105 AS POTENTIALLY A VERY FINE WEAPONS SYSTEM PD
PARA 5 PD I AM FORWARDING BY MAIL TODAY A MORE COMPLETE RECORD OF THE DISCUSSIONS BETWEEN ROBERTSON AND DOUGLAS

AC PARAPHRASE NOT REQUIRED
NO UNCLASSIFIED REPLY OR REFERENCE
PERMITTED IF THE DATE-TIME GROUP IS QUOTED

4 OF 4 PAGES

RC

CRYPTOCENTRE COPY

Telex, National Archives RCAF Files

ANNEX I to APPENDIX G

DEPARTMENT OF DEFENCE PRODUCTION   V-3.4

                                        30th January, 1958.

MEMO TO FILE:

        The Ambassador was the luncheon guest of Secretary James H.
Douglas, Department of the Air Force, who brought along Lt. Gen.
D. L. Putt, Deputy Chief of Staff, Research and Development, U.S.A.F.,
and Major Gen. H. M. Estes, Assistant Chief of Staff for Air Defence
Systems, and Dudley C. Sharp, Assistant Secretary (Materiel), Depart-
ment of the Air Force.

        The Secretary chatted generally over a wide range of topics
including the budgetary position of U.S.A.F. in FY1958 and 1959, the
high cost of programs, the defensive and offensive postures of the
U.S.A.F., and the difficult decisions which must be taken with respect
to types and quantities of new and complex equipments. He also spoke
of the philosophy of the U.S.A.F. which discounts any major build-up
after an outbreak and dictates reliance on forces in being and those
which can be mobilized within a matter of weeks.

        He led into what was obviously the purpose of the get-together
by enquiring concerning the progress of the Canadian CF-105 program.
The Ambassador outlined the position and laid some emphasis on the
fact that with our smaller resources we did not have the choice of
alternatives which an organization as large as U.S.A.F. could elect.
The CF-105, he mentioned. was related to the evaluation of the manned
bomber threat, the rate of development of newer and superseding
weapons, and indeed, whether it made sense for us to commit such a
major portion of our resources and money to a weapons system which
could become virtually obsolescent by the time it is operational.

        The Secretary said that recently they had been looking over their
manned interceptor programs and that the possibilities of the
utilization of the CF-105 in a continental defence role had not escaped
them. The U.S.A.F. problem in its simplest terms, with respect to the
CF-105, is that they have in production the F-101B and F-106 manned
interceptors which they consider to be pretty good and to which he
alluded as being more or less in the CF-105 class as to performance.
The decisions had been taken within the parameters of the FY59 budget
for a decrease in both tactical air squadrons and interceptor strength
in favour of emphasizing other programs. (In this connection he spoke
of the never ceasing problem of trying to maintain the proper balance
of various types of equipments in order to be able to meet the
different capabilities of the potential enemy.) There was no place in
the U.S.A.F. system that he could see for the CF-105. He mentioned
that its cost would make the CF-105 "look like something which might be
picked up in a department store." Quite clearly, the Secretary and his
advisors view the F-108 as being of a much more advanced design and
capability than the CF-105. He stated very firmly that they were going ahead with it, and

        Despite the U.S.A.F. inability to absorb CF-105's into their
interceptor system, the Secretary said that in the context of continental defence he had been thinking in terms of the possibility of
greater utilization of the CF-105 on the basis of some form of U.S.
participation. He elaborated by saying that it was his personal view
that one form which this participation might conceivably take would be
for the Department of the Air Force to purchase CF-105's in squadron
strength, to be integrated into the continental defence system, to
operate from Canadian bases, and to be manned and maintained by R.C.A.F.
personnel.

- 2 -

        The Ambassador commented that this would pose certain problems
against the background of Canada having remained aloof from Lend
Lease and from the acceptance of aid from the U.S. or any other
country. The traditional position has been for Canada to participate
in programs associated with the common defence as a contributor rather
than a beneficiary, and we had hoped that the CF-105 might contribute
something to interceptors of that capability. He mentioned also that
there would be political and other problems associated with the
suggestion made by the Secretary. The Secretary immediately said that
he could understand that to try to implement such an arrangement would
lead to many, many problems. He then dropped the CF-105 subject and
talked about the encouraging possibilities of Bomarc and its increasing
potential as an unmanned interceptor in the U.S. defence plans.

        After a spate of general conversation, he returned to the subject
of the Canadian interceptor. He reiterated his personal view that he
would like to see CF-105's employed in squadron strength in Canada in
greater numbers than was currently being planned for. He also
reiterated that there was no place for the Canadian weapons system in
the U.S.A.F. General Putt, who had not participated up to this point
(as had none of the others), then "wondered aloud" if the end could r
be achieved through NORAD indicating the desired disposition of U.S.
and Canadian interceptor strength on the continent and, on this basis,
showing an essential requirement for a number of squadrons based in
Canada considerably greater than those presently planned for commitment
to continental defence by the R.C.A.F. If it could be presented in
this light, Putt wondered if the fact of U.S. purchase of the aeroplanes might not be cast in the terms of overall continental defence
and thus be more acceptable to Canada. As an alternative, he
mentioned that something in the order of eight SAC refueling bases
were being planned for installation on Canadian soil, and that possibly
some "saw-off" or "swap" arrangement might be worked out, i.e. purchase
of CF-105's in exchange for work which might be done by Canada in
readying the refueling bases to give SAC a longer reach.

        (Incidental to the discussion of the CF-105, it was mentioned to
the Secretary that a sizeable portion of the initial 250 millions or
so being spent on the CF-105 (Arrow Astra System) was actually being
expended in the U.S., including the development program for the I.E.S.
the license for the Sparrow II, the initial hardware for the Sparrow
II, and odds and ends under Reimbursable Aid. It was also intimated
that, particularly on the I.E.S. portion, there would probably be a
continuing U.S. content in the nature of GFAE not manufactured in
Canada.)

        The Ambassador commented that he had certainly been given consider-
able food for thought, and was grateful for the opportunity of hearing
the Secretary's views. The Secretary in turn said that he had been
wanting to present his personal view on the employment of the CF-105.

        It was obvious that the Secretary had been thoroughly briefed on
the Canadian-built weapons system and had also discussed it more than
casually with his top military people. In addition, he showed a famili-
arity with a variety of subjects associated with continental defence
which indicated a knowledge of U.S.A.F.'s interests in Canada. He
also gave evidence of an understanding of associated Canadian problems,
both political and economic. He gave the impression of being a very
capable person.

                                                       3

- 3 -

        While a discussion of this sort could not be anything but
inconclusive, it would appear that, on the basis of the personal views
of the Secretary (as contrasted with an agreed Government view, or
even an agreed Department of the Air Force position), the opportunity
is afforded for discussion, and even possibly negotiation, which might
lead to an acceptable arrangement for greater utilization of the
CF-105 based on U.S. participation.

                                                N. R. Chappell

cc. H.E. The Ambassador
    Mr. D. A. Golden, DDP(O)
    A/C R. A. Cameron, CJS(W)
    Dr. J. J. Green, DRB(W)

DDP Minutes, DHIS/HER

So where are we at?

From the beginning of the Arrow project, the RCAF wanted what it thought was the best. The difficult specification of turns at altitude with a Mach 1.5 interceptor, the electronic detection and sophisticated ground control capabilities and an accurate missile that could assure a kill...all assembled what was to be called the Arrow Weapons System. A.V. Roe Canada Limited wanted it too, and actively lobbied for it from the start. Though Avro did not agree with the choice of Sparrow and Astra, it really had no alternative but to help the RCAF meet its needs, even if it was somewhat misguided.

As the project evolved, Avro built up strength and expertise that outstripped the RCAF, the Chiefs of Staff, the Defence Research Board and the National Aviation Establishment capacity to follow. In the correspondence you sense the frustrations of the RCAF as events unfold. Avro's expertise could be interpreted as arrogance although not intentionally so. Jim Chamberlin, Avro's chief aerodynamicist, is reported to have said," I have no requirement to be fair." Neither did the company, and in the end, neither did the RCAF!

The project got bigger and bigger...it was the biggest defence contract in Canada's history, apart from the Second World War. So many people, 650 suppliers, ambitious management, cocky foreigners, Red sabre-rattling threats, new government unaccustomed to technology and large scale industry, allies that were going supersonic, inter-service rivals who wanted their toys, sudden budget constraints and the damn thing even flew, looked beautiful and might even be the best thing in the western arsenal... at the brink...what do we do?...we do what is known today as "the Canadian thing"...we pull back.

We justify it to ourselves and preside over the destruction with many options considered and discarded. The RCAF, at large, was also fooled into believing that not only must we stop the program, but we have to remove all trace of it. Privately, I have been told, time and time again, that destroying it made sure it wouldn't come back. It would

have become an embarrassment, something to be reminded of at every turn if it was allowed to be around. Some would like it dead and buried and to stay that way, even today.

During that spring of 1958, the full impact of the complexity and the work remaining to develop the weapon was becoming more and more evident. The uncertainty of the threat added fuel to the fire. The military wanted out. Compromise programs, such as only completing the preproduction program were entertained and rejected as impractical, as shown by the internal memo to the right.

Sideline watchers correctly predicted that the cancellation of Astra and the Sparrow missile would spell the death of the whole program. Some would say the Americans convinced us to drop the program. Supposedly, they would cover us if things got hot while we redirected our efforts to purchasing, as opposed to developing our own high performance aircraft. The US supplied key components to the program. Every jet available was a deterrent in the event of nuclear war. There would be no time to rebuild. The U.S. helped in all the programs and learned from us. They paid others to buy our product. They paid us to place Bomarcs on our soil. They offered to help with the Arrow. I have evidence for the foregoing - nothing to indicate otherwise - no smoking gun!

Hugh Campbell was under pressure from all fronts to do the easier thing. You will see that he did. Pearkes believed in the interceptor... but at what cost?

Document, National Archives, RCAF files

Air Marshal Hugh Campbell's plea

Both the Chief of the Air Staff and the Minister of National Defence appeared to agree

The Honourable George Pearkes, speaking at the Arrow's rollout.

Quote, Avro Newsletters

"I do not feel that missiles and manned aircraft have, as yet, reached the point where they should be considered as competitive. They will, in fact, become complementary. Each can do things which the other cannot do, and for some years to come, both will be required in the inventory of any nation seeking to maintain an adequate 'deterrent' to war". —Hon. George R. Pearkes, Canada's Minister of National Defence.

MEMORANDUM   CONFIDENTIAL

The Minister   21 August 58.

CF-105 - Supersonic Interceptor

1   The Air Defence submissions, and in particular the CF-105, now being discussed by you with your Cabinet colleagues at Cabinet Defence Committee are of such a nature and import that I feel I should again make clear my recommendations, in order that there may be no misunderstanding.

2   The Chiefs of Staff have considered at great length and over a long period of time the future of the 105 and associated air defence programmes. The programme initially called for the re-equipping of the nine squadrons from a production run of 169 aircraft, and still does. It was clear that this number of aircraft, if ordered, would substantially increase the Defence Budget, if we went into production while at the same time maintaining the present overall pattern of Canadian forces.

3   As a consequence the Chairman, Chiefs of Staff, attempted to get agreement on a programme of 60 front-line aircraft to keep the Budget within two billion dollars. More recently, on your return from Washington, you announced your decision to recommend to Cabinet the cancellation of the 105 programme in its entirety.

4   As I understand it, you would couple with this recommendation to cancel, the introduction of Automaticity (SAGE) plus two squadrons of Bomarcs for the Ontario/Quebec area, as well as some additional Bomarc squadrons which would be the subject of further

Memorandum, DHIS/HER

- 2 -   CONFIDENTIAL

investigation. The degree to which the United States would share the costs of this programme would be the subject of negotiation.

5   In this connection I should state that the requirement for SAGE and the two Bomarc squadrons to be introduced, as well as a manned interceptor, has been recognised in order to provide a balanced air defence force. I should mention that an air defence system in this time scale requires three main components:

    (a)   ground environment, including SAGE and radars,

    (b)   a surface-to-air missile, and

    (c)   a supersonic manned interceptor.

6   It is clearly not my responsibility to comment on the Budget or its size.

7   It is, however, my responsibility to recommend to you the military requirement as I see it in order that the Royal Canadian Air Force may be capable of carrying out its responsibilities. I believe that we must maintain an air defence component of the North American air defence system that will assist in maintaining and preserving our peace. Consequently, I fully support the SAGE programme and the two Bomarc squadrons. I cannot, however, associate myself with your decision to cancel the 105 programme but must recommend that it proceed as it is presently planned or, alternatively, to couple the cancellation of the 105 with the procurement of a supersonic interceptor to fill the gap. On the basis of present plans, as I remember them, it may be interesting to note that if no action is taken to replace the CF-100 aircraft with a supersonic interceptor Canada will be the only nation in NATO having an Air Force that is not equipped with such an aircraft.

- 3 -   CONFIDENTIAL

I could go on at some length and re-reason the requirement, pointing out the threat as I understand it from the various Intelligence Agencies. I would, however, be covering ground which we have previously discussed on many occasions during the review of this problem. I would simply like to re-state that, as I see it, to help maintain the peace Canada requires a pattern of air defence forces that are efficient, equipped with modern equipment, operationally ready, and the knowledge of its existence should be well known to any would-be aggressor. Consequently, the Royal Canadian Air Force needs the 105 or, alternatively, another supersonic manned interceptor of comparable performance within the time scale in order to continue to assume its responsibilities, and I so recommend.

(signed) "HUGH CAMPBELL"

(Hugh Campbell)
Air Marshal
Chief of the Air Staff

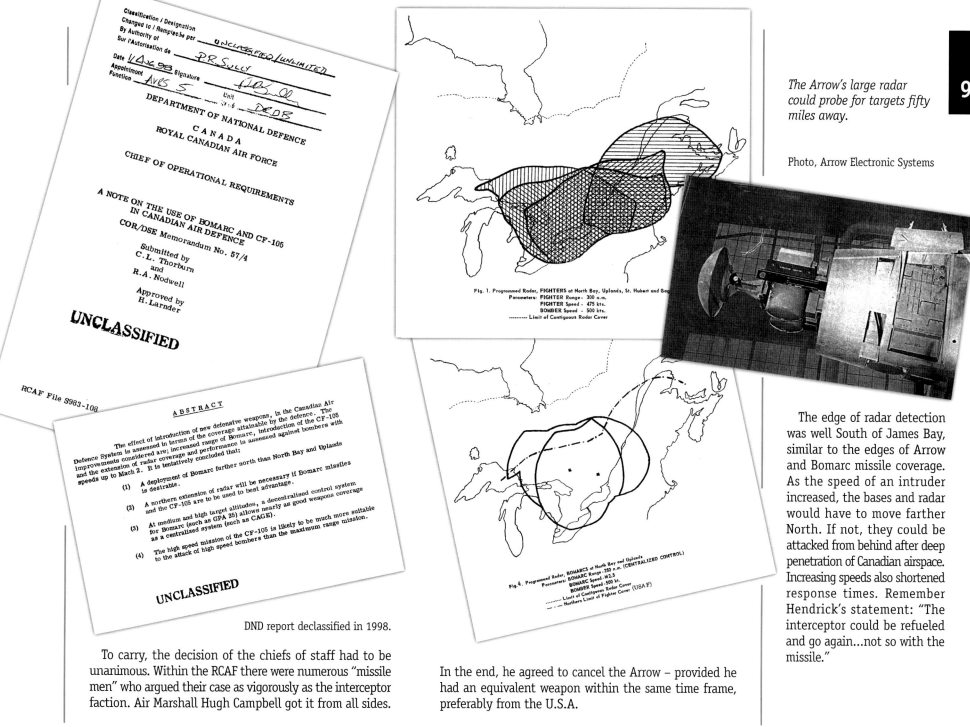

The Arrow's large radar could probe for targets fifty miles away.

Photo, Arrow Electronic Systems

Classification / Designation
Changed to / Remplacée par
By Authority of
Sur l'Autorisation de — UNCLASSIFIED/UNLIMITED
Date 11 AUG 98 Signature — P.R. Sully
Appointment — AVRS S
Function — Unit Grp DRDB

DEPARTMENT OF NATIONAL DEFENCE
C A N A D A
ROYAL CANADIAN AIR FORCE

CHIEF OF OPERATIONAL REQUIREMENTS

A NOTE ON THE USE OF BOMARC AND CF-105
IN CANADIAN AIR DEFENCE
COR/DSE Memorandum No. 57/4

Submitted by
C.L. Thorburn
and
R.A. Nodwell

Approved by
H. Larnder

UNCLASSIFIED

RCAF File S983-108

A B S T R A C T

The effect of introduction of new defensive weapons, in the Canadian Air Defence System is assessed in terms of the coverage attainable by the defence. The improvements considered are; increased range of Bomarc, introduction of the CF-105 and the extension of radar coverage and performance is assessed against bombers with speeds up to Mach 2. It is tentatively concluded that:

(1) A deployment of Bomarc further north than North Bay and Uplands is desirable.

(2) A northern extension of radar will be necessary if Bomarc missiles and the CF-105 are to be used to best advantage.

(3) At medium and high target altitudes, a decentralised control system for Bomarc (such as GPA 35) allows nearly as good weapons coverage as a centralized system (such as CAGE).

(4) The high speed mission of the CF-105 is likely to be much more suitable to the attack of high speed bombers than the maximum range mission.

UNCLASSIFIED

DND report declassified in 1998.

Fig. 1. Programmed Radar, FIGHTERS at North Bay, Uplands, St. Hubert and Bagotville
Parameters: FIGHTER Range - 300 n.m.
FIGHTER Speed - 475 kts.
BOMBER Speed - 500 kts.
-------- Limit of Contiguous Radar Cover

Fig. 4. Programmed Radar, BOMARCS at North Bay and Uplands (CENTRALIZED CONTROL)
Parameters: BOMARC Range - 250 n.m.
BOMARC Speed - M2.5
BOMBER Speed - 500 kt.
-------- Limit of Contiguous Radar Cover (USAF)
— . — . — Northern Limit of Fighter Cover

To carry, the decision of the chiefs of staff had to be unanimous. Within the RCAF there were numerous "missile men" who argued their case as vigorously as the interceptor faction. Air Marshall Hugh Campbell got it from all sides.

In the end, he agreed to cancel the Arrow – provided he had an equivalent weapon within the same time frame, preferably from the U.S.A.

The edge of radar detection was well South of James Bay, similar to the edges of Arrow and Bomarc missile coverage. As the speed of an intruder increased, the bases and radar would have to move farther North. If not, they could be attacked from behind after deep penetration of Canadian airspace. Increasing speeds also shortened response times. Remember Hendrick's statement: "The interceptor could be refueled and go again...not so with the missile."

Unofficial cancellation - August 25, 1958

Members of the CSC – they all agreed to these minutes - they were: Vice Admiral H. D. DeWolf, Chief of Naval Staff; Lieutenant General H.D. Graham, Chief of general Staff; Air Marshal Hugh Campbell, Chief of Air Staff; Dr. A. Zimmerman Head of the Defence Research Board; A/V/M Frank Miller, Deputy Defence Minister; and General Charles Foulkes Chief of the Army as chairman.

AIDE MEMOIRE FOR THE MINISTER   25 Aug 58

ADVANTAGES AND DISADVANTAGES
OF CONTINUING PRODUCTION OF THE CF105

ADVANTAGES

1. **Political**

(a) Will avoid an awkward announcement of closing down the A. V. Roe and Orenda engine plants, which will also involve many subsidiary plants. However it will be realized that even if the CF105 is allowed to proceed, these plants will all have to close down by 1962.

(b) Will avoid an explanation of the waste of $400 million in continuing this development for the last five years. While the responsibility can be placed on the previous government, it should be borne in mind that this government made the decision last October to continue the programme for one year without too close an examination of the future requirements, based mainly on preventing lay-offs in the A. V. Roe and associated industries.

(c) Will avoid a serious political criticism that this government is giving only lip service to the development of scientific and technical development in Canada and that because of financial considerations the government is now turning its back on further scientific and technical developments in the fields of defence, aviation, missilery and defence electronics. Any such action may be interpreted as a serious set-back to scientific and technical development and Canadian industrial potential.

- 2 -   SECRET

2. **Defence Production**

There appears to be considerable defence production advantage in maintaining this development and production, particularly in the defence electronic and missilery fields. While perhaps there is sufficient other aviation production in Canada to allow A. V. Roe to close, this is not the case in the defence electronic industry, which is just beginning in this specialized field. A shut-down of the newly created electronic and missilery development installations may seriously hamper any participation in the development of the defence against the ICBM, which may be a requirement within the next two years.

3. **Labour**

Defence Production points out that the abandonment of this project would mean unemployment in the Toronto area of 25,000 men. There is no alternative production that could be put into A. V. Roe and the Orenda engine plants. Even if a substitute aircraft for the CF105 were selected, it would not meet the immediate situation as it would take twelve to eighteen months to obtain licences, make arrangements for royalties, tooling, etc., for any other aircraft to replace the A. V. Roe aircraft.

4. **Military**

The production of the CF105's would meet the minimum foreseeable military requirements for interceptor aircraft but it is not expected that any other interceptor aircraft will be produced in Canada, and our whole reliance is expected to be placed on ground-to-air missiles in the future.

- 3 -   SECRET

DISADVANTAGES

1. **Military**

The military disadvantages are pointed out in the Cabinet paper already circulated (para. 9):

(a) The changing threat, where it is estimated that the manned bomber will not be the major threat in the period of the life of this aircraft.

(b) The rapid advances in technology, where the missiles such as Bomarc will provide a cheaper and more effective type of defence against the manned bomber.

(c) The diminishing requirements for the manned bomber. The following further points should also be considered:

The need to keep flexibility in our military structure so that there would be sufficient room to do research and development with the United States on defence against the ICBM.

2. **Financial**

(a) A further disadvantage is financial. This is outlined in para. 9 (d) of the Cabinet paper and in the appendices. It is quite clear that this aircraft will require almost $500 million to complete development and then it will likely cost between $10 and $12 million a copy for production. It should be emphasized that these costs cannot be guaranteed, and in the recent study carried out by the Departments of Defence Production and National Defence it was stated:

"No assurances can be given that further increases will not occur. These increases depend on many factors; such as, wage increases, application of overhead, and the volume of business which may be expected from all prime contractors

From this date forward, DND never altered their stance.

- 4 -

If the pattern of past performances follows in the future, we can expect these costs to rise twenty-five to fifty per cent, especially in the electronic and missile part of this project. The adoption of a limited programme would still require all the overhead and additional facilities required for manned aircraft, such as:

Additional facilities on airfields	-	$ 20 million
Supersonic Drones	-	14 million
Flight (Training) Simulators	-	20 million.

(b) On the other hand, Appendix "A" shows very clearly that a programme involving 100 aircraft purchased from the United States could be obtained at much less cost than completing the development of the CF105. It would then be possible to buy spares and replacement equipment from the United States as they are required; whereas if we complete the CF105 we will be required to provide estimated life-time spares as the factories would go out of production on completion of the order. It should be realized, in purchasing a fully developed U.S. aircraft, that the development has been completed and our orders would be tacked onto the end of the U.S. production run. All we would really pay for would be materials and labour costs, as overhead and development would already have been paid for in the U.S. order. Furthermore the United States produce a series of aircraft, which involves anywhere from 600 to 1000 aircraft, and therefore the prices can be much lower.

(c) Considerable savings can be made in the use of missiles instead of manned aircraft:

(i) the numbers required to man a Bomarc battery are between 100 and 200, whereas a squadron of aircraft requires some 400 to 500.

- 5 -

(ii) aircraft are required to operate continuously to keep the crews in shape; missiles do not require any operating costs but just maintenance and a few practice missiles.

Therefore economies can be expected in the operational and maintenance fields by the use of missiles.

(d) There is some concern in the Defence Department that a continuation of the CF105 programme would not leave the programme flexible enough to allow for other urgent projects; such as re-arming of the Air Division, defence against ballistic missiles, development of submarines for anti-submarine work, and development of up-to-date equipment for the Army. A careful study which was made last autumn shows very clearly that there is no room in the present defence programme for major economies which would be required to carry out this programme. Therefore an increased budget must be anticipated if this development and production of the CF105 is to continue.

3. Nuclear Warheads

The abandonment or limitation of manned aircraft in the air defence system and more reliance being placed on ground-to-air missiles would bring about a necessity for arrangements to be made for the use of nuclear warheads for air defence. It is not possible to put a nuclear warhead on the Sparrow missile, and therefore the CF105 with Sparrow cannot be said to be the most modern air defence weapon available. However if more reliance is placed on the use of missiles, then arrangements will have to be made for the storage of nuclear warheads for the use of Canadian missile units in Canadian airspace.

- 6 -

CONCLUSIONS

Therefore I consider that the disadvantages far outweigh the advantages of continuing the CF105 programme. This conclusion has been reached after most thorough study of this problem by the Chiefs of Staff and myself; and the considerations can be summed up briefly as follows:

(1) The decreasing threat may make this aircraft superfluous to requirements before it is completed.

(2) The rapid progress in missile technology is producing ground-to-air missiles which are cheaper, more efficient and more economical to maintain than the manned aircraft. They can be fitted with nuclear warheads and they are possible of further development. I am convinced that the missile will provide more defence per dollar than the manned interceptor, and now that the range of the missile is reaching the range of the interceptor, the advantage appears to be all with the missile. The use of missiles will also save manpower and allow us to take over more U.S. establishments in Canada.

(3) Costs

As I have pointed out, the cost of completing this development is exorbitant and there is no guarantee that these estimated costs will not increase. The acceptance of this programme would mean a budget of more than $2 billion for the next three or four years. The Minister of Finance has stated that the strain which would be placed on the national budget by continuing this programme would be intolerable, which indicates that a $2 billion budget may mean increased taxes.

Chairman, Chiefs of Staff
25 August, 1958.

From the chief's of staff point of view, given the unsettling events of the last year, the overwhelming amount and complexity of work to be completed and ever uncertain increases of costs involved, it is no real wonder that they arrived at this conclusion. The chiefs cannot totally absolve themselves however, since they let it get away on them.

The Arrow Scrapbook - Road To Cancellation

Last days - road to cancellation
Dief's folly

This Iroquois, X-116, came the closest to seeing service by being test-fitted in RL-206 at Avro in February 1959.

Photo, L.Wilkinson

The jewel in the crown was lost for good...
at least to Canada!

Dief's folly...

The Rt. Hon. John Diefenbaker has been criticized for many things, and in retrospect, probably deserves most of what he got. Certainly he can be blamed for letting the Arrow fiasco happen – even if recently released cabinet documents from the period give a kinder view. How could he continue with the purchase of a weapon that the military did not want? He did try to find some compromise.

National Archives

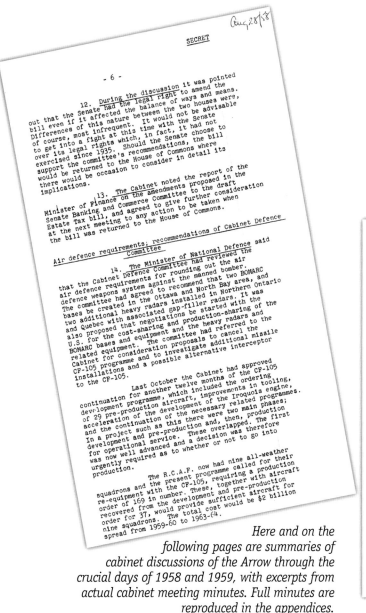

Here and on the following pages are summaries of cabinet discussions of the Arrow through the crucial days of 1958 and 1959, with excerpts from actual cabinet meeting minutes. Full minutes are reproduced in the appendices.

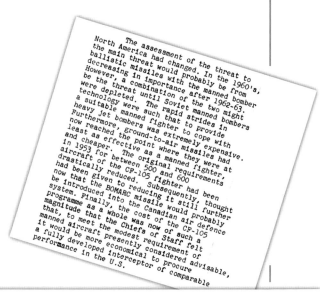

August 28, 1958

There's a review of the latest Cabinet Defence Committee Meeting with Pearkes reporting to the full Cabinet;

- The Chiefs of Staff have reviewed the Air Defence program
- The threat has changed
- Originally 5-600 aircraft were envisioned, now fewer are needed raising the cost per plane. They become too expensive. It is expected that counting the original 37 pre-production models plus 169 additional, it would cost $ 2 billion dollars over 4 fiscal years to have 9, all weather squadrons operational.
- Canada should procure fully developed, comparable fighter interceptors, of same performance, in the USA.
  (possibly F-106C)
- Missiles as effective and cheaper.
- Pearkes recommends program be scrapped entirely.
- After some discussion layoffs most serious drawback. Some 25,000 might be affected.
- No decision. Will keep whole program under review

SECRET

- 11 -

(1) On military or financial grounds it seemed clear that there was no reason to continue the programme. Indeed, many members of the Conservative Party had said in the past that it was quite unwise for a country of Canada's size to attempt to develop an aircraft of this kind in the first place. Instead, they had advocated the manufacture of military aircraft under license. However, to abandon the CP-105 now and undertake to produce the U.S. F-105C, which was physically quite possible, would be a serious political mistake.

17. The Cabinet deferred decision on the recommendations of the Cabinet Defence Committee regarding air defence requirements, including the future of the CP-105 programme.

R.B. Bryce,
Secretary to the Cabinet.

September 7, 1958

- What is the cost of prestige
- Employment and the general economic situation are at stake
- We should agree to cancel on defence aspects
- M. of Finance says the Military wants to cancel it
- My God , we could save $ 400 million...the value of one year's wheat crop

September 3, 1958

John Tory and Fred Smye meet the PM, Pearkes and Fleming to discuss rumours about possible cancellation of the Arrow. A.V. Roe recommends continuation of the engine and airframe programs. The government should drop the RCA Astra / Sparrow agenda, in favour of the Hughes MA-1 / Falcon, fire control and missile respectively. At least $300 million can be saved. Again, the Cabinet discusses this meeting later the same day.

- There is no chance to resume the program once it is cancelled
- Better now than in 2 years after 100 aircraft have been produced
- Manned interceptor is obsolete
- Mr. Smye is said to be very critical of some RCAF decisions and Officers
- The figures presented by Smye should be taken with reserve says Pearkes.
- previous experience with the Company places figures and issues in doubt
- Loss of jobs reported on by the M. of Finance

As this letter of September 16, 1958 makes clear, Avro's Crawford Gordon knew the Arrow program was in trouble well before the official announcement some six months later.

DND, DHIS/HER

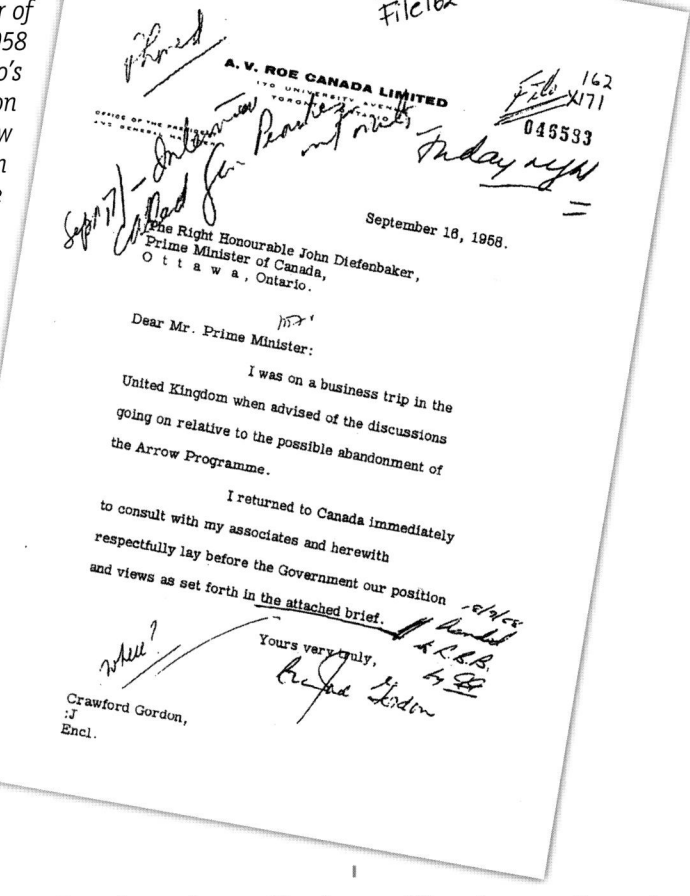

Frequent cabinet meetings set the stage for the announcement that the Arrow will not be put into production at this time, and will face a review by March 1959.

The much dramatized confrontational meeting between Diefenbaker and Gordon seems much more mundane than reported.

September 8, 1958

- Dief asks for time. At least two weeks
- New alternatives should be worked out or compromises reached
- Agree on two new Bomarc Bases and two Heavy Radars

September 21, 1958

- Dief reports seeing Crawford Gordon, first alone and later with Pearkes and Fleming.
- Nothing new... keep going with airframes and engine... stop Astra / Sparrow
- US willing to help with cost on the Hughes system

September 22, 1958

- Cabinet agreed that cancellation likely in March/59, the deadline
- No decision at this time.

Things go quiet for a while. There is lots of activity in the press with all sorts of speculations, pros and cons for cancellation, testimonials, each side taking shots at one another.

A late-1950s map showing the extent of Bomarc missile coverage.

RCAF files, National Archives

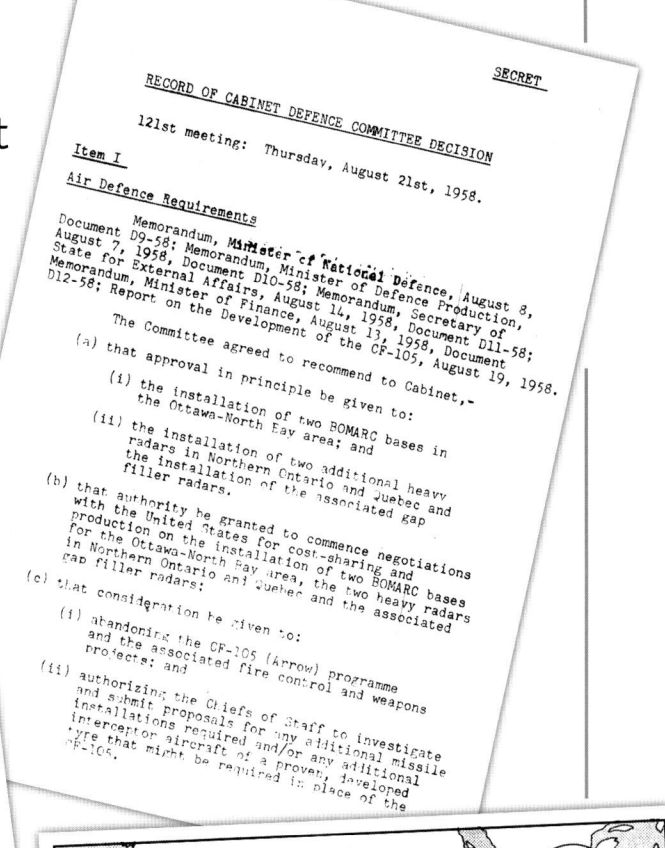

SECRET

RECORD OF CABINET DEFENCE COMMITTEE DECISION

121st meeting: Thursday, August 21st, 1958.

Item I

Air Defence Requirements

Memorandum, Minister of National Defence, August 8, Document D9-58; Memorandum, Minister of Defence Production, August 7, 1958, Document D10-58; Memorandum, Secretary of State for External Affairs, August 14, 1958, Document D11-58; Memorandum, Minister of Finance, August 13, 1958, Document D12-58; Report on the Development of the CF-105, August 19, 1958.

The Committee agreed to recommend to Cabinet,-

(a) that approval in principle be given to:

(i) the installation of two BOMARC bases in the Ottawa-North Bay area;

(ii) the installation of two additional heavy radars in Northern Ontario and Quebec and the installation of the associated gap filler radars.

(b) that authority be granted to commence negotiations with the United States for cost-sharing and production on the installation of two BOMARC bases for the Ottawa-North Bay area, the two heavy radars in Northern Ontario and Quebec and the associated gap filler radars;

(c) that consideration be given to:

(i) abandoning the CF-105 (Arrow) programme and the associated fire control and weapons projects; and

(ii) authorizing the Chiefs of Staff to investigate and submit proposals for any additional missile installations required and/or any additional interceptor aircraft of a proven, developed type that might be required in place of the CF-105.

Bomarc sites will give air-defence coverage over much of North America. The areas shown are based on the 250-mile operational range of the IM-99A Bomarc. The two sites in Canada have been assumed to be at Quebec and North Bay.

OFFICE OF THE PRIME MINISTER
CANADA

Press Release

For Immediate Release
September 23, 1958.

REVISION OF THE CANADIAN AIR DEFENCE PROGRAMME

The Prime Minister, the Right Honourable John Diefenbaker, announced today that in recent weeks the government has fully reviewed the Canadian air defence programme in the light of the rapid development that has taken place during the past year in missiles for both defence and attack. In doing so it has had detailed advice from its military experts on the nature of attacks on North America that might be expected should a major war take place. A number of changes in the air defence programme have now been decided upon.

The government has concluded that missiles should be introduced into the Canadian air defence system and that the number of supersonic interceptor aircraft required for the R.C.A.F. air defence command will be substantially less than could have been foreseen a few years ago, if in fact such aircraft will be required at all in the 1960's, in view of the rapid strides being made in missiles by both the United States and the U.S.S.R. The development of the Canadian supersonic interceptor aircraft, the CF-105 or the "Arrow" was commenced in 1953, and even under the best of circumstances it will not be available for effective use in squadrons until late in 1961. Since the project began, revolutionary changes have taken place which have made necessary a review of the programme in the light of anticipated conditions when the aircraft comes into use. The preponderance of expert opinion is that by the 1960's manned aircraft, however outstanding, will be less effective in meeting the threat than previously expected

It has therefore been decided to introduce the BOMARC guided missile into the Canadian air defence system, to be used in defence against hostile bombers. This is a long range, anti-aircraft missile guided from the ground with the aid of the same radar system as that used in guiding interceptor aircraft. It can be used with

The government has also approved the extension and strengthening of the Pinetree radar control system, which was constructed, and is being operated, jointly by the United States and Canada. Several additional large radar stations will be constructed. These and the existing stations will be supplemented by a considerable number of small intervening stations.

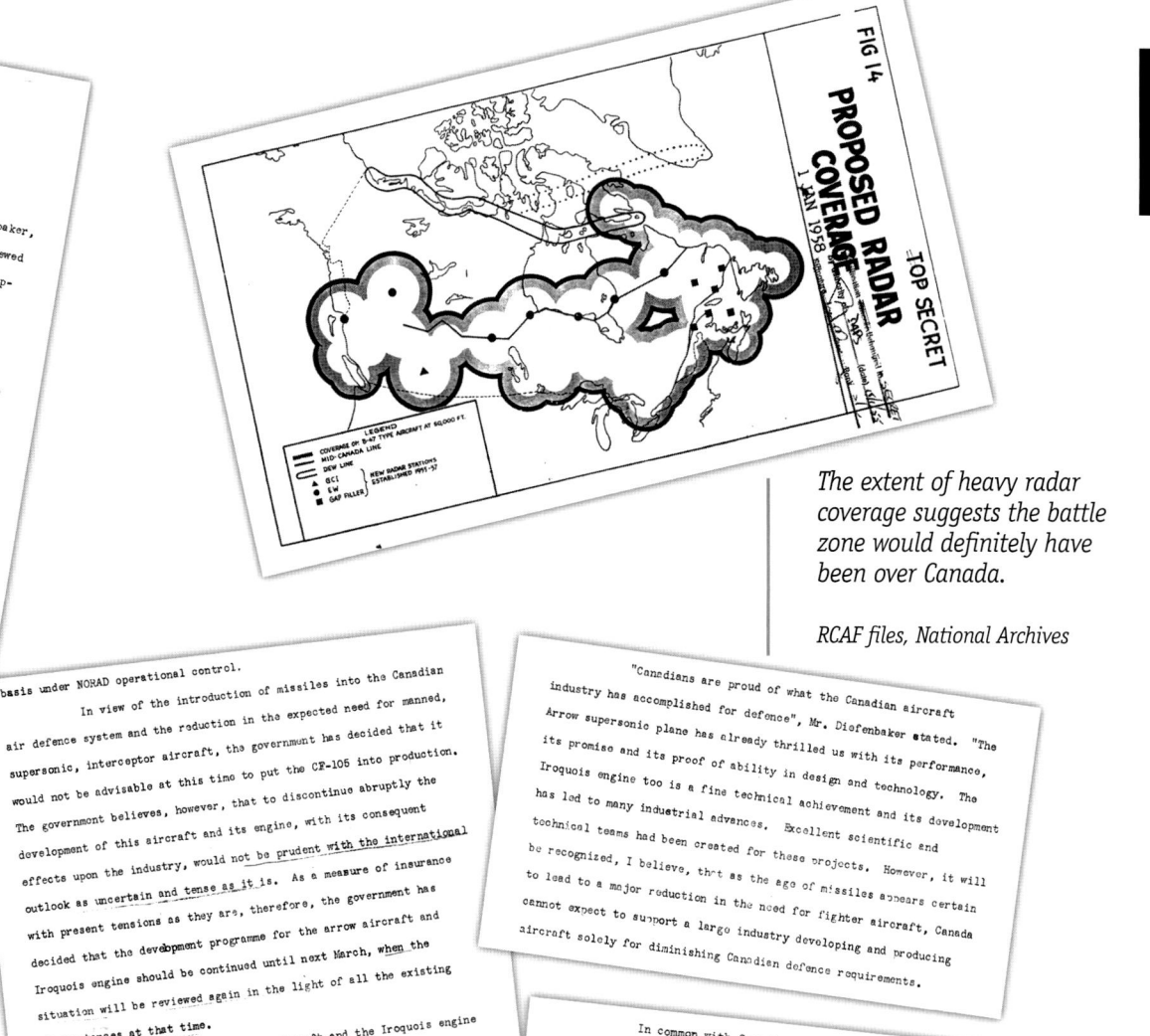

FIG 14

TOP SECRET

PROPOSED RADAR COVERAGE
1 JAN 1958

LEGEND
COVERAGE OF B-47 TYPE AIRCRAFT AT 50,000 FT.
MID-CANADA LINE
DEW LINE
GCI   NEW RADAR STATIONS
EW   ESTABLISHED 1953-57
GAP FILLER

The extent of heavy radar coverage suggests the battle zone would definitely have been over Canada.

RCAF files, National Archives

basis under NORAD operational control.

In view of the introduction of missiles into the Canadian air defence system and the reduction in the expected need for manned, supersonic, interceptor aircraft, the government has decided that it would not be advisable at this time to put the CF-105 into production. The government believes, however, that to discontinue abruptly the development of this aircraft and its engine, with its consequent effects upon the industry, would not be prudent with the international outlook as uncertain and tense as it is. As a measure of insurance with present tensions as they are, therefore, the government has decided that the development programme for the arrow aircraft and Iroquois engine should be continued until next March, when the situation will be reviewed again in the light of all the existing circumstances at that time.

Although both the Arrow aircraft and the Iroquois engine appear now to be likely to be better than any alternatives expected to be ready by 1961, it is questionable whether in any event their margin of superiority is worth the very high cost of producing them by reason of the relatively small numbers likely to be required.

As a further consequence of the reasons given above, the government has decided that it would be clearly unwise to proceed with

"Canadians are proud of what the Canadian aircraft industry has accomplished for defence", Mr. Diefenbaker stated. "The Arrow supersonic plane has already thrilled us with its performance, its promise and its proof of ability in design and technology. The Iroquois engine too is a fine technical achievement and its development has led to many industrial advances. Excellent scientific and technical teams had been created for these projects. However, it will be recognized, I believe, that as the age of missiles appears certain to lead to a major reduction in the need for fighter aircraft, Canada cannot expect to support a large industry developing and producing aircraft solely for diminishing Canadian defence requirements.

In common with Canadians, the Government recognizes the accomplishments and technical quality of the work done, but to continue vast expenditures on aircraft and equipment which military and other expert opinion does not support as the best way to achieve the defence essential to our security would not only be wasteful but unjustifiable.

Many would see this press release from the Prime Minister's office, on September 23, 1958 as an indication that the Arrow program was doomed. It shows a decision not to put the Arrow into production, and a change in defence strategy towards adoption of Bomarc missile bases and heavy radar installations along the Pine Tree Line and away from manned interceptor aircraft.

DND, DHIS/HER

Fred Smye, A.V. Roe's executive vice-president, tried desperately to inform the government that the price for the Arrow, in smaller quantities, would be far cheaper than the $7 to $12 million then quoted in the media. He suggests that a fixed price bid is possible, whereas the contract to date had been open-ended at cost-plus-5 percent. Though Charles Foulkes, chairman of the chiefs of staff, instructed his subordinates to confirm the numbers, the discussion went nowhere.

Letter, RCAF files,
National Archives

A. V. ROE CANADA LIMITED
170 UNIVERSITY AVE. TORONTO. ONTARIO

October 21, 1958

The Hon. George R. Pearkes, V.C.,
Minister,
Department of National Defence,
Ottawa, Ontario.

Dear Mr. Pearkes:

The purpose of this letter is to confirm some of the remarks I made during our meeting in your office on Thursday, October 16th, to the following effect:-

That, on the basis of installing the Hughes MA1 fire control system, and the adoption of the Falcon and/or Genie missiles, and as the result of other substantial economies and savings proposed by the Company, it is now estimated that we can produce and deliver 100 operational Arrow aircraft, complete in all respects including the Iroquois engine and the MA1 fire control system, for approximately $3,500,000. each. This excludes the development and tooling costs, which it is assumed would continue in accordance with existing contracts, and the small amount of GFE presently proposed. However, the originally estimated cost of development, that is, on the basis of the 37 aircraft programme, would also be substantially reduced, inasmuch as the last 17 of these aeroplanes have been calculated as part of the aforementioned 100 operational aircraft.

In order to substantiate the validity of this estimate, and on the basis that it would make a substantial contribution to the Government's deliberations concerning the Arrow programme, it was stated that the Company would be prepared to enter into a fixed-price type of contract on the basis of $3,750,000. for a complete, operational aircraft, including the Iroquois engine and the MA1 fire control system, excluding only GFE.

-2-

It is realised that, in essence, this is a statement of intention in principle, and that a definitive proposal would have to be submitted, outlining the terms of contract, and clarifying and defining the specification in detail in accordance with our normal practice.

Should you wish it, Avro Aircraft and Orenda Engines would be happy to prepare proposals in conjunction with the Officers of your Department and the Department of Defence Production in line with the principles outlined in this letter.

Yours sincerely,

FRED T. SMYE.

fts-dc

Letter, RCAF files,
National Archives

December 31, 1958

- Dief asks Cabinet if anybody objects to or wishes to change the decision on the Arrow program
- No !!
- No one objects...all Cabinet members are there!!!
- Pearkes says that $ 10 million of the fifty allocated for cancellation could be saved if it is done before March 31 / 59.
- Latest best cost for aircraft is $5 million per copy, including Hughes fire control and fire system

OFFICE OF THE CHAIRMAN, CHIEFS OF STAFF
OTTAWA

CONFIDENTIAL

4 November 1958

8310 A

C.A.S.

1. The Minister has forwarded to me a copy of a letter he received from Mr. Fred T. Smye of A. V. Roe Canada Limited, which makes a proposal for a fixed cost estimate for the production of 100 CF105 aircraft, at an approximate cost of $3.5 million.

2. The Minister has directed that the Chiefs of Staff review this matter; and in making any such review it will be necessary to clarify the question of the future costs of this aircraft and to ascertain what will be required to complete development before any fixed price contract can be considered.

3. I would suggest that your officers should discuss this matter with the Department of Defence Production and be able to come up with agreed figures for the cost of completing the development and a clear understanding of what is included in any fixed price contract as suggested in Mr. Smye's letter.

(Charles Foulkes)
General,
Chairman, Chiefs of Staff.

c.c. Mr. D.A. Golden,
Deputy Minister of Defence Production

Jet Arrow Decision Awaits PM

By JAMES A. OASTLER
Of The Star's Ottawa Bureau

OTTAWA, Nov. 26 — Whether or not the Canadian Government will order the resumption of the production of the CF-105 Arrow interceptor will not only have to wait until Prime Minister Diefenbaker returns but almost certainly until the Defence Department concludes a new series of tests sometime in March.

The statement in Colorado Springs on Monday by Air Marshal Slemon, deputy head of NORAD, sparked a great controversy here yesterday.

(Air Marshal Slemon said that the manned interceptor was going to be necessary as far as he could see in the future.)

Clipping, *Montreal Star*

The Arrow Scrapbook - Road to Cancellation

November 27, 1958

Air Marshal C. Roy Slemon, RCAF, deputy Commander NORAD, stationed in the US, gave an interview to the press in which he sees the need for a manned interceptors for the foreseeable future. He stated that the CF-105 was essential for the defence of North America. Furthermore he claimed that no equivalent aircraft exists or will exist for the next 6 years.

Needless to say, this was at odds with the Government's view !

- The cabinet wanted Slemon chastized
- if Slemon's statement were considered accurate it would mean that the advice from the Chiefs of Staff had been rejected by Cabinet
- Slemon should realize this is a Political issue…basically none of his business
- Some MPs want disciplinary action taken

Slemon said that North America needed a manned interceptor. The Arrow could fill the bill until…the F-108 was in service.

Canadian Air Marshall C. Roy Slemon, stationed in the U.S. as deputy commander of NORAD, said in an interview, that he saw the need for manned interceptors for the foreseeable future. He said the Arrow was essential for the defence of North America, and he claimed that no equivalent aircraft existed or would exist for the next six years. Clearly, his views were at odds with the government.

NORAD

Slemon's CF-105 Bid 'For Best'

NOV 28 1958

By ROBERT MARJORIBANKS

COLORADO SPRINGS (Staff) — Air Marshal Slemon, Canadian deputy-commander of Norad, has made the strongest possible bid to get the Avro CF-105 Arrow for North American defence.

Choosing his words carefully, and with Norad commander-in-Chief General Earle T. Partridge standing at his side, Slemon said that if the CF-105 is put into operation it will be the best interceptor available for air defence of the continent until the U. S. F-108 is in operation five or six years hence.

Slemon spoke several times during a day-long briefing for 35 Canadian newsmen on the continuing need for manned interceptors.

This was interesting since our party was organized and brought here by the RCAF, presumably with the approval of the defence minister.

Clippings, *Montreal Star*

The Arrow was not the only military item threatened with cancellation. The Bobcat, an all-terrain personnel carrier being developed by Canadian Steel Car (an A.V. Roe subsiduary) at Fort William, Ont., was also on the chopping block. Employment was the key card once again.

A.V. Roe, 1958 Annual Report

Arrow Likely To Be Scrapped PM Indicates

JAN 2 0 195

The Avro Arrow circles above a thin layer of cloud during a test flight of the controversial plane.

By TIM CREERY
Of The Star's Ottawa Bureau

OTTAWA, Jan. 20 — Prime Minister Diefenbaker has given a virtual kiss of death to the Avro Arrow interceptor.

The Prime Minister, answering a lengthy indictment by Liberal Leader Pearson of Government policies in the Commons yesterday, indicated he was making a statement now because of the heavy pressure brought on the Government to produce the faster-than-sound interceptor.

Mr. Diefenbaker told the Commons it had made the decision announced September 23 to postpone a final decision on the Arrow until March 31 because of the international situation at the time.

There had been fear that the dangerous situation over Quemoy and Matsu islands in the Formosa Straits might lead to a major war.

Technologists Key

The Government was afraid that if it cancelled the Arrow at that time it might lose the technologists who would be vital to a Canadian war effort.

If a decision to stop the Arrow had been made then, said Mr. Diefenbaker, "it would have brought about the demobilization of the technical men who — in the event that hostilities came about — would have purposes other than the production of the Arrow.

The Prime Minister said the advent of intercontinental ballistic missiles and the launching of Lunik made apparent "a tremendous change in the techniques of potential war."

"It is a disagreeable course," he continued, evidently referring to the consequent decision to stop the Arrow after $400,000,000 had been spent on developments.

January 7, 1959

This cabinet meeting is interesting because an A.V. Roe subsiduary Canadian Car of Fort William (Thunderbay) was bidding on the new "Bobcat" for the Army. If they were not considered they would close the plant and move the business to Montreal. This upset Diefenbaker understandably.

January 28, 1959

The Arrow continues to be controversial but no decision is reached.

- The M. of Finance noted that the "cat would be out of the bag" if he tabled RCAF expenditure estimates for 1959 / 60.

- As of April 1 / 59 only cancellation fees were budgeted.

- Wait for further discussion.

Missile on the way in!

This Montreal Star article (opposite page) is typical of the times. All parties have their supporters and lobbyists.

In February / 59 things start to get difficult and the Arrow is discussed in Cabinet, every few days. Rumours abound.

February 3, 1959

- Make final decision now
- PM speaks to the Chiefs of Staff again. There's nothing new.
- Do it now and save some money.

February 4, 1959

- Continue to delay until the Cabinet defence committee meets one more time

February 10, 1959

- Continued vacillation
- The European based Canadian NATO contingent needs to replace its aging Sabres with a new jet fighter. Decisions are needed but this is hardly the time.
- A Cabinet member suggest there is something wrong with Canada buying American fighters to be flown by Canadian Pilots for the defence of Europeans while at home we depend on Americans to help defend Canadian sovereignty.

A point for reflection to be sure!!!

Arrow on the way out!

The decisive day.

February 14, 1959,

- Cabinet is informed that Avro has requested more money to complete the current fiscal year. About 40 million dollars more than budgeted . This is the straw that breaks the Camel's back !!!

- Cabinet is unanimous in stopping the program NOW !

February 17, 1959

- The draft statement is ready…the sooner the better

February 19, 1959

- The 50th anniversary of powered flight in Canada is to be celebrated February 23/59 , the following Monday. The Governor General, who is to announce a new National Aviation Museum is asked by Cabinet , not to talk about it at this time. I wonder why!

The much publicized adversaries, John Diefenbaker and Crawford Gordon. They met only once, on September 17, 1958.

Clippings *Montreal Star* /A.V.Roe 1958 Report

Ottawa Gets Arrow Plea

Canadian Press

FORT ERIE, Ont., Feb. 14 The Aircraft and Guided Missiles Council of Canada has urged the Federal Government not to cancel the Avro Arrow jet fighter program.

The council's conference here said yesterday that curtailment or cancellation of the project would sound the death knell for Canada's aircraft industry.

This statement was included in telegrams to Prime Minister Diefenbaker, Defence Minister Pearkes and Labor Minister Starr.

The council, composed of representatives of all production phases of the aircraft industry, decided to advise every organized worker in the country of the economic consequences that the cancellation of the program would bring.

It will attempt to enlist the support of organized labor in convincing the Government that the Avro Arrow program should be continued—at least until there is a sound alternative.

Avro's Fred Smye wrote that year-end cost-overruns on the Arrow were normal. But this time the timing was bad and the amount too high.

Fred Smye,
Canadian Aviation and The Avro Arrow

---

92   FRED SMYE

if the contracts were, in effect, cancelled or were about to be cancelled so that the company could work with the Government in the orderly wind down or termination of the work. These pleas always fell on deaf ears.

From the day of the election of the Diefenbaker Government, there was virtually no interchange, as between the Government and the company. The company was cut off, more so than the military, for the same reason--suspicion. The company like the military was a product of the Liberal Government. For their efforts, the company executives were chastised and branded as lobbyists. The company had every right to be involved and should have been consulted, as it had been in the past. The companies were the designers and producers of the airplane and its engine and did feel responsible for the welfare of its 15,000 people. A large body of the personnel had a deep interest and concern for the defence of the country. This concern and commitment was one of the reasons they were devoting their talents to the creation and production of advanced military equipment.

In the past, it was the Government's practice to appropriate funds for each fiscal year ending March 31. These amounts were established as ceilings in the contracts from year to year. Traditionally these limits were exceeded, usually due to the Government's cumbersome paper system, but this was understood and agreed to by the appropriate Government officials. Technically, in the strictest, legal sense the Government was not bound to reimburse the company above the limits in the contract.

In January, 1959 it became apparent that some of the contract limits were about to be exceeded. The amount was estimated to be approximately $20,000,000 by the end of March. There would be an additional amount of some $40,000,000 in outstanding commitments. As indicated previously, in the past the company would carry the over run with the concurrence of the Government.

The situation was now very different. The officers of the Department of Defence Production would not or could not discuss the matter as all matters concerning the Arrow were in the hands of the politicians. I was unable to contact the acting Minister of that Department, Mr. Green, as he refused to see me. In desperation I wrote a letter dated February 9, 1959 to the Minister outlining the situation and saying that, although technically the

$10 million saved by cancelling now

CONFIDENTIAL

RECORD OF CABINET DECISION

Meeting of February 17th, 1959. *S 1038CN-180*

Arrow (CF-105) aircraft; Report of Cabinet Defence Committee; decision to terminate development

The Cabinet,—

(a) agreed that the development of the Arrow aircraft and Iroquois engine be discontinued; effective as of the time of announcement;

(b) that an announcement concerning this decision and also production sharing with the United States and the acquisition of atomic weapons be made in the House of Commons, probably on Friday;

(c) that the contractors be notified of the termination of their contracts at the same time; and,

(d) that an agreement be made with the United States, in the form of an exchange of notes, for the implementation of the agreed arrangements on the sharing of the costs of Bomarc and S.A.G.E. installations in Canada and the associated extension of radar coverage.

February 27, 1959.

sgd (Mrs. Duncan)
Chief Secretary

VCAS				
CPlansI	AMTS	COMPT	AMP	SCR
COR	CMat	CFin		LPA
COps	CAE			
CTel				

For your information.

(J. [signature]) W/C
CAS/EA
6-6175

Arrow (CF-105) aircraft; report of Cabinet Defence Committee; decision to terminate development
(Previous reference Feb. 14)

12. **The Prime Minister** said a draft announcement on the termination of the development contract for the Arrow had been prepared. It included a section on arrangements with the United States for production sharing and a section on the acquisition by Canada of nuclear weapons for defence. He had gone over the draft in great detail but it was not yet in the right form to be made that day.

13. **The Minister without Portfolio (Mr. Macdonnell)** reported that, the previous day in Toronto, the Premier of Ontario had spoken to him in strong terms about the effects of terminating the Arrow contract upon the municipalities in the vicinity of Malton.

14. **The Minister of Finance** said Mr. Frost had also spoken to him in pungent language about work on the Arrow being stopped. Mr. Frost had complained about so little notice being given to Avro, and had asked why other contracts could not be given to the company. He had replied that the matter had been exhaustively considered, that all possible alternatives had been reviewed, and that the decision would be taken in the light of the best military advice available. He had also told Mr. Frost that, right from the outset, it had never been said that actual production would proceed and that everyone understood that the matter was to be reviewed year by year.

15. **During the discussion** the following points emerged:

(a) The sooner the announcement could be made the better, because the decision to terminate was bound to leak out and the longer the announcement was delayed the more would be the cost.

(b) The most appropriate time for the announcement appeared to be the following Friday. This, as proposed, should refer not only to the Arrow termination but also to the acquisition of nuclear weapons. The Prime Minister's statement should be followed by one by the Minister of Defence Production, which would deal in greater detail with production sharing. In considering this question of timing, the possibility of a motion to adjourn the house to discuss a matter of urgent public importance should not be overlooked.

- 11 -

SECRET

Courts of Canadian citizenship; establishment
(Previous reference Feb. 12)

27. The Cabinet agreed that the Minister of Citizenship and Immigration be authorized to establish citizenship courts,—

(a) in those areas handling a large number of applications for citizenship or where ordinary courts cannot provide adequate facilities for handling these applications in a judicious and expeditious manner; or,

(b) in areas where applicants are being charged fees in excess of those provided in the Canadian Citizenship Act and Regulations.

National Aviation Museum; proposed speech by Governor General

28. The Minister of Northern Affairs and National Resources said the Governor General wished to make a speech in favour of the establishment of a National Aviation Museum.

29. During the discussion it was pointed out that this was a matter of government policy which had not yet been discussed by the Cabinet. It would be improper for Mr. Massey to speak about the subject at this time.

30. The Cabinet agreed that the Governor General be advised not to speak publicly in support of a National Aviation Museum at this time.

R. B. Bryce,
Secretary to the Cabinet.

Cabinet is finally of one mind on February 14, 1959 – triggered by A.V. Roe's request for more funds.

Black Friday - February 20, 1959

Fred Smye - Executive Vice President, A.V. Roe Canada Limited.

National Archives

Their faces say it all!

Decision Deferred As Avro Talks End

By JAMES A. OASTLER
Of The Star's Ottawa Bureau

MAR 4 1959

OTTAWA, March 4.—Talks between cabinet members and top officials of A. V. Roe Limited have concluded for the time being with no decision reached on proposals for work to occupy the Avro and Orenda plants at Malton, Ont.

After a 10-minute talk with Defence Minister Pearkes yesterday, Sir Roy Dobson, A. V. Roe board chairman who flew from Britain over the weekend, finally talked to newspapermen who had been chasing him for two days.

Indicative of his frame of mind was his answer to a question whether the prospects of his Canadian subsidiaries affected by cancellation of the Arrow jet interceptor contract had been enhanced by his visit.

"I wish I knew," he said. "We've tried hard enough. But that's still the $64 question."

Sir Roy said it suited his purpose not to comment on possible contracts which Avro might get from the Government. "The less we can say about it the better."

Work For Engineers

He was, however, willing to talk about the future of Avro engineers. If there was no work for them in Canada he was quite willing to take them back to Britain, "and that includes the top."

Defence Minister Pearkes had earlier said that only minor proposals had been made by the company. Sir Roy indicated he didn't quite agree but would not elaborate, saying only that any proposals presented to the Government were secret.

He said the alternatives he had proposed would, if accepted, employ quite a few men but he didn't know just how many. The proposals were extensions of those put forward last week by Avro president Crawford Gordon, Sir Roy said.

Relations With Ottawa

It was apparent that uppermost in Sir Roy's mind was the n... to bolster relations of the c... pany with the Government...

Earlier, Sir Roy met w... fence Production O'Hurley, who report... cabinet. The visitor... to see Prime Min... baker, but he was... debate in the Hou...

Under furthe... Roy insisted h... talk about... Government... that they... But Go... of the fi... curtain... Roy's...

Thirteen thousand Avro and Orenda workers are suddenly laid off

Jobless Aircraft Workers

FEB 21 1959

A gate guard at Avro waves goodbye to workers as they leave the aircraft plant under notice of dismissal.

Ten thousand subcontractor workers would be laid off in the weeks to come, 6500 in Canada and 3500 in the U.S.A.

John Plant - President and General Manager, Avro Aircraft Limited.

National Archives

February 23, 1959

The previous Friday, the PM announced the cancellation of the whole Arrow program...the fallout was now coming in fast and furious. A defensive Cabinet met and exclaimed;

- **Avro claim of 'no notice'...unfair**
- **Assistance for those laid off considered with reluctance**
- **No call to be delicate with the Company**

February 26, 1959

- There is suggestion from A.V. Roe to pay 6 months for technical staff 'on hold' costs...250 people at Orenda and 200 at Avro
- MPs say...why should the Government pay anything? The Company made more than $ 34 million in the last four years. Why can't they help!
- We should help each other.
- Cabinet agrees the next day... a 50/50 cost sharing budget, $1,650,000 of matching funds from the government, over six months.

Reportedly, Air Vice Marshal Easton convinced the Chief of the Air Staff, Hugh Campbell to scrap the Arrow.

House of Commons Debates

Volume 103 · Number 28 · 2nd Session · 24th Parliament

OFFICIAL REPORT

Monday, February 23, 1959

Speaker: The Honourable Roland Michener

THE QUEEN'S PRINTER AND CONTROLLER OF STATIONERY
OTTAWA, 1959

Air Vice-Marshal John Easton signed a memo informing other armed forces departments of the cancellation of the Arrow program. Some ex-RCAF officers claim that it was he who pushed for missiles over interceptors and argued for the destruction of the Arrows and their plans.

Photo, DND DHIS/HER

The Arrow Scrapbook - Road to Cancellation

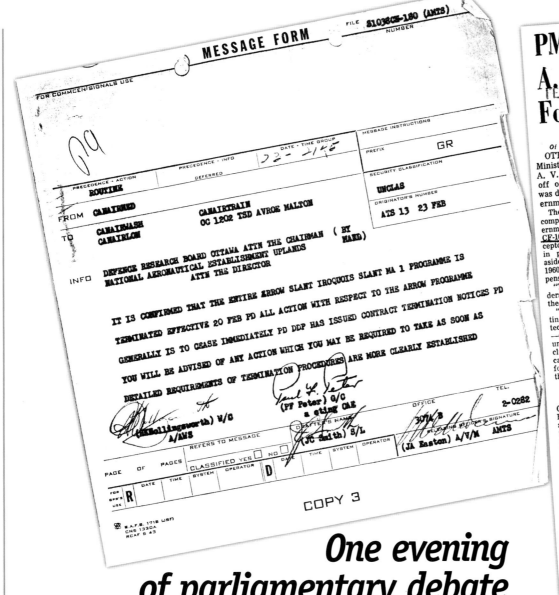

PM Chides A. V. Roe For Layoffs

FEB 24 1959

By TIM CREERY
Of The Star's Ottawa Bureau

OTTAWA, Feb. 24 — Prime Minister Diefenbaker says the A. V. Roe (Canada) Ltd. lay-off of 14,000 workers Friday was done to embarrass the Government.

The Prime Minister said the company had warning of the Government decision to cancel the CF-105 Arrow supersonic interceptor and knew that $50,000,000 in public funds had been set aside in the estimates for 1959-1960 to cover winding-up expenses.

"The company had no misunderstanding whatsoever," he told the Commons yesterday.

"I say that its attitude in letting out thousands of workers—technical workers and employes—on Friday was so cavalier, so unreasonable, that the only conclusion any fair-minded person can come to is that it was done for the purpose of embarrassing the Government."

Emergency Debate

The statement was cheered by Government supporters. The Prime Minister was replying in an emergency debate to Opposition criticism that the Government had made no orderly plan for the winding up of the Arrow and possible other work for A. V. Roe.

Mr. Diefenbaker put the onus on the company to come forward with "practicable" alternative proposals. He said he hoped to hear them today from Avro president Crawford Gordon Jr. and senior officers of the company meeting him in Ottawa.

Mr. Gordon conferred for more than an hour this morning with Prime Minister Diefenbaker. The Prime Minister said there had been "preliminary discussions" and that talks would continue throughout the day.

He said Mr. Gordon and Fred T. Smye, a Roe vice-president, will fully outline their suggestions during the day to a cabinet committee comprising Defence Minister Pearkes, Finance Minister Fleming, Transport Minister Hees, Labor Minister Starr and Defence Production Minister O'Hurley.

Mr. Diefenbaker confirmed to Parliament shortly after 2:30

The Arrow

THE debate on scrapping the Arrow blew into Commons and blew out again just as quickly. There was not enough in this issue to sustain a major debate, and this the Opposition knew.

In fact, the debate would not have cropped up so suddenly in Commons except for the dramatic and political stroke in which 14,000 people were cut adrift on Friday at Malton. Avro officials explained there had been no advance warning. It came as a shock. Sympathizers spoke of the body blow to the aviation industry.

FEB 25 1959

If this was a body blow, then never in the history of industrial combat has a punch been so obviously telegraphed. Any fighter wise in the ways of the political ring could have seen that haymaker coming up all the way from the floor. As early as 1955 the worried Liberals said they would review it on an annual basis. On that October day in 1957 that Avro unveiled the Arrow with such fanfare, their Tory successors said they would take the same cautious approach. Last September the Prime Minister wrote on the wall for all to see. This month there was a $50 millions item in estimates, and this was pointedly explained as being available for a sort of severance pay if the contract were cancelled. And still Friday's announcement was treated as a bombshell.

It was significant that the Liberal CCF speakers did not dwell on the military virtues of the Arrow. These were considerable, but not as considerable as they once were thought to be. The Opposition contented itself with concern for national economy the dislocation of industry and professional skills, of more of us becoming a defence satellite of the U.S. In fact, the Arrow was killed because of its much reduced value in light of advances in other fields, its inordinate cost in relation to the dollar, and the sad fact that we wanted to share it with ...

... course, there must be serious efforts to relate the upheaval at Avro, to what else would have become of the Arrow. This too if the cancellation is confirmed. Sound alternative work is needed. The Government has a proposal to build short-range jets at $2,500,000 each. Then the question of turboprops cost $3,000,000. Another was to use all this energy into the exploration of space. How much will this cost? Can one hot potato simply to exchange for another one.

Clippings,
Montreal Star and
Toronto Telegram

One evening of parliamentary debate is all the Arrow gets!

Diefenbaker claims that there is no need to be delicate with the company... especially after the embarrassing lay-offs.

In the end, the government and the military faced

- the closing of the Avro, Orenda and subcontractor plants laying off some 25,000 skilled workers.
- the contradiction of why the Arrow was cancelled after five years and $400 million had been poured into it.
- the charge that the government was paying only lip service to scientific and technical development in Canada and curtailing industrial potential.

An inept government had a chance to put it right but was "overtaken by events" itself.

"At the assembly bay door stood the first Iroquois-powered Arrow and, behind it, stood more in various stages of completion. The silence was deafening. Row upon row of the most modern machine tools stood idle in both Avro and Orenda plants with their work partially finished."

Fred Smye, *Canadian Aviation and The Avro Arrow*

DANGER 550 VOLTS

25206

25000

Although cancellation was still to come, this "after-hours" view of the Arrow Mk II assembly shop floor gives a hint of the quiet that lay ahead. The Arrow metal mockup is in the foreground. RL-206 leads the line.

Photo, L Wilkinson

Road to Cancellation - The Arrow Scrapbook

An Arrow Mk II, probably RL-207, being dismantled, not cut up as the Mk Is were.

Photo, L. Wilkinson

The dirty business begins

S1038GN-180 (CAS)

APR 10 1959

MEMORANDUM   7 Apr 59

The Minister (Through Deputy Minister)

Arrow Cancellation - Progress Report

1   In executing the details involved in the termination of the Arrow, the RCAF has been working in close collaboration with DDP. This has been achieved by meetings and daily contacts both in Ottawa and at the contractors' plants of the Termination Committees duly established within DDP and the RCAF. In this connection I would like to give you a short summary of the present status of the termination proceedings.

2   We have advised DDP to arrange for the disposal of new materiel, work in process and tooling. DDP have also been advised to dispose of the wooden and metal mockups of the Arrow. Arrangements have been completed with the USAF to accept the return of the B47 in its present state and DDP have been advised to return the B47 to the USAF. Arrangements have also been completed through DDP for the return of the MA-1 Systems to the USAF. AMCHQ has been requested to screen all equipment on loan and to withdraw to RCAF units equipment that can be used and to arrange for disposal through CADC of equipment not required.

3   In my 1038GN-80 (CAS) dated 26 March 59, I reported at your request the proposed method of disposal of the Arrow airframes and Iroquois engines. If this method receives your approval, DDP will be so advised. This I feel will materially assist in physically clearing out the residual work in the AVRO and Orenda plants.

(Hugh Campbell)
Air Marshal
Chief of the Air Staff

cc: Deputy Minister

Hugh Campbell's further admission of the RCAF's role in getting rid of the Arrow

National Archive, RCAF Files

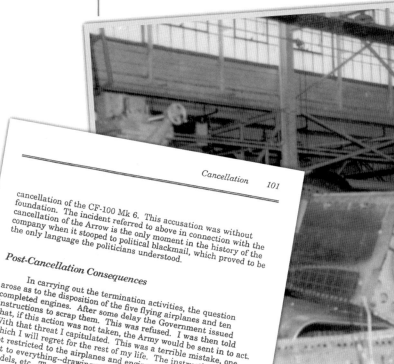

cancellation of the CF-100 Mk 6. This accusation was without foundation. The incident referred to above in connection with the cancellation of the Arrow is the only moment in the history of the company when it stooped to political blackmail, which proved to be the only language the politicians understood.

Post-Cancellation Consequences

In carrying out the termination activities, the question arose as to the disposition of the five flying airplanes and ten completed engines. After some delay the Government issued instructions to scrap them. This was refused. I was then told that, if this action was not taken, the Army would be sent in to act. With that threat I capitulated. This was a terrible mistake, one which I will regret for the rest of my life. The instructions were not restricted to the airplanes and engines and their components but to everything--drawings, technical data, micro-film, photos, models, etc. The existence of the airplane and the engine was to be erased without trace. $400,000,000 of the taxpayer's investment in advanced technology was deliberately destroyed. Not the slightest attempt was made to salvage anything from this gigantic investment.

It is impossible to convey the scenes which prevailed in these two enormous, empty plants: Avro, 1,600,000 sq ft, and Orenda 1,200,000 sq ft; a relative handful of dejected employees, scattered here and there, endeavouring to do their little bit of work; the big skin milling machines standing idle, with partially processed aluminum slabs lying on their beds; the gigantic presses standing hauntingly still. At the assembly bay door stood the first Iroquois-powered Arrow and, behind it, stood more in various stages of completion. The silence was deafening. Row upon row of the most modern machine tools stood idle in both plants with their work partly finished. In the flight test hangar stood the five majestic Arrows which had flown above 50,000 ft at twice the speed of sound. They were awaiting the arrival of the blow torches in the hands of the men who built them.

At about this time Sir Roy Dobson arrived from the U.K. to survey the wreckage. He had conversations with the Government leading him to the opinion that the management was not without blame. Mr. Gordon and particularly myself wished Dobson to state the true facts in the case so that the company might retain

An excerpt from Fred Smye's unpublished memoir, Canadian Aviation and the Avro Arrow, in which he relates the unhappiness which Avro officials and workers felt in having to destroy the technical marvel they had earlier created.

Randy Smye.

The cut line, on a fragment now in the National Aviation Museum, Ottawa.

Photo, Peter Zuuring

IN REPLY PLEASE QUOTE No. 610380N-180(DMP)

Department of National Defence

CANADA

OTTAWA, Ontario.
April 14, 1959.

Director,
Aircraft Branch,
Department of Defence Production,
No. 4 Building,
Ottawa, Ontario.

Attention: Mr. J. Bush

Dear Sir:

Cancellation of Arrow Program
Disposal of Airframes and Engines

The RCAF has no requirement for any of the Arrow airframes or Iroquois engines. It is therefore requested that you arrange for disposal of these as soon as possible. In your arrangements will you please ensure that any items installed in either the airframe engine that can be disposed of in whole state to better advantage disposed of in this manner.

The balance of the airframe and engine will be reduced to scrap and disposed of through CADC as you have previously indicated. We do not wish to have the airframe and engine disposed of in the whole state.

With this decision will you please advise if there are any other matters which require further clarification before you can proceed with the complete disposal arrangements.

As has been indicated in verbal conversation, AMC personnel will screen RCAF requirements of any items. In addition, there will be a section of the fuselage with the pressurized cabin for the Institute of Aviation Medicine.

Any further items that are required will be cleared by AMC through Mr Hoare, if this is satisfactory, or directed through your office if preferred.

Will you please advise AMC which method you prefer.

Yours truly,

A. H. Lieff
Group Captain
for Chief of the Air Staff

c.c. 1202 T&D Malton
c.c. AOC AMC

Obviously, RL-206 was cut up, as the mangled junction here shows. Following an RCAF directive, the nose piece was sent to the Institute for Aviation Medicine in Toronto for research purposes. It was moved quickly during the night from the Avro plant at Malton, with a hole in a wall at the institute being made to admit the nose piece, then being repaired and repainted before morning. There was no publicity and no photos. It is said that the rest of RL-206 was flattened with a bulldozer. A fanciful version perhaps, but who knows?

RCAF Group Captain Abe Lieff makes it quite clear that the force has no need for any leftover pieces of the Arrow program.

Letter, National Archives

Delays – and madcap destruction

At least one delay in the destruction of the Arrows was an apparent interest in the aircraft by the Royal Aeronautical Establishment of Great Britain. Though no direct correspondence has been found, several former Avro employees maintain that the RAE was interested but was discouraged from asking so that the Canadian government would not have to say no.

Letter,
National Archives, RCAF files

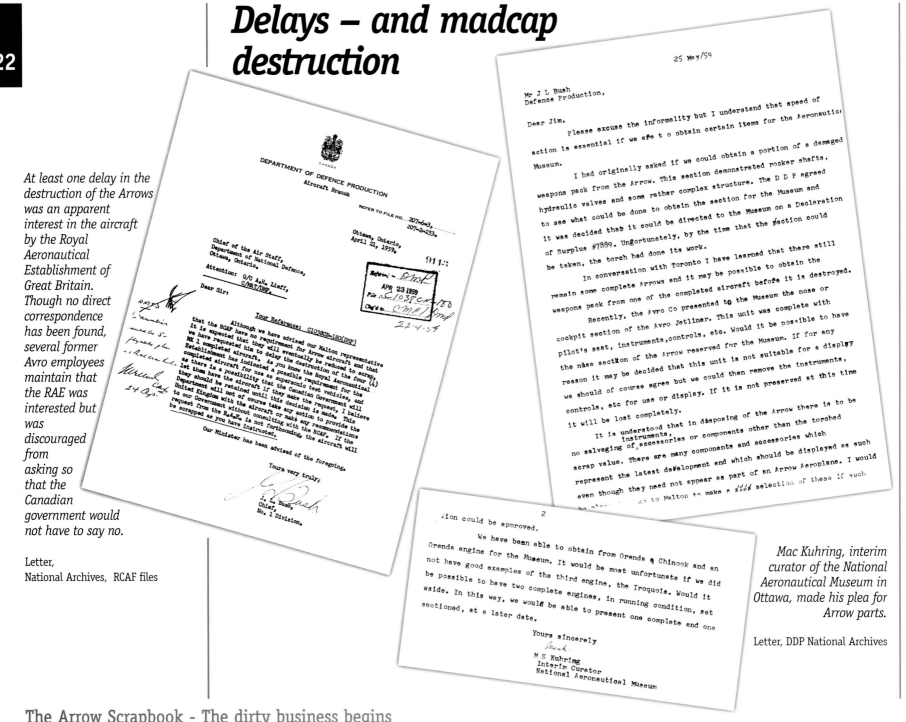

Mac Kuhring, interim curator of the National Aeronautical Museum in Ottawa, made his plea for Arrow parts.

Letter, DDP National Archives

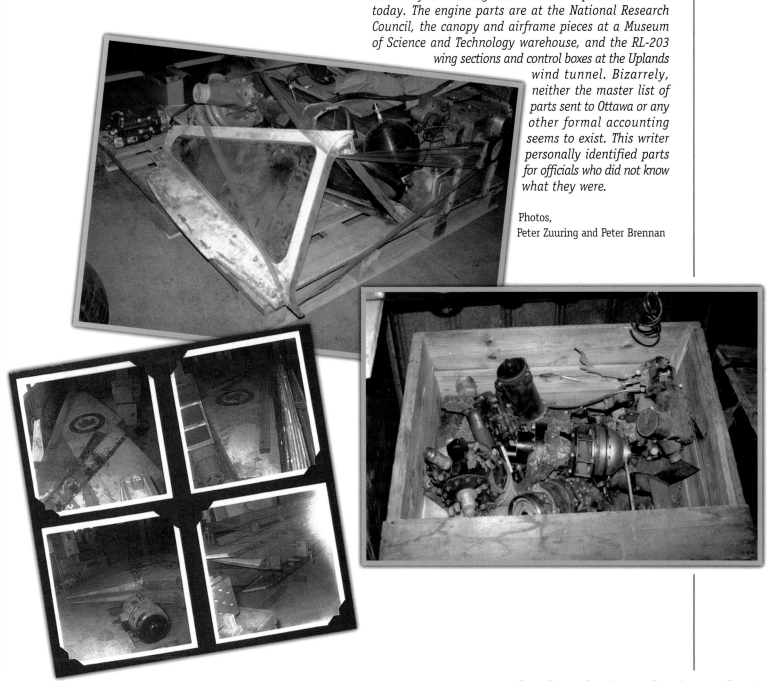

Results of the Kuhring initiative: Arrow pieces in Ottawa today. The engine parts are at the National Research Council, the canopy and airframe pieces at a Museum of Science and Technology warehouse, and the RL-203 wing sections and control boxes at the Uplands wind tunnel. Bizarrely, neither the master list of parts sent to Ottawa or any other formal accounting seems to exist. This writer personally identified parts for officials who did not know what they were.

Photos,
Peter Zuuring and Peter Brennan

Death row, sometime after May 8, 1959 - taken by a British visitor and smuggled out of the plant. Note engine removal in progress on RL-204 and dismantling of RL-202.

The Arrow Scrapbook - The dirty business begins

RL 202

202

The dirty business begins - The Arrow Scrapbook

Do it quickly...

and quietly

Department of Defence Production report

A view of Waxman's junk yard in Hamilton, Ont., from an article entitled *"Flight into disaster: the Avro Arrow story"* in a June 1962 issue of The Canadian. It cites government lies and company arrogance, and laments the sudden loss of many jobs, industrial potential and national prestige.

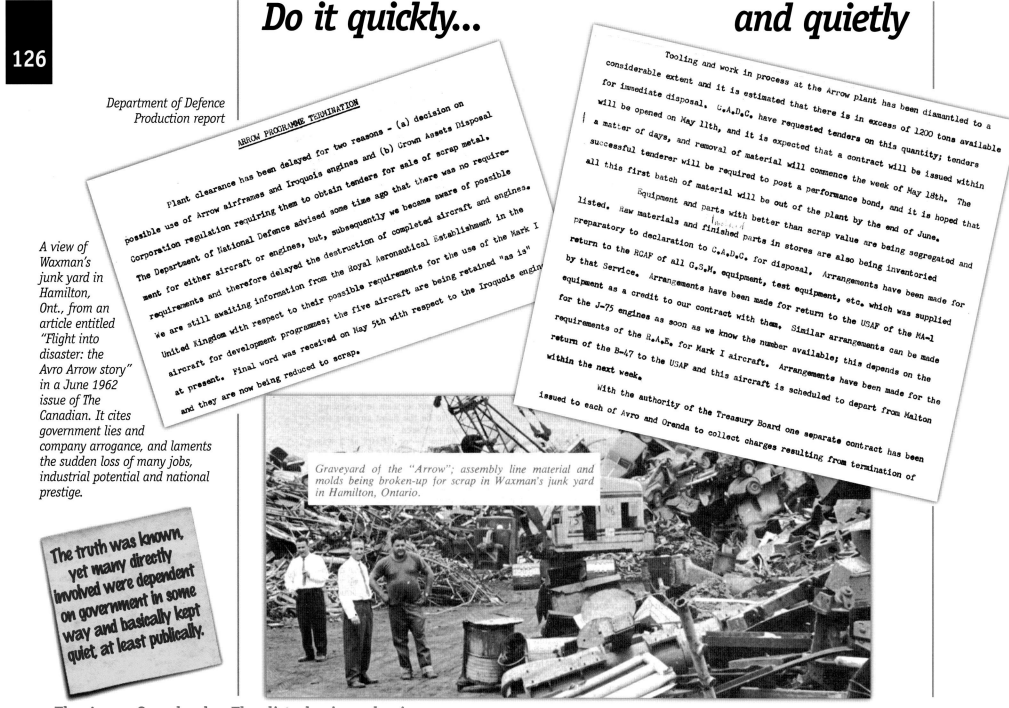

ARROW PROGRAMME TERMINATION

Plant clearance has been delayed for two reasons - (a) decision on possible use of Arrow airframes and Iroquois engines and (b) Crown Assets Disposal Corporation regulation requiring them to obtain tenders for sale of scrap metal.

The Department of National Defence advised some time ago that there was no requirement for either aircraft or engines, but, subsequently we became aware of possible requirements and therefore delayed the destruction of completed aircraft and engines.

We are still awaiting information from the Royal Aeronautical Establishment in the United Kingdom with respect to their possible requirements for the use of the Mark I aircraft for development programmes; the five aircraft are being retained "as is" at present. Final word was received on May 5th with respect to the Iroquois engine and they are now being reduced to scrap.

Tooling and work in process at the Arrow plant has been dismantled to a considerable extent and it is estimated that there is in excess of 1200 tons available for immediate disposal. C.A.D.C. have requested tenders on this quantity; tenders will be opened on May 11th, and it is expected that a contract will be issued within a matter of days, and removal of material will commence the week of May 18th. The successful tenderer will be required to post a performance bond, and it is hoped that all this first batch of material will be out of the plant by the end of June.

Equipment and parts with better than scrap value are being segregated and listed. Raw materials and finished parts in stores are also being inventoried preparatory to declaration to C.A.D.C. for disposal. Arrangements have been made for return to the RCAF of all G.S.M. equipment, test equipment, etc. which was supplied by that Service. Arrangements have been made for return to the USAF of the MA-1 equipment as a credit to our contract with them. Similar arrangements can be made for the J-75 engines as soon as we know the number available; this depends on the requirements of the R.A.E. for Mark I aircraft. Arrangements have been made for the return of the B-47 to the USAF and this aircraft is scheduled to depart from Malton within the next week.

With the authority of the Treasury Board one separate contract has been issued to each of Avro and Orenda to collect charges resulting from termination of

Graveyard of the "Arrow"; assembly line material and molds being broken-up for scrap in Waxman's junk yard in Hamilton, Ontario.

The truth was known, yet many directly involved were dependent on government in some way and basically kept quiet at least publically.

Sam Lax got the contract to scrap the Arrow and related jigs, fixtures and tooling. According to the Department of Defence Production, the Ancaster-based metals dealer put up a performance bond of $300,000 and committed to clearing the plant within ninety days. Apparently it had to be done quickly and

with the cabinet's decision to allow photographs since all sensitive materials had now been removed. Avro's scrap was dealt with in a hurry and a paper trail exists. Not so with Orenda and the Iroquois programs. To this day it is not really known who got to scrap the engines and related tooling. Apparently, some spare parts are still to be found today at Orenda.

27 Chatham Street
Brantford, Ontario
May 8, 1959

Prime Minister J. Diefenbaker
House of Commons
Parliment Hill
Ottawa, Ontario

Dear Mr. Diefenbaker:

I would like to ask you and your government not to scrap the Avro CF-105 Arrow RL 201 if such is your intention.

I believe that this Arrow should be kept for historical purposes. It was the first Canadian aircraft to exceed one thousand miles per hour and it is one of the finest achievements in Canadian aeronautical engineering to date.

To-day in Canada there are many people who are trying to salvage the historical items in the aviation field. The Ryerson Aeronautical Club of the Ryerson Institute of Technology are trying to find a Vickers Vedette to rebuild, so as to fill in one of the gaps in the history of this country. However, none of these efforts will be effective if we do not preserve what we already have and then when the damage is done same way we did the Bluenose and now in some scrap heap, first jet transport in North America and now in the Jetliner, Is not this country proud enough to want to wish we had it back. Will the Arrow follow the same path as save any of its achievements?

If it is a matter of storage, I am sure that if you asked there would be a company or individual who would take it to preserve it. If not then if you give it the Ryerson Aeronautical Club of which I am President I am sure we could find a place for it.

If security prevents you from giving it away then perhaps Avro could keep it until such time as it would be safe for the craft to be allowed out.

Whatever is done this craft must be saved to show future generations of Canadians what their forefathers did.

Yours truly

Robert MacMillan

Letter National Archives,
RCAF files

Photo, L. Wilkinson

Arrow Scrap Sold For $304,370

OTTAWA, March 8 — The government sold 2,785 tons of scrap from the Arrow jet interceptor program for $304,370 after the project was junked a year ago, it was reported yesterday.

The figures were given by the Defence Production Department in a tabled Commons reply for Paul Hellyer (L., Toronto Trinity).

About $500,000,000 was sunk into the cancelled program by the government.

The scrap, sold through crown assets disposal corporation, was mostly steel but there were also quantities of various other metals.

quietly. Bid tenders went out on May 7, 1959. Bids were opened on May 11...the deal closed on the 15th and work started on May 18, 1959. Sam Lax was well known to Crown Assets Disposal Corp., Avro and Orenda. He had been dealing with all three for years. It is unlikely, given the short time frame that there were many other bidders, if any at all. By the end of July 1959, most of the destruction was complete. Strangely enough, it coincided

Photo, P. Brennan

The letter (at far left) was one of many requests to save something from the Arrow program. Meanwhile, cut-up Arrow Mk I pieces were assembled for transport to the scrapyard and to safety in Ottawa.

An engine yard-sale

Proof that the Department of Defence Production did indeed loan an Arrow engine to the British firm Bristol Siddeley. Today, such an engine in pieces is said to be stored at a Royal Air Force Museum in the U.K.

Letter, DDP file National Archives

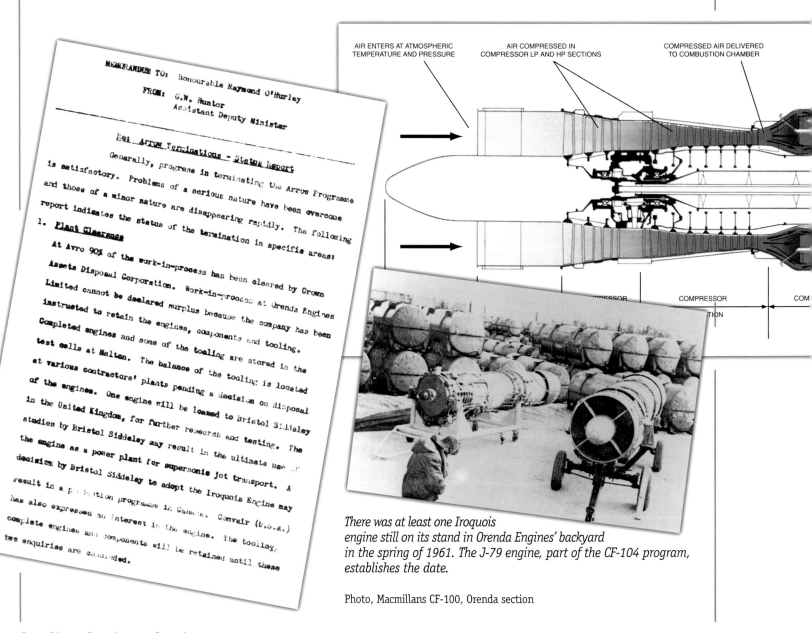

MEMORANDUM TO: Honourable Raymond O'Hurley

FROM: G.W. Hunter
Assistant Deputy Minister

Re: Arrow Terminations - Status Report

Generally, progress in terminating the Arrow Programme is satisfactory. Problems of a serious nature have been overcome and those of a minor nature are disappearing rapidly. The following report indicates the status of the termination in specific areas:

1. Plant Clearance

At Avro 90% of the work-in-process has been cleared by Crown Assets Disposal Corporation. Work-in-process at Orenda Engines Limited cannot be declared surplus because the company has been instructed to retain the engines, components and tooling. Completed engines and some of the tooling are stored in the test cells at Malton. The balance of the tooling is located at various contractors' plants pending a decision on disposal of the engines. One engine will be loaned to Bristol Siddeley in the United Kingdom, for further research and testing. The studies by Bristol Siddeley may result in the ultimate use of the engine as a power plant for supersonic jet transport. A decision by Bristol Siddeley to adopt the Iroquois Engine may result in a production programme in Canada. Convair (U.S.A.) has also expressed an interest in the engine. The tooling, complete engines and components will be retained until these two enquiries are concluded.

AIR ENTERS AT ATMOSPHERIC TEMPERATURE AND PRESSURE

AIR COMPRESSED IN COMPRESSOR LP AND HP SECTIONS

COMPRESSED AIR DELIVERED TO COMBUSTION CHAMBER

COMPRESSOR

COMPRESSOR

COM

TION

There was at least one Iroquois engine still on its stand in Orenda Engines' backyard in the spring of 1961. The J-79 engine, part of the CF-104 program, establishes the date.

Photo, Macmillans CF-100, Orenda section

Air was sucked into the giant Iroquois engine at the rate of 300 pounds per second. Only 25 percent of the air combusted one pound of fuel per pound of dry thrust. Afterburning increased thrust by 30 percent to 26,000 pounds, but doubled the fuel flow.

and then collapse

Illustration, Iroquois Mk II manual

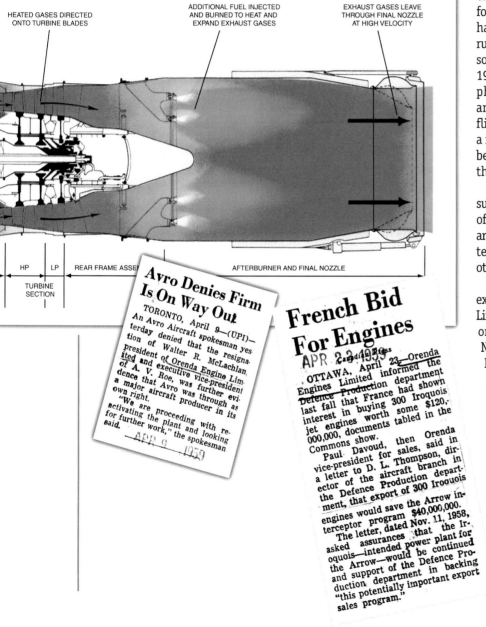

HEATED GASES DIRECTED ONTO TURBINE BLADES

ADDITIONAL FUEL INJECTED AND BURNED TO HEAT AND EXPAND EXHAUST GASES

EXHAUST GASES LEAVE THROUGH FINAL NOZZLE AT HIGH VELOCITY

HP | LP | REAR FRAME ASSE | AFTERBURNER AND FINAL NOZZLE

TURBINE SECTION

Avro Denies Firm Is On Way Out

TORONTO, April 9—(UPI)— An Avro Aircraft spokesman yesterday denied that the resignation of Walter R. McLachlan, president of Orenda Engine Limited and executive vice-president of A. V. Roe, was further evidence that Avro was through as a major aircraft producer in its own right.

"We are proceeding with reactivating the plant and looking for further work," the spokesman said.

APR 8 1959

French Bid For Engines

APR 23 1959

OTTAWA, April 23 — Orenda Engines Limited informed the Defence Production department last fall that France had shown interest in buying 300 Iroquois jet engines worth some $120,000,000, documents tabled in the Commons show.

Paul Davoud, then Orenda vice-president for sales, said in a letter to D. L. Thompson, director of the aircraft branch in the Defence Production department, that export of 300 Iroquois engines would save the Arrow interceptor program $40,000,000.

The letter, dated Nov. 11, 1958, asked assurances that the Iroquois—intended power plant for the Arrow—would be continued and support of the Defence Production department in backing "this potentially important export sales program."

At the time of cancellation only one Iroquois engine X-116, had been delivered to Avro, cleared for ground running trials. Its mating engine, X-115, had thrown a blade during the 50 hour preliminary run-in period. X-117/8 were scheduled for delivery sometime in late March, ready for first flight in May 1959...not before! Lou Wise, Avro's former head of photography explained to me during the 40th anniversary dinner celebrating the Arrow's first flight, that any of the pictures we see today are as a result of some publicity shots showing an Iroquois being fitted in RL-206. In fact, this stunt indicated that a fair bit of match-up was still required.

When the RCAF declared the airframes and engines surplus to their needs, telexes were sent to get them off the official inventory. All engines, except X-116, are accounted for on one Orenda telex. A subsequent telex from Avro shows the de-commissioning of the other engine (X-116) that they had in their possession.

By the summer of 1959 all the well known executives such as Gordon, Smye, Floyd, Chamberlin, Lindley, etc. had either retired, gone back to England or had taken a lucrative position with a US firm. Now the head of Orenda was also leaving...Sir Roy Dobson, Hawker Siddeley Canada's original founder was left to pick up the pieces. By 1962 A.V. Roe Canada Ltd. ceased to exist at all.

With all this interest in the Iroquois engine, why didn't Orenda complete its development? The contract with the Department of Defence Production allowed for third-party licensing. A possible deal with Curtis-Wright never came to fruition.

Clippings, *Montreal Star* 1959/60

U.S. Company Considering Iroquois Jet

OTTAWA, July 28—A United States aircraft company is giving "serious consideration" to purchase of the Iroquois jet engine from Orenda Engines Limited, Malton, Ont., the Commons was told today by Defence Production Minister O'Hurley.

He said he could not identify the company for fear it would prejudice negotiations.

Mr. O'Hurley made the statement as he opened Commons debate on his department's spending estimates for the current fiscal year.

Development of the Iroquois engine, originally planned for use in the CF-105 Arrow jet interceptor, was suspended when the government cancelled the Arrow program in 1958.

Mr. O'Hurley said that 13 complete prototypes of the Iroquois engine and parts for seven more are in storage at Malton.

He said the U.S. aircraft firm was one of several companies which have been interested in using the Iroquois as a power plant. A United Kingdom company also had asked that one engine be sent to it.

Clipping, *Montreal Star*, 1960

The RCAF gave instructions to retain Arrow engineering data, and apparently a complete set of microfilms was made. Later reviews called for the destruction of all materials, but exactly when and where this was done, and how much was destroyed, remains unclear.

No room for doubt?

There is no doubt that the cut-up was a sensitive situation for all concerned. It was impossible to keep it under wraps without something getting out. The fly-overs that have been recorded start with the May 8, 1959, Fednews photo credited to Russel. Because all five Mk I Arrows are present, all other photos must be later.

So at least three other passes at different times were made.

These fly-over photos show the cutting-up process, from five Arrows on the ground to just one, RL-203.

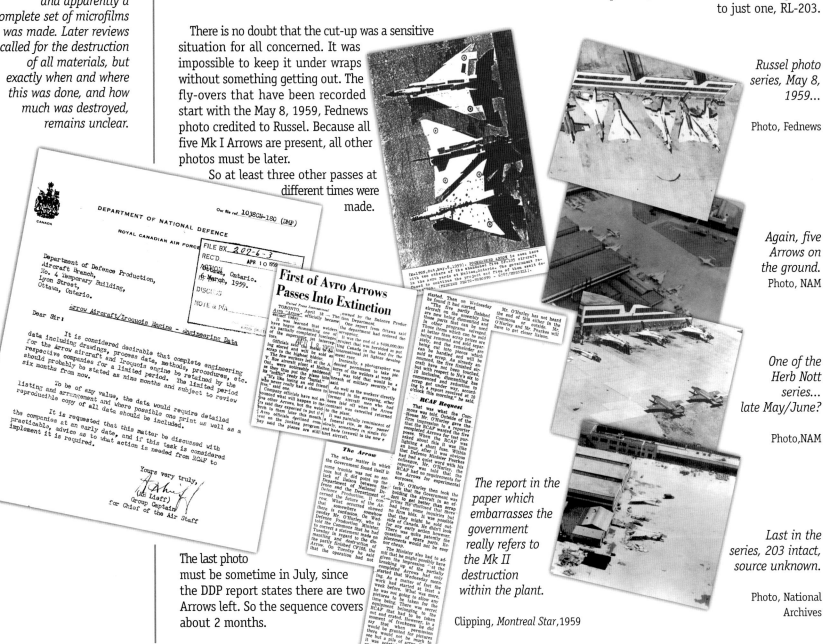

Russel photo series, May 8, 1959...

Photo, Fednews

Again, five Arrows on the ground.

Photo, NAM

One of the Herb Nott series... late May/June?

Photo, NAM

Last in the series, 203 intact, source unknown.

Photo, National Archives

The report in the paper which embarrasses the government really refers to the Mk II destruction within the plant.

Clipping, *Montreal Star,* 1959

The last photo must be sometime in July, since the DDP report states there are two Arrows left. So the sequence covers about 2 months.

First of Avro Arrows Passes Into Extinction

United Press International

TORONTO, April 13 — ...

The Arrow ...

RCAF Request ...

June Callwood,the Toronto based, well respected journalist, took reporting the Arrow and Iroquois programs progress to heart. She even went so far as to get a ride in a USAF B-47 so she could report first hand how it felt to control the big bomber in the air. Her reporting was at a gut level...the short paragraph reproduced to the left of her photo was, I believe, the start of the "One got away" legend. My findings clearly show all Arrows in various stages of destruction. The photos show RL-203 to be last...since its wing tips are at NAM, it did not fly away either. When I showed June these findings she stopped talking...slowly tears welled up in her eyes... years of hope that one did get away were shattered with the realization that nothing flyable did! Of course we know today that lots of the Arrow did escape the wreckers furnace but basically at the hands of a very few persistent and ironically, government employees.

A Department of Defence Production memo discussing the Arrow dismantling process at Avro's Malton plant. The J-75 engines fetched less money than expected when sold back to the U.S.

Memo, DDP file, National Archives

Department of Defence Production

July 6, 1959.
207-6-3

CF-105 Termination Status

Status of completed Aircraft and Iroquois Engines

Three of the five completed Mark I aircraft have been completely dismantled. The fourth and fifth will be finished about July 10th and 17th respectively. The partially completed Mark II aircraft has already been dismantled.

All completed Iroquois engines together with spare parts and tooling will be retained for the time being and are being moved to the test cells at Malton for storage.

Reclaimed Equipment

During the dismantling operation all reuseable equipment is being salvaged either for use by the Department of National Defence or for disposal by Crown Assets Disposal Corporation at the best current prices.

The J-75 engines which had been purchased from the United States government will be resold to that government at the original price less a discount for the use they received during the CF-105 programme and consideration for packing, handling and transportation costs. These prices are now being negotiated.

The United States government has also agreed to repurchase the MA-1 Electronic system at the original cost less packing, handling and transportation costs.

Our house is in Toronto's west end but distant enough from the airport that we rarely hear planes. The next morning, I was wakened before dawn by the loudest airplane engine sound I have ever heard. Its shattering roar filled the sky for a long moment and then suddenly was gone.

"The Arrow!" I thought in amazement. Nothing else could make such a racket. Someone has flown an Arrow to safety.

Maybe so. Maybe somewhere, perhaps packed in straw in a barn, one poignant Arrow remains. Dreams aren't mortal. □

MACLEAN'S/JANUARY 13, 1997 **57**

Zooming in ...

A Herb Nott Photo

Journalist June Callwood hitching a ride in a USAF B-47 in 1958.

Photo, *Macleans Magazine*, 1958

Herb Nott's famous photograph showed the public for the first time that the Arrow was being cut up. The photo was taken in early June 1959 but could not be published until a photo ban was lifted in late July.

Some say that this photo was the catalyst that led to the eventual downfall of the Diefenbaker government.

Mid-August, 1959 issue of Weekend Magazine

Photo, L. Wilkinson

The dirty business begins - The Arrow Scrapbook

M2-9-74
M4-N7-32

5 June, Ontario,
1959.

Mr. I.M. MacKinnon,
Assistant General Manager,
Crown Assets Disposal Corporation,
Room 2094, Trade and Commerce Building,
Wellington Street,
Ottawa, Ontario.

Dear Mr. MacKinnon:

I have just returned from Malton, and would like to express my
thanks for the assistance given to me by Mr. Cassidy and Mr. Larsen.

Following our recent discussion regarding the possibility of
obtaining materials and equipment which would be of use to the National
Research Council and to the National Aeronautical Museum, I visited Malton
and discussed with Mr. Cassidy the feasibility of moving to an isolated
cage in Bay 1 of the Avro plant, the materials which I considered would
be most useful. Arrangements were made with Mr. Harry Beffort and Mr. J.
Tause to use such a space, and Mr. Tause supplied two men to assist in the
moving. This material is now isolated, and Mr. Cassidy and Mr. Tause
know where it is.

The materials selected for submission to Crown Assets for approval
fall into several classes:

1. Materials, sheet and rolled or formed sections which were originally
   issued for use in the plant, and which are now being disposed of.

2. Miscellaneous aircraft parts which were made up by Avro for construction of the aeroplanes. In this group is a number of parts which are
   unfinished, and they will show the steps in manufacture.

3. Miscellaneous components such as hydraulic pumps, valves, fuel tank
   gauges, etc. Most of these items seem to have been used.

In addition to the above there are certain instruments and components which are the property of the RCAF, and it is my understanding
that these are not being put up for disposal but will be retained by the
RCAF. I propose initially to ask the Department of Defence Production or
the RCAF if some of these may be diverted to the NRC.

In addition to the materials and equipment requested from the
Avro plant there are numerous items in the Orenda plant which I examined
through the assistance of Mr. Larsen, and while I realize that at the
moment there is to be no action taken on the materials in this plant I
enclose herewith a list of the items desired--so that, if it is decided
to declare the items surplus, we may receive consideration.

I expect to be away from Ottawa for the next two weeks, and will
get in touch with you upon my return. If arrangements can be made for us
to obtain the materials and equipment listed, we would be pleased to make
whatever arrangements you suggest, to move it to Ottawa.

Yours sincerely,

Original Signed by
SECTION HEAD
Engine Laboratory

M.S. Kuhring,
Head, Engine Laboratory, N.R.C.
and

Interim Curator,
National Aeronautical Museum.

MSK:ht
Enc.

The Arrow Scrapbook - Vignettes

Post-cancellation vignettes and curiosities

Entry to main communications and command centre for the Diefenbunker, CFB Carp, near Ottawa.

The Canadian people have rung, have knocked and are waiting for the truth of what really happened to the Avro Arrow.

Photo, Peter Zuuring, at CFB CARP

These short excerpts are very interesting and shed some new light on some very controversial issues.

Mac Kuhring's letter to the DDP representative at Malton speaks for itself. He isolated and brought to Ottawa a significant number of Arrow parts and finished pieces. I have only found some of them. If the list is real, there is a lot more to come.

Letter, National Archives, DDP Files

The Institute for Aviation Medicine

The nose of RL-206 (the first Mk II Arrow) was removed just after cancellation and used for some years at the Institute for Aviation Medicine (IAM) in Toronto as a low-pressure chamber to test pilots' reactions to simulated high-altitude conditions. The general purpose pipe fitting in the nose wheel bay was the suction point. An RCAF pilot is shown rigged out for a test, with headpiece, pressure waistcoat and anti-gravity suit. Flying at an altitude of 50,000 feet is not, as a rule, a comfortable business.

Photos, Peter Zuuring/National archives, RCAF files

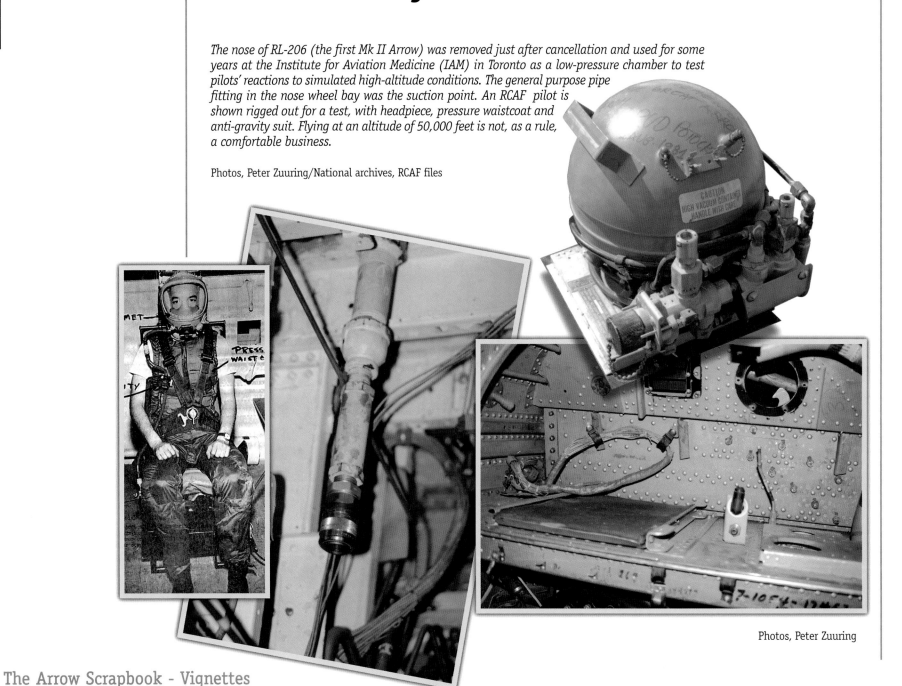

Photos, Peter Zuuring

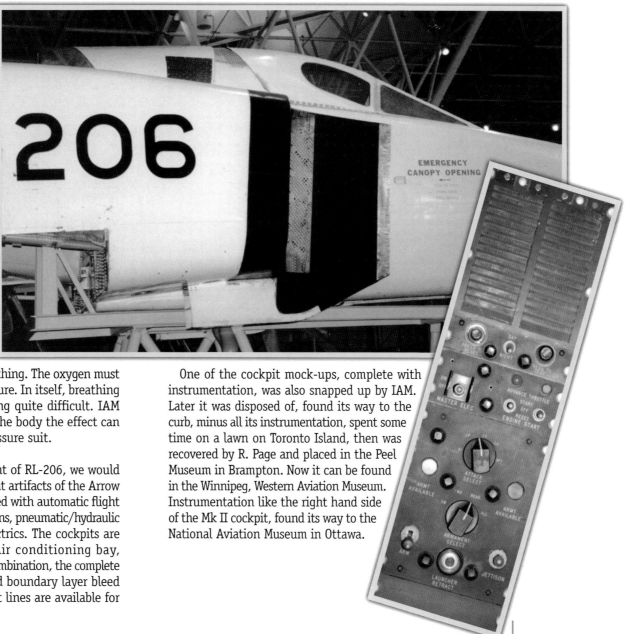

The platform on the left is just behind the observer's head. Small blow-in doors can be seen above the rubber pad. Spud Potocki's oxygen reservoir is shown above it. IAM determined that an increasing amount of oxygen was needed to maintain body functions as pressure dropped at increasingly higher altitudes. By 32,000 feet, the pilot was breathing pure oxygen compared to 20 percent at ground level. Atmospheric pressure above 34,000 feet is insufficient to maintain normal breathing. The oxygen must be forced into the lungs under pressure. In itself, breathing pressured oxygen can make exhaling quite difficult. IAM found that by putting pressure on the body the effect can be reduced...hence the use of a pressure suit.

If IAM had not requested the front of RL-206, we would be missing one of the most important artifacts of the Arrow program. The nose wheel bay is packed with automatic flight control system items, electrical junctions, pneumatic/hydraulic components and ramp de-icing electrics. The cockpits are intact and partially equipped. Air conditioning bay, depressurizing turbine/water boiler combination, the complete intake ramp, shock wave wedge and boundary layer bleed design are also intact. The basic loft lines are available for rebuilding.

One of the cockpit mock-ups, complete with instrumentation, was also snapped up by IAM. Later it was disposed of, found its way to the curb, minus all its instrumentation, spent some time on a lawn on Toronto Island, then was recovered by R. Page and placed in the Peel Museum in Brampton. Now it can be found in the Winnipeg, Western Aviation Museum. Instrumentation like the right hand side of the Mk II cockpit, found its way to the National Aviation Museum in Ottawa.

Thanks to Mac Kuhring

Mac Kuhring was the head of the National Research Council Engine Laboratory in Ottawa at the time of cancellation. He had the foresight to contact the Department of Defence Production which was redirecting assets from Avro and Orenda. During the summer of 1959, a twenty-six-page list of items, set aside for Mac, was compiled. It was very comprehensive, covering engines, fuselage parts, system components, wing tips, hydraulic cylinders and accessories...anything that would show the evolution of the Arrow and its power plant. He succeeded in carting the whole lot to the Montreal Road and Uplands campuses of the NRC. When the RCAF technical library was unloading files, Mac and the staff of the Parkin Library accepted the lot although it was still classified and required locked storage. It wasn't until Tom Dugelby, a retired high school teacher and ex-Avro employee, wanted to publish a volume on Arrow technology that the files were finally declassified.

Today the National Aviation Museum's collection, with the exception of the RL-206 nose-piece, is due almost exclusively to the work of Mac Kuhring. Others have more recently come forward when either guilt or death comes calling and Arrow stuff sees the light of day again.

Fortunately, the list of saved items survived. Unfortunately, many of the items listed are not traceable. If they are still lingering in the dusty storage sheds or behind partitions is still to be determined. Understandably, NAM does not know the origin of all its Arrow collection. There are many pallets of unidentified, uncatalogued items, shelves of small parts, a nearly complete set of Mk I service manuals...on and on it goes.

The NRC also got rid of known Arrow parts during routine cleanups. Where are those pieces today? What else can be found in DND facilities? Rumours abound! Have you got a lead, a part, drawing, photo or manual?

Yes...ARROWMANIA!

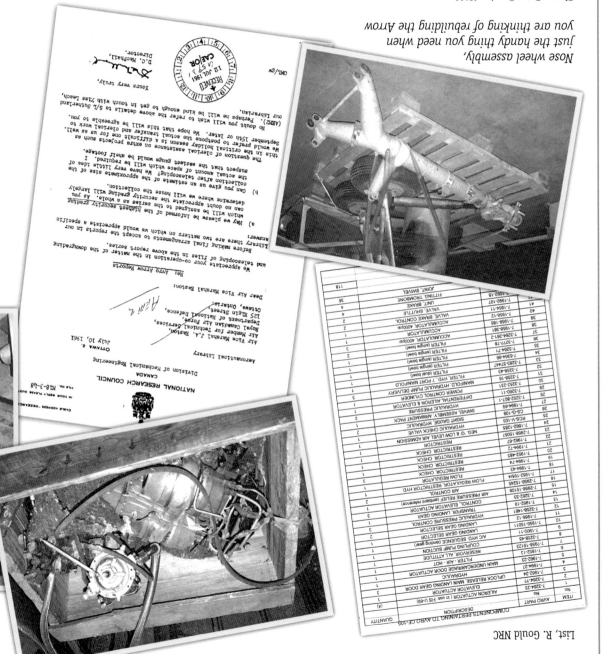

Photo, Peter Zuuring NAM

Nose wheel assembly, just the handy thing you need when you are thinking of rebuilding the Arrow

More than 700 Arrow documents were transferred to the Parkin Library in the early 1960s. Curiously, Air Vice-Marshal Easton, implicated in the destruction of the Arrow program, was later involved in saving Arrow files and information.

Photo, Peter Zuuring / NRC

More of the same, turbine and compressor parts ... some in mint condition!

Photo, Peter Zuuring / NRC

More Quonset hut material, engine pumps and hydraulic parts.

List, R. Gould NRC

Part of the legacy that Mac Kuhring left us. Most of these have found their way to NAM via the NRC.

Status of RL-206
February 20, 1959

RL-206 not ready to fly or taxi.

Memo and report,
National Archives,
RCAF and DDP files

June Callwood's article, in a *Maclean's* magazine of the period, romanticized the possibility that "One got away." Equally, CBC's recent mini-series *"Shutting Down The National Dream,"* portrayed a ready RCAF pilot who got the nod to take one of the still-fueled Arrows and fly it to safety? Many Arrow fans have said the same thing...why didn't they just fly RL-206 out of there, show the world what it could do and then they would never dare to go ahead with cancellation.

Remember when RL-201 was between rollout and first flight...daily progress reports were issued because everyone was nervous about the Arrow's progress and wanted everything done that could be done to ensure a safe first flight. Anything less would have been a disaster. In the Mk II program, RL-206 was planned to be the first to have the Iroquois installed in it and to be flown with it. Weekly progress reports sufficed at this stage.

I was fortunate enough to come across the particular report for February 20, 1959, "Black Friday," after which all worked stopped. The report is short and to the point. RL-206 was not ready for flight. It was not ready for taxi trials. Indeed, it was not ready to go anywhere as yet. Engine availability and general clean-up work was

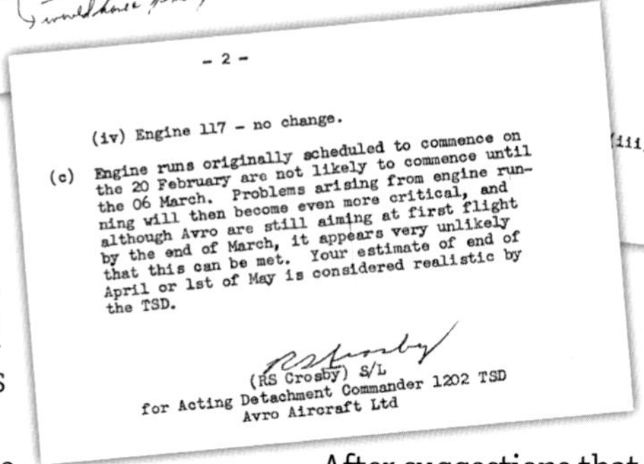

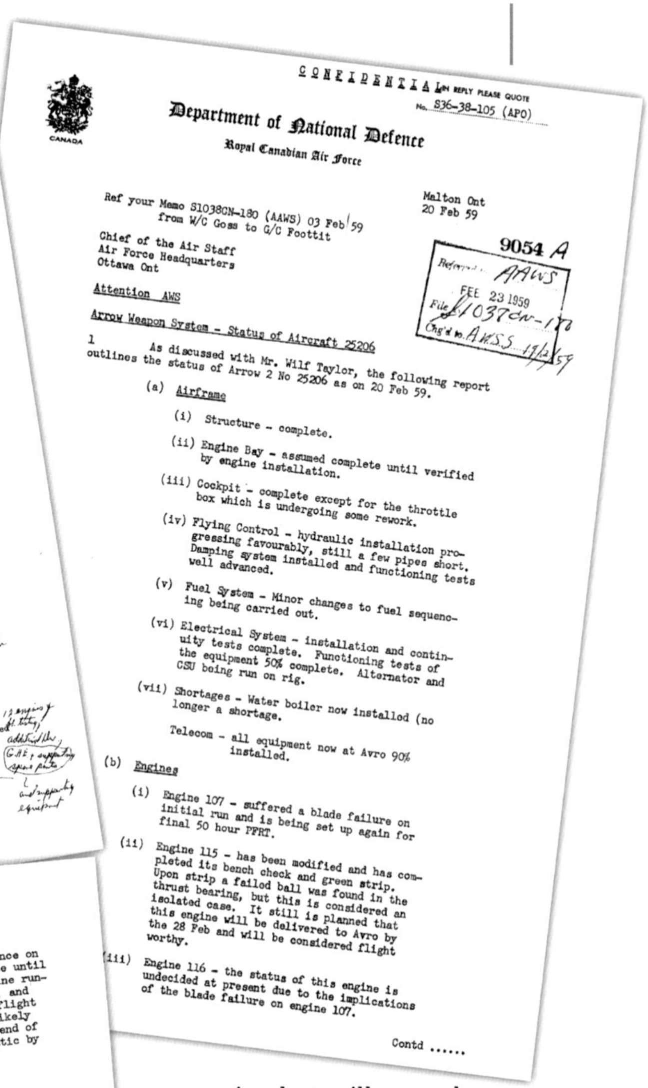

progressing but still several weeks away from saying..."We have an aircraft ready to go."

After suggestions that a world speed record might have been possible with a Mk II Arrow, DDP did analyze what would be involved, as the memo on the left shows. Again costs are just too high to even consider taking it further. It was considered, which is more than some would have given credit for.

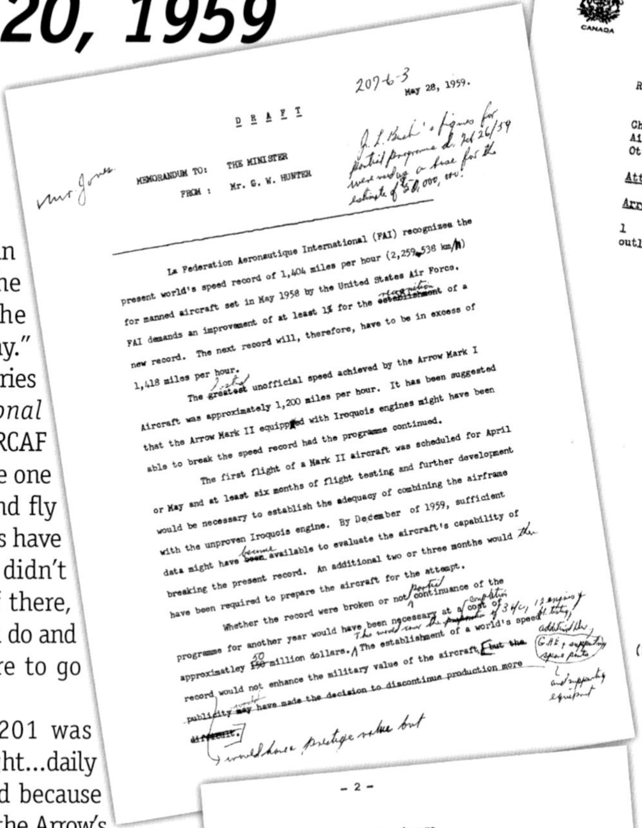

The Arrows are gone...but, Bomarc garages remain

It is curious to see and walk around these, early 1960s Cold War, Bomarc missile launchers. You can see that the northern climate would have played havoc with the roof opening system...snow and ice could easily have jammed the sideways sliding roofs. The U.S. paid about 90 percent of the Canadian RCAF Bomarc program cost . Why could we accept money for these but call it "lend lease" for the Arrow and let it go at that?

These pictures were taken in the fall of 1998, on the outskirts of North Bay, Ontario. An aviation maintenance school associated with a local community college shares the site.

Photos, Peter Zuuring

CF-104 Manipulations...
Avro shut-out/Orenda under licence

Within four months of cancelling the Arrow program, the Diefenbaker government was ready to buy 214 F-104g, Lockheed Starfighters for $420 million. This did not include any of the so-called weapons system extensions for armament and fire control. That this happened so soon after the demise of the Arrow didn't appear to phase anyone.

During the debate it was clear that the chiefs of staff had better be in agreement and make the necessary recommendation, before the decision is made public, to avoid possible embarrassment to the government should the chiefs feel otherwise. Furthermore, it was recognized that delivery to squadrons would take five years to complete. Imagine, this was with respect to an already developed aircraft...you will recall the gasps of consternation because of program delays with the Arrow..."obsolete before its time" is not to be heard. The debate also made it plain that the public was to be informed that in no way could the Arrow have fulfilled the role that the CF-104 was now to be considered for. The fact that the F-104 was designed as a defensive interceptor whose role was changed to an attack day fighter/bomber apparently went over most people's heads.

The choice of airframe contractor was manipulated to suit overall government policy. After much discussion, public tenders for the airframe were requested. Avro had the lowest bid. How the contract ended up in Canadair's hands is a true lesson for anyone bidding on government business. The phrase "best value to the Crown" is the catch-all which makes it palatable...at least for those in power.

Wheat for the West Aerospace for Quebec and Cars for Ontario

The engine contract was easy since there were only two suppliers, Orenda and Pratt& Whitney Canada. The U.S. giant, General Electric, was not going to be happy with a competitor manufacturing its product under licence, so Orenda being independent, got the engine, the J-79. Because Avro and Orenda were under Hawker Siddeley Canada, fairness was deemed to have been exercised by giving something to all parties.

The cabinet discussions around Canadair, the fact that it was American owned (General Dynamics) and had never received any business from its parent company and the fact that the name made Canadians feel that the company must be Canadian, all figured into the decision. Regionality also played a role in moving and maintaining aviation business in Montreal.

The Canadian government's policy to have wheat in the West, aerospace in Quebec and auto makers in Ontario was as in vogue then, as it is today!

The complete text of the cabinet deliberations on this subject are in the appendices.

An interesting side reference is about taking photos of the cancelled Arrow. By mid-July 1959 the government has decided that sensitive materials have now been removed and photos are to be allowed. They neglected to say that the cut-up was also complete and there was nothing left to take pictures of. The embarrassing Herb Nott aerial photos were finally published in an August 1959 issue of *Star Weekly Magazine* as you have seen in the Dirty Business chapter.

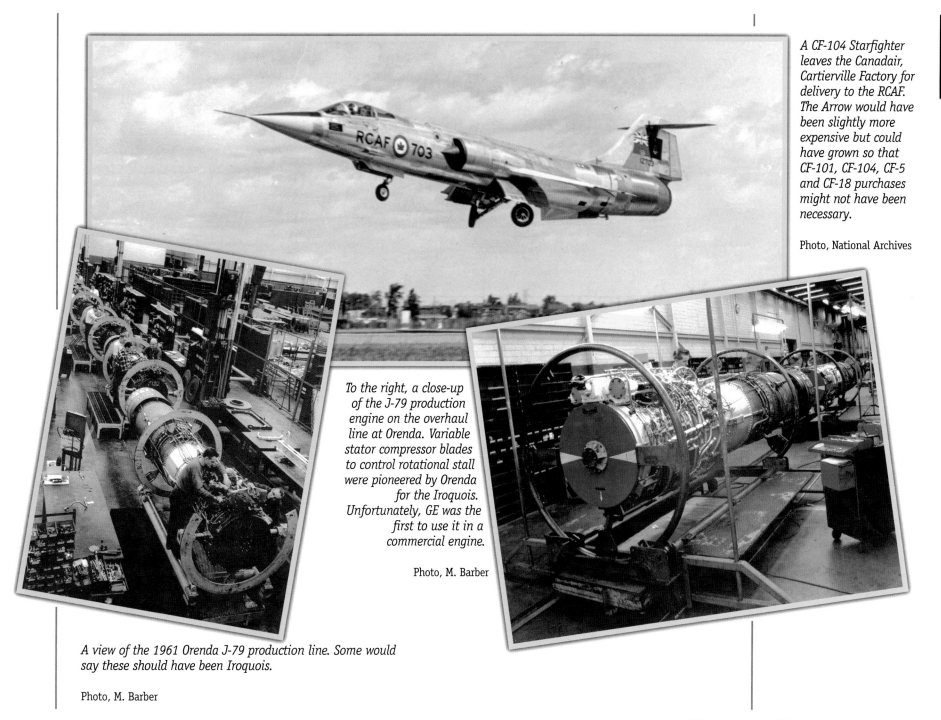

A CF-104 Starfighter leaves the Canadair, Cartierville Factory for delivery to the RCAF. The Arrow would have been slightly more expensive but could have grown so that CF-101, CF-104, CF-5 and CF-18 purchases might not have been necessary.

Photo, National Archives

To the right, a close-up of the J-79 production engine on the overhaul line at Orenda. Variable stator compressor blades to control rotational stall were pioneered by Orenda for the Iroquois. Unfortunately, GE was the first to use it in a commercial engine.

Photo, M. Barber

A view of the 1961 Orenda J-79 production line. Some would say these should have been Iroquois.

Photo, M. Barber

Final Arrow program costs

In the end, Arrow Program costs were lower than expected.

This post-cancellation cost analysis came from the Department of Defence Production files at the National Archives. It is clear that cost estimates bandied around to justify cancellation were in excess by some 30 percent over what they actually were. Note the breakdown of the different programs. Although the full thirty-seven airframes and engines were not completed, their construction was well underway. These final costs do include the in-progress Arrows sitting in various stages of completion both at Avro and Orenda and the subcontractors. Compare these to the 1958 escalations....

Costing Table, National Archives, DDP Files

3. Summary of Costs

Payments under all terminated contracts ceased with effect from June 30, 1959.

The totals paid out against these contracts are:

	Final Payment	Previous Estimate
AVRO	180.5 million	178.5 million
ORENDA	127.5 "	128.8 "
TOTAL	308.0 million	307.3 million

These contracts are now being audited but no further charges will be made against them. Any adjustments which may be necessary will be made against the termination contracts. The estimated costs of the termination contracts are as follows:

The Department of Defence Production's, Assistant deputy-Minister, G.W. Hunter, reports that the final Arrow termination program costs were below estimate. As well, the final Avro and Orenda costing is less than the April estimate by some $8 million. The planned return of the nineteen J-75 Pratt & Whitney engines to the USAF only netted a little more than $2 million. Pearkes made sure that the monies went directly to the RCAF to be used as a discretionary slush fund. Finally, fifteen J-75-p5 engines were returned and four J-75-p3s were retained by the NRC for large-scale engine correlation studies.

Costing memo, National Archives

NAE Arrows... too expensive

The cable from London to Canadian headquarters discusses the RAF's, chief of the air staff's view, that something should be saved. Further, he states that the decision was probably based on economics and not operational effectiveness.

Cable, National Archives, RCAF Files

RAF reaction

SECRET
S1038GN-180 (AWS/MP2)

MEMORANDUM

4 Mar 59

AWS

NAE Arrow Programme - Estimated Cost

1   In response to your request for an estimate of the cost of operating (a) 2 Arrow Mk 1 aircraft and (b) doing ground test running on Iroquois engines I have made a rough approximation of the cost of what I consider will be involved. The following assumptions have been made:

(a) **Operation of Two Arrow Mk 1 A/C for 3 Years**

(i)   only one will be flown and it will be flown from Malton.

(ii) the second aircraft will be used as a ground static test vehicle.

(iii) an absolute minimum organization will be retained at AVRO.

(iv) NAE will only monitor - all engineering will be done by AVRO.

(v)   The aircraft will not be employed on further development of the Arrow or extension of the flight envelope already explored i.e. will be used for air testing of other equipments.

(b) **Operation of Two Test Cells at Orenda Ltd. for 3 Years**

(i)   that 2 cells will be adequate.

(ii) that the altitude test facility will be required.

(iii) that the 6 to 8 engines available will be adequate.

(iv) that support spares on hand will be generally adequate.

(v)   that the total running time will be 120 hours/year.

(vi) that further development of the Iroquois Engine is not intended.

2   Based on the foregoing assumptions, I have made the following
estimate:

(a) **Operation of Two Arrow Mk 1 A/C for 3 Years**

(i)   Support for 2 A/C for 3 years - almost all spares are assumed to be available for the airframe and J75's. $1,500,000

...../2

SECRET

- 2 -

(ii) 65 engineers and technicians @ $12,000 per year   2,340,000

(iii) overhaul and repair of equipment not replaceable by cannibalization.   600,000

(iv) Flt. Testing - 25 hrs. per year @ $1500/hour.   112,000

(v)   Static Testing - 50 hrs. per year @ $500/hour.   75,000
                                                    ──────────
                                                    $4,677,000

(vi) Abnormal overhead - 50%   2,338,500
                                   ──────────
                    Total $7,015,500

(b) **Operation of Two Test Cells for Iroquois Testing for 3 Years**

(i)   Running 120 hrs/year @ $1,000 per hr.   360,000

(ii) 60 engineers and technicians @ $12,000/year.   2,160,000

(iii) Spares for new builds and labour (2 builds per year) (spares are generally assumed to be on hand or obtainable by cannibalisation)   600,000

(iv) Altitude Tunnel (most of this cost is a fixed charge to Ontario Hydro - believed to be $16,000 to $25,000 per month)   800,000
                                                    ──────────
                                                    $3,920,000

(v)   Abnormal Overhead - 50%   1,960,000
                                   ──────────
                    Total $5,880,000

Estimated Cost of Aircraft and Iroquois Project $12,895,500

Average Cost Per Year $ 4,223,875

You will recognise the extremely rough nature of this estimate. However, I think it will suffice as an order of magnitude.

(Sgd) JW Cook F/L
For (JC Smith) S/L
AWS/MP2
2-0282

Our RCAF was not stupid! This analysis evaluates a plan to keep some Arrows for research purposes, and what the economic impact of such a decision might be. Obviously it was too rich for the NAE and was not pursued. It begs the question whether or not a similar analysis was done for the potential use of the the Arrow by the RAE (the U.K. version of an experimental air research facility) and maybe rejected for the same reason, i.e. the difficult job of maintaining an aircraft in the absence of the manufacturer.

Memo, National Archives, RCAF Files

The "Diefenbunker"

Computers, switching gear and telecommunications equipment filled the bunker's main communication room.

Photo, Peter Zuuring

"If war should come...there are...responsibilities which rest on a government to ensure a continuance of government, for without government and with a completely separate group of ministers you would have chaos."

Prime Minister John Diefenbaker, 1961

Anyway, who would be left to govern after an atomic war? Our vacillating defence policy sure let the Russians know that resistance would be light over Canada. If and when conflict came, some selected officials would board the secret train in Ottawa, head out to Carp and bury their heads in the sand, leaving the rest of Canada to fend for itself!

When it came to protecting the men in power there was no "cancellation." There was nothing "too costly." There was no "overtaken by events." Close to $30 million was spent building and outfitting the four-story, 100,000-square-foot underground safe haven. To protect the main entrance vault door, a perpendicular corridor directed the main atomic blast away. Spring-loaded equipment ensured the survival of the bunker.

A long blast corridor leads to the main entrance. The bunker is, in effect, a huge concrete cube about eighty feet underground.

Photo, Peter Zuuring

Constructed over a two-year period when nuclear fear was at its zenith, the Central Emergency Government Headquarters began operation in 1961. Intended to be a secret relocation centre for Canadian government leaders, civil servants and military personnel in the event of a nuclear war, it quickly became the focus of media and public speculation. Initially the government firmly maintained that the massive new structure was an army signals establishment. However, information about the bunker's real purpose soon leaked out, and the media dubbed it "the Diefenbunker" after John Diefenbaker, the prime minister at the time.

Protective construction was virtually a new field in engineering in the late 1950's. Composed of 32,000 cubic yards of concrete and 5,000 tons of steel, the 100,000 square-foot, four-story hardened shelter is floated on a five-foot gravel pad surrounded by a thick envelope of gravel allowing the building to absorb the shock of an explosion. Equipment such as air conditioning units and boilers sit on giant springs. The entrance to the bunker is located at a right angle midway down an open-ended tunnel. This design feature meant that an explosive blast above ground would sweep through the tunnel without affecting the double air-lock doors at the front of the building.

Communication is essential in a crisis situation, and the bunker was the central hub of a sophisticated national communications network. Throughout its 33-year lifetime the communications sector of the building remained highly restricted and in operation 24 hours a day.

Areas of particular interest in the Diefenbunker are the CBC radio studio; the hospital and the morgue; the bedrooms for the governor general and prime minister; the Bank of Canada vault with its separate tunnel access; the decontamination unit; the machine room and the filter room; and the huge kitchen and cafeteria with the capacity to serve the over 300 people that might be housed there for 30 days during a nuclear war. Even food storage, and sewage and garbage disposal, required specialized designs.

The Diefenbunker was decommissioned in 1994 when CFS Carp closed. Recently it has emerged in a new role as a tangible reminder of the Cold War and a testament to the menace of nuclear conflict.

In 1997 the Historic Sites and Monuments Board of Canada declared the Diefenbunker "the most important surviving Cold War site in Canada."

A panel (right) sampled outside air and determined the extent of radioactivity. The boiler (below) was mounted on springs, allowing it to jiggle in the event of a major explosion but not break loose.

Photos, Peter Zuuring

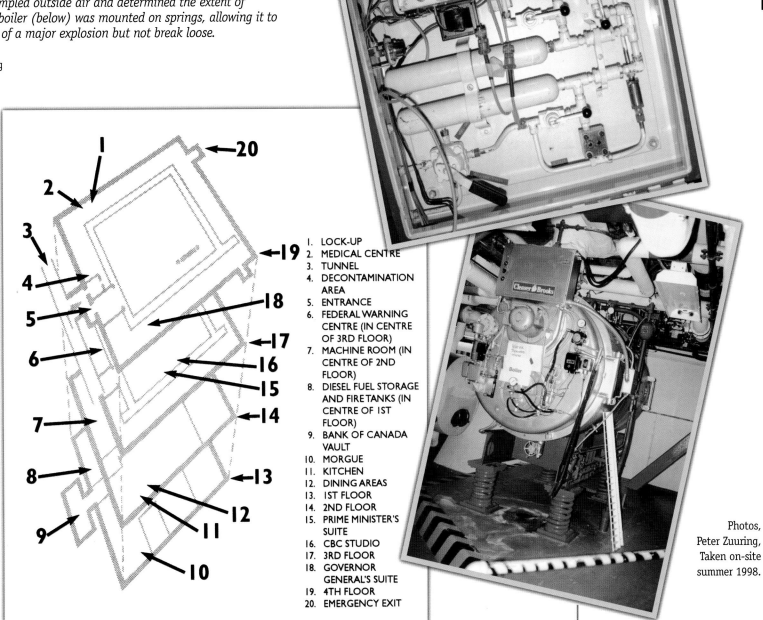

Text and plan,
Canada's Cold War
Museum,
Carp., Ont.

1. LOCK-UP
2. MEDICAL CENTRE
3. TUNNEL
4. DECONTAMINATION AREA
5. ENTRANCE
6. FEDERAL WARNING CENTRE (IN CENTRE OF 3RD FLOOR)
7. MACHINE ROOM (IN CENTRE OF 2ND FLOOR)
8. DIESEL FUEL STORAGE AND FIRE TANKS (IN CENTRE OF 1ST FLOOR)
9. BANK OF CANADA VAULT
10. MORGUE
11. KITCHEN
12. DINING AREAS
13. 1ST FLOOR
14. 2ND FLOOR
15. PRIME MINISTER'S SUITE
16. CBC STUDIO
17. 3RD FLOOR
18. GOVERNOR GENERAL'S SUITE
19. 4TH FLOOR
20. EMERGENCY EXIT

Photos,
Peter Zuuring,
Taken on-site
summer 1998.

Mystery and...

Did A.V. Roe U.K. receive plans for the Arrow?

The CF-100 book by MacMillan has a section on Orenda Engines Limited. One of the pictures shown is the one on the right, with a caption reading "Completed engines in the Rheem container area behind Orenda plant." Close examination reveals a J-79 engine from the CF-104 program and an Iroquois Mk II as indicated by the inlet guide vanes.

The first production J-79 was early 1961. What is an Iroquois engine still doing at Orenda when the program terminated two years earlier? Apparently, some engines were retained for potential use by Bristol-Siddeley and Curtis-Wright ....but this long?

MANCHESTER,England,May 13 1960 REVIVE THE AVRO ARROW?? The Manchester Guardian has called for the re-birth of the Avro Arrow (CF-105).Stating that there is still a great demand for manned interceptors,the authorative report said that the United States could make good use of the top flight fighter. "FEDNEWS"

An article about British defence policy in the Manchester Guardian in May 1960 called for the restoration of the Arrow program. The information could only have come from Hawker Siddeley, which had knowledge of the Arrow. But since Arrow plans were supposedly destroyed, how could British Avro have considered such a proposal unless it had complete plans? It seems reasonable that the parent company of a Canadian operation would indeed have had been given such documents.

Neglect

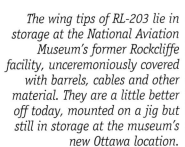

The wing tips of RL-203 lie in storage at the National Aviation Museum's former Rockcliffe facility, unceremoniously covered with barrels, cables and other material. They are a little better off today, mounted on a jig but still in storage at the museum's new Ottawa location.

Photo, Marc-André Valiquette

The nose of RL-206 fared little better than 203's wing tips; it spent years in storage at the National Museum of Science and Technology in Ottawa. Now it is on prominent display at the National Aviation Museum. But for many people working there, it is nothing special..."just another part of our collection," they say.

Photo, Marc-André Valiquette

Privileged information

In the fall of 1978, the CBC was planning a twenty-year retrospective documentary on the Arrow. Executive producer George Robertson asked then Deputy Defence Minister, C.R. Nixon, for access to relevant records. Though the response was negative, internal correspondence within the Department of National Defence, now unclassified, sets the record straight as to...

"Who ordered the Arrows cut-up?"

The manner in which the whole affair was handled, although understandable, leaves no doubt that the military wanted the information to remain privileged.

The CBC apparently had planned to broadcast the story earlier. In keeping with neutrality, it was postponed because of a federal election. (See *Montreal Star* news clipping).

Clipping,
Montreal Star

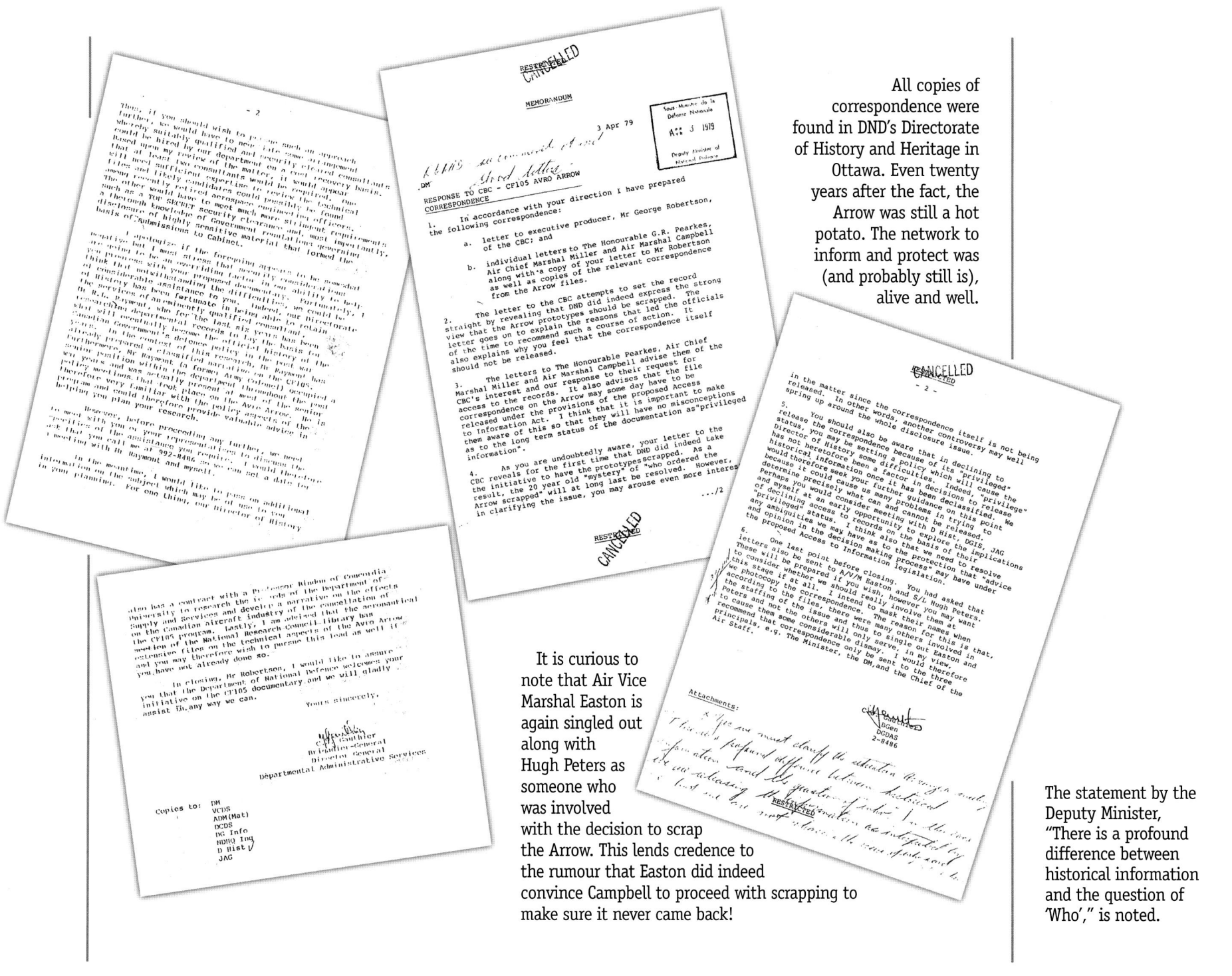

All copies of correspondence were found in DND's Directorate of History and Heritage in Ottawa. Even twenty years after the fact, the Arrow was still a hot potato. The network to inform and protect was (and probably still is), alive and well.

It is curious to note that Air Vice Marshal Easton is again singled out along with Hugh Peters as someone who was involved with the decision to scrap the Arrow. This lends credence to the rumour that Easton did indeed convince Campbell to proceed with scrapping to make sure it never came back!

The statement by the Deputy Minister, "There is a profound difference between historical information and the question of 'Who'," is noted.

Vignettes - The Arrow Scrapbook

Privileged information, cont'd.

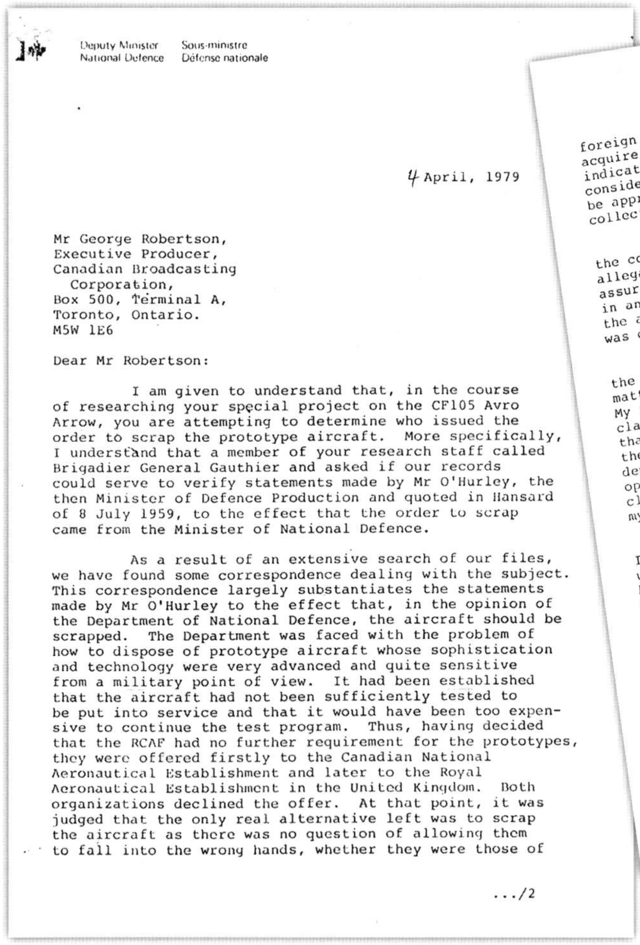

Letter 1 (left):

Deputy Minister   Sous-ministre
National Defence   Défense nationale

4 April, 1979

Mr George Robertson,
Executive Producer,
Canadian Broadcasting
Corporation,
Box 500, Terminal A,
Toronto, Ontario.
M5W 1E6

Dear Mr Robertson:

I am given to understand that, in the course of researching your special project on the CF105 Avro Arrow, you are attempting to determine who issued the order to scrap the prototype aircraft. More specifically, I understand that a member of your research staff called Brigadier General Gauthier and asked if our records could serve to verify statements made by Mr O'Hurley, the then Minister of Defence Production and quoted in Hansard of 8 July 1959, to the effect that the order to scrap came from the Minister of National Defence.

As a result of an extensive search of our files, we have found some correspondence dealing with the subject. This correspondence largely substantiates the statements made by Mr O'Hurley to the effect that, in the opinion of the Department of National Defence, the aircraft should be scrapped. The Department was faced with the problem of how to dispose of prototype aircraft whose sophistication and technology were very advanced and quite sensitive from a military point of view. It had been established that the aircraft had not been sufficiently tested to be put into service and that it would have been too expensive to continue the test program. Thus, having decided that the RCAF had no further requirement for the prototypes, they were offered firstly to the Canadian National Aeronautical Establishment and later to the Royal Aeronautical Establishment in the United Kingdom. Both organizations declined the offer. At that point, it was judged that the only real alternative left was to scrap the aircraft as there was no question of allowing them to fall into the wrong hands, whether they were those of

.../2

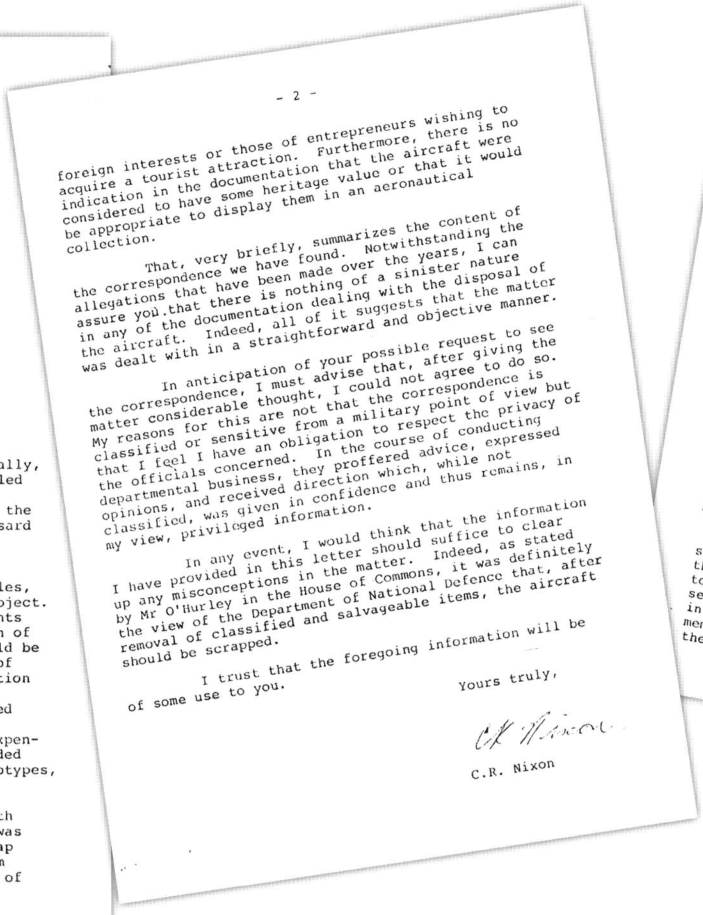

Letter 2 (center):

- 2 -

foreign interests or those of entrepreneurs wishing to acquire a tourist attraction. Furthermore, there is no indication in the documentation that the aircraft were considered to have some heritage value or that it would be appropriate to display them in an aeronautical collection.

That, very briefly, summarizes the content of the correspondence we have found. Notwithstanding the allegations that have been made over the years, I can assure you that there is nothing of a sinister nature in any of the documentation dealing with the disposal of the aircraft. Indeed, all of it suggests that the matter was dealt with in a straightforward and objective manner.

In anticipation of your possible request to see the correspondence, I must advise that, after giving the matter considerable thought, I could not agree to do so. My reasons for this are not that the correspondence is classified or sensitive from a military point of view but that I feel I have an obligation to respect the privacy of the officials concerned. In the course of conducting departmental business, they proffered advice, expressed opinions, and received direction which, while not classified, was given in confidence and thus remains, in my view, privileged information.

In any event, I would think that the information I have provided in this letter should suffice to clear up any misconceptions in the matter. Indeed, as stated by Mr O'Hurley in the House of Commons, it was definitely the view of the Department of National Defence that, after removal of classified and salvageable items, the aircraft should be scrapped.

I trust that the foregoing information will be of some use to you.

Yours truly,

C.R. Nixon

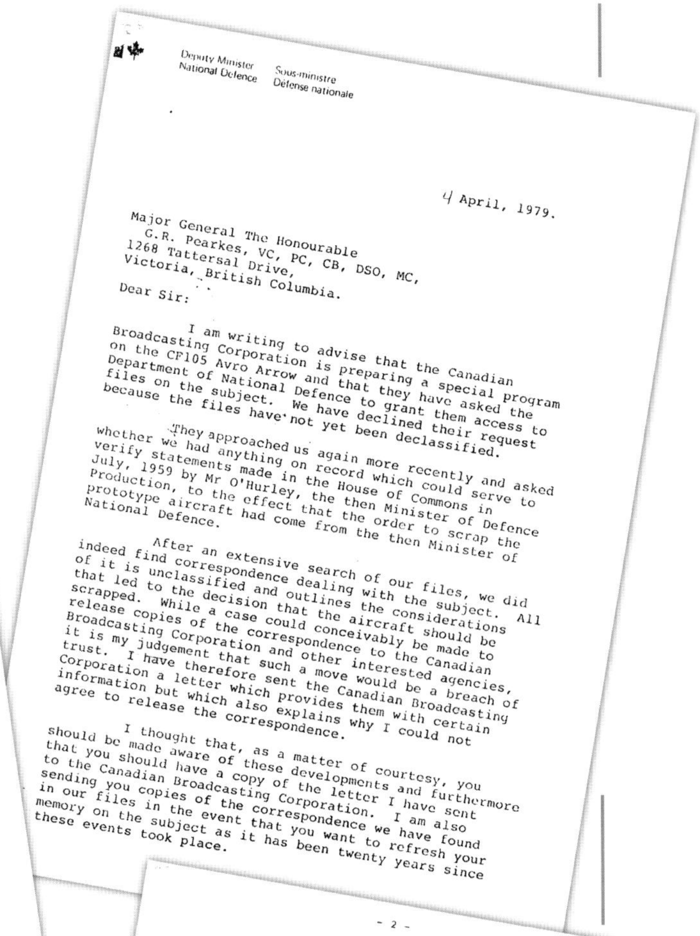

C.R. Nixon

Letter 3 (right):

Deputy Minister   Sous-ministre
National Defence   Défense nationale

4 April, 1979.

Major General The Honourable
G.R. Pearkes, VC, PC, CB, DSO, MC,
1268 Tattersal Drive,
Victoria, British Columbia.

Dear Sir:

I am writing to advise that the Canadian Broadcasting Corporation is preparing a special program on the CF105 Avro Arrow and that they have asked the Department of National Defence to grant them access to files on the subject. We have declined their request because the files have not yet been declassified.

They approached us again more recently and asked whether we had anything on record which could serve to verify statements made in the House of Commons in July, 1959 by Mr O'Hurley, the then Minister of Defence Production, to the effect that the order to scrap the prototype aircraft had come from the then Minister of National Defence.

After an extensive search of our files, we did indeed find correspondence dealing with the subject. All of it is unclassified and outlines the considerations that led to the decision that the aircraft should be scrapped. While a case could conceivably be made to release copies of the correspondence to the Canadian Broadcasting Corporation and other interested agencies, it is my judgement that such a move would be a breach of trust. I have therefore sent the Canadian Broadcasting Corporation a letter which provides them with certain information but which also explains why I could not agree to release the correspondence.

I thought that, as a matter of courtesy, you should be made aware of these developments and furthermore that you should have a copy of the letter I have sent to the Canadian Broadcasting Corporation. I am also sending you copies of the correspondence we have found in our files in the event that you want to refresh your memory on the subject as it has been twenty years since these events took place.

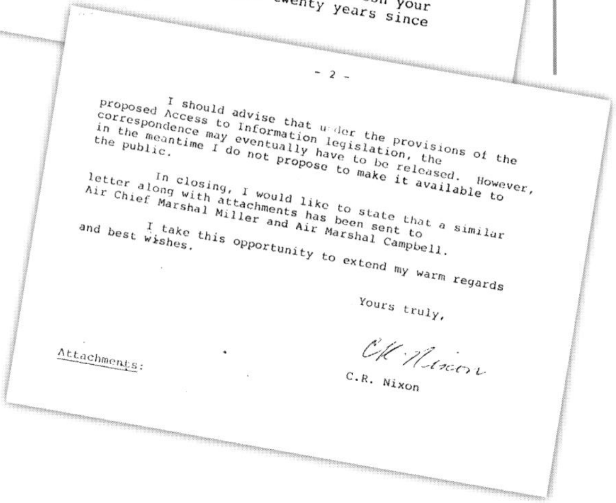

Letter 3, page 2 (bottom right):

- 2 -

I should advise that under the provisions of the proposed Access to Information legislation, the correspondence may eventually have to be released. However, in the meantime I do not propose to make it available to the public.

In closing, I would like to state that a similar letter along with attachments has been sent to Air Chief Marshal Miller and Air Marshal Campbell.

I take this opportunity to extend my warm regards and best wishes.

Yours truly,

C.R. Nixon

C.R. Nixon

Attachments:

Deputy Defence Minister, C.R. Nixon, wrote to CBC executive producer George Robertson in 1979 during production of the documentary, "There never was an Arrow," and confirmed that it was indeed the Department of National Defence that ordered the scrapping of the Arrows.

2125-1
1325-7
1325-500/00

21 April 1980

NOTE TO FILE

CBC Programme on the Avro Arrow

1. Early in 1980 the CBC aired a programme on the Avro Arrow. During research the producer requested access which could not be given into DND files concerning the Arrow. The Deputy Minister did, however, answer some specific questions about the order for destroying the aircraft prototype. This correspondence is to be found on file number 2125-4 TD 8285.

2. The programme itself turned out to be a moderate and relatively accurate interpretation of events. The following observations were made by the Director at the time of the programme.

3. The reason for cancelling the Avro jet liner was not convincing, nor could it be supported by documentation. This is a subject that requires proper historical analysis.

4. The rank of LtGen "Reggie" Lane was consistently given as Brig Gen.

5. The programme argues that it is not known who ordered the destruction of the prototype. In fact the Deputy Minister explained in his letter to the producer that the order for destruction stemmed from advice given by the Chief of Air Staff, the Deputy Minister of National Defence and the Department of Defence Production.

6. The programme left the impression that no opportunity had been given for various agencies to acquire the prototype. As the Deputy Minister's letter pointed out, this is not true.

7. The programme was interesting in that it left the viewer with the feeling that Mr. Crawford Gordon's personality clash with Mr. Diefenbaker was instrumental in bringing about cancellation of the Arrow. This impression could even be interpreted to suggest that Mr. Gordon himself might have ordered the destruction of films and blueprints relating to the Arrow. It must be emphasized that there is no evidence of such actions.

8. The programme concluded that no American interests were involved in the decision. On the face of it this seems a remarkably innocent point of view. Previous accounts have suggested with some reason that the American aviation industry would not have been comfortable with the Arrow as competition and therefore was not likely to give the Canadian firm much opportunity to compete.

W.A.B. Douglas
Ottawa, 21 April 1980

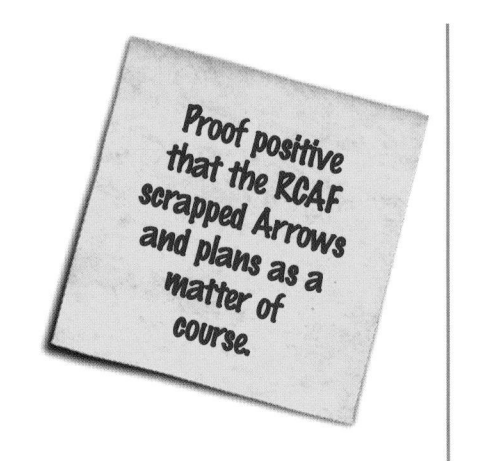

Proof positive that the RCAF scrapped Arrows and plans as a matter of course.

A reaction to the documentary was filed in April 1980. It states that:

• the Chief of Air Staff, the Deputy Minister of National Defence and the Department of Defence Production had all advised destruction of the Arrow prototype.

• other agencies (possibly the Canadian National Aviation Establishment and the British Royal Aviation Establishment) had been offered a chance to acquire an Arrow.

• there is no evidence that Crawford Gordon gave the order to destroy Arrow plans and blueprints, implying that the Department of National Defence had done that as part of the program wrap-up.

• the U.S. would not have been happy with the Arrow as competition and might have blocked attempts to sell it.

• the cancellation of the Avro Jetliner deserves more investigation.

Engine tales

In the mid 1980s, the National Research Council was cleaning house and sold several engines via Crown Assets Disposal Corporation to a wrecker called McEwen in Moncton, N.B. Les McGuiness, a CP Air pilot on the lookout for collectibles, was contacted. McEwen, I have been told, was not sure what he had bought since the container was marked PS-10, yet was too heavy for an Orenda. Similarly, he mistook the two larger Rheem containers included in the batch to be J-57s from the Voodoo CF-101 program. At any rate, Les bought the containers and noticed there were, mysteriously, actually four. It was soon determined that an Iroquois was in two pieces in two separate containers, while the other two really contained J-75s-p3s. Obviously these were from the Arrow program.

I learned since that these engines were part of the cache that Mac Kuhring of the Ottawa NRC Engine lab had put away after the demise of the Arrow. In fact, there were four J-75s, two are still in Ottawa,

A forklift cracking a container and finding...an Iroquois engine. When Howard Carter opened Tutankhamon's tomb he said he saw "wonderful things." We felt the same way.

Photo,
Peter Zuuring

A long journey for an Iroquois engine, from Orenda to the National Research Council to a wrecking yard in Moncton, N.B., to the Canadian Warplane Heritage Museum in Hamilton, Ont., and back to the National Research Council where it is now being restored.

Photo, Peter Zuuring

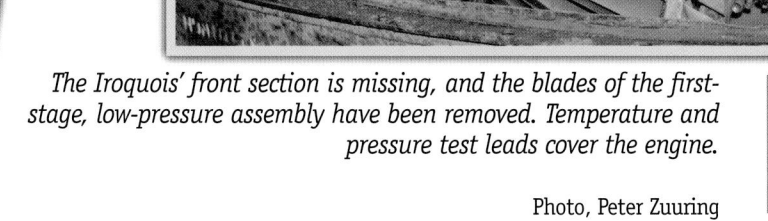

The Iroquois' front section is missing, and the blades of the first-stage, low-pressure assembly have been removed. Temperature and pressure test leads cover the engine.

Photo, Peter Zuuring

The exit from the low-pressure turbine at the aft end of the engine. All the second high-pressure turbine blades are gone.

Photo, Peter Zuuring

One way to ensure an engine won't be used again: cut a large hole in the cowling. Imagine workers seeing something that required so much care ruined in a moment.

Photo, Peter Zuuring

one at the NRC and the other recently removed to NAM. The J-75s had been acquired by the NRC to perform correlation studies between predicted and actual performance of large jet engines. The standby use of one engine to supply high pressure air was being considered. According to Mark Chappell, one of the first jobs he had was to go to Malton and return with recovered parts for the NRC. He remembers having an engine trailer flat tire on highway 7 in the middle of the night.

Phil Nelson, a director of the Canadian Warplane Heritage Museum in Hamilton, acquired the lot from Les for a hefty tax receipt. For the last fifteen years the engine has been sitting, surviving a fire and being periodically shown during airshows. The afterburner disappeared after the

fire. It was recently recovered from the airport dump. The nose section is nowhere to be found. There was some speculation that the engine was the one that flew in the B-47. Today we know that the engine was a development version; views of it in the test cells have been found. The amount and type of instrumentation pretty well determines it was a Mk I variety. CADC burned massive holes in the high-pressure compressor and high-pressure turbine areas to make sure it was disabled. Apart from the Iroquois in the National Aviation Museum, no other engines have been recovered. Supposedly Bristol Siddeley, in the U.K., got one. Where are they all?

An Iroquois afterburner found and recovered from a dump at Hamilton airport.

Photo, Peter Zuuring

Where are the rest?

An Iroquois engine, then...

Three views of an Iroquois engine about 1957 at the Orenda Engines plant in Malton, being prepared for testing, then being rolled in and rolled out of the test cell.

The same Iroquois engine back at the National Research Council in Ottawa undergoing restoration. Jim MacLeod of the NRC's Engine Lab has taken the project under his wing.

Photo, Jim MacLeod

The afterburner found at Hamilton airport, in the NRC being restored by the sheet metal group under the direction of Ron Gould.

Photo, Peter Zuuring

...and now

The Iroquois' front end has been removed and major components dismantled. Steve Giguère is doing the work.

Photo, Peter Zuuring

Arrow free-flight models at Point Petre in the 1950s

Key to Photos

1. Assembly of transmitter in model
2. Setting up telemetry communications
3. Final adjustments; note Avro truck in background
4. Rolling out the model to the launch area
5. In the control room looking down range
6. Radar tracking using doppler techniques for speed verification
7. In the Avro data collection van
8. Stabilizing the launch frame and switching on equipment
9. Plan of the Point Petre range
10. Free-flight model on its way; Nike boosters functioned well
11. Free-flight model on course; charges tested lateral stability

1.

4.

The free-flight program was extremely successful in that drag coefficients were calculated and the airframe's lateral and longitudinal stability was ascertained. The models achieved between Mach 1.7 & Mach 1.8, each flight lasting from thirty to forty seconds. They have not been recovered to date.

3.

2.

All coloured photos, Aviation Videos. Black and white photos are from free-flight model reports dated June 1955 through July 1957, NRC, except no. 8, Ross Richardson.

5.

6.

7.

8.

9.

10.

11.

Free-flight model schematic and report covers that give flight details at the time of the shots. The models were partly magnesium so they may have corroded in the water.

All reports,
NRC Ottawa

Free-flight models today

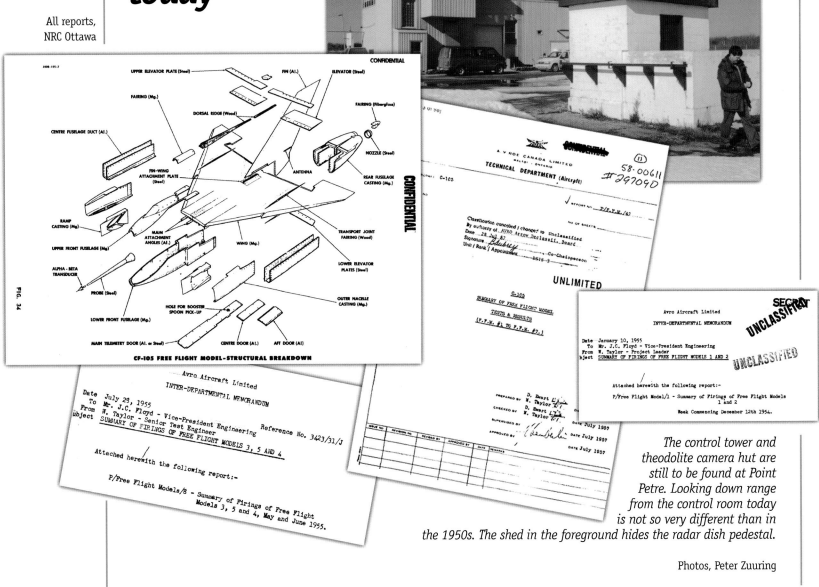

The control tower and theodolite camera hut are still to be found at Point Petre. Looking down range from the control room today is not so very different than in the 1950s. The shed in the foreground hides the radar dish pedestal.

Photos, Peter Zuuring

The chart below shows velocity versus time for a typical flight. Some twenty-five seconds, averaging about 1000 feet per second, makes the search zone obvious. The direction is clear from the map and photo.

Chart, Peter Zuuring

SEARCH ZONE

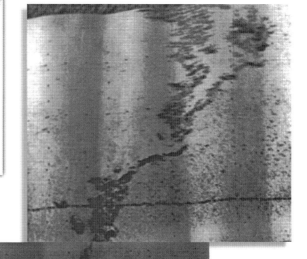

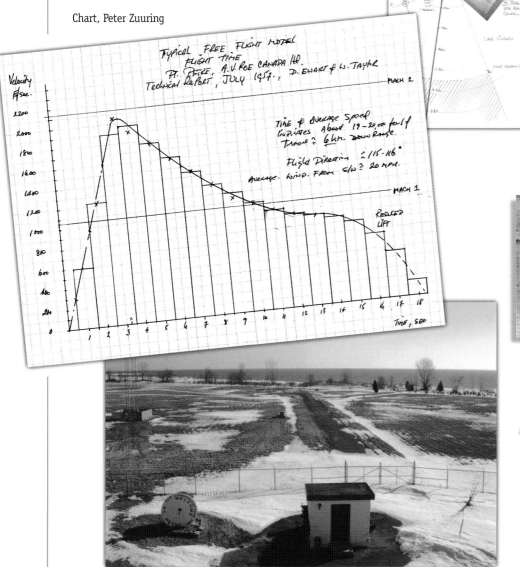

Within hours, using side-scan sonar (supplied by Ocean Scan Systems), a trace on the Lake Ontario bottom shows a tell-tale track: something hitting hard , slithering over the bottom and coming to rest at trail's end, an object about ten feet long. Three more tracks have been identified.

Model recovery is making progress.

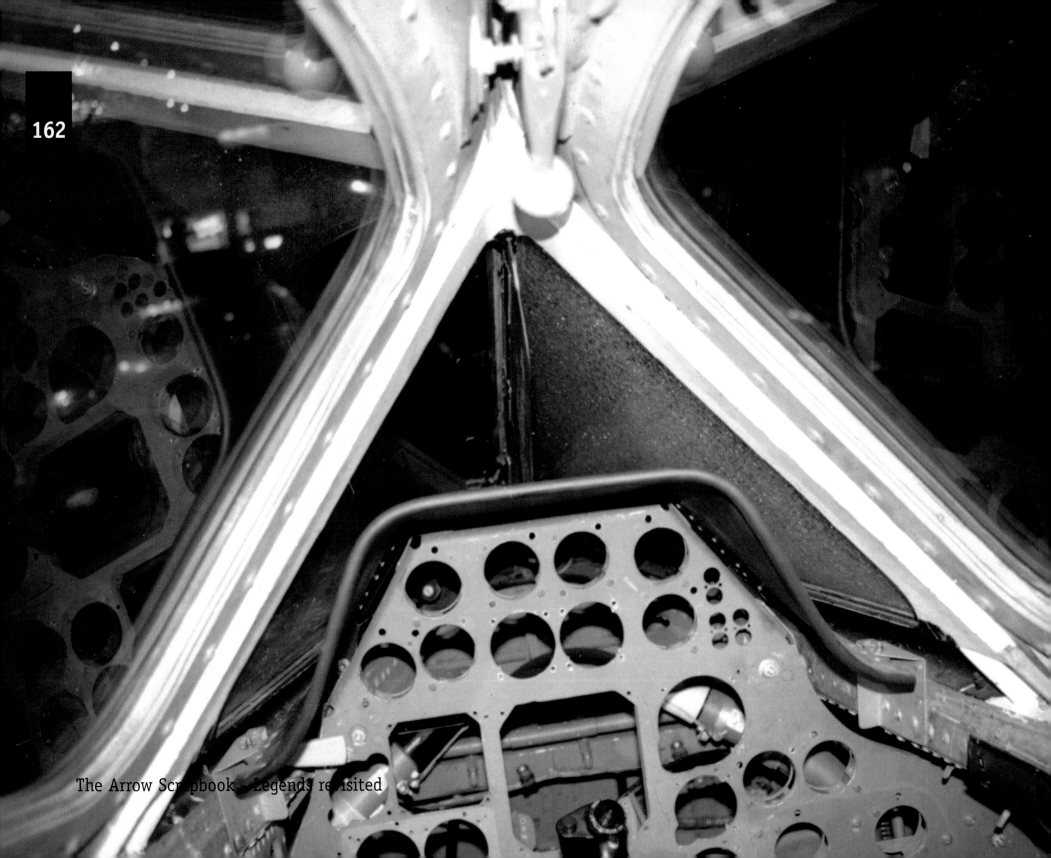

The Arrow Scrapbook - Legends revisited

Legends revisited

1. Diefenbaker did it. Anyway he did not like Crawford Gordon and that contributed.
2. The Americans were probably behind it and did not want us to compete with them.
3. It was too expensive.
4. No one else wanted to buy it.
5. It would probably have broken up because it was technically flawed.
6. It was obsolete and over taken by events.
7. It was twenty years ahead of its time.
8. One got away.

As you probably noted, some of these legends are in direct contradiction, one with the other.

In this chapter, based on my findings as evidenced by what you have seen and read, I try to put together a scenario of what happened and why. I think it's the best one yet! Further more, I review the technology of the time and draw fair conclusions about the Arrow's place.

The inside of RL-206 with the canopy closed. The reflections are striking. When you are inside it is smaller than you think...but what power behind you.

Photo, Peter Zuuring/NAM

What really happened -the best explanation yet

The stuff of legends!

The Arrow would have kept pace. Here is the Allen Jackson model at Winnipeg while shooting the CBC miniseries.

Photo, DND Photo Unit

Having read and seen the evidence presented so far, I believe it is clear that our Department of Defence, through its Chiefs of Staff Committee was responsible for the birth and the demise of the Arrow program. They arrived at their conclusions, not in isolation, but through deliberation. They knew the consequences exactly. They kept the secret hidden for twenty years as indicated by their internal correspondence and admissions when the CBC wanted to do its first retrospective in 1979.

Officially, the government of the day did make the final decision. Diefenbaker could have visited the plant - seen first-hand the extent of the commitments made and the spirit of the workforce that put it all together. He didn't! He could have found the compromise that he talked about in cabinet. He could have found the money needed to complete the program to its first delivery phase. Sixty percent of every dollar spent on the program stayed in Canada...even the lowliest worker understood the idea of

being a Canadian and buying Canadian. There were no problems in finding the money to buy the CF-104 Starfighter within three months of cancellation!

The project was huge for the day. It was in the so called "Shop Window." It looked good and it flew. Hawker-Siddeley Canada was a transplant, yet was slowly becoming Canadian like all the other foreigners that flocked to Canada at that time. Avro and Orenda did successfully put an airframe and an engine together, not without teething pains, but they did what was considered inadvisable.

So the problem was homegrown. We can come up with every excuse in the book, but the bottom line is we did it to ourselves. Many would have us believe that we were forced into it, that no one else wanted it, that it was too expensive, that the technology was so far ahead that it had to be destroyed for security reasons, that it was also technically flawed and that in time it would fall apart ...what a contradiction...

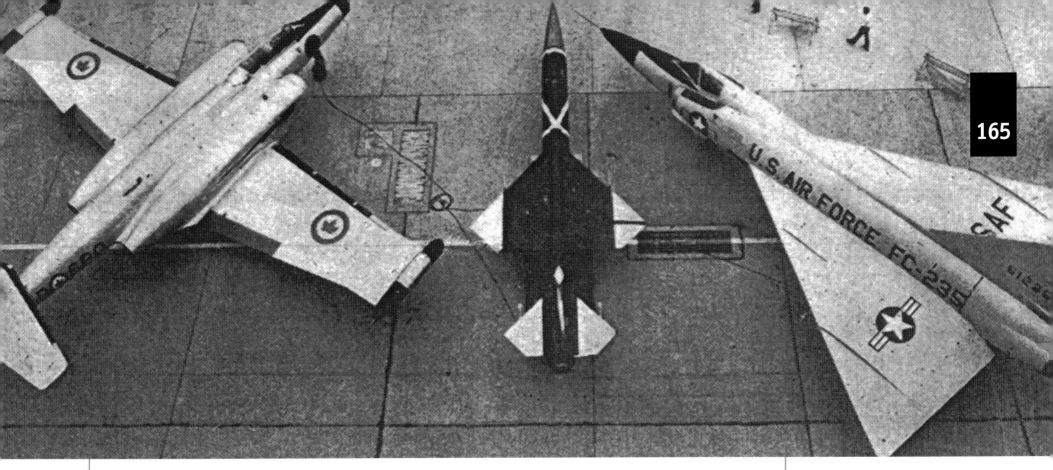

The Arrow saga has grown to mythological proportions.

Canada was the underdog, trying the impossible, daring to push the envelope. Big Brother took it away from us. An interfering government lost our moment in the sun. The loss was sudden. Cancellation affected many. Unsatisfactory explanations sowed seeds of doubt. What were the real reasons? The speed, secrecy and extent of the destruction raised suspicions. Why was it necessary to destroy all our work? Was there a hidden agenda? If it was that good, why did we get rid of it? It looked beautiful. We were told it could have broken the world speed record. These questions have been seething under our skins for years and they haven't gone away...

... The stuff of legends!

Once we start to peel away the veneer, layer by layer, the root cause of cancellation, I believe, was the breakdown of the working relationship between the company and the RCAF. A loss of confidence viscerally affected the program. Can we have the Arrow in time, to specification, and within budget? It wasn't the fact that a development project of this magnitude and depth would have uncertainties, this was understood. It was the realization that the targets were ever moving with no end in sight, that's what made the chiefs and the government nervous. It was embarrassing. It was deceiving. The military and the government can take some of the blame for letting the program get out of hand. No one likes to have their failures paraded around in public. It was easier to get rid of it.

Too bad they had to lie about it!

Good enough for Canada's defence: a CF-100, Bomarc and an American F-102 shown here at Boeing Field, Seattle in the early 1960s.

Photo, DND clipping

Root cause of cancellation? Poor working relations!

Dr. John Parkin of the National Aeronautical Establishment, 1956

Photo, Aircraft Magazine

Arrow Technology... product of the times ?

"It flew through the air with the greatest of ease, Too far and too fast Prince Albert to please."

Paul Hellyer's so-called parliamentary act of impudence when chiding Diefenbaker that an Arrow should be preserved for the new National Aviation Museum.

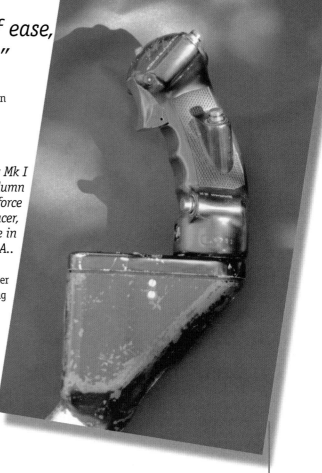

Arrow Mk I control column grip and force transducer, both made in the U.S.A..

Photo, Peter Zuuring

Much has been said about the Arrow's performance potential, both then and now. On one hand, there were predictions of complete disaster. National Research Council pundits like Dr. J.H. Parkin and Julius Lukasiewicz claimed in the1950s, that the plane would not fly supersonically and if it did, it would fall apart through structural failure. On the other, enthusiasts since have maintained that the Arrow, in its 1959 state, would have flown faster and higher than any other aircraft.

Certainly, the Arrow was considered by many observers to have had the potential to be the "best in the west." As an airframe, it appeared to work and exceeded expectations even with the original J-75 engines. Installing the Iroquois would have lightened the aircraft by some 5000 pounds, and increased its speed beyond Mach 2 to push it to the air-intake design limit. Any speed much greater than Mach 2.3 however, would have put an induced shock wave into the throat of the air duct inlet, leading to cavitation and possible engine choking. Since the J-75s already pushed the airframe close to the design limit, the Iroquois would certainly have got it there at reduced power levels. Intake geometry is usually considered the tell-tale of an aircraft's design-speed limitations.

The Iroquois, had it continued, would definitely have distinguished itself. The weight-to-thrust ratio of 1:5 was phenomenal. The 4500-pound cylinder had the first fully variable afterburner, kicking another 30 percent power boost out the rear end. It was powerful! Dry fuel consumption was about one pound/hour/pound of thrust (so about one hour of flight time with 20,000 pounds of fuel and 20,000 pounds of thrust). Use of the afterburner increased thrust by 30 percent but nearly doubled the fuel requirement.

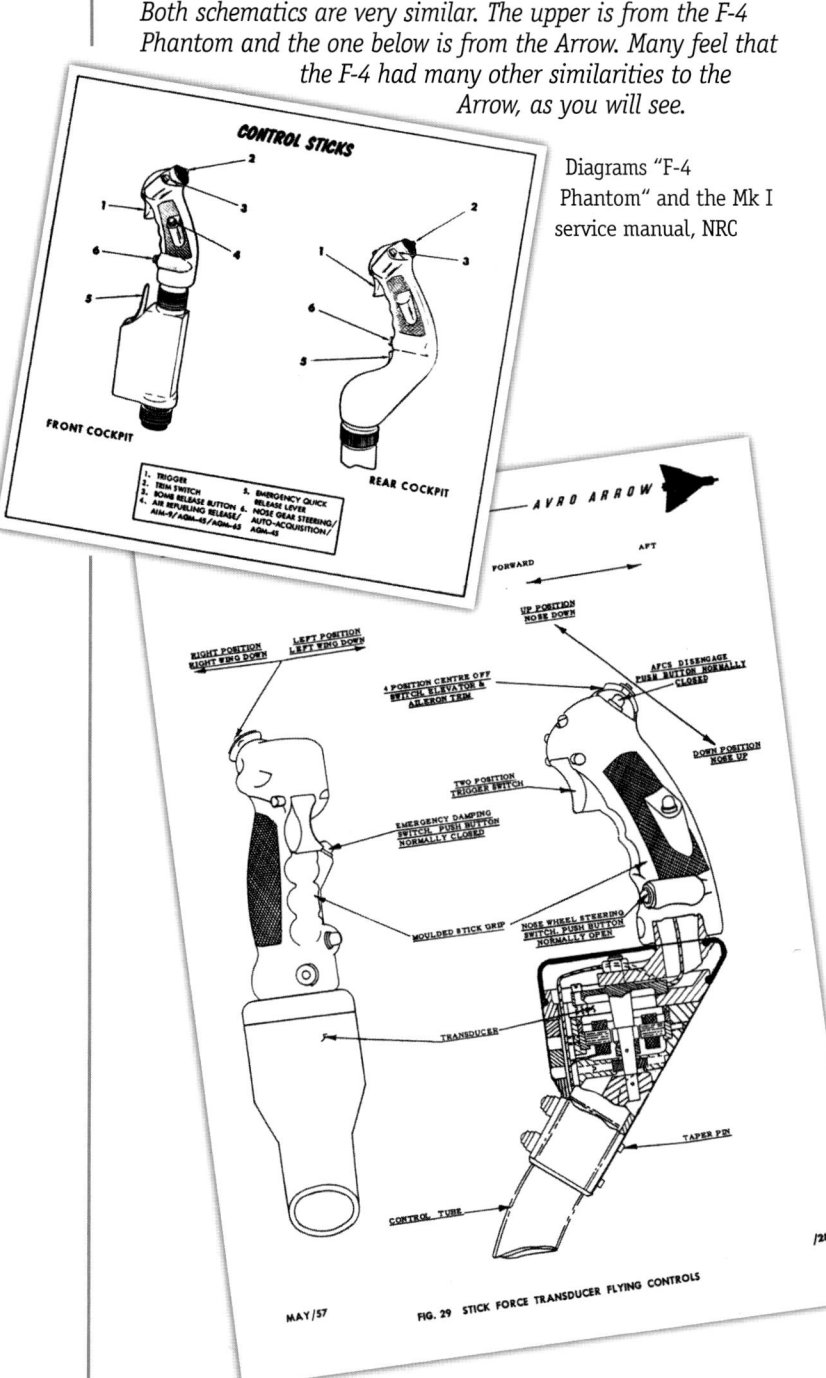

Both schematics are very similar. The upper is from the F-4 Phantom and the one below is from the Arrow. Many feel that the F-4 had many other similarities to the Arrow, as you will see.

Diagrams "F-4 Phantom" and the Mk I service manual, NRC

A - American
B - British and
C - Canadian

There were ABC pilots who cross-trained with different aircraft and helped to design the cockpit layouts of new ones so that transition training would be at a minimum should war break out.

So what were Canada's allies doing and how did we stack up?

The Second World War brought the Canadian military closer to the U.S. and British forces more than ever before. They shared the captured German research records, experts and equipment, the so-called "Missing Paper Clips." They learned from each other and developed long-standing fraternal relationships that spilled over into post-war commerce and development. There was a habit of sharing secrets. The post-war air forces of all three nations continued to work together, not only because of war camaraderie, but through common interests to defeat the new evil lurking behind the Iron and Bamboo Curtains. For the most part, nothing was withheld. They all knew what the others had. They gave to each other freely, yet jealously guarded their independence with respect to what was actually implemented. This was without a doubt applicable to the U.S. and to a slightly lesser extent, to the British. A.V. Roe tried and succeeded with the CF-100 and the Orenda, but failed with the Jetliner, Arrow and the Iroquois. The practice of sharing continues in today's military. Even though it is less so within industry, information destined for the host military gets shared via the forces' "need-to-know" old-boy networks.

Remember that the roots of the Arrow lay in the USAF F-102 Delta Dagger

The internal weapons bay was necessary to have minimal drag. As engine power increased, external weapons stores would come back.

The USAF, Convair, Avro and the RCAF all lost no time in applying the new "Coke bottle" design - actually called AREA ruling. The drag of a bullet-shaped cylinder could be preserved if the frontal area of any wings or appendages was taken away from the waist area of the new shape. Hence the pinched - in look.

From the Mk I brochure

BULGES AT TAILPIPE are a design trick to improve speed. YF-102A was built in only six months, went past Mach 1 on second flight.

Design Changes Make F-102 Supersonic

Half-a-dozen design changes, built around more power, less drag and lower weight, make Convair's YF-102A delta-winged interceptor supersonic in level flight.

On its second flight, made at Edwards AFB Dec. 21, the big plane passed through the Mach 1 mark in a climb to 35,000 ft. At that altitude, Convair engineering test pilot Richard Johnson leveled out and accelerated further into the supersonic range.

He reported no buffeting and good control characteristics through the transonic range.

These first photos of the modified airplane, which was built in 117 working days after completion of engineering, detail some of the layout changes. (Other YF-102A pictures are on p. 9.)

• **Newer Look.**—From needle nose to blistered tail, the YF-102A is new in aerodynamic detail. The nose has been lengthened and apparently drooped a little further to give better visibility over the radome at high angles of attack.

• Canopy has been redesigned to take out the side bulges; it now features a near-flat side panel and layout similar to the canopy on Convair's F2Y Sea Dart. Below the canopy, new air inlets feed the bigger Pratt & Whitney J57 turbojet, rated at 16,000 lb. thrust with afterburner on.

• Wing leading edge has been cambered to improve lift characteristics of the very thin airfoil; the camber stops just short of the tip and the transition from it to the unmodified tip section gives an "upswept" wingtip.

• Two huge fairings jut aft at each side of the tailpipe exit, presumably to fill in the channel section between

AVIATION WEEK, January 10, 1955

LATEST F-102 (left) shows many changes compared with earlier model next to it.

NEW CANOPY has flatter side panels, fewer braces. Air intakes also are different.

wing, fuselage and vertical tail and thus delay flow breakaway. This is a standard stratagem to increase critical Mach number by a few hundredths.

Work on the delta-winged interceptor is done at the San Diego plant of Convair division of General Dynamics Corp.

15

ADDED
REDUCED
ADDED
REDUCED
TAIL CONE ADDED
'BUMP' DELETED
LOWER SHOULDER LINES MODIFIED CROSS SECTION REDUCED
NACELLE LINES MODIFIED CROSS SECTION REDUCED
ADDED

Forward
bulkhead
index
(aft of nose)

_ng attach points

Aft fuselage
tooling accessories

Forward
fixture-section
(movable)

Aft
Fixture-section
(movable)

Center
fixture-section
(fixed)

The same tooling techniques were employed using heavy rigid framed jigs to assemble components into a final aircraft. The bottom photo shows the centre section jig of the F-102 at Convair's factory in San Diego. We saw, in the chapter, "Back in the Fifties," the jigs and floor disposition of the Avro plant - the above, if anything, looks more primitive than that. It is hard to see how this particular jig was loaded or unloaded. Avro's centre wing marry-up jig is above...just a bit bigger.

Photo, P. Brennan

REGISTERED

S1038-113 (AMTS/DDA)

Air Member,
Canadian Joint Staff,
2001 Connecticut Avenue, NW,
Washington 8, D.C.,
U.S.A.

4 May 54   Ontario,

ABC
IN ACTION!

CF105 Aircraft - Transition from Prototype to Production

1   There are various approaches to the problem of the evolution of a line of production aircraft from the basic prototype machine, and the merits and demerits of each is the subject of a report being prepared by the Directorate of Development A.

2   The method usually employed in the past was to hand-build the prototypes in the experimental shop to experimental drawings and with a minimum of tooling. Upon successful flight testing of the prototype, the experimental drawings were re-drawn and issued as production drawings, tooling was designed and ordered and after a long delay the production aircraft finally appeared.

3   The trend in the UK appears to be towards increased overlap between the prototype and production aircraft by issuing production type drawings for the prototype and by the use of prototype tooling which, by some elaboration, is suitable for production. This is, of course, a limited risk program in that, any re-design of the prototype involves subsequent modification to the tooling.

4   It is understood that this method is also being used in the United States, in particular, at Convair for the production of the F102 and is called the "Craige - Cooke" method.

5   May information on the "Craige-Cooke" method of transition from prototype to production aircraft be obtained and forwarded as soon as possible. In particular, information as detailed below is required:

(a) General report on "Craige-Cooke" method.

(b) The extent that production type tooling is procured for prototype aircraft, i.e. fuselage, wings, details, etc.

(c) Appreciation of the risk due to subsequent re-design of aircraft, e.g. scrappage of tooling, re-issue of drawings etc.

(d) Specific figures for (b) and (c) for the F101 and F102 aircraft or others.

(e) USAF opinion of this method.

HR Foottit) A/C
for CAS

The "Cooke-Craigie" method of slow manufacture was adopted and dropped by nearly all airframe manufacturers. It was supposed to speed up final delivery to squadron. A larger number of pre-production planes were needed to wring out the production tooling. The above letter is proof positive of the ABC group in action.

Letter, National Archives, RCAF files

The USAF's "century jets"

The USAF jets with three digit identification became known as the "century jets". All of them went supersonic. All of them incorporated irreversible control surfaces actuated with high-pressure hydraulic systems. Similarly, various damping and automatic flight controls were common.

Before the Arrow flew, the U.S. already had plenty of experience with supersonic fighters. The USAF did not hesitate to share information. In fact, most of the complicated equipment for the Arrow was manufactured by U.S. suppliers.

F-103, The Republic XF-103, Mach 3 Fighter/Interceptor was cancelled at the mockup stage August 1957.

F-104, "Starfighter" (Lockheed)

F-100, "Super Sabre" (American)

In 1958 , the F-104 achieved the world speed record of 1404 miles per hour and at the same time the world altitude record by zooming to 100,000 feet.

F-101, "Voodoo" (McDonnell)

F-102, "Delta Dagger" (Convair)

Again, internal weapon bays were popular only until raw jet engine power exceeded the need for very clean lines. The increased drag of outboard weapon racks was only a problem with the early jets, when engine power could only just get the plane through the sound barrier.

F-105, "Thunderchief" (Republic)

This first flight time-line shows clearly that the Arrow was later than most of its competitors in getting into the air. Not only did the USAF, the RAF and the French Armeé de L'air beat the Canadians, but the Swedes, with the Draken, did it, too.

The F-4 Phantom went Mach 2 on its maiden flight just one month after the first flight of the CF-105 Arrow.

We were definitely part of the pack but not leading it by any stretch. However, the CF-105 was the biggest of all these jets.

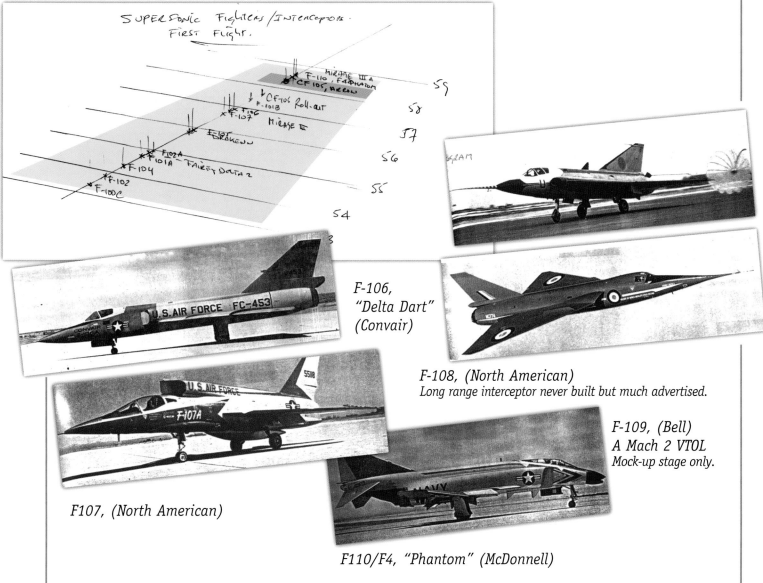

The Europeans were going supersonic too. The Swedish Dracken, the British Fairey Delta II and the French Mirage III were part and parcel of the same series.

F-106, "Delta Dart" (Convair)

F-108, (North American)
Long range interceptor never built but much advertised.

F-109, (Bell)
A Mach 2 VTOL
Mock-up stage only.

F107, (North American)

F110/F4, "Phantom" (McDonnell)

In fact, everybody was going supersonic

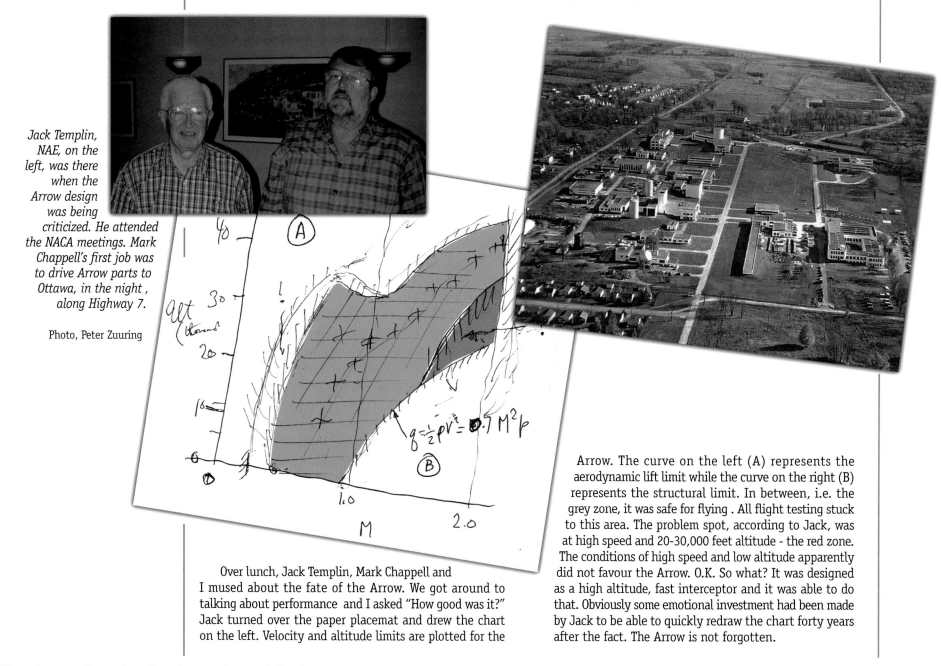

Jack Templin, NAE, on the left, was there when the Arrow design was being criticized. He attended the NACA meetings. Mark Chappell's first job was to drive Arrow parts to Ottawa, in the night , along Highway 7.

Photo, Peter Zuuring

Over lunch, Jack Templin, Mark Chappell and I mused about the fate of the Arrow. We got around to talking about performance and I asked "How good was it?" Jack turned over the paper placemat and drew the chart on the left. Velocity and altitude limits are plotted for the

Arrow. The curve on the left (A) represents the aerodynamic lift limit while the curve on the right (B) represents the structural limit. In between, i.e. the grey zone, it was safe for flying . All flight testing stuck to this area. The problem spot, according to Jack, was at high speed and 20-30,000 feet altitude - the red zone. The conditions of high speed and low altitude apparently did not favour the Arrow. O.K. So what? It was designed as a high altitude, fast interceptor and it was able to do that. Obviously some emotional investment had been made by Jack to be able to quickly redraw the chart forty years after the fact. The Arrow is not forgotten.

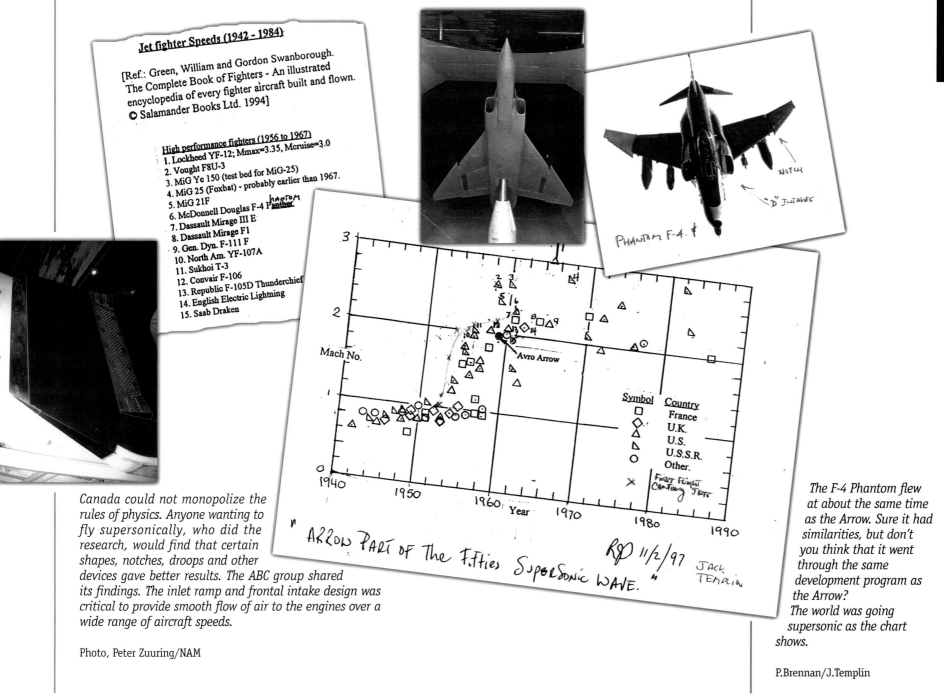

Jet fighter Speeds (1942 - 1984)

[Ref.: Green, William and Gordon Swanborough. The Complete Book of Fighters - An illustrated encyclopedia of every fighter aircraft built and flown. © Salamander Books Ltd. 1994]

High performance fighters (1956 to 1967)
1. Lockheed YF-12; Mmax=3.35, Mcruise=3.0
2. Vought F8U-3
3. MiG Ye 150 (test bed for MiG-25)
4. MiG 25 (Foxbat) - probably earlier than 1967.
5. MiG 21F
6. McDonnell Douglas F-4 Phantom *Panther*
7. Dassault Mirage III E
8. Dassault Mirage F1
9. Gen. Dyn. F-111 F
10. North Am. YF-107A
11. Sukhoi T-3
12. Convair F-106
13. Republic F-105D Thunderchief
14. English Electric Lightning
15. Saab Draken

PHANTOM F-4. ↑

NOTCH
"D" INTAKES

Mach No.

Avro Arrow

Symbol | Country
□ | France
◇ | U.K.
△ | U.S.
○ | U.S.S.R.
 | Other.
× | FIRST FLIGHT Century JETS

1940   1950   1960 Year 1970   1980   1990

" ARROW PART OF THE Fifties SuperSonic WAVE. "

RP 11/2/97 JACK TEMPLIN

Canada could not monopolize the rules of physics. Anyone wanting to fly supersonically, who did the research, would find that certain shapes, notches, droops and other devices gave better results. The ABC group shared its findings. The inlet ramp and frontal intake design was critical to provide smooth flow of air to the engines over a wide range of aircraft speeds.

Photo, Peter Zuuring/NAM

The F-4 Phantom flew at about the same time as the Arrow. Sure it had similarities, but don't you think that it went through the same development program as the Arrow?
The world was going supersonic as the chart shows.

P.Brennan/J.Templin

...and so was Canada.

Former Chief of the Air Staff, Wilf Curtis, was a director of A.V. Roe Canada Limited during that crucial spring of 1958. The newspaper debates ranged far and wide about the Arrow's capacity and sensibility of having it. Curtis explains that, just because next year's model is being discussed, does not make this years model obsolete. Furthermore, keeping our developments in Canada is good for everyone – it circulates the money and builds our capacity.

In my opinion the Arrow was a product of the times. Believe it or not, it was designed conservatively, building on the available know-how. Advances were made and limits were extended. (for example 3000 to 4000 – pound hydraulics,allowing a thinner wing.)

The Iroquois program broke more new ground than the Arrow. A whole book could be dedicated to finding out what really happened to it and why.

Manufacturing techniques and quality control became more exacting. Management skills and methods were learned. Thousands of people improved their abilities and pulled together. When you hear of everyday workers going into Avro early so that they could walk through the plant and see the progress of the Arrow, you can't help but be impressed. Something special was going on in Malton during those days!

Not only was the Arrow shot down – so was our pride and spirit.

It does not need to be repeated.

He Defends➡

"To relate the total development costs of such a program to a single Arrow is like saying that the first Edsel car cost the hundreds of millions of dollars the Ford company is reported to have spent on its design, tooling and marketing. . . . If you have a 1958 model car, I'm sure you don't consider it obsolete just because a later model is already on the way."

A/M W. A. CURTIS

Our Fastest Weapon . . .

'The Avro Arrow NOT Obsolete'

FINANCIAL POST — MAY 17 1958

It did NOT cost Canadian taxpayers $200 million just to put the first Arrow in the air.

Missiles are NOT the only threat against Canadian security.

These are the major points in a statement on Canadian defence policy and airplane costs made this week by Air Marshal W. A. Curtis, vice-president, A. V. Roe Canada Ltd.

Here is a digest of his address to the RCAF Benevolent Association in Ottawa:

One thing about the Arrow, it had capacity to grow. With inlet changes, new skin metallurgy and a Mach 3 Iroquois, voila a Mach 3 Arrow.

Sketch,
Marc André
Valiquette
collection

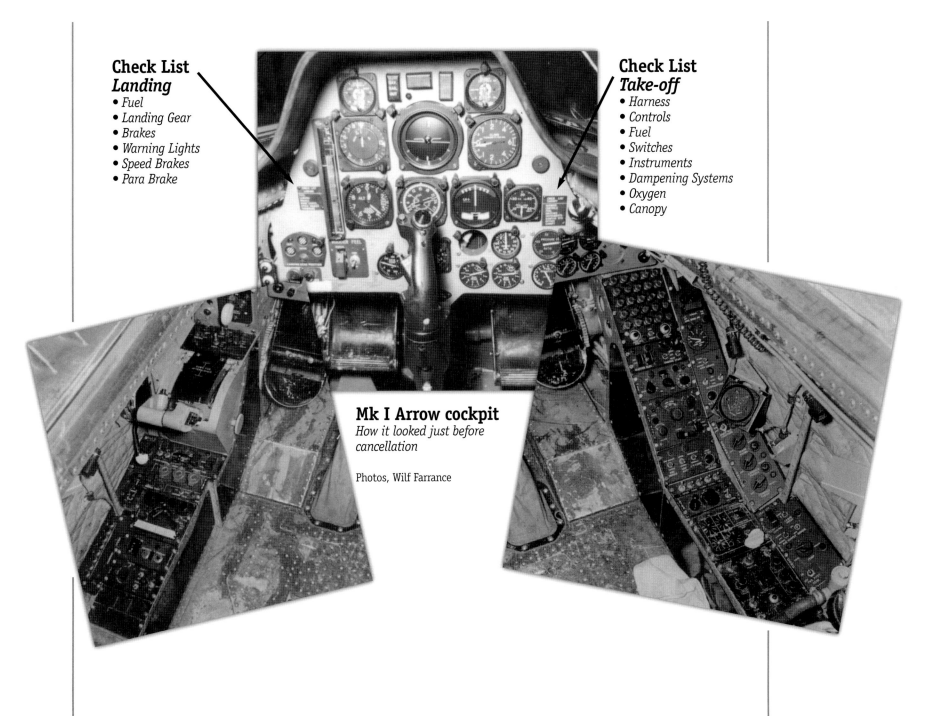

Check List
Landing
- *Fuel*
- *Landing Gear*
- *Brakes*
- *Warning Lights*
- *Speed Brakes*
- *Para Brake*

Check List
Take-off
- *Harness*
- *Controls*
- *Fuel*
- *Switches*
- *Instruments*
- *Dampening Systems*
- *Oxygen*
- *Canopy*

Mk I Arrow cockpit
How it looked just before cancellation

Photos, Wilf Farrance

Brett Reid

A beautiful colour cutaway of the Mk I Arrow, rendered by Brett Reid and published by Art & Design, Toronto (whereabouts unknown).

Photo, Peter Zuuring

The Arrow legacy

- Recovered parts
- Recovered plans, photos and other documentation
- Places - still intact
- A.V. Roe Canada spirit - pioneers, lateral thinkers and sci-fi dreamers
- And those who were there

The big pieces

The nose section of Arrow Mk II RL-206 at the National Aviation Museum, Ottawa. It went from Avro to the Institute for Aviation Medicine in Toronto to the National Museum of Science and Technology in Ottawa, then to the museum.

Mk I Arrow control boxes and a half-section Mk II aileron at the National Aviation Museum, Ottawa. Its route? From Avro to the National Research Council at Uplands airport, Ottawa, then to the museum.

Outer wings of Arrow Mk I RL-203 at the National Aviation Museum, Ottawa. Route: Avro to the National Research Council at Uplands airport, then to the museum.

Photos, Peter Zuuring

A J-75 P-3 jet engine from an Arrow Mk I, at the National Research Council, Ottawa. It went from Avro to the NRC; now it's at the National Aviation Museum.

An afterburner from a J-75 engine, at the Canadian Warplane Heritage Museum in Hamilton. Route: from Avro to the National Research Council to the McEwen scrapyard to the CWHM. It will go to the Arrow Alliance.

An Iroquois development engine at the Canadian Warplane Heritage Museum in Hamilton, Ont. It travelled from Avro to the National Research Council, next to the McEwen scrapyard in Moncton, N.B., then to the CWHM. Now it's back at the NRC, undergoing restoration.

An Arrow Mk II Iroquois, X-104, engine at the National Aviation Museum. From Orenda Engines at Malton, Ont., to the National Research Council, then to the museum.

Photos, Peter Zuuring

Smaller pieces
Results of the Mac Kuhring initiative

Arrow spare parts including this canopy, on a pallet at a National Aviation Museum warehouse in Ottawa.

Iroquois low-pressure turbine, in storage building no. 22 at the National Research Council, Ottawa.

Iroquois turbine hub in mint condition, still wrapped in its original oiled paper.

Arrow Mk II simulator and instrumentation. They went from Avro to the Institute for Aviation Medicine in Toronto to the National Aviation Museum in Ottawa.

Photos, Peter Zuuring

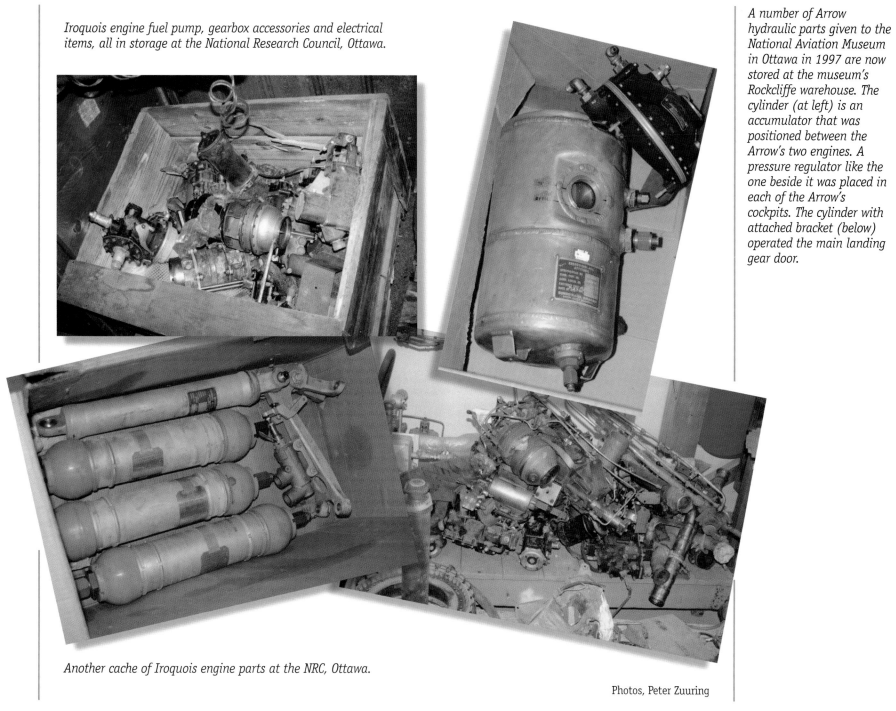

Iroquois engine fuel pump, gearbox accessories and electrical items, all in storage at the National Research Council, Ottawa.

A number of Arrow hydraulic parts given to the National Aviation Museum in Ottawa in 1997 are now stored at the museum's Rockcliffe warehouse. The cylinder (at left) is an accumulator that was positioned between the Arrow's two engines. A pressure regulator like the one beside it was placed in each of the Arrow's cockpits. The cylinder with attached bracket (below) operated the main landing gear door.

Another cache of Iroquois engine parts at the NRC, Ottawa.

and more pieces

Hydraulic actuator,
in new condition.

Hot-air de-icing control valve for inlet and
bullet of the Iroquois.

Iroquois engine fuel
pumps and gear box.

Recently uncovered Mk II
air brakes, mint condition.
There are two!

Photos, Peter Zuuring

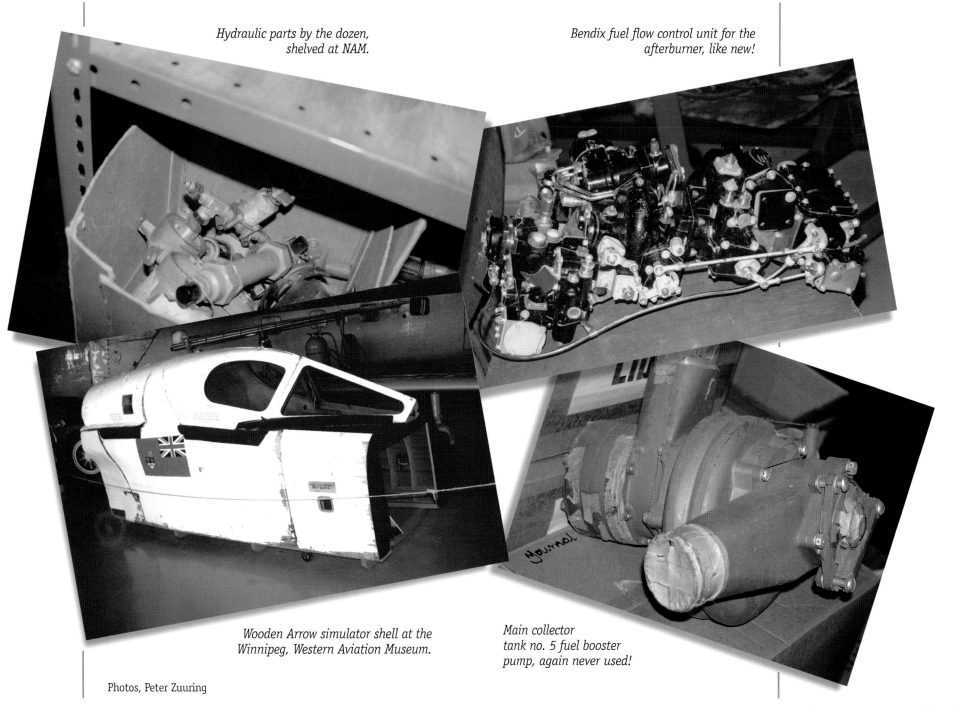

Hydraulic parts by the dozen, shelved at NAM.

Bendix fuel flow control unit for the afterburner, like new!

Wooden Arrow simulator shell at the Winnipeg, Western Aviation Museum.

Main collector tank no. 5 fuel booster pump, again never used!

Photos, Peter Zuuring

Arrow Mk II, pilot's position

Photo, Peter Zuuring, NAM

The business end of any aircraft is naturally the cockpit. At the on-set of the Arrow program, it was recognized that the advanced performance capabilities of the Arrow called for advanced flight-control instrumentation. For the Mk II version, the Astra fire control and Sparrow II missile systems were chosen by the RCAF. Avro agreed to manage the development of the overall "weapons system," although it only had direct control over the airframe and engine, not the fire control or missile. RCA of the U.S. and Minneapolis/Honeywell were two of the main suppliers for Astra and its associated controls. Avro and RCA jointly prepared a report on the instrumentation design and manufacture for the Arrow Mk II system. Both the pilot's and the observer's instruments were covered by the report. These were presented at the September 17, 1958 Mk II mock-up conference at Avro in Malton. Apparently the work progressed quite slowly and was way behind schedule by the fall of 1958 when the Sparrow/Astra programs were cancelled. Wilf Farrance, in charge of cockpit implementation at the time, told me that there was a scramble to equip the cockpits with replacements. The early Mk I layouts were of a much more conventional style. For example, true ground speed could only be determined after a flight by reviewing the radar traces. A new Mach meter, fed by datalink was to be installed

Arrow Mk II, observer's position

in RL-206. Most front panel instruments were conventional other that the horizontal situation and destination indicators.

The pilot normally handled the control stick with his right hand. Consequently, critical equipment requiring hand control was placed on the left console.

Because the position of the throttle quadrant is fixed, remaining left-hand controls were arranged forward and behind in order of their importance. The aircraft emergency and engine functions are located just behind the throttle, followed by the automatic flight control panel and surface position indicator. Farthest forward is the landing gear control just ahead of the anti-skid, canopy and light switches

Other than the engine start switches, the right console provides room for instruments needing excellent visibility (the right stays on the stick). Therefore warning lights, oxygen level, cockpit pressure and weapons system status components are placed there.

The rear cockpit also consists of a central, left and right consoles. The front panel contained the radar indicator and associated equipment needed to navigate the Arrow. The side panels contained supporting equipment, a hand control for target acquisition with arm rest for comfort. Normal housekeeping function of the aircraft could be monitored by the observer as much as the pilot could in the cockpit. Bailout indicators were prominent on both front panels. Details of the pilot and observer positions follow on the next two pages.

Photo,
Peter Zuuring, NAM

The photographs, charts and diagrams here and on the following pages form the most complete picture yet of what the Arrow Mk I, Mk II and Mk II simulator looked like.

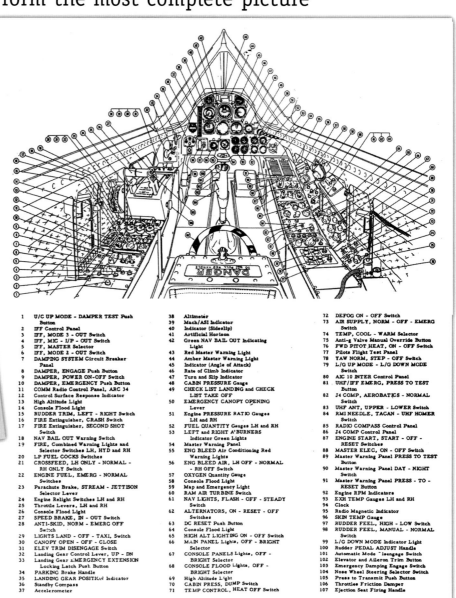

Photo, Wilf Farrance

The real Mk I cockpit as it was flown. Note the G-meter, a vertical tube and ball beside the air speed indicator. Engine indicators are at the bottom right. The two meters at the top are for sideslip and angle of attack. The diagram at right is supposed to be a Mk II layout but it does not correspond to Arrow RL-206.

1	U/C UP MODE - DAMPER TEST Push Button
2	IFF Control Panel
3	IFF, MODE 3 - OUT Switch
4	IFF, MIC - I/P - OUT Switch
5	IFF, MASTER Selector
6	IFF, MODE 2 - OUT Switch
7	DAMPING SYSTEM Circuit Breaker Panel
8	DAMPER, ENGAGE Push Button
9	DAMPER, POWER ON-OFF Switch
10	DAMPER, EMERGENCY Push Button
11	COMM Radio Control Panel, ARC 34
12	Control Surface Response Indicator
13	High Altitude Light
14	Console Flood Light
15	RUDDER TRIM, LEFT - RIGHT Switch
16	FIRE Extinguisher, CRASH Switch
17	FIRE Extinguisher, SECOND SHOT Switch
18	NAV BAIL OUT Warning Switch
19	FIRE, Combined Warning Lights and Selector Switches LH, HYD and RH
20	LP FUEL COCKS Switches
21	CROSSFEED, LH ONLY - NORMAL - RH ONLY Switch
22	ENGINE FUEL, EMERG - NORMAL Switches
23	Parachute Brake, STREAM - JETTISON Selector Lever
24	Engine Relight Switches LH and RH
25	Throttle Levers, LH and RH
26	Console Flood Light
27	SPEED BRAKE, IN - OUT Switch
28	ANTI-SKID, NORM - EMERG OFF Switch
29	LIGHTS LAND - OFF - TAXI, Switch
30	CANOPY OPEN - OFF - CLOSE
31	ELEV TRIM DISENGAGE Switch
32	Landing Gear Control Lever, UP - DN
33	Landing Gear EMERGENCY EXTENSION Locking Latch Push Button
34	PARKING Brake Handle
35	LANDING GEAR POSITION Indicator
36	Standby Compass
37	Accelerometer
38	Altimeter
39	Mach/ASI Indicator
40	Indicator (Sideslip)
41	Artificial Horizon
42	Green NAV BAIL OUT Indicating Light
43	Red Master Warning Light
44	Amber Master Warning Light
45	Indicator (Angle of Attack)
46	Rate of Climb Indicator
47	Turn and Slip Indicator
48	CABIN PRESSURE Gauge
49	CHECK LIST LANDING and CHECK LIST TAKE OFF
50	EMERGENCY CANOPY OPENING Lever
51	Engine PRESSURE RATIO Gauges LH and RH
52	FUEL QUANTITY Gauges LH and RH
53	LEFT and RIGHT A'BURNERS Indicator Green Lights
54	Master Warning Panel
55	ENG BLEED Air Conditioning Red Warning Lights
56	ENG BLEED AIR, LH OFF - NORMAL - RH OFF Switch
57	OXYGEN Quantity Gauge
58	Console Flood Light
59	Map and Emergency Light
60	RAM AIR TURBINE Switch
61	NAV LIGHTS, FLASH - OFF - STEADY Switch
62	ALTERNATORS, ON - RESET - OFF Switches
63	DC RESET Push Button
64	Console Flood Light
65	HIGH ALT LIGHTING ON - OFF Switch
66	MAIN PANEL Lights, OFF - BRIGHT Selector
67	CONSOLE PANELS Lights, OFF - BRIGHT Selector
68	CONSOLE FLOOD Lights, OFF - BRIGHT Selector
69	High Altitude Light
70	CABIN PRESS, DUMP Switch
71	TEMP CONTROL, HEAT OFF Switch
72	DEFOG ON - OFF Switch
73	AIR SUPPLY, NORM - OFF - EMERG Switch
74	TEMP, COOL - WARM Selector
75	Anti-g Valve Manual Override Button
76	FWD PITOT HEAT, ON - OFF Switch
77	Pilots Flight Test Panel
78	YAW NORM, STEP - OFF Switch
79	L/G UP MODE - L/G DOWN MODE Switch
80	AJC 10 INTER Control Panel
81	UHF/IFF EMERG, PRESS TO TEST Button
82	J4 COMP, AEROBATICS - NORMAL Switch
83	UHF ANT, UPPER - LOWER Switch
84	RMI NEEDLE, TACAN - UHF HOMER Switch
85	RADIO COMPASS Control Panel
86	J4 COMP Control Panel
87	ENGINE START, START - OFF - RESET Switches
88	MASTER ELEC, ON - OFF Switch
89	Master Warning Panel PRESS TO TEST Button
90	Master Warning Panel DAY - NIGHT Switch
91	Master Warning Panel PRESS - TO - RESET Button
92	Engine RPM Indicators
93	EXH TEMP Gauges LH and RH
94	Clock
95	Radio Magnetic Indicator
96	SKIN TEMP Gauge
97	RUDDER FEEL, HIGH - LOW Switch
98	RUDDER FEEL, MANUAL - NORMAL Switch
99	L/G DOWN MODE Indicator Light
100	Rudder Pedal ADJUST Handle
101	Automatic Mode Disengage Switch
102	Elevator and Aileron Trim Button
103	Emergency Damping Engage Switch
104	Nose Wheel Steering Selector Switch
105	Press to Transmit Push Button
106	Throttles Friction Damper
107	Ejection Seat Firing Handle

PILOT'S COCKPIT LAYOUT

Chart, Peter Brennan

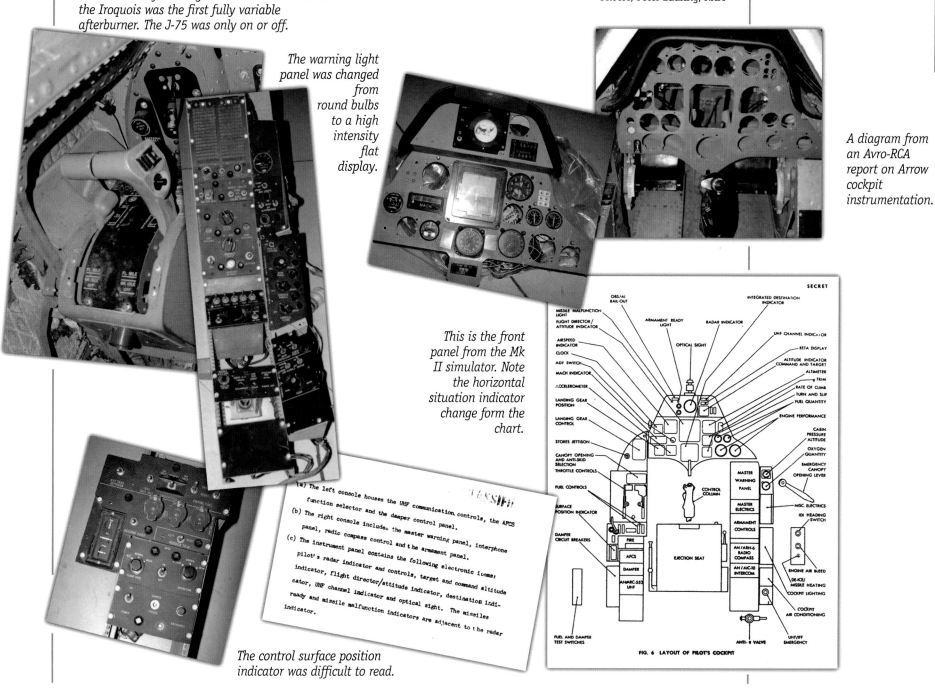

There were major changes to the throttle in that the Iroquois was the first fully variable afterburner. The J-75 was only on or off.

Photos, Peter Zuuring, NAM

The warning light panel was changed from round bulbs to a high intensity flat display.

A diagram from an Avro-RCA report on Arrow cockpit instrumentation.

This is the front panel from the Mk II simulator. Note the horizontal situation indicator change form the chart.

(a) The left console houses the UHF communication controls, the AFCS function selector and the damper control panel.

(b) The right console includes the master warning panel, interphone panel, radio compass control and the armament panel.

(c) The instrument panel contains the following electronic items: pilot's radar indicator and controls, target and command altitude indicator, flight director/attitude indicator, destination indicator, UHF channel indicator and optical sight. The missiles ready and missile malfunction indicators are adjacent to the radar indicator.

The control surface position indicator was difficult to read.

SECRET

OBS/AI BAIL-OUT
MISSILE MALFUNCTION LIGHT
FLIGHT DIRECTOR / ATTITUDE INDICATOR
INTEGRATED DESTINATION INDICATOR
ARMAMENT READY LIGHT
RADAR INDICATOR
UHF CHANNEL INDICATOR
AIRSPEED INDICATOR
OPTICAL SIGHT
BETA DISPLAY
CLOCK
ALTITUDE INDICATOR COMMAND AND TARGET
ADF SWITCH
ALTIMETER
MACH INDICATOR
g TRIM
RATE OF CLIMB
ACCELEROMETER
TURN AND SLIP
FUEL QUANTITY
LANDING GEAR POSITION
ENGINE PERFORMANCE
LANDING GEAR CONTROL
CABIN PRESSURE ALTITUDE
OXYGEN QUANTITY
STORES JETTISON
EMERGENCY CANOPY OPENING LEVER
CANOPY OPENING AND ANTI-SKID SELECTION
THROTTLE CONTROLS
MASTER WARNING PANEL
FUEL CONTROLS
MASTER ELECTRICS
MISC ELECTRICS
SURFACE POSITION INDICATOR
ARMAMENT CONTROLS
IDI HEADING SWITCH
CONTROL COLUMN
DAMPER CIRCUIT BREAKERS
FIRE
AFCS
AN/ARN-6 RADIO COMPASS
DAMPER
AN/AIC-10 INTERCOM
ANARC-552 UHF
EJECTION SEAT
ENGINE AIR BLEED
DE-ICE/ MISSILE HEATING
COCKPIT LIGHTING
COCKPIT AIR CONDITIONING
FUEL AND DAMPER TEST SWITCHES
ANTI-g VALVE
UHF/IFF EMERGENCY

FIG. 6 LAYOUT OF PILOT'S COCKPIT

With the Arrow's canopy closed, the observer was tightly enclosed in a relatively small workspace. The RCAF expressed some unhappiness with the lack of visibility. Only one flight was recorded with an observer on board. The Arrow could operate independently of ground control or it could operate under "SAGE" a ground-based, radar-directed guidance system. The observer would scan the sky ahead with a hand-operated radar dish mounted in the nose. If a target was acquired, an intercept heading was calculated with time and distance indicated. The Arrow Mk II was to be equipped with infrared heat trail-seeking devices to assist detection of enemy aircraft.

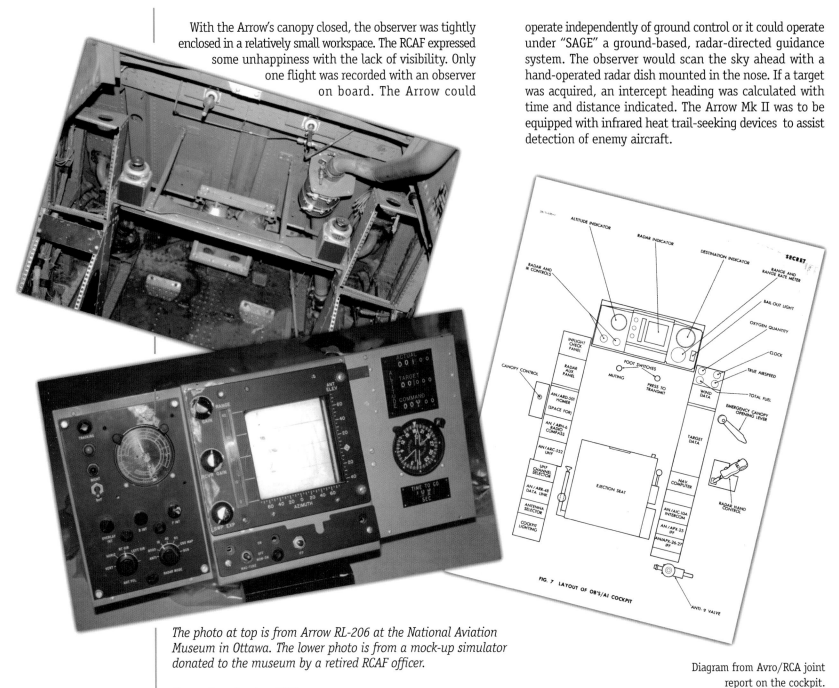

The photo at top is from Arrow RL-206 at the National Aviation Museum in Ottawa. The lower photo is from a mock-up simulator donated to the museum by a retired RCAF officer.

Photos, Peter Zuuring, NAM

Diagram from Avro/RCA joint report on the cockpit.

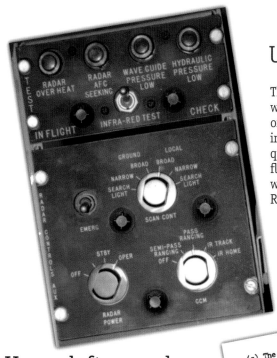

Upper left console

Upper right console

The upper right console included warning lights for cabin pressure, oxygen reserve and bailout indicator. It also showed fuel quantities (not visible here) and flight data. Bearing and distance were shown in the Position Data Reference panel.

Lower left console

(a) The left console contains the data link control, UHF communication controls, radio compass control, radar homer control and indicator space provision only, antenna selector, auxiliary radar control panel and radar test panel. A signal data converter unit is installed under the forward end of the left console.

(b) The right console incorporates the wind data display, target data display, interphone controls, IFF controls, and the navigation computer controls. The radar hand control is installed above the right console and a signal data converter unit is located under the forward end of the right console.

(c) The OBS/AI's instrument panel contains the radar indicator and controls, destination indicator, radar/IR control panel, range and range rate meter, target and command altitude indicator and UHF channel indicator.

Lower right console

Mk II instrument, observer's position at NAM.

Photos, Peter Zuuring

The CF-100 ejection path required the one-piece canopy be blown upward and backward so the pilots could escape. Wind forces were such that pilots or observers could not pull the handle above their heads to release the ejection seat. Because of this poor track record, great effort was made, in the case of the Arrow, to make ejection fast and safe.

Clamshell canopy and ejection

On the right, the Martin-Baker Mk 5c ejection seat used in the Arrow.

Photo, W.Farrance

Below, the external switches that opened the canopy.

Photo, Peter Zuuring, NAM

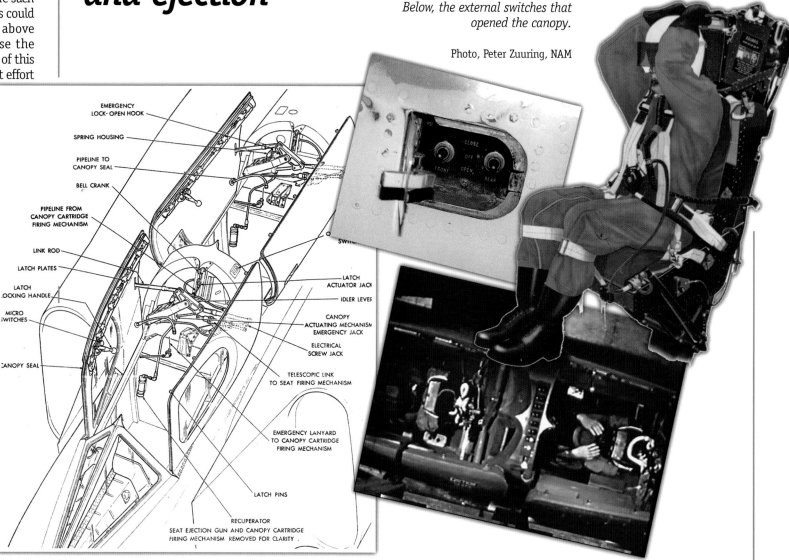

EMERGENCY LOCK-OPEN HOOK

SPRING HOUSING

PIPELINE TO CANOPY SEAL

BELL CRANK

PIPELINE FROM CANOPY CARTRIDGE FIRING MECHANISM

LINK ROD

LATCH PLATES

LATCH LOCKING HANDLE

MICRO SWITCHES

CANOPY SEAL

SWITCH

LATCH ACTUATOR JACK

IDLER LEVER

CANOPY ACTUATING MECHANISM EMERGENCY JACK

ELECTRICAL SCREW JACK

TELESCOPIC LINK TO SEAT FIRING MECHANISM

EMERGENCY LANYARD TO CANOPY CARTRIDGE FIRING MECHANISM

LATCH PINS

RECUPERATOR

SEAT EJECTION GUN AND CANOPY CARTRIDGE FIRING MECHANISM REMOVED FOR CLARITY.

Numerous trials such as this top view of the Arrow cockpits show the process and ejection mechanism at work. The overhead pull was designed to keep the back straight.

Photo, Aviation Videos

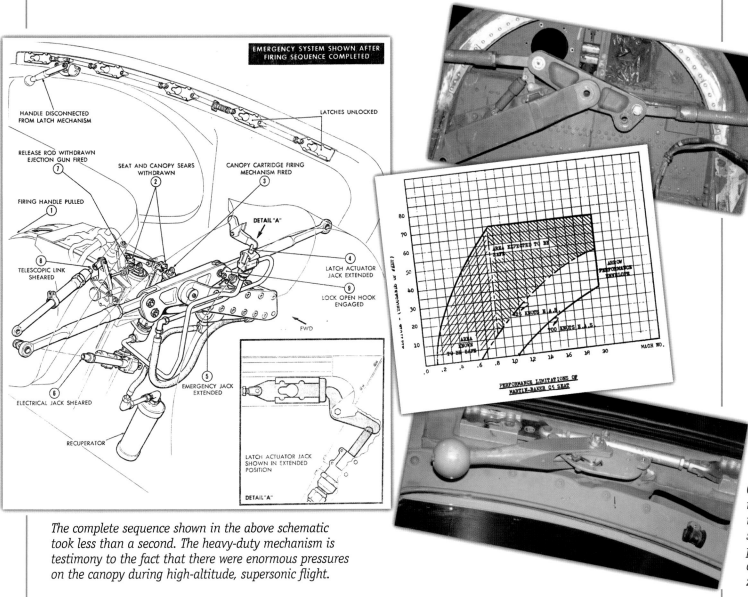

EMERGENCY SYSTEM SHOWN AFTER
FIRING SEQUENCE COMPLETED

HANDLE DISCONNECTED
FROM LATCH MECHANISM

LATCHES UNLOCKED

RELEASE ROD WITHDRAWN
EJECTION GUN FIRED
(7)

SEAT AND CANOPY SEARS
WITHDRAWN
(2)

CANOPY CARTRIDGE FIRING
MECHANISM FIRED
(3)

FIRING HANDLE PULLED
(1)

DETAIL "A"

(8)
TELESCOPIC LINK
SHEARED

(4)
LATCH ACTUATOR
JACK EXTENDED

(9)
LOCK OPEN HOOK
ENGAGED

FWD

(6)
ELECTRICAL JACK SHEARED

(5)
EMERGENCY JACK
EXTENDED

RECUPERATOR

LATCH ACTUATOR JACK
SHOWN IN EXTENDED
POSITION

DETAIL "A"

PERFORMANCE LIMITATIONS OF
MARTIN-BAKER C5 SEAT

The observer's canopy toggle mechanism. The plastic sheet just above it covers blown-in doors that retained cabin pressure at altitude.

Photo, Peter Zuuring, NAM

The complete sequence shown in the above schematic took less than a second. The heavy-duty mechanism is testimony to the fact that there were enormous pressures on the canopy during high-altitude, supersonic flight.

Diagram, NRC, Mk I Service manual

Once the handle was closed, it must be pulled forward and rotated further to inflate the seals that ensured a pressurized cabin. The above chart shows the safe ejection zone.

Photo, Peter Zuuring, NAM Chart, the Mk I Service manual NRC

Stick and pedal

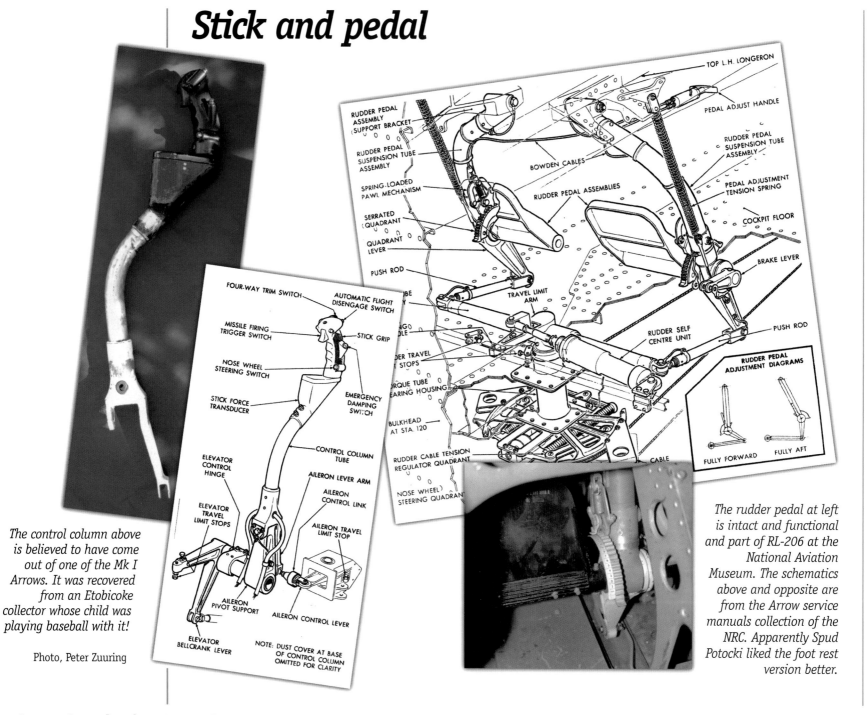

Schematic labels (right diagram):

TOP L.H. LONGERON
PEDAL ADJUST HANDLE
RUDDER PEDAL ASSEMBLY (SUPPORT BRACKET)
RUDDER PEDAL SUSPENSION TUBE ASSEMBLY
RUDDER PEDAL SUSPENSION TUBE ASSEMBLY
BOWDEN CABLES
PEDAL ADJUSTMENT TENSION SPRING
SPRING-LOADED PAWL MECHANISM
RUDDER PEDAL ASSEMBLIES
COCKPIT FLOOR
SERRATED QUADRANT
QUADRANT LEVER
PUSH ROD
TRAVEL LIMIT ARM
BRAKE LEVER
RUDDER SELF CENTRE UNIT
PUSH ROD
RUDDER TRAVEL STOPS
TORQUE TUBE BEARING HOUSING
BULKHEAD AT STA. 120
RUDDER CABLE TENSION REGULATOR QUADRANT
NOSE WHEEL STEERING QUADRANT
CABLE
RUDDER PEDAL ADJUSTMENT DIAGRAMS
FULLY FORWARD   FULLY AFT

Schematic labels (stick grip diagram):

FOUR-WAY TRIM SWITCH
AUTOMATIC FLIGHT DISENGAGE SWITCH
MISSILE FIRING TRIGGER SWITCH
STICK GRIP
NOSE WHEEL STEERING SWITCH
STICK FORCE TRANSDUCER
EMERGENCY DAMPING SWITCH
CONTROL COLUMN TUBE
ELEVATOR CONTROL HINGE
AILERON LEVER ARM
AILERON CONTROL LINK
ELEVATOR TRAVEL LIMIT STOPS
AILERON TRAVEL LIMIT STOP
AILERON PIVOT SUPPORT
AILERON CONTROL LEVER
ELEVATOR BELLCRANK LEVER
NOTE: DUST COVER AT BASE OF CONTROL COLUMN OMITTED FOR CLARITY

The control column above is believed to have come out of one of the Mk I Arrows. It was recovered from an Etobicoke collector whose child was playing baseball with it!

Photo, Peter Zuuring

The rudder pedal at left is intact and functional and part of RL-206 at the National Aviation Museum. The schematics above and opposite are from the Arrow service manuals collection of the NRC. Apparently Spud Potocki liked the foot rest version better.

Control surface mechanism

The large casting levers that connected the control box and the control surface are clearly visible in these pictures. The outer wing was so thin that streamlined cowlings were required to cover the linkage mechanism. The half aileron at left shows the internal structure. The control surfaces were not longer than four feet and were built in sections to prevent buckling in use.

Photo, Peter Zuuring, NAM

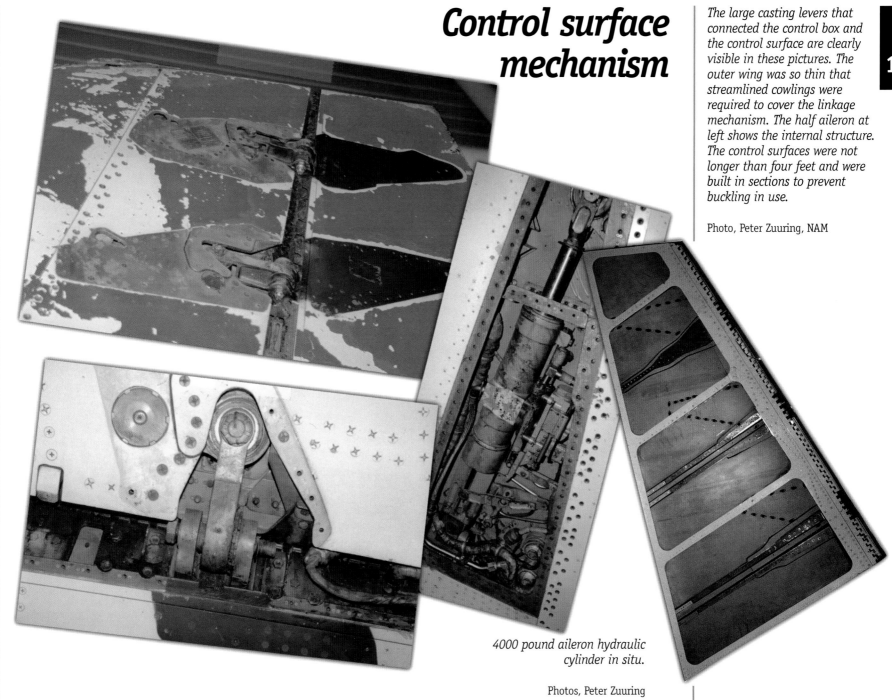

4000 pound aileron hydraulic cylinder in situ.

Photos, Peter Zuuring

Aileron and rudder

The photo shows the aileron cable quadrant, black trim and feel unit, and the hydraulic booster jack, installed to help overcome system friction causing high breakout forces at the stick. The linkage mechanisms are clear as is the schematic of the damping system. Supersonic planes need irreversible controls since aerodynamic forces are too great to be held manually.

Photo, RL-206 nose wheel well at NAM, Peter Zuuring

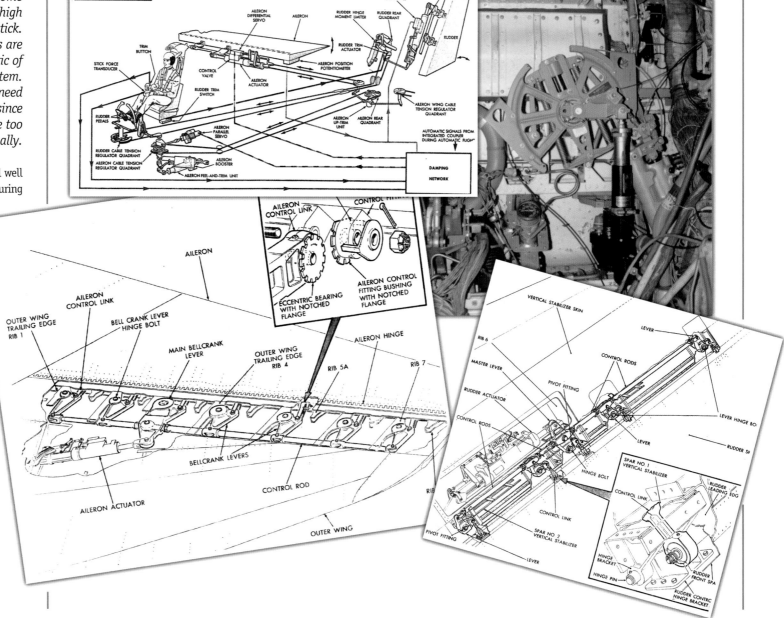

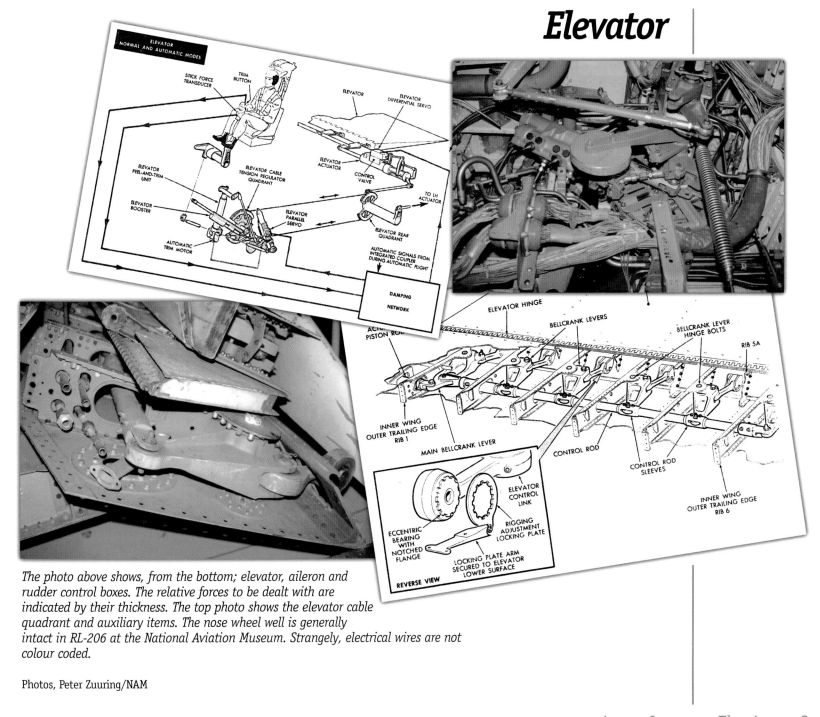

The photo above shows, from the bottom; elevator, aileron and rudder control boxes. The relative forces to be dealt with are indicated by their thickness. The top photo shows the elevator cable quadrant and auxiliary items. The nose wheel well is generally intact in RL-206 at the National Aviation Museum. Strangely, electrical wires are not colour coded.

Photos, Peter Zuuring/NAM

The main landing gear of the Arrow had to go through three movements as it retracted, i.e., shortening, twisting and bogie wheel pull up, so that it could fit snugly into the very thin wing. The 4000 pound utility hydraulic system was chosen so that the retraction cylinder could be small enough to fit into the wing. The photo at right shows RL-201 being repaired after its June 1958 accident. The parts that were worked on are clearly visible. Brake efficiency was borderline from the start. Many a flight was delayed because differential braking was used to steer the aircraft. On some landings, the brake housing got so overheated that the tires blew.

The left side landing gear schematic complements the photo on the right. Note the hydraulic swivel joints as opposed to flexible tubing.

Drawing, Mk I Service Manual, NRC

Main landing gear

The sheer size of the Arrow's wing is easily seen in the angle of this photo of RL-201. The details of the gear can be traced on the schematic. Note the depth of the notch!

Photo, L. Wilkinson

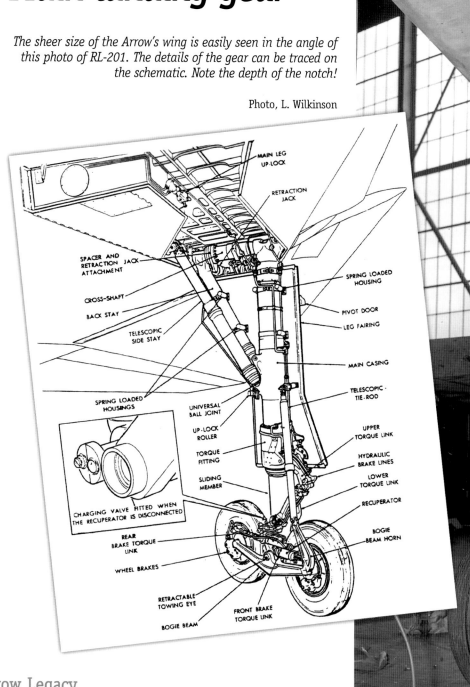

MAIN LEG UP-LOCK

RETRACTION JACK

SPACER AND RETRACTION JACK ATTACHMENT

SPRING LOADED HOUSING

CROSS-SHAFT

PIVOT DOOR

BACK STAY

LEG FAIRING

TELESCOPIC SIDE STAY

MAIN CASING

SPRING LOADED HOUSINGS

TELESCOPIC TIE-ROD

UNIVERSAL BALL JOINT

UP-LOCK ROLLER

UPPER TORQUE LINK

TORQUE FITTING

HYDRAULIC BRAKE LINES

SLIDING MEMBER

LOWER TORQUE LINK

RECUPERATOR

CHARGING VALVE FITTED WHEN THE RECUPERATOR IS DISCONNECTED

REAR BRAKE TORQUE LINK

BOGIE BEAM HORN

WHEEL BRAKES

RETRACTABLE TOWING EYE

FRONT BRAKE TORQUE LINK

BOGIE BEAM

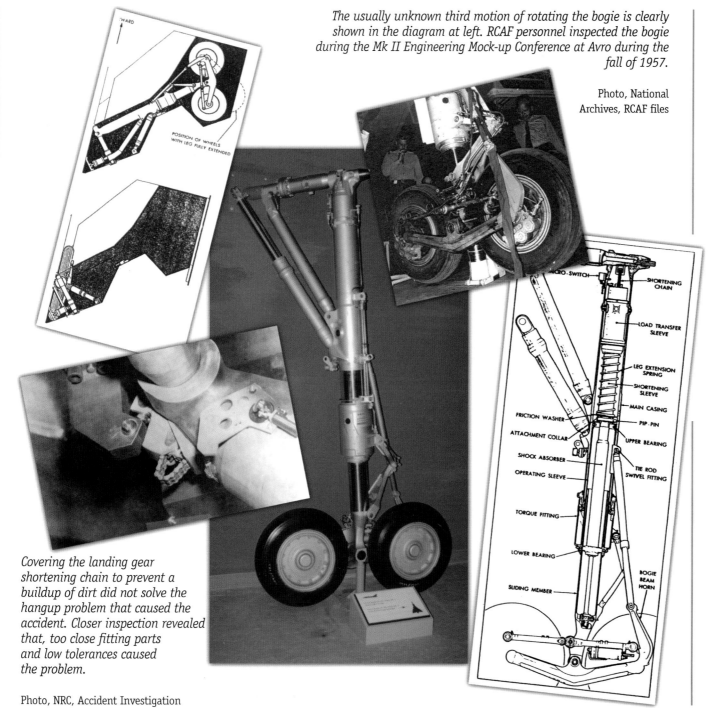

The usually unknown third motion of rotating the bogie is clearly shown in the diagram at left. RCAF personnel inspected the bogie during the Mk II Engineering Mock-up Conference at Avro during the fall of 1957.

Photo, National
Archives, RCAF files

UPWARD

POSITION OF WHEELS
WITH LEG FULLY EXTENDED

Covering the landing gear shortening chain to prevent a buildup of dirt did not solve the hangup problem that caused the accident. Closer inspection revealed that, too close fitting parts and low tolerances caused the problem.

Photo, NRC, Accident Investigation

MICRO-SWITCH

SHORTENING CHAIN

LOAD TRANSFER SLEEVE

LEG EXTENSION SPRING

SHORTENING SLEEVE

MAIN CASING

FRICTION WASHER

PIP-PIN

ATTACHMENT COLLAR

UPPER BEARING

SHOCK ABSORBER

TIE ROD SWIVEL FITTING

OPERATING SLEEVE

TORQUE FITTING

LOWER BEARING

SLIDING MEMBER

BOGIE BEAM HORN

Jan Zurakowski told me that when Dowty, the manufacturer of the main gear, first announced the design, one of the engineers is reported to have said that he had designed the most complicated gear ever. Jan kept quiet but said to himself, "As a test pilot I wish he had told me that it was the simplest design." It seems that landing gear is always trouble in an aircraft development program. The Jetliner belly-landed because the Dowty gear hung up. The CF-100 had gear problems with lock mechanisms. Jan recalls landing and as he touched down, retraction started. He was blamed until a mechanic slapped the fuselage after reporting all was well, and the gear started to retract.

The gear, on the left, is in NAM, saved by the Kuhring initiative.

Photo, Peter Zuuring, and Drawing NRC, Mk I manuals

197

Nose gear

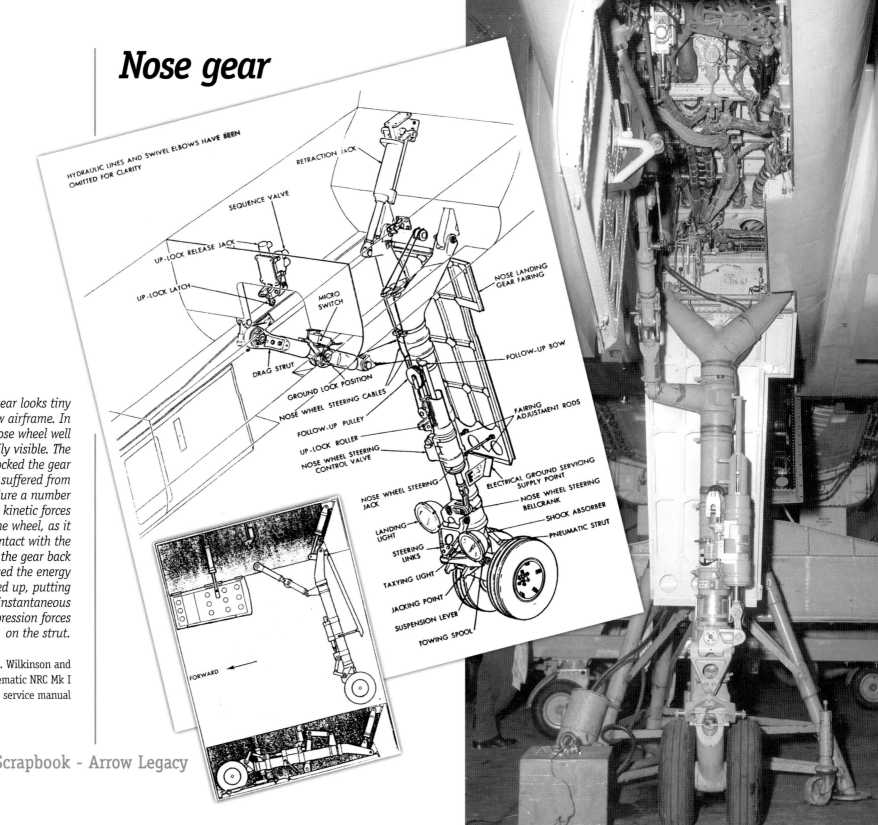

HYDRAULIC LINES AND SWIVEL ELBOWS HAVE BEEN OMITTED FOR CLARITY

RETRACTION JACK

SEQUENCE VALVE

UP-LOCK RELEASE JACK

UP-LOCK LATCH

MICRO SWITCH

DRAG STRUT

GROUND LOCK POSITION

NOSE WHEEL STEERING CABLES

FOLLOW-UP PULLEY

UP-LOCK ROLLER

NOSE WHEEL STEERING CONTROL VALVE

NOSE WHEEL STEERING JACK

LANDING LIGHT

STEERING LINKS

TAXYING LIGHT

JACKING POINT

SUSPENSION LEVER

TOWING SPOOL

NOSE LANDING GEAR FAIRING

FOLLOW-UP BOW

FAIRING ADJUSTMENT RODS

ELECTRICAL GROUND SERVICING SUPPLY POINT

NOSE WHEEL STEERING BELLCRANK

SHOCK ABSORBER

PNEUMATIC STRUT

FORWARD

The front nose gear looks tiny beside the Arrow airframe. In the photo, the nose wheel well details are easily visible. The drag strut that locked the gear in place suffered from compression failure a number of times. The kinetic forces spinning up the wheel, as it made contact with the runway, pulled the gear back and then released the energy as the wheel sped up, putting large instantaneous compression forces on the strut.

Photo, L. Wilkinson and schematic NRC Mk I service manual

The nose wheel was pulled up into the well, locked and stowed snugly as the schematic (opposite) shows. The photos were taken in the Lancaster Road storage facility of the National Aviation Museum in Ottawa. Many of the Mac Kuhring parts found their way there over time. Many are not yet registered, simply because their history is not well known. Recently, air brakes, air-to-air heat exchangers from the air conditioning equipment and many smaller pieces from the fuel and emergency barking system were found.

Nose wheel steering was attempted during the early taxi trials. To my knowledge it was abandoned and the wheel allowed to caster and follow the track created by main gear differential braking. Take-off did not require steering since the bogie tandem wheels kept the plane in line once the roll had been initiated. A cable and follower system was tried in which the pilot engaged nose wheel steering from the control grip. Centering of the rudder pedals was required before steering was locked in. All the drawings showed nose wheel lights in place for taxiing and landing. None were installed on RL-206 or for that matter on any of the Mk Is.

Photo, Peter Zuuring,
Drawing NRC, Mk I Service manuals

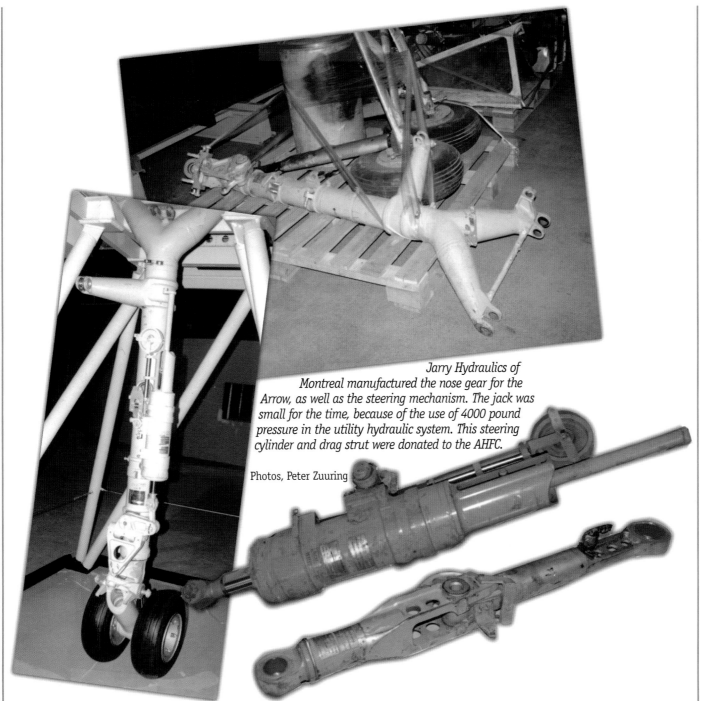

Jarry Hydraulics of Montreal manufactured the nose gear for the Arrow, as well as the steering mechanism. The jack was small for the time, because of the use of 4000 pound pressure in the utility hydraulic system. This steering cylinder and drag strut were donated to the AHFC.

Photos, Peter Zuuring

The Arrow, when first designed, was to have engines that dropped out the bottom for easy change and service access, hence the overhead wing design. It became apparent that, due to the high operating temperatures and the need to cool the engine, a tunnel construction was needed, forcing rear entry and exit. A rail system was chosen that supported the engine on one side as it was pushed off the cradle dolly. Five mounting points were designed that would accommodate the various load conditions, but mainly it was hung from the inner-wing box structure. A large central spigot, toward the front of the engine, transferred forward thrust to the airframe. Suspension of the inboard side took care of lateral forces while the rear two side supports accommodated longitudinal changes in dimension by as much as four inches at operating temperatures. The rear central attachment aligned the thrust direction with the airframe through an off-set cam.

Photo, L. Wilkinson

Mounting the Iroquois...

The photo at right, shows the central spigot, part of A-104 Iroquois engine at NAM. The central mount and inboard side supports are clearly indicated on the schematic at right. The engine was literally suspended from the centre wing. In this manner the engine would not be distorted as the wing flexed, which it did.

Photo, Peter Zuuring, NAM

The engine throttle connections could be made from either side.

Drawing NRC, Mk I
Service Manual

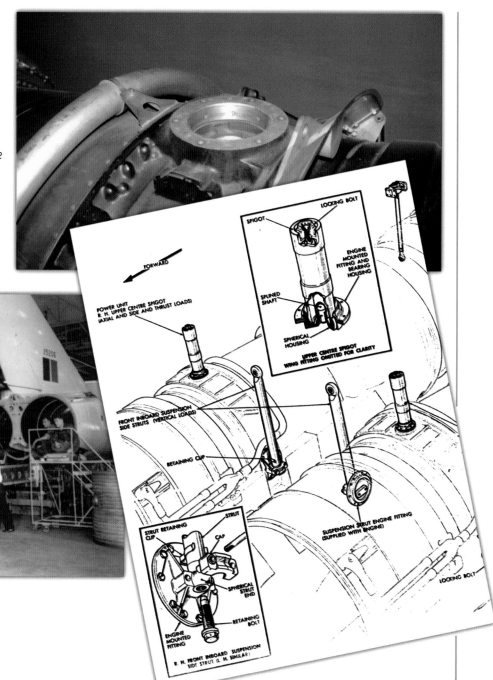

The drawing shows the rail system used to install the engine. The weight of the Iroquois was about 4500 pounds, some 1500 pounds less than the Pratt & Whitney J-75. All these mounting brackets had to pass through the titanium tunnel walls. All accessories had to be hooked up, including the gear box drive shafts to the hydraulic and fuel pumps. Considering the operating temperatures and thrust forces at play, the fact that airframe distortions could not be transmitted to the engine and that the engine expanded while operating, it is amazing that the tremendous forces available from the engines were harnessed as they were. The photo below and at right pictures the side mounts as they existed.

A-104 at NAM...in mint condition!

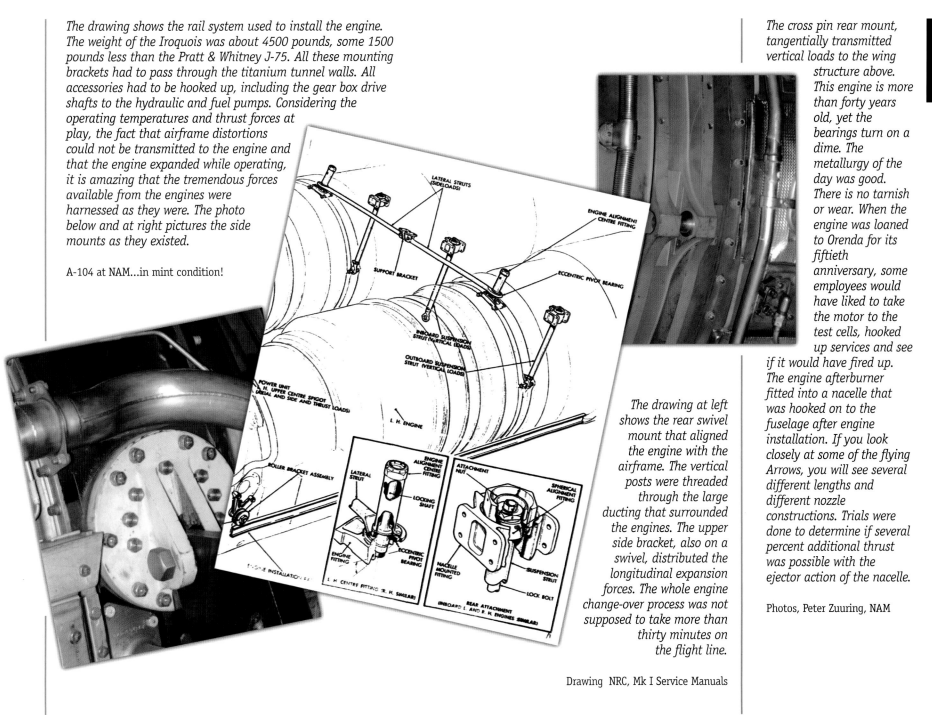

The drawing at left shows the rear swivel mount that aligned the engine with the airframe. The vertical posts were threaded through the large ducting that surrounded the engines. The upper side bracket, also on a swivel, distributed the longitudinal expansion forces. The whole engine change-over process was not supposed to take more than thirty minutes on the flight line.

Drawing NRC, Mk I Service Manuals

The cross pin rear mount, tangentially transmitted vertical loads to the wing structure above. This engine is more than forty years old, yet the bearings turn on a dime. The metallurgy of the day was good. There is no tarnish or wear. When the engine was loaned to Orenda for its fiftieth anniversary, some employees would have liked to take the motor to the test cells, hooked up services and see if it would have fired up. The engine afterburner fitted into a nacelle that was hooked on to the fuselage after engine installation. If you look closely at some of the flying Arrows, you will see several different lengths and different nozzle constructions. Trials were done to determine if several percent additional thrust was possible with the ejector action of the nacelle.

Photos, Peter Zuuring, NAM

A special fuel test rig simulated all flying aspects, except dynamic loadings, to be encountered while flying the envelope of the Arrow. All eight tanks could be accessed, altitudes simulated, fuel temperatures and their effects on operations tested, and the pressurization no-air pickup points and proportioning system evaluated. The building still stands today on Airport Road at Derry.

Fuel and relight system

Throttle positions are self evident. Air brake extension and push-to-talk button are on the side. Note the variable idle and afterburning positions.

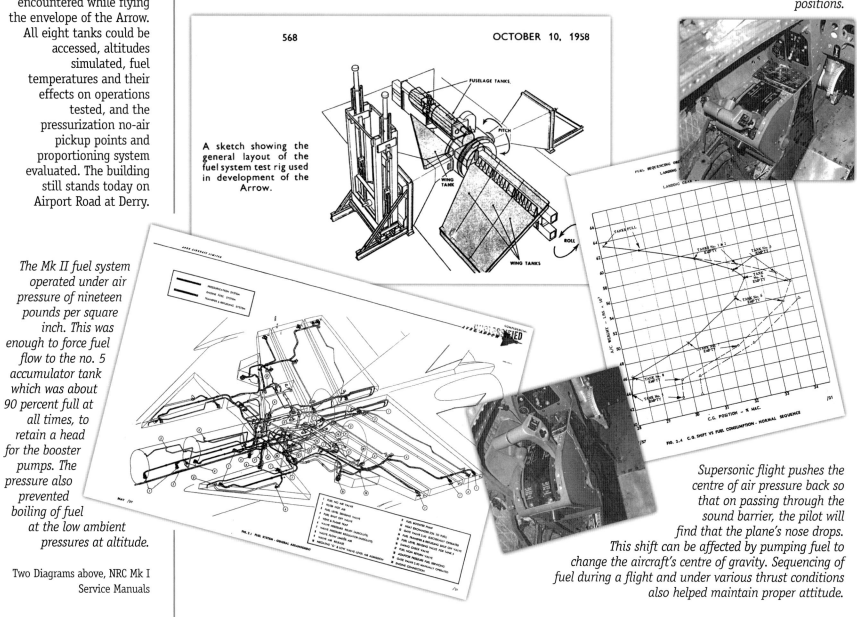

568 OCTOBER 10, 1958

A sketch showing the general layout of the fuel system test rig used in development of the Arrow.

The Mk II fuel system operated under air pressure of nineteen pounds per square inch. This was enough to force fuel flow to the no. 5 accumulator tank which was about 90 percent full at all times, to retain a head for the booster pumps. The pressure also prevented boiling of fuel at the low ambient pressures at altitude.

Two Diagrams above, NRC Mk I Service Manuals

Supersonic flight pushes the centre of air pressure back so that on passing through the sound barrier, the pilot will find that the plane's nose drops. This shift can be affected by pumping fuel to change the aircraft's centre of gravity. Sequencing of fuel during a flight and under various thrust conditions also helped maintain proper attitude.

The booster pumps, shown in the recovered parts section, have been located at NAM. They were mounted in the bottom of the main collector, tank no. 5. Fuel was used to cool hydraulic fluid as the small heat exchangers at the bottom show.

Diagram Mk I service manual, NRC

A high-altitude relight system, high-pressure oxygen cylinder is intact at the bottom of the A-104 Iroquois engine at NAM. Note the pressure gauge. The grey box to the left is the ignition high tension electrical supply to start the engine on the ground.

Photo, Peter Zuuring

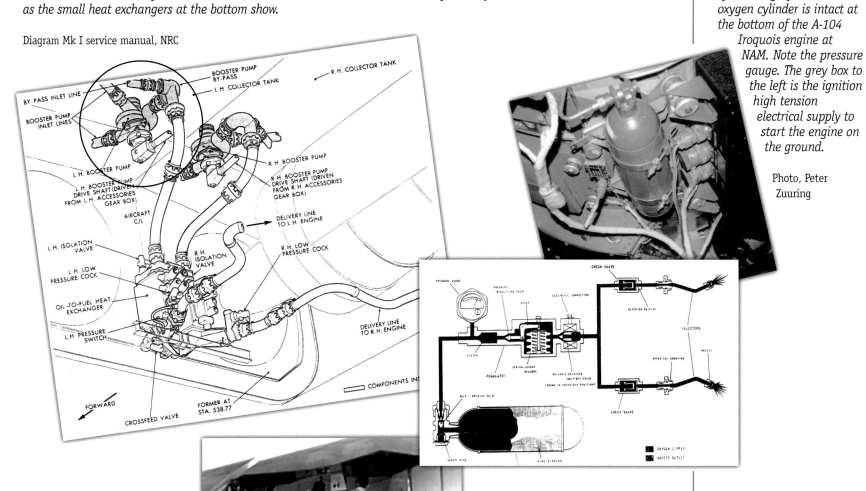

RL-203 being fueled. It has just been rolled out of the experimental building after an RCAF getting-to-know you-conference. Fueling interfered with cycling the main landing gear doors.

Photo, Aviation Videos

Orenda patented the high-altitude relight system. It was very basic and it worked. Simply, pure oxygen was injected into the annular combustion zone, and the fuel ignited via a button on each forward part of the throttles.

Diagram, NRC Mk II Iroquois Service Manual

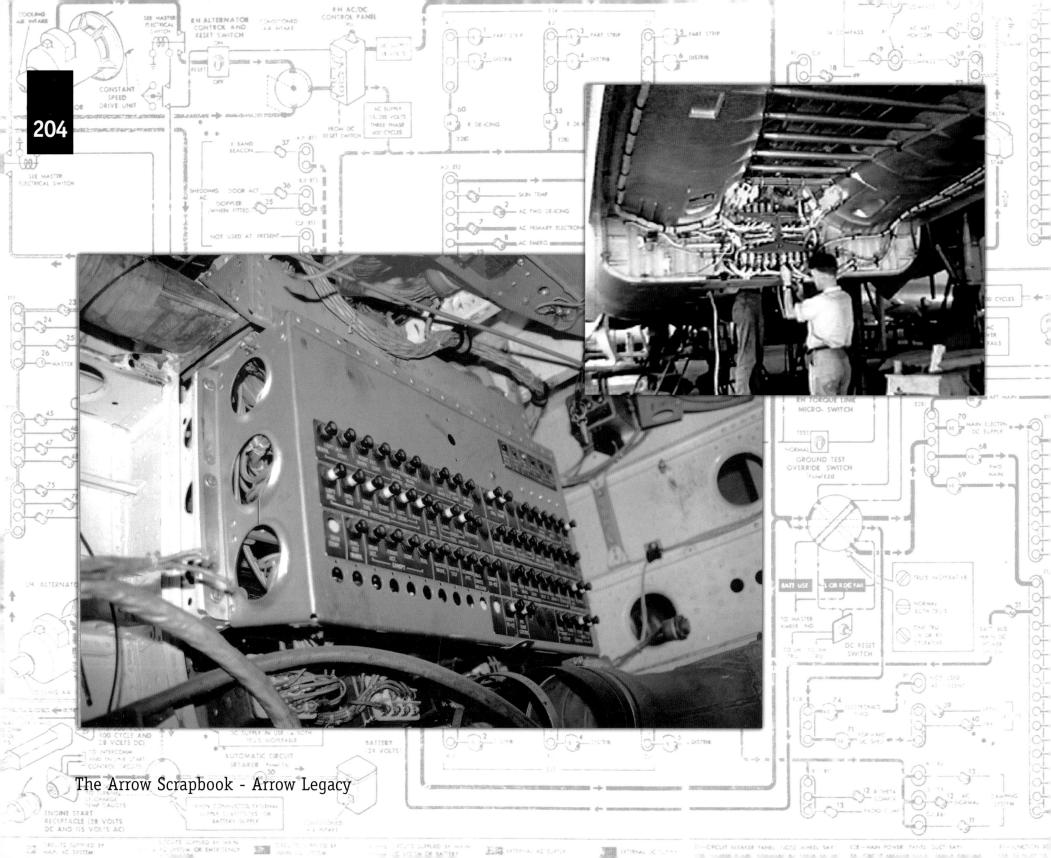

The Arrow Scrapbook - Arrow Legacy

Electrical and emergency fire control

The front nose wheel bay and weapons pack bay at station 485 housed major electrical fuse and junction boxes and terminals. The picture opposite,top is of the Mk II wooden mockup; the one below it is RL-206 at NAM. Both DC and AC power systems were in use.

Photos, Peter Zuuring and Aviation Videos

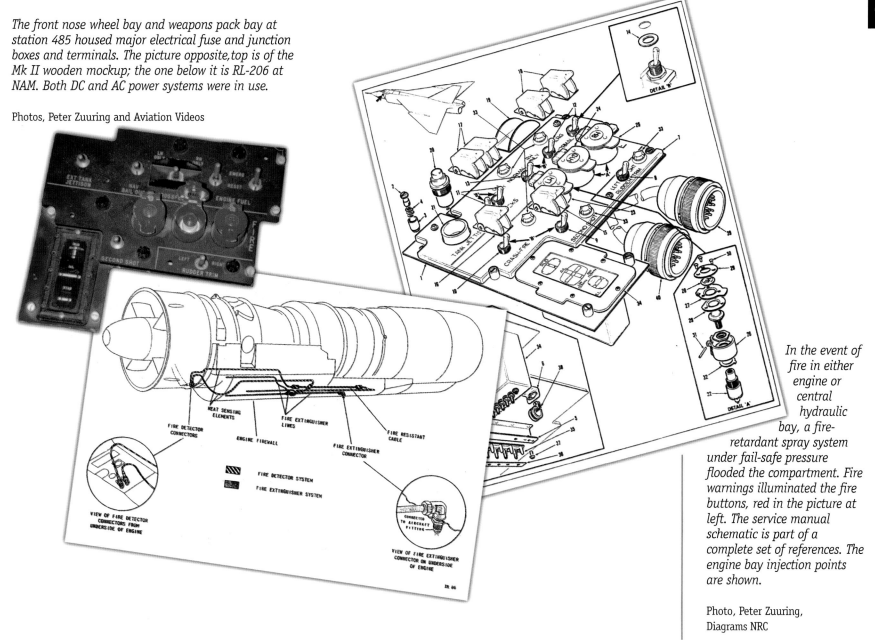

In the event of fire in either engine or central hydraulic bay, a fire-retardant spray system under fail-safe pressure flooded the compartment. Fire warnings illuminated the fire buttons, red in the picture at left. The service manual schematic is part of a complete set of references. The engine bay injection points are shown.

Photo, Peter Zuuring,
Diagrams NRC

Hydraulics

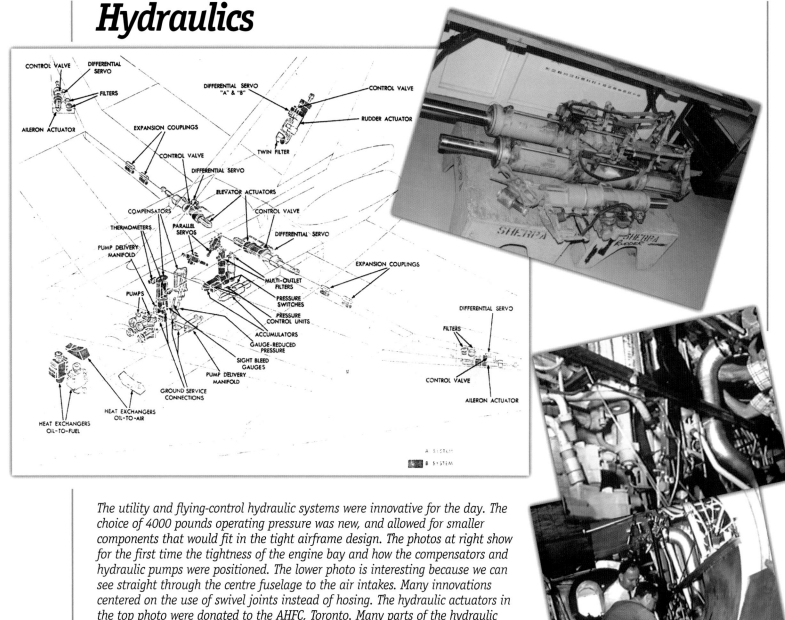

The utility and flying-control hydraulic systems were innovative for the day. The choice of 4000 pounds operating pressure was new, and allowed for smaller components that would fit in the tight airframe design. The photos at right show for the first time the tightness of the engine bay and how the compensators and hydraulic pumps were positioned. The lower photo is interesting because we can see straight through the centre fuselage to the air intakes. Many innovations centered on the use of swivel joints instead of hosing. The hydraulic actuators in the top photo were donated to the AHFC, Toronto. Many parts of the hydraulic system have been recovered.

Photo, Peter Bullman, Diagram NRC Mk I Service Manuals

Photos,
Aviation Videos

De-icing air intakes

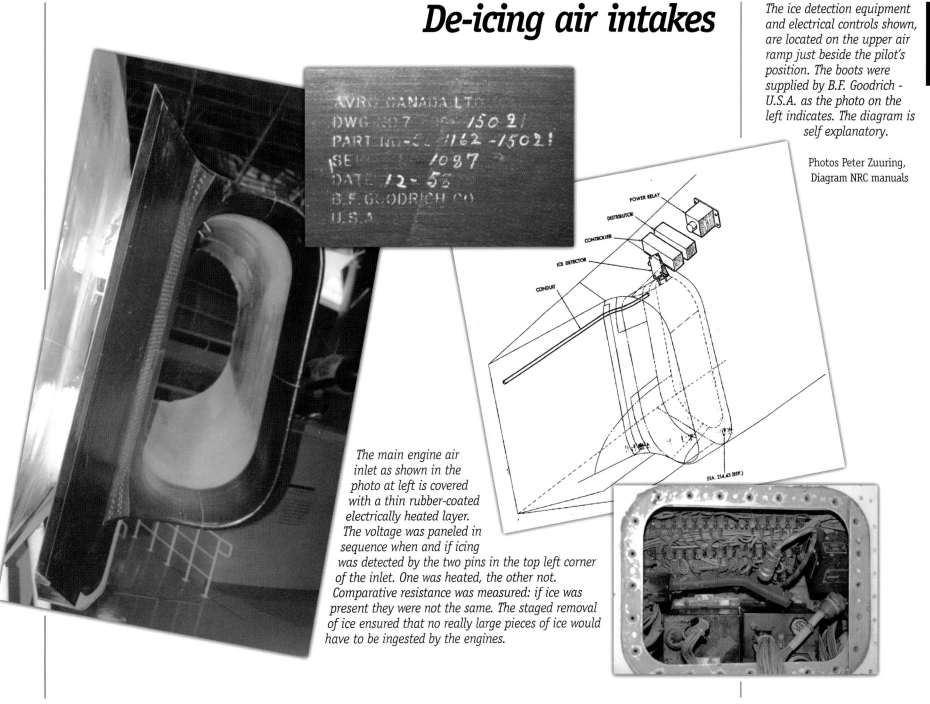

The ice detection equipment and electrical controls shown, are located on the upper air ramp just beside the pilot's position. The boots were supplied by B.F. Goodrich - U.S.A. as the photo on the left indicates. The diagram is self explanatory.

Photos Peter Zuuring, Diagram NRC manuals

AVRO CANADA LTD
DWG NO 7 ... 1502/
PART NO. CL 1162 -/502/
SER ... 1087
DATE 12 - 5?
B.F. GOODRICH CO
U.S.A.

POWER RELAY

DISTRIBUTOR

CONTROLLER

ICE DETECTOR

CONDUIT

STA. 214.43 (REF.)

The main engine air inlet as shown in the photo at left is covered with a thin rubber-coated electrically heated layer. The voltage was paneled in sequence when and if icing was detected by the two pins in the top left corner of the inlet. One was heated, the other not. Comparative resistance was measured: if ice was present they were not the same. The staged removal of ice ensured that no really large pieces of ice would have to be ingested by the engines.

Air conditioning

The air conditioning system received pressurized air from the tenth stage of the Iroquois engine. It was hot. It was rooted to the air-to-air heat exchanger that was fed by fuselage, ram pressure, boundary layer air, to cool it. The pressure was reduced through an air turbine that worked to dissipate energy, but not before it had gone through a water boiler – yes, water boiler! – that compensated for lack of cool boundary layer air (skin heating during supersonic flight). Water simply absorbed heat and was vented overboard to the rear. The whole heat-exchange process was reversible in that, when pressures were low in the air intakes, as during taxiing, air was sucked back into the air-inlets from the top of the spine through the normal vent. At right is the air conditioning bay, situated just behind the observer's seat. The ram air turbine was not installed yet. This would provide power in the event of complete system failure.

About 10 percent of the air flow that went through the engines ended up in the air conditioning system. Important areas to have controlled temperature and pressure were the cockpit, armament pack, radome and wheel well.

Diagram, NRC

Photo, Peter Zuuring

Main air conditioning bay intact at NAM. An electrical junction box is in the foreground.

Photo, Peter Zuuring, NAM

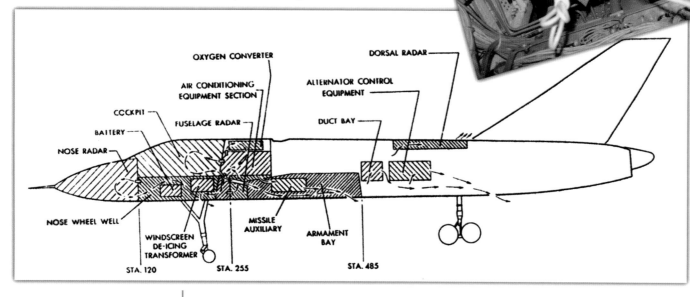

OXYGEN CONVERTER
DORSAL RADAR
AIR CONDITIONING EQUIPMENT SECTION
ALTERNATOR CONTROL EQUIPMENT
COCKPIT
FUSELAGE RADAR
DUCT BAY
BATTERY
NOSE RADAR
NOSE WHEEL WELL
WINDSCREEN DE-ICING TRANSFORMER
MISSILE AUXILIARY
ARMAMENT BAY
STA. 120
STA. 255
STA. 485

Schematic of the air flows in the primary section of the air conditioning system. Note the return flow doors for the low pressure engine intake case.

Diagram, NRC Mk II manuals

The wooden mockup shows the size of the engine high-pressure air lines to the air-to-air main heat exchanger. The main vent aft is in between.

Photo, Aviation Videos

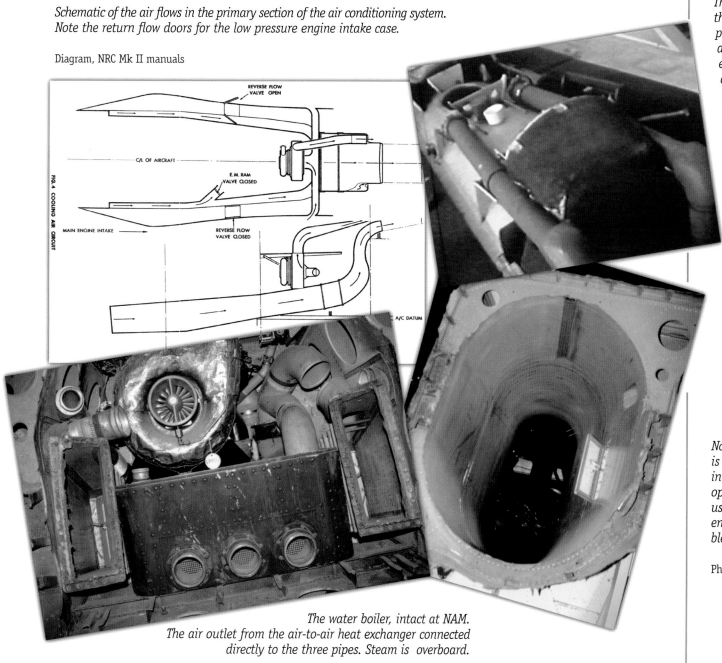

REVERSE FLOW VALVE OPEN

C/L OF AIRCRAFT

E.M. RAM VALVE CLOSED

FIG. 4 COOLING AIR CIRCUIT

MAIN ENGINE INTAKE

REVERSE FLOW VALVE CLOSED

A/C DATUM

The water boiler, intact at NAM. The air outlet from the air-to-air heat exchanger connected directly to the three pipes. Steam is overboard.

Photo, Peter Zuuring, NAM

Note the return-flow air door is open in the engine air intake. Also note the other opening, the air turbine inlet, used to reduce energy of the engine high-pressure air bleed.

Photo, Peter Zuuring, NAM

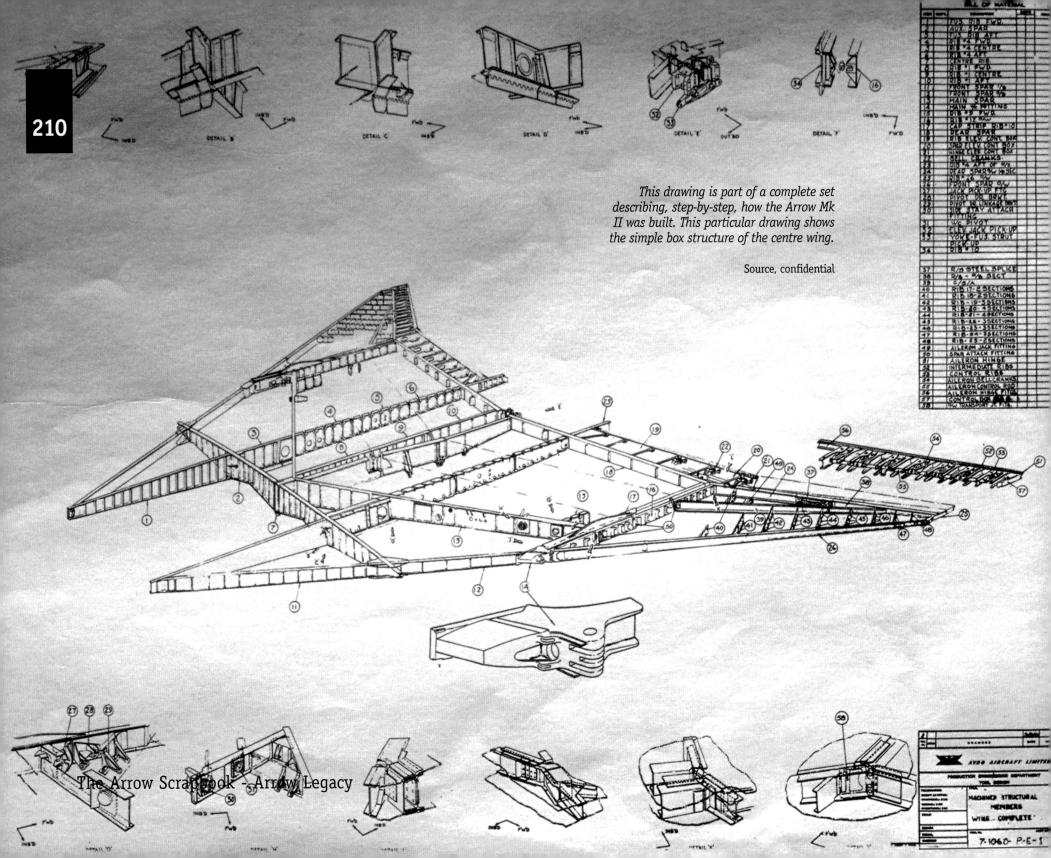

This drawing is part of a complete set describing, step-by-step, how the Arrow Mk II was built. This particular drawing shows the simple box structure of the centre wing.

Source, confidential

These report cover titles are typical of the Arrow collection at the NRC. The document on the right is particularly important in that it is the last known complete specification of the Arrow Mk II. It is dated January 1959, as near to cancellation as one might get.

Documents, NRC Parkin Library and DSIS

ARROW 2

FLYING CONTROLS HYDRAULIC SYSTEM

REPORT NO. 72/SYSTEMS 32/25

JUNE 1957

This brochure is intended to provide an accurate description of the system(s) or service(s) for purposes of the Arrow 2 Mock-up Conference, and is not to be considered binding with respect to changes which may occur subsequent to the date of publication.

COMPILED BY _D. Royston._   APPROVED BY _Alan R Bulay_

ENGINEERING DIVISION

AVRO AIRCRAFT LIMITED

MALTON — ONTARIO

72/MS/1
JUNE 1958
REISSUED JANUARY 1959

AVRO AIRCRAFT LIMITED

Classification cancelled / changed to Unclassified
By authority of AVRO Arrow Declassif. Board
Date 28 Jul 87
Signature _Edubiey_ , Co-Chairperson
Unit / Rank / Appointment DSIS 3

MODEL SPECIFICATION

FOR

ARROW 2 AIRFRAME

AND

GOVERNMENT SUPPLIED MATERIAL INSTALLATIONS

(SERIAL NO. 25206)

59-02141
314763

NUMBER OF PAGES	272
COPY NUMBER	47
ASSIGNED TO	R.C.A.F.

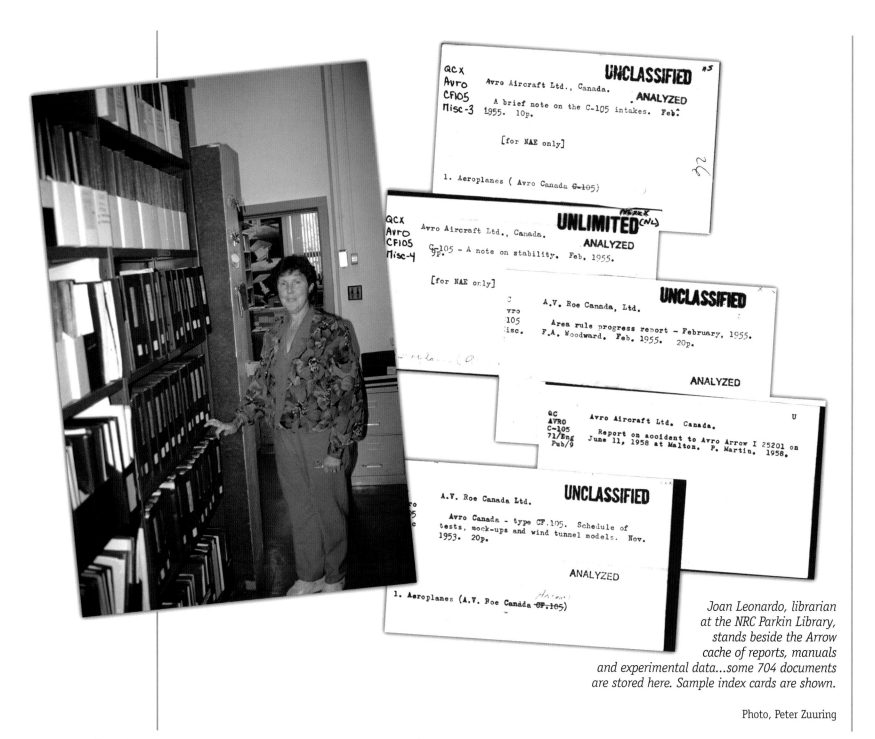

QCX
Avro
CF105
Misc-3

Avro Aircraft Ltd., Canada.

UNLIMITED *#5*

ANALYZED

A brief note on the C-105 intakes. Feb. 1955. 10p.

[for NAE only]

1. Aeroplanes (Avro Canada C-105)

QCX
Avro
CF105
Misc-4

Avro Aircraft Ltd., Canada.

UNLIMITED *(NL)*

ANALYZED

C-105 - A note on stability. Feb. 1955. 9p.

[for NAE only]

A.V. Roe Canada, Ltd.

UNCLASSIFIED

Area rule progress report - February, 1955.
F.A. Woodward. Feb. 1955. 20p.

ANALYZED

QC
AVRO
C-105
71/Eng
Pub/9

Avro Aircraft Ltd. Canada.

U

Report on accident to Avro Arrow I 25201 on
June 11, 1958 at Malton. P. Martin. 1958.

A.V. Roe Canada Ltd.

UNCLASSIFIED

Avro Canada - type CF.105. Schedule of
tests, mock-ups and wind tunnel models. Nov.
1953. 20p.

ANALYZED

1. Aeroplanes (A.V. Roe Canada CF.105)

*Joan Leonardo, librarian
at the NRC Parkin Library,
stands beside the Arrow
cache of reports, manuals
and experimental data...some 704 documents
are stored here. Sample index cards are shown.*

Photo, Peter Zuuring

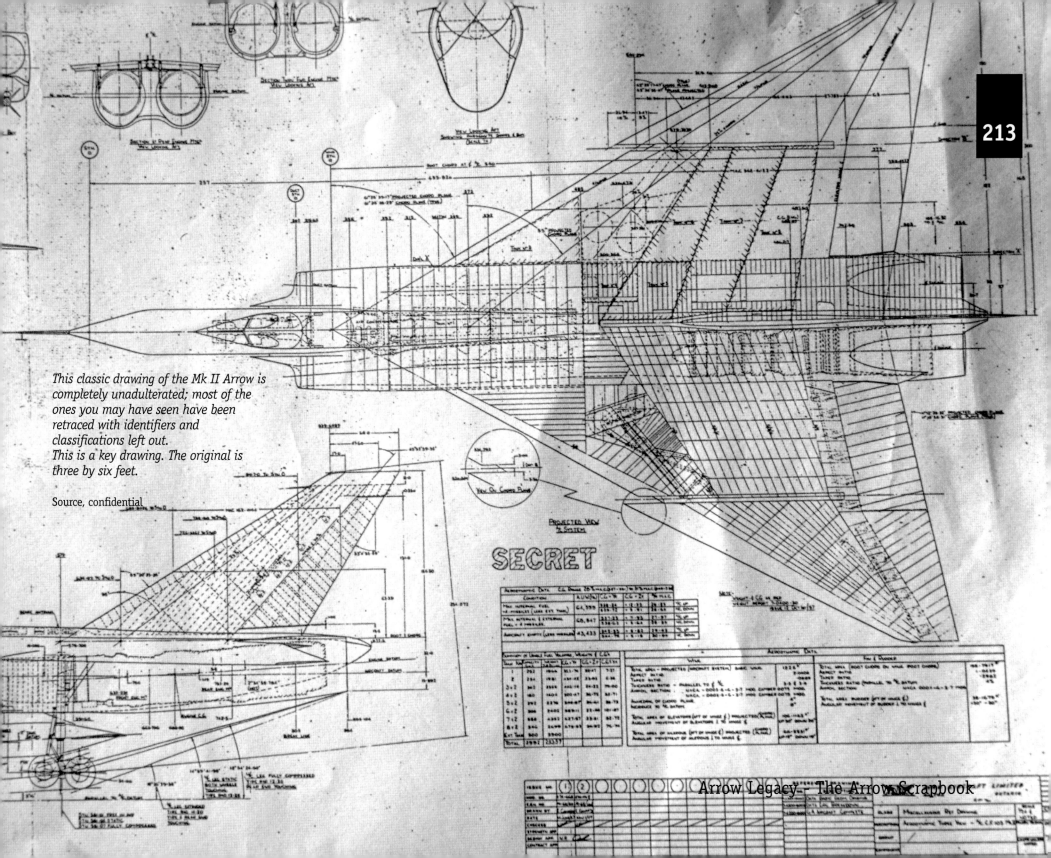

This classic drawing of the Mk II Arrow is completely unadulterated; most of the ones you may have seen have been retraced with identifiers and classifications left out.
This is a key drawing. The original is three by six feet.

Source, confidential

SECRET

Facilities still remain...

but for
how long?

Uplands Wind Tunnel

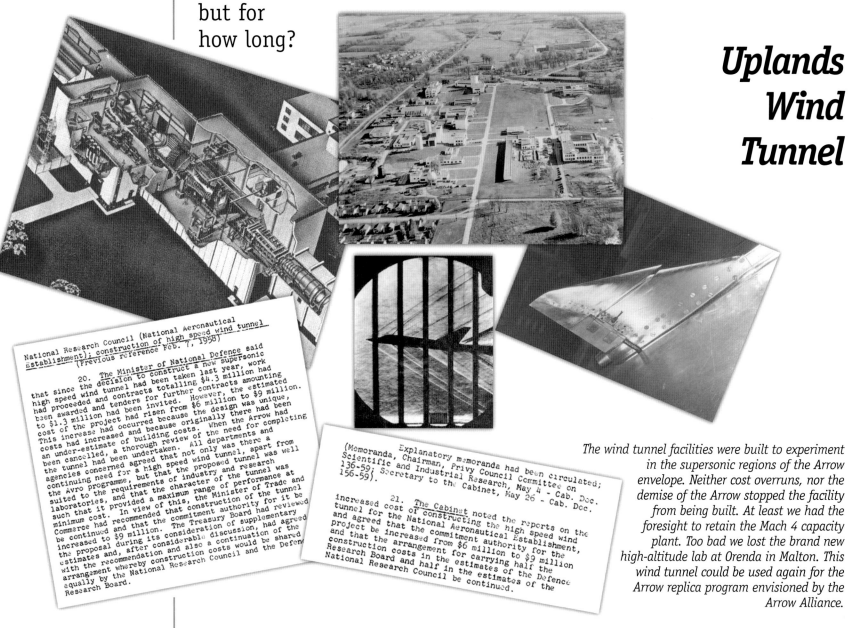

National Research Council (National Aeronautical Establishment); construction of high speed wind tunnel (Previous reference Feb. 7, 1958)

20. The Minister of National Defence said that since the decision to construct a new supersonic high speed wind tunnel had been taken last year, work had proceeded and contracts totalling $4.3 million had been awarded and tenders for further contracts amounting to $1.3 million had been invited. However, the estimated cost of the project had risen from $6 million to $9 million. This increase had occurred because the design was unique, costs had increased and because originally there had been an under-estimate of building costs. When the Arrow had been cancelled, a thorough review of the need for completing the tunnel had been undertaken. All departments and agencies concerned agreed that not only was there a continuing need for a high speed wind tunnel, apart from the Avro programme, but that the proposed tunnel was well suited to the requirements of industry and research laboratories, and that the character of the tunnel was such that it provided a maximum range of performance at minimum cost. In view of this, the Minister of Trade and Commerce had recommended that construction of the tunnel be continued and that the commitment authority for it be increased to $9 million. The Treasury Board had reviewed the proposal during its consideration of supplementary estimates and, after considerable discussion, had agreed with the recommendation and also a continuation of the arrangement whereby construction costs would be shared equally by the National Research Council and the Defence Research Board.

(Memoranda, Explanatory memoranda had been circulated; Scientific and Chairman, Privy Council Committee on 136-59; and Industrial Research, May 4 - Cab. Doc. 156-59). Secretary to the Cabinet, May 26 - Cab. Doc.

21. The Cabinet noted the reports on the increased cost of constructing the high speed wind tunnel for the National Aeronautical Establishment, and agreed that the commitment authority for the project be increased from $6 million to $9 million and that the arrangement for carrying half the construction costs in the estimates of the Defence Research Board and half in the estimates of the National Research Council be continued.

The wind tunnel facilities were built to experiment in the supersonic regions of the Arrow envelope. Neither cost overruns, nor the demise of the Arrow stopped the facility from being built. At least we had the foresight to retain the Mach 4 capacity plant. Too bad we lost the brand new high-altitude lab at Orenda in Malton. This wind tunnel could be used again for the Arrow replica program envisioned by the Arrow Alliance.

Photos, Peter Brennan

The Malton plant of Avro is still intact. Rumours abound that Boeing, the current owner, may not be there for long. This Canadian heritage site should be preserved and returned to the Canadian people. "Canada" has already disappeared from the rollout door. Let's not lose the rest!

Background photo, Les Wilkinson, others Peter Zuuring

215

Arrow Legacy - The Arrow Scrapbook

Pioneers, the Jetliner...

What might have been

Jetliner

The Avro Jetliner over the Ontario country side.

Photo, Ross Richardson.

This unusual view of the Jetliner shows the wing spread dramatically. Born in the late 1940s, the Jetliner showed how passenger air travel could be revolutionized. It had the distinction of being the first commercial jet to fly in North America. It could have been in the world, but through some strange circumstance, the Malton Airport authority decided to close and repair the runways for two weeks, coinciding with the first flight of the Comet in England – complicity?

The Arrow Scrapbook - Arrow Legacy

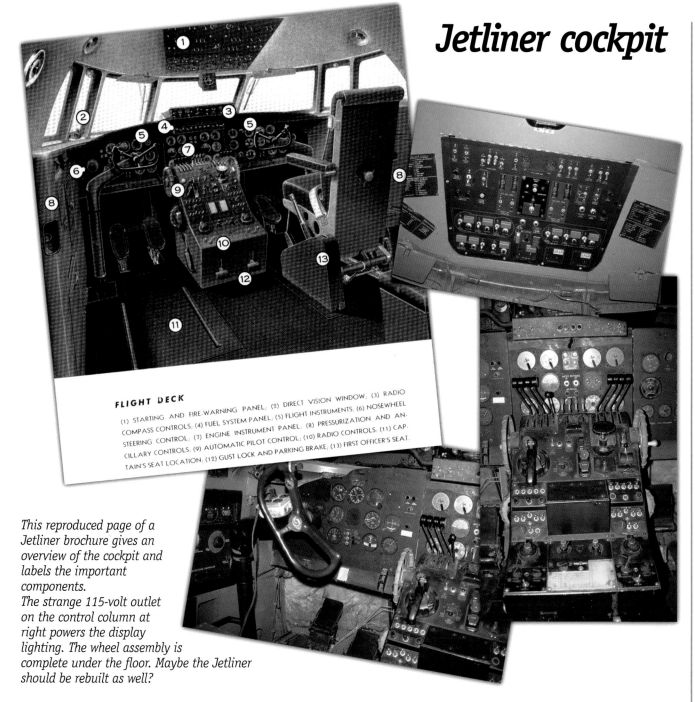

FLIGHT DECK

(1) STARTING AND FIRE-WARNING PANEL; (2) DIRECT VISION WINDOW; (3) RADIO COMPASS CONTROLS; (4) FUEL SYSTEM PANEL; (5) FLIGHT INSTRUMENTS, (6) NOSEWHEEL STEERING CONTROL; (7) ENGINE INSTRUMENT PANEL; (8) PRESSURIZATION AND AN-CILLARY CONTROLS; (9) AUTOMATIC PILOT CONTROL; (10) RADIO CONTROLS; (11) CAP-TAIN'S SEAT LOCATION; (12) GUST LOCK AND PARKING BRAKE; (13) FIRST OFFICER'S SEAT.

These cockpit pictures were taken when the nose of the Jetliner was being incorporated into the "Pushing the Envelope" exhibit at NAM, Ottawa.

Photo, Peter Zuuring, NAM

This reproduced page of a Jetliner brochure gives an overview of the cockpit and labels the important components.
The strange 115-volt outlet on the control column at right powers the display lighting. The wheel assembly is complete under the floor. Maybe the Jetliner should be rebuilt as well?

Brochure, Avro Publication, Ross Richardson

Lateral thinkers...

Jet truck

Orenda developed the OT-4 turbine power plant to be used in vehicles, tanks and boats. It was an extension of the successful power-generating series that preceded it. A complete Mack Truck was built and driven across Canada... where is it today?

Photo, M.Barber

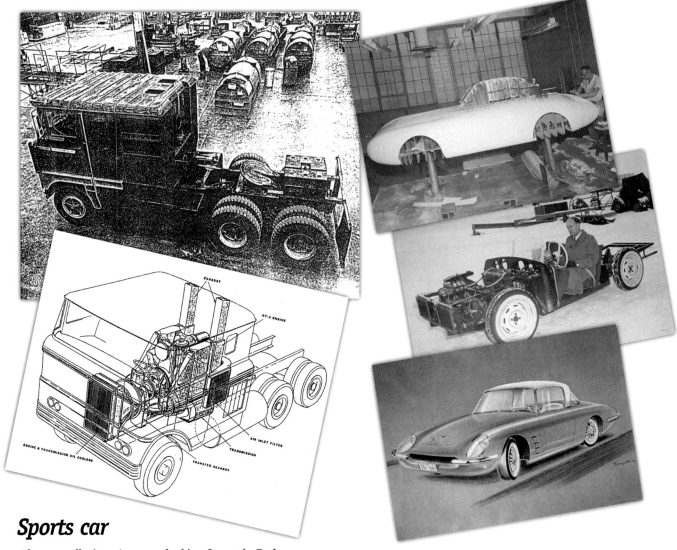

Sports car

After cancellation, Avro was looking for work. Earl Brownridge, an Orenda executive, enjoyed cars and thought that a market existed for a snappy sports car. A prototype was built along the same lines of an airplane.

Photo, AHFC

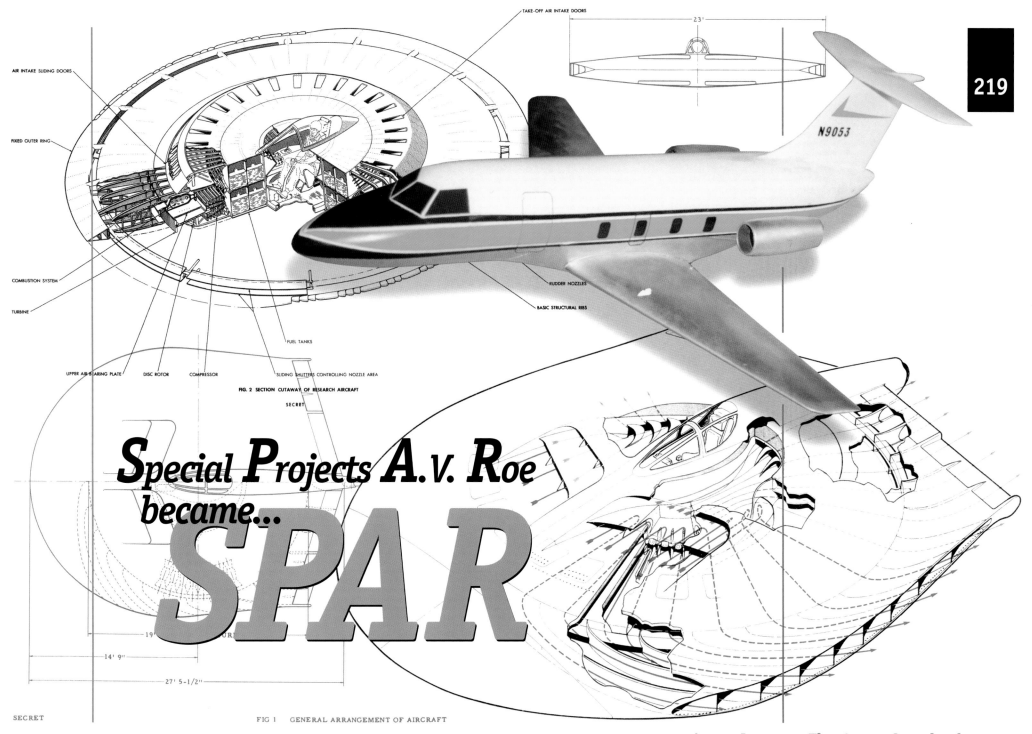

AIR INTAKE SLIDING DOORS

FIXED OUTER RING

COMBUSTION SYSTEM

TURBINE

FUEL TANKS

UPPER AIR-BEARING PLATE   DISC ROTOR   COMPRESSOR   SLIDING SHUTTERS CONTROLLING NOZZLE AREA

FIG. 2 SECTION CUTAWAY OF RESEARCH AIRCRAFT

SECRET

TAKE-OFF AIR INTAKE DOORS

23'

N9053

RUDDER NOZZLES

BASIC STRUCTURAL RIBS

*Special Projects **A**.v. **R**oe became...*

SPAR

19'

14' 9"

27' 5-1/2"

SECRET

FIG 1   GENERAL ARRANGEMENT OF AIRCRAFT

*Spud Potocki at
the controls.*

Canada's skunk works.

The Avrocar was jointly financed by the U.S. Army and the USAF. The idea was to have a fast battlefield VTOL that could get in and out of any terrain. Today there are Harrier Jump Jets and Helicopters. Ground effect and a lack of vertical thrust kept the Avrocar barely above the ground...strangely, the project barely got off the ground. The Smithsonian, in Washington, wants to return the Avrocar to Canada. Yeah!

Jump gyros

That's what they were called. The idea was to have a flat disc with inner compressor, radial combusters and outer turbine sections. The spinning disc acted like a gyro. Torque applied to the vertical would effect turning motion. Streamlining and pass-through would give it extremely low drag and hence high speed at altitude.

Mockups were built. After cancellation, rumour has it, some were built and flown out of Georgetown, Ontario. Science fiction...Avro Spirit!

Documents, Ross Richardson

Those who were there...

outstanding talent I have had the pleasure to meet...

Peter Brennan, Orenda

Jim Floyd, Avro

Jan Zurakowski, Avro

Ken Barnes, Avro and Orenda

Ron Page, Orenda

Ray Foottit, RCAF

Les Wilkinson - Canadian

Jack Templin, NAE

In 1989 Doug Moore,
an aeronautical designer/engineer,
ex-Avro, ex-De Havilland retired from
McDonnell Douglas Canada Ltd.
Jan Zurakowski was there and sums up the spirit
that touched nearly all who experienced those heady
days at Malton, in the fifties.

" You are the last member in the great team of engineers who have
maintained continuous employment in the former Avro facility,
who participated in the development of Canada's greatest gift
and technical contribution to aviation,

Our Avro Arrow."

"As you enter your golden years we, who touched the Arrow,
can cherish the dream and memories of our wonderful team
and the incredible airplane we produced."

What more could possibly be said!

The Arrow Alliance

Rebuilding a dream and a nation

Achievement through initiative,
hands-on participation and team work

Forty years to the day, after the Arrow's cancellation, Peter Zuuring, a Dutch born Canadian, announces a project to rebuild the Arrow.

Clipping, *The Toronto Star*

A18 THE TORONTO STAR Friday, February 19, 1999

Flying high and straight as an Arrow

Entrepreneur leads charge to rebuild jet

BY NICOLAAS VAN RIJN
STAFF REPORTER

Arrowmania.

Peter Zuuring has it, and now — 40 years after the death knell sounded for the Avro Arrow — he'd like to give it to the rest of us.

"The Avro Arrow was, at the time, the finest aircraft ever built in Canada," said Zuuring, founder and director of the Arrow Alliance, a not-for-profit group being organized to keep the dream alive. "It's too much to let go of."

His dream?

Zuuring wants to build a fully functional, flyable replica of the famed jet fighter that was officially killed off by then-prime minister John Diefenbaker 40 years ago tomorrow — Feb. 20, 1959 — and have it ready to cross the country in 2009, to mark the 100th anniversary of flight.

A Dutch-born University of Toronto engineering graduate with more than 30 years of entrepreneurial experience, Zuuring now has focused his life on the Arrow, and is determined to see the jet back in the skies of Canada.

"We can do it," he stressed.

To fund the $40 million to $50 million project, Zuuring's Arrow Alliance has devised a scheme of donations and investments that he hopes will also fund Arrow scholarships in Canada's high schools. Although Arrow Alliance now has only some 70 members, Zuuring said, the group continues to draw new recruits with every talk he gives about the storied fighter.

As a first step, Zuuring is working on an Arrowmania weekend to coincide with the CNE's Air Show in September.

"Even though the official order went out in 1959 to destroy everything having to do with the Arrow, we are learning about more and more boxes of parts, diagrams, blueprints and other bits and pieces that were

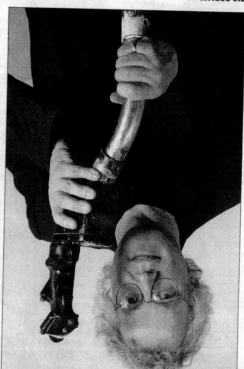

BIG DREAMS: Peter Zuuring has an ambitious plan. He wants to build a fully functional, flyable replica of the Avro Arrow, the famed jet fighter officially killed off by the Canadian government 40 years ago tomorrow.

DAVID COOPER/TORONTO STAR

squirrelled away by employees of A.V. Roe," the Arrow's manufacturer, Zuuring said.

Brandishing a control stick from one of the original planes, Zuuring detailed discoveries that have come to light.

He said enough parts and "bits and pieces" have already been located to rebuild 45 per cent of the white fighter jet that set hearts aflutter when it blazed a trail through the skies over Malton in the 1950s.

Six engines, including two iroquois built by Orenda Engines Ltd. of Malton, have been located, along with instruments, hydraulics and chunks of wing panels.

Zuuring, who is just finishing a book, Arrow Scrapbook,

scheduled for publication this spring, says his goal is to identify every Arrow part left in existence.

"I'm not hoarding anything. I'm just making it happen."

His proposed Arrowmania Weekend would play a key role in encouraging people who once worked on the Arrow project to give up parts they may have held on to as souvenirs.

"There is a lot of stuff in peo-

ple's hands," he said, noting that many of the 40,000 Roe employees who worked on the Arrow smuggled parts and drawings home with them after the project was killed off.

"Imagine a call to action that would uncover that hoard.

"That's why we need to develop a weekend where people can see what there is, what is left."

Making things happen is an old habit for Zuuring, who has worked on projects ranging from Wayne Gretzky's hockey blades to big business petrochemicals and computer pinball games.

For this project, Zuuring wants to reclaim a section of the old McDonnell Doug-

las/Boeing plant at Malton, an Elvis-era 10-building site where the jet was built.

Initially, the site would be used to reconstruct an Arrow from existing parts.

Eventually, Zuuring said, he'd like to see a living air museum on the site, where static displays are accompanied by live flights, classes and a pilot training centre.

He's also excited by the apparent discovery of four large-scale Arrow test models in Lake Ontario last fall.

Sonar scanning has discovered lakebed traces off Trenton that appear to be made by the models, which were fired into the lake on missiles to test the design's aerodynamics.

Initiative

Sir Roy Dobson was not a Canadian, yet he believed in us. Look up, Canada!

Photo, National Archives

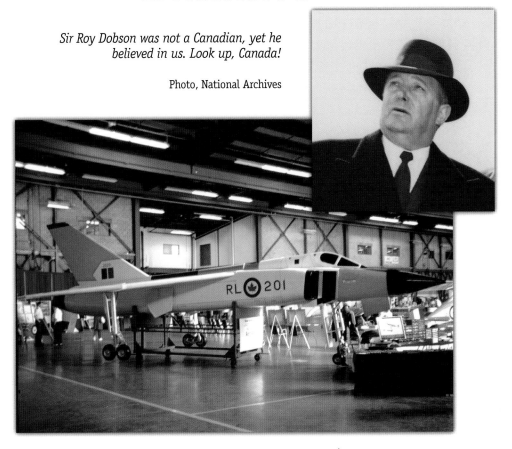

When Sir Roy Dobson came to Canada after the Second World War to set up a new post-war aircraft factory, he didn't have to do it. He was chairman of the Hawker Siddeley group, king of the castle, so to speak. Did he need another headache?

What he knew was that Canada, a largely agrarian society, had managed, during the war years, to build 16,000 planes from scratch. Many of these were of better quality than those built back in the U.K. What an opportunity! The facilities were intact, management was available, a trained work force could be skimmed and a whole host of subcontractors and suppliers were interested in work.

Roy Dobson had a vision that the development of Canada, and North America for that fact, was going to be tied to the development of a commercial aviation business. Furthermore, the growing Communist threat was only going to be deterred, in large part, by a strong America which emerged victoriously from the war years. So, both civil and military airplanes would be needed. What better jumping off ground than Canada? Roy Dobson had initiative and a vision!

The Avro Arrow became the symbol of this renewed vision and represented Canada's technical competence and our ability to compete in a growing scientific world. When the Arrow was cancelled our government told us that we were involved in something beyond our capacity, that we aimed too high and should be content with less. Sound familiar? Our pride was struck and injured. We knew it was a lie. We couldn't even keep the knowledge...it had to be destroyed. Canadians went along with it. Until today!

Peter Zuuring, after a significant "Outward Bound " experience, decided to get involved with youth, so they could learn some of life's secrets early on, as opposed to in their fifties. Involvement in a leadership camp proved that demoralized students and cash-strapped parents are difficult to recruit. Something to rally around, something significant that would spark our imagination, something that would touch the very fibre of Canada was needed. He found it!

"Our Avro Arrow."

Although models of the Arrow are good, such as the one above used in the stage play "There never was an Arrow", it was only half scale. People seeing it said, "I thought the Arrow was bigger than that." Only the real thing will do!

Photo, at Trenton Air Show, Marc André Valiquette

Hands-on Participation

An Avro team, getting their hands dirty, building the Arrow Mk II nose section.

Photo,
Avro Magazine, summer 1958

A national project to rebuild the Arrow, to hook a new generation, to rally the country...now that's a program to embrace. How could you do it? Just dreaming about it won't make it happen. You have to get your hands dirty...get involved.

You have learned that, from a technical viewpoint, there is enough information, there are parts and there are capable people able to rebuild the Arrow. Can we do it? It's a question of will. President Kennedy inspired a nation by saying that before the 1960s were out, a man would walk on the moon. I say to you, before this next decade to the 100th anniversary of flight is out, we should have our Arrow and fly it from one end of the country to the other!

The Arrow Alliance is the umbrella group that I have set up to to make this happen. Its stated mission is dedicated to reminding and encouraging Canadians that they can do great things. The process must be on-going. The demonstration project must be national in character. It must involve a cross-section of our population so that mentoring and understanding is fostered. The Arrow is the first project of many.

So how can this be funded? Asking Canadians for money every year will become tiring for all concerned. Governments come and go. We will need a method that is self-perpetuating and independent of manipulation. Widespread support is needed to make funding less vulnerable. I have three steps in mind.

Firstly, the usual membership, donation, government largess and promotional sale programs will be established and sought after. This will kick-start the program but will never see it blossom.

Because the national project builds something of significance it will involve industry. Secondly, there is an Arrow Scholarship Program centred on local high schools and funded by local small business. I propose a $5000 amount, half goes to the student and half goes to the Alliance's national project. Local businesses could act in concert or independently, to come up with the money. Local initiative shows results and commitment. Arrow Scholars would be chosen based on their interest and skills demonstrated in science/technology and entrepreneurship. Their peers will play a role in choosing that high school's Arrow scholar. A one week leadership experience and two weeks helping to build their portion of the national project is part of the scholarship.

Once a ground swell of Arrow scholars is available, they can, if they so choose , become involved in the third program, The Arrow Reliance...an education tuition savings plan operating as an RESP. Today there are five major Canadian RESP programs. USC and Canadian Scholarship Trust Fund are examples. Typically the trust fund aspect of their operations is "not for profit". The exclusive management and sales contracts are private and take out annually some $6 million and $12 million respectively. This is not explained in their program pitches but is available from the perpetual offering statement which is included in all their paperwork. The Arrow Alliance will setup its own RESP offering, involve students to sell the program, help to pay their way through university and provide a cut for the national project.

In addition to providing a financial vehicle to pay for members' future tuition, the Alliance will get more involved by offering a host of education-related services which will set it apart. Recognizing that paying for education is only part of the problem , the Alliance will be involved in ensuring there is even a seat available. Trust funds will have to be invested...the Reliance will do so in post-secondary education and participate with others to ensure that facilities and trained staff are there. Imagine a Canadian MIT equivalent with at least one campus in each province, a uniform standard of excellence, granting national degrees. Goals are to graduate 100 percent of students as opposed to the current tragedy of only a third.

An Orenda team, getting their hands dirty, working on the Iroquois development and project "Northwind."

Photo, Les Wilkinson

The Arrow Alliance - The Arrow Scrapbook

Lucas-Rotax advertisement of the late 1950s. The implication of engine and airframe working together, leading to a safe nation, parallels the Alliance's goals of rebuilding a strong Canada using as one of our strengths, a well-informed and motivated youth.

Ad, *Aircraft* magazine appropriately August 1958

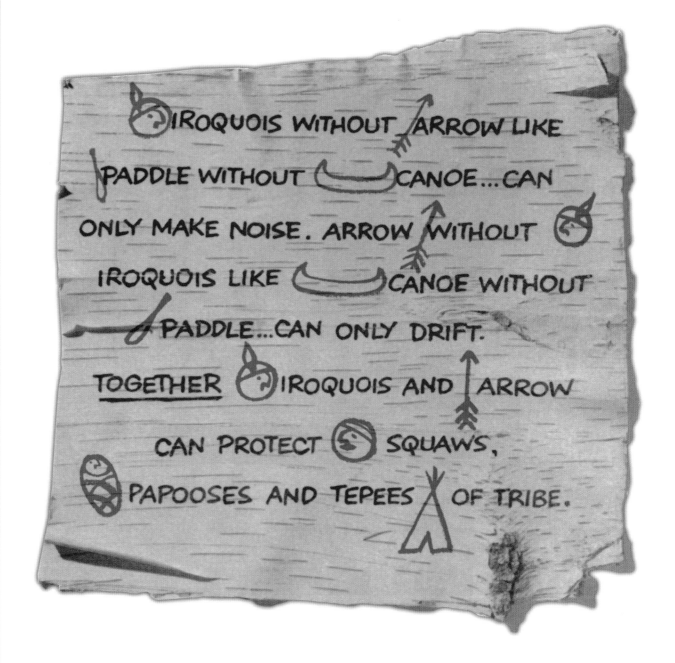

IROQUOIS WITHOUT ARROW LIKE PADDLE WITHOUT CANOE...CAN ONLY MAKE NOISE. ARROW WITHOUT IROQUOIS LIKE CANOE WITHOUT PADDLE...CAN ONLY DRIFT. TOGETHER IROQUOIS AND ARROW CAN PROTECT SQUAWS, PAPOOSES AND TEPEES OF TRIBE.

The program structure is being put together. How do we build an airplane?

I propose that it is to be tackled in a two-step process.

The first, is the building of an accurate static display version. It would incorporate any existing parts and be filled in-between with new material. It would be built up out of the same sections that the original Arrow followed. The engines, both the J-75 and the Iroquois, would be similarly restored with one set installed in the model and the other sectioned for viewing.

The second, would be the building of an accurate flying replica. Using all the modern tools of CAD/CAM, laser-cutting, numerical control milling, aeronautical know-how and manufacturing facilities in place, we should be able to do it without all the manual steps and tooling of the 1950s. A workable engine is the Pratt & Whitney F-100, currently used in the USAF's F-15 and F-16. It is a stable and proven engine that would reduce the risk involved and money needed in trying to rebuild the Iroquois. The F-100 thrust and dimensions are within the Iroquois design envelope so it would, more than adequately, power and fit into a new Arrow.

Regulatory bodies are very much involved in today's aircraft businesses. In part, they have contributed to the excellent safety record of the aviation world. Unfortunately, their extensive regulation and inspection processes have also resulted in major increases in costs and time to certification. I am told that this would apply to any rebuilding of the Arrow. One way around this is to once again place the Arrow under the umbrella of the military, which up until now, has been exempt from such regulations. Will DND get involved? It would be a fitting solution and make up for the roll it played in getting rid of it. The Minister of Defence said at the 1998's National Capital Airshow that the rebuilding of the Arrow is a great project..."but don't ask me for any money!"

DND should be involved. Certainly, the rank and file has not been aware of the role that the military bosses, played in the demise of the Arrow. Obviously, the facts would not have sat very well with serving men and women of the day, so it was kept from them. Today all levels of the military might participate in rebuilding the "Phoenix." On the other hand, some of the more senior staff may not wish the wounds to be reopened, as per General Baril's comments at the same airshow. Nonetheless, including the military would make the rebuilding easier. Furthermore, we need someone to fly it.. Snowbird Pilots have expressed an interest!

Back to rebuilding the Arrow. Many former employees and related families have collected pieces, documents, drawings and other items related to the Arrow. Many tell of officials coming into the workplace, filling bins with information to be taken away for destruction, only to be found once again at the curb-side for garbage pick-up. One guess as to who picked it up!

Earlier, people were nervous about letting it be known that they possessed "secret" material and be subject to prosecution under the Official Secrets Act. This was a factor during the twenty-fifth anniversary of first-flight celebrations. No global official cancellation of "secret" status has been issued, yet at some expense and assistance from the Freedom of Information Act, large-scale declassification has happened. The fact that I was able to obtain the documents presented here, through official government channels is testimony to that fact. Furthermore, the greatest amount of parts and materials are interestingly in government hands, mysteriously right from the beginning, even when it was all supposed to have been destroyed.

"Arrowmania," a Toronto-based event, to gather under one roof any and all things Arrow-related, will go a long way to encouraging people and institutions to bring in their collections and allow an accurate inventory of "what's available" to be made.

> ## "Oh very young... What will you leave us this time?"
> A Cat Stevens inspiration

100 years of flight... coming up!

Building Alliance membership, selling this book, establishing the Arrow Scholarship program and Arrow Reliance saving plan are first priorities. Building the core team of about twenty -five to thirty professionals to head up the organization and lead the teams to build the static display version is key. There are two places where this could be done.

In Ottawa, proximity and access to parts, documents and national institutions can assist the project. The possible move of the National War Museum to Rockcliffe could herald the merging of the aviation and war museums under one administration, making it easier for an extensive Arrow display to bridge both organizations.

Malton, however, is the preferred place. After all, it was built there and the facilities still exist. There is a large financial base and skill reserve in the region. Boeing, which recently acquired the site through its purchase of McDonnell Douglas Canada, has removed the "Canada" sign over the old rollout doors. Happily, the old Avro plant is still intact and complete. There are many rumours, however, that this may not be the case for long. It is a piece of prime real estate and many would want it for their own purposes. I say right now, that the only people who should have this site are the people of Canada. It is the quintessential historical aviation spot in all of Canada. The envelope was pushed here from the beginning. It should be viewed as a national treasure and designated as a national heritage site. This should not be allowed to become a question of

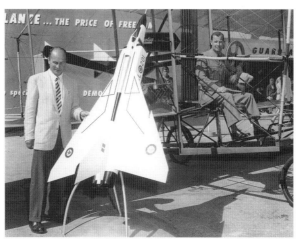

money. The people of metropolitan Toronto, particularly, and Canadians as a whole, are going to have to become very vocal to protect this facility and get it back from our neighbours who occupy it now. This is a call to action!

At the fiftieth anniversary of flight, Jan Zurakowski, the civilian and Jack Woodman, the soldier, are both represented at the celebration. The Silver Dart replica was there. It will cost more to rebuild the Arrow. I expect to see it at the 100th anniversary, rolling out for its flight across a wintery Canada, as the scene on the right so aptly portrays.

The CF-105 was conceived during mid-1950s optimism and destroyed in controversy. It raised aspirations of a generation and resulted in the biggest single lay-off in Canada's corporate history. Even today, many Canadians can point to a relative or acquaintance who was somehow connected to the project. Again at the time, the Arrow was a symbol of technical competence and national pride. A rebuilt Arrow can revive and inspire a new generation to set their goals at an elevated level, achieve them and feel a sense of accomplishment.

In summary, the Arrow Alliance can mobilize and inspire Canadians at large and its youth in particular. Rather than sitting back and waiting for others to take the lead, the Alliance will demonstrate to its members that individual initiative, hands-on participation and team effort can bring tangible results. The outcome of this story is still unclear. Time will tell what Canadians are really made of!

February 23, 2009, Malton...
the Arrow flies again!

Photo, in memory of Les Wilkinson, 1923-1999

RL 204

The Arrow Alliance - The Arrow Scrapbook

What started out as a search for a national leadership project led Peter Zuuring into the bizarre and fascinating world of the Avro Arrow. He was not the first to be so smitten. The story and the myths surrounding the construction and sudden destruction of the great aircraft has captured the imagination of millions of Canadians.

A dream of rebuilding the Arrow, to bring closure to the loss of such a magnificent achievement, led the author down many paths. Some were immensely rewarding, like the discovery of significant parts or engineering data. Others were frustrating, like the secret classifications that still block access to pertinent information. Discussions with important players, including Avro personnel Jim Floyd, Ray Foottit, Ken Barnes and Pete Brennan, and test pilot Januz Zurakowski, to name just a few, have shed new light on events and issues not previously known.

I have collected hundreds of significant Arrow papers, letters, technical manuals, photos, parts and conversations, and presented them here, in The Arrow Scrapbook. I hope you have learned from the original sources about the birth of the Arrow, its development, its growth, its final collapse and destruction.

Peter Zuuring, on the road, promoting the Arrow Alliance.

Now, let's get it back... join the Alliance!

Application form on last page of the Appendices

Appendices

S E C R E T
Appendix "A" to
CEPE Letter S51-05-03

CEPE ARROW DETACHMENT COMMENTS ON

THE FIRST THREE FLIGHTS OF THE ARROW 1

1   The Arrow Mk 1 has flown three flights reaching an indicated Mach. of 1.1 at an indicated altitude of 40,000 feet on its third flight. During these three flights only approximately 18 parameters were recorded; 12 on telemetry and 6 on oscillograph. All recorded parameters were related to the stability of the airplane and to the directional damper system. In no case were any parameters recorded to indicate altitude or speed.

2   Three possible problem areas have appeared during these three flights. They are:

(a)   The take-off and approach speeds appear to be higher than was expected by the company. The F47 cameras (on the ground) in one instance showed a take-off speed of 186-196 knots when estimates indicated it should have been 160-170 knots. Estimated approach speeds are of the order of 180 knots but the pilot reported approach speeds ranging from 190-210 knots. If these indications are valid then it indicates that the lift curve slope is smaller than expected and that more elevator angle will be required to trim the airplane at high Mach. numbers. This will mean increased drag, decreased speed, and decreased "g" capability.

(b)   During the acceleration from the Mach. 0.95 to Mach. 1.1 only 93% RPM was being registered on the cockpit gauge even though both after burners were lit. The pilot reported that he did not feel that the airplane could have reached a much higher speed under these conditions. If this is the case, then it would indicate that either the engines are not developing full thrust or the aircraft's drag is higher than expected.

(c)   During elevator step inputs at the speed range 300-400 knots I.A.S. stick-free divergent longitudinal oscillations occurred. This oscillation was thought to be due to sticky valves in the flying control system. The frequency of the oscillations were such that the pilot could control them. Since there are so many valves in the flying control system this could be an indication that very particular attention will be required in the maintenance of the flying control system. Further more, it is possible that such oscillations could become uncontrollable.

At present, there is no cockpit indicator to show when the after burners are lit. The company's pilot has had two occasions when he was not aware of whether the after burners were working. In one case during a take-off

. . . /2

S E C R E T
Appendix "A" to
CEPE Letter S51-05-03

- 2 -

(2 cont'd)

run he applied additional pressure to the undercarriage selector by using the throttles as a fulcrum. This accidently lit one of the after burners. The pilot was unaware of this except from throttle position. In the second case, during an after burner climb both after burners were selected but from ground observations it would appear only one lit. The pilot had no indication of which one was lit.

(K. Owen) S/L

Left Page

ARROW I FLIGHT TESTING   S E C R E T

PROGRESS REPORT FOR PERIOD 7 JUNE 58 - 3 NOV 58

(Compiled and Submitted by CEPE)

Introduction

1   This report is forwarded for record and reference purposes.

General

2   Thirty one flights took place during the period 7 Jun 58 to 3 Nov 58 and 35:55 flying hours were acquired. Details are as follows:

Aircraft 25201 - 3 flts (4:25 hrs)(1st flt 25 Mar)

Aircraft 25202 - 20 flts (21:20 hrs)(1st flt 1 Aug)

Aircraft 25203 - 7 flts (9:00 hrs) (1st flt 22 Sep)

Aircraft 25204 - 1 flt (1:10 hrs) (1st flt 27 Oct)

3   The total number of flight test aircraft - months that were available during the period (Calculated from date of first flight for each a/c except a/c No. 1 which is calculated from 6 June) was approximately 9½ which averages out to approximately 4 hours flying time per aircraft per month.

4   The four aircraft have been allocated to programmes as follows:

(a) #25201 - Systems check-out and back-up for 25202.

(b) #25202 - Optimization of the damper and flying control systems, stability investigation and structural integrity.

(c) #25203 - Initially assigned to the Phase 2 programme but later switched to trial installation of the Hughes Fire Control system.

(d) #25204 - Initially assigned to u/c and weapon pack work but is now assigned to Phase 2 performance.

5   AVRO Report #71/FAR/30 which covers the detailed flight test programmes for the first 3 Arrow I aircraft is out of date. The company have been requested to revise it and include the early Arrow 2 aircraft.

Discussion

6   Specific items that have been watched in the flight test programme are performance, flight envelop exploration, buffeting, stability and control and any snags that have occurred. These are covered separately below.

7   Performance - The company's main objective in many of their flights on the Arrow 1 has been to establish its speed capability as quickly as possible. During the period the aircraft achieved M1.86 (indicated) at 50,000 ft while still accelerating.

.../2

Right Page

8   -2-   S E C R E T

8   Two flights have been carried out to establish the difference in drag between the cylindrical ejector and the convergent - divergent ejector. The difference between the two types of ejectors does not appear to be significant although the instrumentation used for the evaluation was very meagre. Because of the limited instrumentation that has been available and because the engines have not been calibrated any attempt to get a reasonable value for drag is highly questionable. The results did show however the excess thrust available is constant up to 1MN 1.7 at 50,000. This result alone shows the performance is better than was estimated.

9   Flight Envelope Exploration - This is closely associated with performance, however will be discussed separately. Appendix A shows the portion of the speed envelope covered during the period. It should be noted the greater part of this envelope which contains the divergent stability (with yaw dampers inoperative) region still remains to be explored.

10   On the load factor side of envelope exploration the following table gives details on the progress made to date.

Aircraft/ Flight No.	Alt.	IAS or IMN	"n"	a/c Wt.	"n"V	"n" at 55,000 lbs.
202/8	5,000	400	3	58,625	175,875	3.2
202/18	7,000	430	~ 1.50	62,000	-93,000	~ 1.7
202/18	7,500	450	3.60	63,000	226,800	4.1
201/5	8,000	475	3.25	63,500	206,400	3.8
202/15	10,000	450	2¼	57,900	144,750	2.6
201/6	10,000	400	3.0	52,000	156,000	2.8
202/14	14,000	440	2.5	65,400	163,500	3.0
202/15	16,000	0.7	+3.0 -2.0	64,325	192,975	3.5
202/15	20,000	0.70	3	58,000	174,000	3.2
202/15	25,000	0.80	3.00	59,600	178,800	3.3
202/10	30,000	0.90	2.50	60,500	151,250	2.8
202/18	36,000	1.6	2	59,125	182,500	3.3
202/18	39,000	1.32	2.75	53,300	146,600	2.7
202/13	42,000	1.40	2.75	55,500	152,600	2.6
	50,000	1.5	1.25	57,825	72,281	1.3

. . ./3

-3-

11   No serious load factor work has been attempted, probably because the flying control system is still not satisfactory. No strain gauge readings have been obtained as yet.

12   Buffeting – Airframe – Some buffeting occurs when pulling 2 "g" between 250 – 300 knots and also when pulling 1.25 "g" at M1.5 @ 50,000 feet IAS. The cause has not been determined as yet.

– Intakes – The engine intakes have caused no difficulty. An engine chop at IMN – 1.72 @ 50,000 ft caused a compressor stall, but later investigation showed the air bleed valves had not been activated. With this one exception (the fault has subsequently been rectified) the engines have behaved very well.

13   Stability and Control – This work has been carried out primarily on a/c #25202. This programme has been a "fly and fix" programme supported by about 10 channels of telemetry. Control taps are made periodically to check for control buzz at supersonic speeds and control flutter at low altitude and high "g". Very little quantitative information has obtained because of the lack of instrumentation. Compared to Convair's approach made on the F106A, the approach made on the Arrow is rather primitive.

14   Flight tests for the period show the following:

(a)   Normal and emergency yaw dampers are very reliable and provide adequate damping.

(b)   Roll damper is only partially satisfactory since it behaves well when no stick steering is used, but hesitates with stick steering. No serious problems appear to exist, just a matter of time and guessing correctly. Aileron stick force per degree of aileron is still being changed in order to obtain better feel.

(c)   Turn co-ordination still is a question mark. The co-ordination is apparently working as designed but does not appear to be satisfactory from a handling point of view.

(d)   Pitch damper has not received much attention because of the longitudinal flying control problem. The aircraft is very sensitive to control displacement at high subsonic speeds. With linear control gearing, this sensitivity makes it very touchy to fly at these speeds. In addition, the control system free play, control valve friction and linear stick force per "g" feel have contributed to the problems. The main endeavour on the last few flights of Aircraft 25202 has been to obtain a clearer picture. The plan is to remove control boosters and to move the parallel servo onto the rear quadrant, hence returning to the original design. In addition a non linear stick vs control angle relationship is being designed.

(e)   Spurious oscillations still occur on all control surfaces without or without dampers. These oscillations are generally of low magnitude and low frequency (4-10 cps.). On one flight, elevator oscillations produced 4 cycles of +3g – 1½g, much to the discomfort of the pilot.

(f)   Some of the oscillations are in sympathy with fundamental and lateral wing bending modes, others do not relate to any known aircraft mode.

.../4

-4-

(g)   There have been several cases of damper disengagement in the air and during landing. No explanation exists to-date.

(h)   Elevator angle to trim and per "g" appear to be generally in agreement with predictions; angles to trim are slightly less and angle per "g" more. Results have been rough and should be considered accordingly.

(i)   The "g" vane is prone to zero shift.

(j)   The aircraft has been flown in the clean configuration to IMN – 1.45 at 48,000 ft. and to IMN – 1.45 at 48,000 ft. IMN – 1.7 at 50,000 ft. and to IMN – 1.45 at 48,000 ft. Limited control kicks have been attempted in these regions and indications are that the aircraft is near predictions at 50,000 ft. but below predictions at 1.45 and 42,000.

(k)   Control taps over the speed envelope covered, indicate that both the structural modes and control surface modes are damped. No flutter or buzz has been recorded though damping was quite low at high IAS at 42,000 ft.

15   Aircraft Snags – The unserviceabilities on the four aircraft have primarily been associated with the undercarriage, air conditioning, fuel system gauges, parabrakes and the master warning panel. Each are covered separately below:

(a)   Undercarriage – A malfunction of the port u/c on Aircraft 25201 occurred on 11 June which caused the a/c to be damaged on landing. Modification to the undercarriage system has prevented this recurring. Some mild walking of the main legs has been experienced from time to time, but adjustments of struts etc. appears to eliminate this. Severe u/c door vibration still occurs between approximately 220-250 knots and the outer u/c doors were sucked off at 500 knots IAS – 9,000 feet. On the last flight of 25203 a leak in the utility hydraulic system occured which necessitated the use of the emergency braking system. This proved adequate for the conditions prevailing at the time; very little differential brake was required because of the small amount of cross wind and because of the failure of the chute. In addition to the above, during retraction tests the u/c retraction jack leg pick-up sheared which required a modification to the leg.

(b)   Air Conditioning System – The air conditioning problem has been primarily a function of the temperature controller. Over-heating, pressure fluctuations and delayed pressure control have been the result. Also during F/L Woodman's last flight the air conditioning turbine seized and caused a fire warning light indication.

(c)   Master Warning Light – This light is now known as the nuisance light and is not fulfilling the function it was designed for. The cause will probably be sorted out on a system aircraft. The light is on most of the time and it would appear as if there is no logical reason for this.

(d)   Fuel System – Fuel migration has been a common occurance on all aircraft, when they are left with partial fuel loads for a period of time – i.e. 24 – 36 hours. Fuel remaining gauges have been highly erratic.

.../5

-5-

(e)   Parachute Operation – No problem has been encountered with the chute release from the aircraft except on the last flight of 25203, the chute was jettisoned on selection. All the problems have been with the chute itself. There has been many failures of the chute. Other times only the complete failures of the risers and at least 4 – 5 gores have ripped out. Most of the time after the chute does deploy, it streams either on the top or to the side of the jet efflux. This latter situation puts considerable increased demand on the brakes, especially with no nose-wheel steering.

DECLASSIFIED
AUTHORITY: DHD3-12
BY _____
FOR DHIST NDHQ
DATE: OCT - 1 1997

CANCELLED

SECRET

ROYAL CANADIAN AIR FORCE

AIR MATERIEL COMMAND

CENTRAL EXPERIMENTAL AND PROVING ESTABLISHMENT

REPORT NO. 1364

RCAF FLIGHT NUMBER TWO

ARROW MARK I AIRCRAFT

REFERENCE:

AMC Experimental Project 58/33
Issue 2, dated Aug 58.

COMPILED BY:

J.F. Woodman, Flight Lieutenant,
Project Test Pilot.

SUBMITTED BY:

J.N. Brough, Wing Commander,
Senior Project Officer.

APPROVED BY:

D.L.S. MacWilliam, Group Captain,
Commanding Officer, CEPE,
for AOC AMC.

CANCELLED

SECRET
iii

SUMMARY

Flight No. 2 of CEPE's Phase 2 Flight Test Programme on Arrow Mark I, Serial No. 25202 was carried out Sunday, 28 September 1958 by F/L J.F. Woodman. Flight duration was 1 hour. The flight was carried out using mainly the emergency mode of control. The control stick steering system (which will be the normal mode of control) functions when either the roll and/or pitch dampers are engaged. The yaw and roll dampers were functioning but not the pitch damper.

In general, the handling characteristics of the Arrow Mark I have been improved considerably since the RCAF first flight. The yaw damper is performing quite reliably, although turn co-ordination appears questionable in some areas. The roll damper is not optimized as yet, but, it is still easier to fly the aircraft with the damper engaged than with it disengaged. Longitudinal control is sensitive at high IAS.

This will be investigated further with and without the pitch damper functioning.

NOTE

The problem of optimizing the feel and trim units for both elevator and aileron control systems for all conditions of flight is being investigated by the contractor. At present, in both systems, a linear gearing exists between stick displacement and control surface movement. This is satisfactory only for certain conditions of flight and a non-linear gearing system has been designed for the elevator and will be installed for evaluation in the near future.

RCAF FLIGHT NUMBER TWO

ARROW MARK I AIRCRAFT

CANCELLED

INTRODUCTION

1.   Flight No. 2 of CEPE's Phase 2 Flight Test Programme on the Arrow I was carried out on Sunday, 28 Sep 58 on aircraft No. 25202. The flight lasted 1 hour. An attempt was made to fly the supersonic mission profile from take-off, however, the general purpose of the flight was familiarization and evaluation over the area of the flight envelope covered thus far by the contractor.

CONDITION OF THE AIRCRAFT

2.   The condition of aircraft No. 25202 was as follows:-

(a) Starting weight 67, 430 lbs.
(b) Centre of gravity 28. 97% MAC (undercarriage up).
(c) Limitations:

 (i)   EAS 500 knots Max
        160 knots Min

 (ii)   Mach No. 1. 9

 (iii) Normal accelerations:

        Subsonic +3. 4, -2. 3
        Supersonic +2. 9, -1. 3.

 (iv)   Roll 90 degrees.

(d) Roll and yaw dampers were functioning.

3.   Significant changes to the aircraft relative to Flight No. 1 on 22 April 58 were as follows:

(a) Roll damper was functioning.

(b) Control stick break out forces were increased; in roll from 1 lb to 3 lbs and in pitch from 3 lbs to 5 lbs.

(c) Hinge moment limiter was set at a fixed value of 150 lbs for 20 degrees rudder movement.

(d) There was positive self-centering in the hinge moment limiter.

(e) The lost play in the control circuits was reduced.

CANCELLED
2

4   TESTS CARRIED OUT

        Flying was carried out over approximately 90 percent of the flight envelope and a brief qualitative handling assessment covered the following points:

(a) Ground handling.
(b) Take-off and climb.
(c) Handling at 50, 000 feet at Mach Nos. of 1. 5, 1. 6 and 1. 7.
(d) Descent.
(e) Handling at 15, 000 feet at low IAS.
(f) Approach and landing.

RESULTS OF TESTS CARRIED OUT

Ground Handling

5   At a weight of approximately 67, 000 lbs the aircarft started to move with 75% engine RPM. Once started, idle RPM provided sufficient thrust to keep rolling. Differential braking was required to steer the aircraft during taxiing. The feel of the brakes was still inadequate to accurately control the heading of the aircraft without one or two overshoots. However, this could be due partly to a lack of handling familiarization. During the taxi run to the take-off position the aircraft shook and vibrated slightly as if a tire or an oleo leg was flat. Apparently this was not the reason, however. This aircraft vibration was not noticed when taxiing in after the flight.

Take-off and Climb

6   The aircraft was lined up on the runway and stopped. The engines were opened to 100% RPM against the brakes. The aircraft started to roll when the brakes were released and the afterburners were lit after a short stabilizing roll. There was no audible notice of the afterburners lighting separately, however, a slight swing did develop, necessitating differential brake. Here again, the lack of brake feel resulted in 2 or 3 overshoots and corrections. Initially, correction was attempted with rudder only but the response at the low speed was insufficient.

7   The handling technique used for take-off was the same as outlined in CEPE Report No. 1325, with all dampers out. Acceleration at maximum thrust was very high. The nose wheel lifted and the aircraft became airborne at approximately the same speeds quoted in the referenced report, however, the times were noticeably reduced. The take-off roll was estimated at 3, 200 to 3, 500 feet.

8   A yawing oscillation of 2 or 3 degrees was created when the undercarriage was selected up. This oscillation damped out when the undercarriage was fully retracted. Shortly after take-off the normal gear-up mode was selected and yaw and roll dampers were engaged. The climb was carried out at 350 to 375 knots IAS to 20, 000 feet and at Mach 0. 90 (indicated) to 40, 000 feet. At this altitude the nose was pushed over to a level flight attitude and the aircraft allowed to accelerate to Mach 1. 3. The climb was then resumed (still accelerating but at a slower rate) until 50, 000 feet and Mach 1. 5 were achieved.

9   It was possible to carry out a stable climb at supersonic speeds. Control feel and response was generally satisfactory. However, at 350 to 375 knots (indicated) below 20, 000 feet and at Mach . 90 between 20, 000 and 40, 000 feet it was extremely difficult not to over control the aircraft and a continuous 2 or 3 degrees of yaw and roll resulted (i. e. Dutch rolling). The control system as it exists is too sensitive in these subsonic speed ranges.

CANCELLED

Handling at 50,000 Feet

10   At this altitude with the yaw and roll dampers still engaged a level 180 degrees turn was attempted at Mach 1.5. Approximately 1.25G was required to maintain altitude at 45 degrees angle of bank. The altitude, however, did vary somewhat and the speed dropped to Mach 1.4. It is felt the drop in speed was due to the variation in altitude. A continuous slight airframe vibration was felt throughout the turn. It did not feel like a buffet boundary or a stall warning but it did feel like an aerodynamic effect of some sort. When the turn was completed an acceleration to Mach 1.7 was carried out with only yaw damper engaged as the roll damper was not cleared beyond Mach 1.5. No manoeuvres were attempted at this speed but the aircraft was very stable and the control feel was very good.

Deceleration and Descent

11   At Mach 1.6 and still at 50,000 feet while decelerating, the starboard engine was throttled from 100% RPM to idle in approximately 3 seconds. There was no indication of a compressor stall or intake pressure fluctuations and directional control problems were negligible. The other engine was then throttled to idle and the dive brakes were selected out at Mach 1.3. There was a very slight nose-up change of trim but a barely detectable effect on drag. As speed decreased below Mach 1.1 the effect of the brakes became more noticeable. The descent was stabilized at Mach .8, and at 20,000 feet the angle of descent was approximately 45 to 50 degrees. There was no indication of windscreen misting or cabin pressure fluctuation.

Handling at 15,000 Feet

12   At 15,000 feet the roll damper was re-engaged and the aircraft trimmed to fly level at 160 knots IAS. Approximately 90% RPM was required to maintain steady level flight at this speed with an angle of incidence of 13 degrees. With undercarriage down approximately 93% RPM was required. It was not particularly difficult to fly the aircraft in this condition, however, at 160 knots there was an indication of neutral longitudinal stability with stick fixed. At 200 knots IAS, the starboard engine was throttled to idle and level turns were carried out using the port engine and with the undercarriage up and down. There was adequate power available to maintain altitude and there was no problem handling the aircraft in either configuration. In the normal gear down mode (roll and yaw damper engaged) the aircraft sideslipped 4 to 5 degrees when entering each turn. This sideslip was eliminated with approximately 15 to 20 lbs foot force and 2 to 3 degrees of rudder. It would have been very difficult to make the proper correction without the "beta" (sideslip) indicator providing a reference.

13   Power on the idling engine was restored and speed was increased to 250 knots IAS and then 350 knots IAS. At each speed, level turns were carried out (yaw and roll dampers engaged) and 1.75G and 2.5G respectively were pulled. On rolling into a turn (at any speed in this range) if a normal rate of aileron movement was applied, a jerky aileron motion was felt. If a very slow entry was made this jerky motion did not occur. It is obvious the gain settings for the roll rate gyro and the aileron differential servo for these conditions of flight have not been optimized.

14   When speed was increased to 450 knots IAS, lateral control was generally acceptable. Longitudinal control, however, above 400 knots IAS became increasingly sensitive. At 450 knots IAS, approximately only 3 lbs of stick force (1/5 of an inch travel of control column) was required per 1/2G normal acceleration. A longitudinal oscillation was experienced at this speed where the aircraft pitched through 3 or 4 degrees for approximately 5 cycles lasting 3 or

---

CANCELLED

14 (Cont'd)

4 seconds. The pilot was unable to damp this oscillation, however, it stopped as suddenly as it started. Slight elevator taps were carried out at this speed, and the aircraft displayed positive dynamic longitudinal stability, stick free.

Landing

15   The handling technique employed for landing was approximately the same as that described in CEPE Report No. 1325. Four to five degrees of sideslip was experienced on all turns with the undercarriage down and yaw damper only engaged. Corrections were made by using the sideslip indicator as a reference. The final approach was made at 180 knots IAS using 11 to 12 degrees of incidence. Touch down speed was approximately 155 knots. (Landing weight for the aircraft was later estimated to be approximately 51,000 lbs). The drag chute was selected at approximately 145 knots, however, it failed to deploy and the aircraft was brought to a full stop without difficulty using moderate braking, intermittently. The full length of the runway was used to accomplish this.

NOTE

The apparent reason that the drag chute did not deploy was because it was wet (thus reducing the porosity of the chute) and 10 suspension lines failed when the chute was streamed.

CONCLUSIONS

The conclusions are as follows:

16

(a)   The handling characteristics of the Arrow Mark I have been improved considerably since the first RCAF flight.

(b)   The yaw damper functioned reliably although turn co-ordination needs to be improved in some areas.

(c)   The roll damper required more optimization to provide smooth control responses throughout the subsonic speed range.

(d)   Longitudinal control is still too sensitive at high subsonic speeds. However, with the pitch damper and control stick steering system functioning, the longitudinal control characteristics should be very good once the system is optimized.

Aug 28/58

SECRET

- 6 -

12. During the discussion it was pointed out that the Senate had the legal right to amend the bill even if it affected the balance of ways and means. Differences of this nature between the two houses were, of course, most infrequent. It would not be advisable to get into a fight at this time with the Senate over its legal rights which, in fact, it had not exercised since 1935. Should the Senate choose to support the committee's recommendations, the bill would be returned to the House of Commons where there would be occasion to consider in detail its implications.

13. The Cabinet noted the report of the Minister of Finance on the amendments proposed in the Senate Banking and Commerce Committee to the draft Estate Tax bill, and agreed to give further consideration at the next meeting to any action to be taken when the bill was returned to the House of Commons.

Air defence requirements; recommendations of Cabinet Defence Committee

Start Here 8/28/58

14. The Minister of National Defence said that the Cabinet Defence Committee had reviewed the air defence requirements for rounding out the air defence weapons system against the manned bomber. The committee had agreed to recommend that two BOMARC bases be created in the Ottawa and North Bay area, and two additional heavy radars installed in Northern Ontario and Quebec with associated gap-filler radars. It was also proposed that negotiations be started with the U.S. for the cost-sharing and production-sharing of the BOMARC bases and equipment and the heavy radars and related equipment. The committee had referred to the Cabinet for consideration proposals to cancel the CF-105 programme and to investigate additional missile installations and a possible alternative interceptor to the CF-105.

Last October the Cabinet had approved continuation for another twelve months of the CF-105 development programme, which included the ordering of 29 pre-production aircraft, improvements in tooling, acceleration of the development of the Iroquois engine, and the continuation of the necessary related programmes. In a project such as this there were two main phases; development and pre-production and, then, production for operational service. These overlapped. The first was now well advanced and a decision was therefore urgently required as to whether or not to go into production.

The R.C.A.F. now had nine all-weather squadrons and the present programme called for their re-equipment with the CF-105, requiring a production order of 169 in number. These, together with aircraft recovered from the development and pre-production order for 37, would provide sufficient aircraft for nine squadrons. The total cost would be $2 billion spread from 1959-60 to 1963-64.

SECRET

- 7 -

A study of the implications of continuing this programme, its impact on the whole defence programme and the necessity of considering future requirements, such as defence against intercontinental ballistic missiles, had necessitated a review of the air defence programme. The Chiefs of Staff had undertaken such a review. The main points that were considered were the following:

The assessment of the threat to North America had changed. In the 1960's, the main threat would probably be from the manned bomber, ballistic missiles with the manned bomber decreasing in importance after 1962-63. However, a combination of the two might be the threat until Soviet manned bombers were depleted. The rapid strides in technology were such that to provide a suitable manned fighter to cope with heavy jet bombers was extremely expensive. Furthermore, ground-to-air missiles had now reached the point where they were at least as effective as a manned fighter, and cheaper. The original requirements in 1953 for between 500 and 600 aircraft of the CF-105 fighter had been drastically reduced. Subsequently, thought had been given to reducing it still further now that the BOMARC missile would probably be introduced into the Canadian air defence system. Finally, the cost of the CF-105 programme as a whole was now of such a magnitude that the Chiefs of Staff felt that, to meet the modest requirement of manned aircraft presently considered advisable, it would be more economical to procure a fully developed interceptor of comparable performance in the U.S.

The Minister proposed that the recommendations of the Cabinet Defence Committee on the BOMARC bases, the heavy radars, the gap fillers, and on negotiating with the U.S. regarding cost-sharing and production-sharing be approved, and that consideration be given to abandoning the CF-105 and to authorizing the Chiefs of Staff to investigate an alternative for it and to consider any additional missile installations that might be required. He himself recommended cancelling the CF-105 programme in its entirety and deferring for a year any decision to order interceptor aircraft from the U.S.

An explanatory memorandum had been circulated, (Minister's memorandum, Aug. 22, 1958 - Cab. Doc.247-58).

SECRET

- 8 -

15. Mr. Pearkes explained that the CF-105 programme consisted of four major projects; the airframe, development of which was being undertaken by AVRO in Toronto; the Iroquois engine at Orenda Engines Ltd., also in Toronto; the fire control system (ASTRA) on which Westinghouse in Hamilton was co-operating with a U.S. company, and the weapon (SPARROW) on which Canadair in Montreal was co-operating with a U.S. company. There were, of course, several sub-contractors in many parts of Ontario and Quebec. He outlined some limitations of the aircraft, some details of the costs involved, and some of the difficulties that had been encountered since the programme's inception. Not long ago he had been disposed to recommend that it go ahead and aircraft be ordered for squadron service. However, the change in the nature of the threat and the very great cost of development and production had brought him to make the recommendation he had. He was fully aware of its seriousness but he had made it after very careful study of all the factors involved.

He went on to describe the semi-automatic ground environment (S.A.G.E.) system and the steps that had to be taken to introduce it, whether or not the government decided to proceed with the CF-105. He also described the U.S. intentions on BOMARC and how they related to Canada. In addition to installing two such missile sites in central Canada, it might also be desirable to install one base in the Vancouver area and one in the Maritimes. There were considerable advantages in adopting BOMARC. It was cheaper than the CF-105, in terms of men and money, and just as effective. The missile could be fitted with an atomic warhead and the U.S. would probably supply heads on the same basis ("key-to-the-cupboard"), as they made atomic weapons available to the U.K.

As regards aircraft, the U.S. authorities had made it quite clear that they did not intend to buy any CF-105s. Their own F-106C was comparable in performance to the CF-105, it would be available for squadron service several months earlier, and it cost less than half as much. The U.S. was also developing the F-108, a huge aircraft with a range of approximately 1,000 miles.

His recommendation to abandon the CF-105 and investigate other aircraft and missile possibilities meant that the government would have a year to decide whether it should re-equip air defence fighter forces wholly with the BOMARC, or an alternative aircraft, or a combination of both. Within that time there should be a better understanding of Soviet intentions as to whether they were likely to introduce more or better bombers, or go completely into missiles.

SECRET

- 9 -

Decisions could be taken in the light of the then existing information. Abandoning the CF-105 would of course be a rude shock to the aircraft industry, but it would not mean its complete cessation. DeHavilland would not be affected nor would the transport and marine aircraft sections at Canadair.

16. During the long discussion the following points emerged:

(a) It was doubtful if the BOMARC missile or components could be manufactured in Canada. However, the launchers might be.

(b) Layoffs involved in abandoning the CF-105 would amount to well over 25,000 and there was some doubt as to whether these workers could obtain alternative employment. This would have an extremely adverse effect on the economy which now needed every push it could get. This was the most serious aspect of the proposal.

(c) It was argued, on the other hand that, surely, in an economy as potentially vigorous as Canada's, employees would soon be absorbed in other jobs. There was no more expensive way of keeping people at work than by the CF-105 programme.

(d) If the CF-105 were not abandoned, it would mean an increase in the defence budget of $400 million a year for several years. Even without this the deficit in 1959-60 would be as much as in the current year. If it were at all responsible, the government would have no alternative but to increase taxes should the 105 be put into production. Adding it to the present overall rate of deficit would mean the wrecking of Canada's credit and the stimulation of inflation.

(e) The CF-105 would be of no use against ballistic missiles. It would, however, be effective against air-breathing, unmanned bombers. There was no chance of having an anti-missile missile by 1960 or 1961. The Sparrow, with which the CF-105 was to be equipped, could not be fitted with an atomic warhead.

SECRET

- 10 -

(f) Although it would be most helpful if the facilities presently used on the CF-105 programme could be converted for the development of missiles, this was highly unlikely. The best possibility for the future was a production programme of partnership with the U.S. The U.S. authorities had indicated they would be willing to allocate a significant share of future missile development to Canada, but this would not occur for some time and would mean considerable discussions with them. The U.S. had not yet reached a decision on the type of anti-missile missile they would require.

(g) The United Kingdom would not buy the CF-105 and it was most unlikely that any other N.A.T.O. country would either. The U.K. was practically out of the interceptor field and was concentrating on missiles, many of which were being acquired from the U.S. Indeed, the whole trend in Europe was towards missiles, but the air defence problem there was different to that in North America.

(h) One means of helping the aircraft industry would be to manufacture transport aircraft, under licence for Trans-Canada Air Lines and possibly other domestic users.

(1) The evidence available indicated that the U.S.S.R. did not intend to match the U.S. with a long range air force similar to the Strategic Air Command, or come anywhere near it. Recently, the U.S. thought the Russian bomber force was bigger than we did. Now this was not the case. The intelligence authorities were coming to the view that the U.S.S.R. would not launch an attack until it was clearly superior in ballistic missiles to the U.S.

(j) The U.S. was planning to equip its air defence forces half with missiles and half with aircraft. Should not Canada plan to do roughly the same thing? If the CF-105 were discontinued Canada would be completely dependent on the U.S. for equipment for the R.C.A.F.

(k) The CF-100 would soon be obsolete and there was no demand for it here or from abroad. No help for the industry, therefore, could be expected by way of more orders for it.

SECRET

- 11 -

(1) On military or financial grounds it seemed clear that there was no reason to continue the programme. Indeed, many members of the Conservative Party had said in the past that it was quite unwise for a country of Canada's size to attempt to develop an aircraft of this kind in the first place. Instead, they had advocated the manufacture of military aircraft under license. However, to abandon the CF-105 now and undertake to produce the U.S. F-106C, which was physically quite possible, would be a serious political mistake.

17. The Cabinet deferred decision on the recommendations of the Cabinet Defence Committee regarding air defence requirements, including the future of the CF-105 programme.

R.B. Bryce,
Secretary to the Cabinet.

SECRET

Sept 3/58

- 2 -

(re Arrow)

Visit of the Queen and Prince Philip in 1959

1. **The Prime Minister** said he had asked to have this brief meeting to inform the Cabinet of the announcement he intended to make, when the House of Commons met, that the Queen and the Prince Philip would visit Canada from approximately mid-June to the end of July next year. It had been thought advisable to make this announcement at once to prevent leaks that were otherwise bound to occur.

2. **The Cabinet** noted with approval the Prime Minister's intention to announce that the Queen and the Prince Philip would visit Canada from mid-June to the end of July of next year.

Air defence requirements; recommendations of Cabinet Defence Committee (Previous reference Aug. 28)

3. **The Minister of National Defence** said that, since this subject had last been discussed, Mr. John Tory, one of the directors of A.V. Roe, and Mr. F.T. Smye, Vice-President of Avro Aircraft Ltd., had discussed the future of the CF-105 with the Prime Minister, the Minister of Finance, and himself. These men recommended that the airframe and Iroquois engine elements of the programme be continued but that the fire control system (ASTRA) and the weapon (SPARROW) projects be dropped and substitutes obtained in the United States. Instead of ASTRA and SPARROW they had suggested the U.S. Hughes MA-1 system and the FALCON, respectively. He had had cost estimates prepared on this suggestion and comparisons made with other alternatives. These were as follows:

Expenditures for 100 aircraft, from September 1st, 1958:

105/Astra-Sparrow	$1,261.5 million or	$12.61 million each
105/Hughes MA-1-Falcon	$ 896 million or	$ 8.91 million each
U.S. 106	$ 559 million or	$ 5.59 million each
BOMARC (to provide roughly equivalent defensive strength)	$ 520.3 million	4 batteries of 60 missiles each (no cost-sharing with the U.S.)

4. **During the discussion** the following further points emerged:

(a) If it turned out in a year's time that the U.S.S.R. was going to equip its air force with newer, more modern bombers, then Canada would have to buy BOMARC or an interceptor from the U.S., or both, assuming the CF-105 was abandoned.

SECRET

- 3 -

(b) If, on the other hand, it was clear at that time that the U.S.S.R. was not producing bombers, arrangements would have to be made with the U.S. for defence against missiles.

(c) There would be no chance of resuming the CF-105 programme once it was cancelled. It would be better to cancel it now than to be confronted with no more work for Avro, and the other companies involved, after production of 100 aircraft was drawing to an end in 1961 and 1962. It was unwise to encourage the aircraft industry to continue to produce equipment that could quite well be obsolete by the time it was available.

(d) BOMARC might possibly be manufactured in Canada, under licence, by Canadair, which had the closest connections with the company in the U.S. doing this work. Avro and the other companies in the CF-105 programme would probably not be involved in such a project.

(e) It had been said by some that not only were manned interceptors becoming obsolete but so also were naval surface vessels. The latter eventuality, however, was further in the future than the first. Nuclear-powered anti-submarine submarines would be the most useful defence against enemy submarines equipped to launch atomic weapons. But they were very expensive. Failing that, the surface ships and the anti-submarine aircraft, with which Canadian forces were being equipped, provided a reasonable defence against possible assaults from the sea.

(f) The Chiefs of Staff were divided on the question of the CF-105. The Chief of the Air Staff felt there was a useful role for the manned interceptor, but the specific type of equipment and armament he preferred would depend upon the amount of money that was available. The heads of the other two services felt the nature of the threat was changing so quickly that the situation should be kept under review for a year. They did feel that the CF-105 programme, as it presently stood, was not the best way to spend so much money. The Chairman was of the view that BOMARC would give the best defence for the money likely to be available.

Start Here 9/3/58

SECRET

- 4 -

(g) The truth was that no one could forecast with reasonable precision what the requirement might be a year hence. Each of the military services had their own special reasons for the views they held. The Navy and the Army were particularly concerned that going ahead with the CF-105 might mean less money for them in the future. However, it would be unwise to look for reductions in these two services, even with the CF-105, unless some very drastic steps were taken.

(h) The Conservative Party, right from Confederation, had always been a vigorous protagonist of the theory that Canada's needs should be met from within Canada. To abandon the CF-105 even though it was so expensive and might be obsolete would be hard to explain. On the other hand, it would be equally hard to explain, in three or four years, why the government had spent vast sums of money on a relatively small number of aircraft which might by then be virtually useless.

5. The Minister of Finance reported on the representations made to him by Mr. Tory and Mr. Smye of Avro. The CF-105 programme supported 25,000 persons in employment. If it were abandoned, the highly skilled pool of talent drawn together for the project would be dispersed and many of the people concerned would go to the United States, never to return. No portion of Avro's profits had been invested in other sectors of the group industry. Although controlled by the Hawker-Siddley group, of which Avro was now a part except in the aircraft Avro was in large part owned by Canadians. They had stated that the R.C.A.F. had made a major mistake three years ago by recommending the adoption of SPARROW and ASTRA. A great deal of money could be saved by using the FALCON and the Hughes fire control system. Finally, they said that, if the programme with their proposed modification were continued, their company would have a reasonable opportunity before the end of 1962 to look for other business. If they found little or none, then Avro would be in real difficulties.

Mr. Fleming said he had pointed out to Messrs. Tory and Smye that their arguments, that the Falcon missile and Hughes fire control system developed by the United States should be good enough for Canada, could also be used against them in regard to the airframe and engines which they wanted produced in Canada by their own firm. Mr. Smye, in particular, had been very critical of some R.C.A.F. decisions and officers.

SECRET

- 5 -

6. The Minister of National Defence felt bound to say that the R.C.A.F. had conscientiously made the recommendations they thought would be the best in the interests of the defence of Canada. The government of the day was responsible for the decisions reached and the present government would be responsible for any decision on the future of the CF-105. He also said that the figures on savings mentioned by Mr. Smye should be treated with reserve. The latter had not been aware, for example, that there were a number of types of FALCON.

7. The Cabinet deferred decision on the recommendations of the Cabinet Defence Committee regarding air defence requirements, including the future of the CF-105 programme.

R. B. Bryce,
Secretary to the Cabinet.

SECRET

Sept 5/58

- 16 -

(b) an effort being made to interest others at the conference in the possibility of establishing a Commonwealth financial institution to assist in financing the development of the new and emerging members of the Commonwealth; and,

(c) the understanding that there would be reasonable consultation with Commonwealth governments affected before concessional sales of agricultural surpluses were made.

Air defence requirements; recommendations of Cabinet Defence Committee
(Previous reference Sept. 3)

42. The Prime Minister opened the further discussion of the proposal of the Minister of National Defence to cancel the CF-105 programme by stating that although ministers were relatively well agreed on the purely defence aspects, the serious problem still requiring consideration was the effect on employment and the general economic situation.

43. The Minister of Finance said that in considering matters of defence he naturally put the safety of the country ahead of finance. When it had been recommended a year ago that the CF-105 programme be continued, he supported the recommendation. Now, however, the military view was that the programme should be cancelled. In these circumstances, he did not see how the government could decide not to discontinue it. The arguments for continuing were that Canadian military requirements should be found in Canada, that cancelling the programme would throw upwards of 25,000 men out of work with serious effects on the economy, and that national prestige should be taken into account.

As regards the first, other things being equal or nearly so, military equipment should be produced in Canada. But in this case the cost per aircraft was twice as much as the cost of a comparable unit which could be obtained in the U.S., and, more important, the military authorities had now decided that the aircraft was not necessary. On the employment aspect, while a decision to discontinue would undoubtedly be painful, nevertheless, the workers involved would in time be absorbed in the national economy. There would still be an important aircraft industry in Canada without the CF-105. Finally, one had to agree that not going ahead would be a blow to national prestige. But no one even knew now what the price for maintaining this aspect of our prestige might be.

SECRET

- 17 -

44. Mr. Fleming said he had asked himself if there was a middle course between cancelling the programme and going into production. Unfortunately, there was not. Once production was ordered the government would be committed. There was no time that was the right time for a decision like this one. He was sure, however, that it would be better to cancel now than be faced with a final shut down of the plants three or four years hence. Another factor to be kept in mind was that, by deferring cancellation, the programme, in effect, become the present government's programme, whereas in cancelling now it could be said that the government had considered all aspects of a project started by the previous administration and had come to the conclusion that the best course was to abandon it. Finally, one had to keep in mind that by going ahead, and thereby adding approximately $400 million a year for four years to the defence appropriation, air defence would assume a disproportionate share in the defence budget. This was nearly the value of a year's wheat crop. An increase in railway freight rates, which was being considered, was a trifle by comparison. A good deal of northern development could be undertaken for much less. In short, cancelling the programme would be of much greater help to the economy as a whole than continuing it.

45. During the discussion the following further points emerged:

(a) In the forthcoming winter, unemployment would be higher than it was last year. Cancelling now, apart from the effect on the employees concerned, might well be the one psychological factor which would result in a break in the economy and lead to a drastic down-turn from which recovery would be extremely difficult. The programme should be allowed to continue over the winter and a decision taken then as to its future. During that period, management could consider what their plants might do in the future.

(b) On the other hand, continuing the programme, even for only six months, meant that orders had to be placed now for materials for production. Did this proposal mean that the pre-production order of 37 should be completed? If this were the case, only a few planes for identification purposes would be available and the individual costs would be astronomical.

(c) The U.S.S.R. had always said that western economies would ultimately collapse. Carrying on a project like this involving so much of the taxpayers' money and whose returns were questionable was surely only playing into Russian hands. The money could be put to better use elsewhere.

SECRET

- 18 -

(d) On the other hand, while cancellation might be sound in theory, it might result in a recession. If employment prospects were better, the project could be dropped quickly. Continuing, even for only a few months, involved insignificant amounts compared with what would have to be spent during a real depression.

(e) If the project were abandoned, arrangements could quite probably be made with the U.S. to purchase 106Cs and also to secure atomic heads for the weapon with which they would be equipped. The U.S. authorities had also indicated in the last few days that they would be prepared to consider seriously cost-sharing and production sharing of defence equipment. They had also said they would be prepared to relocate northwards some of their proposed Bomarc installations. These Bomarc bases hardly seemed to cover Canada at all. They were most concerned at the moment over improvements to the warning system.

(f) Surely the Canadian public would give credit to the government in the long run for good housekeeping and it appeared that on defence and on sound economic grounds it was good housekeeping to discontinue the programme now.

46. The Cabinet deferred decision on the recommendations of the Cabinet Defence Committee regarding air defence requirements, including the future of the CF-105 programme.

R.B. Bryce,
Secretary to the Cabinet.

SECRET

- 6 -

Sept 8/58

(b) It was impossible to commit a specific amount of $50 million in gifts. The whole question must be looked at carefully and there must be no tying of hands. On the other hand, what could be done in 1958-59 could be used at the Commonwealth Trade and Economic Conference and discussions initiated with India.

8. **The Cabinet** approved in principle the recommendations of the Minister of Trade and Commerce as to assistance for the export of wheat to Commonwealth countries under the Colombo Plan by some form of grants or gifts and agreed that,-

(a) the sum of $10 million be made available immediately from unused appropriations for assisting wheat export under the Colombo Plan;

(b) that, if possible, another $10 million be made available in 1958-59, by arrangement with Commonwealth countries in the plan to hold back expenditures on capital projects and use the amounts for gifts of wheat;

(c) that authority from Parliament for reimbursement of the second $10 million be sought in the Final Supplementary Estimates, 1958-59;

(d) that no commitments be made at this time as to the degree of any aid of this nature in 1959-60, but that talks could be instituted with the Commonwealth countries concerned as to the possible programme; and,

(e) that the whole matter be reviewed early in the coming year.

Start Here 9/8/58

Air defence requirements; recommendations of Cabinet Defence Committee
(Previous reference Sept. 7)

9. **The Prime Minister** said he felt a final decision on the recommendations of the Cabinet Defence Committee about air defence requirements should be deferred for a week or two, in the hope that new alternatives could be worked out, or a compromise reached.

10. **The Minister of National Defence** said that consideration could be given to the completion of 20 development and preproduction CF-105 aircraft and then producing another 48 aircraft. This would give a total of 68, divided into 5 squadrons, which would be the minimum operational aircraft required. The order would only slightly reduce employment at the Avro plant and would cost $400 million for the next two years, if the production rate were kept up. Before 1961 the

- 7 -

programme might be slowed up and then come to a stop. 68 aircraft would also be the minimum if it were decided to purchase U.S. F106 C planes. If hostilities broke out, we should have to use the CF-100 and he would urge immediately starting on an anti-missile missile project. However, apart from this aspect of the problem, it was essential that some decision be taken on the installation of 2 Bomarc bases in the Ottawa-North Bay area and the installation of two additional heavy radars in Northern Ontario and Quebec and the installation of the associated gap filler radars.

He recommended that approval be given in principle to this part of the programme and that he be authorized to begin negotiations with the U.S. for cost-sharing and production.

11. **The Cabinet** agreed,-

(a) that decision be deferred for some two weeks on what should be done with the present CF-105 (Arrow) programme pending further examination of various alternatives; and,

(b) that the Minister of National Defence be authorized to begin negotiations with the United States for cost-sharing and production sharing on the following:-

(i) the installation of 2 Bomarc bases in the Ottawa-North Bay area; and,

(ii) the installation of 2 heavy radars in Northern Ontario and Quebec and the installation of associated gap-filler radars.

Railway labour dispute

12. **The Minister of Transport** spoke on developments arising out of the threatened railway strike by the non-operating unions.

The indications were the unions would accept the majority recommendation of the arbitration board regarding a wage increase. In a sense, this would place them in a strong position. In presenting their case to the public, it was good psychology for them to appear to be giving in for the sake of harmony and agreeing to abide by the majority report of an independent body.

The Presidents of the C.N.R. and C.P.R. were convinced that, if the unions were not granted the increase recommended in the majority report, they would go on strike. The railways took the position that they could not grant the wage increase unless they were guaranteed a compensating increase in freight rates. The C.N.R. was in a serious

SECRET

Sept 21/58

- 4 -

(c) If, as an alternative move, Canada suggested an amendment to the resolution stressing that, under the present circumstances, it was not opportune to consider the matter, this amendment would be considered by the United States as a formal unfriendly act.

(d) In the Province of Quebec public opinion was against the United States attitude and the people did not want to see Canada get involved in a major conflict over Quemoy or Formosa. Chiang Kai-Shek was not popular in Quebec. Many of the clergy (including the clergy in the United States) considered the present situation as ridiculous. The French Ambassador had inquired from Mr. Fulton about the Roman Catholic point of view in Canada. The reasons for his inquiry appeared to be that, because of non-recognition, there was no possibility of protecting Roman Catholic missionary interests in China.

5. The Cabinet agreed that the Secretary of State for External Affairs vote in favour of a procedural motion postponing consideration of the issue for a fixed period such as for the duration of the 13th session of the General Assembly and that he deliver a statement in the Plenary Session along the lines proposed during the discussion.

(At a subsequent meeting held later in the day the draft statement was discusssed and approved).

Government purchasing policy; purchase for defence programme
(Previous reference Sept.7)

Start Here 9/21/58

6. The Minister of Finance said he had now had a chance to discuss the implications of the new government purchasing policy directive, which had been approved by Cabinet, with the Minister of Defence Production who had not been able to be present when it was considered. The Deputy Minister of Defence Production would be in Washington shortly to carry out negotiations and it would be desirable that he be in a position to explain that the new directive did not affect the pattern of government defence purchases based upon strategic consideration.

He hoped to be able to say something on this subject privately to the United Kingdom and to ask them not to press the Canadian government on this matter. The British had expressed some concern about the "buy in America" policy of the United States. He thought it preferable to soft-pedal the purchasing directive rather than jeopardize negotiations with the United States. Mr. O'Hurley was also of this opinion.

7. The Cabinet noted the report of the Minister of Finance on the recent government purchasing policy directive and agreed that it be withheld for some time.

SECRET

Sept 21/58

- 9 -

He recommended that Canada accede to the latest request from the United Nations Secretary General.

19. The Minister of National Defence said that it would be possible for the Army to provide the necessary personnel although the number going would pinch a bit. It was most desirable, however, that an officer of the rank of lieutenant-colonel be sent with this new group with whom defence headquarters could correspond and who would be responsible for discipline and personnel problems for the group. A lieutenant-colonel had already been sent to Lebanon but he could not fulfill these responsibilities and if he also had to play the role of observer. The lieutenant-colonel would act as a sort of "pater familias" to the Canadian contingent.

20. The Cabinet approved the recommendation of the Secretary of State for External Affairs that an additional group of 50 officers be provided for U.N.O.G.I.L., subject to the reservation that one of these officers be of the rank of lieutenant-colonel and be responsible for the discipline and behaviour of the Canadian group.

Air defence requirements; recommendations of Cabinet Defence Committee
(Previous reference Sept. 7)

Start Here 9/21/58

21. The Prime Minister reported that he had seen Mr. Crawford Gordon, President of A.V. Roe Company, who had also interviewed Mr. Pearkes and Mr. Fleming. Mr. Gordon had recommended that production of the Arrow aircraft and the Iroquois engine be undertaken but the programmes for the Astra fire control equipment and the Sparrow missile be cancelled. There was nothing essentially new in his proposal.

22. The Minister of National Defence and the Minister of Finance reported on their conversations with Mr. Gordon and noted that he had made certain assertions in regard to the willingness of the U.S. government to provide fire control and missiles that would be suitable for the Arrow aircraft. He had mentioned some large figures of possible savings that might be made by obtaining such equipment from the United States but had been unable to be precise about these and the figures appeared to be exaggerated.

23. In the course of a further long discussion on this matter, the following points emerged:

(a) Few ministers had changed their minds on the desirabilit of cancelling the contracts for the Arrow and its associated equipment. The Cabinet was clearly divided in its view on the central question.

SECRET

- 10 -

(b) The chief concern of those who wished to have the Arrow contracts continued was the probable shock to the employment situation of such a major termination of work as would be involved in the cancelling of these contracts. It was recognized that the major impact would be psychological, not simply financial and it was very difficult to judge just how important an economic factor it would be.

(c) Some ministers felt, on the other hand, that the effect of continuing this work would be to impose an unnecessarily high cost upon the Canadian economy, which would contribute to the inflationary dangers and the high cost of exports that were handicapping Canada in securing and maintaining export markets. A decline in employment on these projects would be inevitable several years from now in any event, and that might be a worse time to suffer it than this year.

(d) If production of the Arrow and its associated equipment went forward, it was likely to become publicly known that this was done contrary to military advice and there was a danger that the government would be accused of wasting many hundreds of millions of dollars for what were political or economic reasons. That might seriously shake the confidence in the government of the man in the street.

(e) There was some question as to just what the views of the Chiefs of Staff really were on this issue and how much reliance should be placed upon them. Their recommendation for termination of the programme now appeared to be at variance with their views earlier, although it should be noted that only the Chairman of the Chiefs of Staff Committee was a member of that committee at the time the original recommendations were made. The Chief of the Air Staff recommended that the R.C.A.F. should have interceptor aircraft but preferred to purchase U.S. aircraft if the amount of money available to him for aircraft were fixed.

(f) The current international tension would make it appear foolhardy to cancel an important development programme such as that of the Arrow and Iroquois, although it was noted that, if in fact war broke out, it would be necessary to use current types of aircraft and possibly to concentrate on the CF-100 rather than proceed with the CF-105.

SECRET

- 11 -

(g) To carry on the development of the Arrow aircraft and the Iroquois engine until next March would cost in the neighborhood of $86 million; the economy might be better able to stand the shock of cancellation of the programme in March than at present and the international situation might be less tense at that time.

24. The Prime Minister suggested that a compromise should be considered on which possibly the Cabinet could agree. He thought such a compromise might involve carrying on the development programme until next March but not beginning the production programme on the Arrow or the Iroquois at this time. This continuation of development might be regarded as a form of insurance in the present tense situation.

25. During the discussion of the compromise proposal, consideration was given to whether or not it would be possible to carry on only the Canadian elements in the development of the Astra and Sparrow, and it was recognized that further consideration would have to be given to that possibility, bearing in mind the undesirability of spending large amounts to continue development work in the United States and also the undesirability of terminating all this advanced work on electronics and missiles in Canada.

26. The Cabinet,-

(a) approved in principle, the installation of two Bomarc bases in northern Ontario and Quebec and the installation of two additional heavy radars in northern Ontario and Quebec and associated gap-filler radars in the Pinetree system;

(b) decided that the development programme for the Arrow aircraft and the Iroquois engine should be continued until March 31st, 1959, within the scope made possible by the amounts available for it in the estimates for the current fiscal year;

(c) decided that production of the Arrow aircraft and Iroquois engine should not be ordered at the present time;

(d) agreed that a careful and comprehensive review of the requirements for the Arrow aircraft and Iroquois engine should be made before March 31st, 1959, in order to reach a decision before that date as to whether development should be continued or production ordered;

SECRET

- 2 -

Sept 22/58

Air defence requirements; Astra and Sparrow
(Previous reference Sept. 21)

1. The Minister of National Defence referred to the decisions of the preceding day concerning the continuation of development of the Arrow aircraft and Iroquois engine, and in particular the proposal to continue the development of the Astra fire control equipment and Sparrow missile in so far as that could be done within Canada. He said that investigation of the latter proposal this morning indicated that it was necessary either to continue the development programmes in toto for these items or to cancel them, as it was not possible to continue the Canadian portions alone. The major portion of the expenses this winter would be in the United States, particularly in respect of the Astra.

2. During the discussion:

(a) Various suggestions were made for continuation or expansion of electronic work of one kind or another in Canada, including the possibility of a rapid development of the electronic equipment under consideration for the Post Office, and on which some $3 million had already been spent.

(b) It was agreed that any decision on this matter should be deferred until later in the day when the Minister of Defence Production could be present after returning from the Commonwealth Conference in Montreal.

3. The Minister of Defence Production noted, on resumption of the meeting in the afternoon, that, if the development of the Arrow aircraft were to be carried on, there was great advantage in deciding forthwith about the future of the Astra. He noted that one alternative was to stop development of both Astra and Sparrow and switch to the American counterparts already developed, making the necessary modifications in the air-frame development. Another alternative would be to transfer the whole development of the Astra immediately to Canada, adapt the Falcon missile to it, and close out the development of the Sparrow.

4. The Minister of National Defence expressed the view that if, as seemed likely, the development of the Arrow would be terminated at the end of March, the sensible thing to do would be to terminate the development of the Astra and Sparrow at the present time. Even if it were decided to continue with the production of a small number of the Arrow aircraft, it would still appear sensible to terminate the highly expensive Astra development. The electronic engineers and other technical personnel would be better employed to get to work on missiles and receive special training rather than continue the expensive work on the Astra and Sparrow. It would be necessary to modify the Arrow to use the alternative fire control system in it.

SECRET

- 3 -

5. The Cabinet agreed that the programme for the development of the Astra fire control equipment and the Sparrow II missile should be terminated forthwith, and that this decision should be announced the following day along with those decisions on the air defence programme taken the preceding day.

Binding of rates of duty under the British preferential tariff
(Previous reference Sept. 21)

6. The Prime Minister suggested that the recommendation of the Minister of Finance that the government agree to bind the present British preferential rates of duty on the list of tariff items attached to his memorandum might now be approved, and the decision might be made public in such manner and at such time as the Minister of Finance might decide.

7. The Cabinet, after further discussion, agreed to bind the British preferential rates of duty, in the manner provided by the General Agreement on Tariffs and Trade, on the list of tariff items attached to the memorandum of the Minister of Finance on this subject, dated September 19th (Cab. Doc. 269-58).

Lisbon Conference on the revision of the Convention for the Protection of Industrial Property
(Previous reference Sept. 8)

8. The Secretary of State reported that it would be in order for Mr. Christopher Robinson, Q.C., to be technical advisor and alternate delegate at the diplomatic conference for the revision of the Convention for the Protection of Industrial Property to be held in Lisbon beginning October 6th. He himself was planning to be present at this conference on or about October 15th. Dr. Philippe Panneton, the Canadian Ambassador to Lisbon, would act as head of delegation until he arrived in Lisbon.

9. The Cabinet noted with approval the report of the Secretary of State concerning the Canadian delegation at the forthcoming conference in Lisbon on the revision of the Convention for the Protection of Industrial Property.

Income Tax Appeal Board; appointments

10. The Cabinet approved the recommendations of the Minister of National Revenue,-

(a) that Mr. Cecil L. Snyder, Q.C., Assistant Chairman of the Income Tax Appeal Board, be appointed Chairman of the board for the period September 22nd, 1958, to January 31st, 1964; and,

SECRET — NOV 25/58

- 7 -

Unemployment Insurance regulations re fishermen

15. The Minister of Labour recalled that the Unemployment Insurance Act had been amended in 1956 to permit "coverage" under the act for self-employed fishermen. The regulations were complicated and difficult to apply and in the light of experience it had been shown that some simplification should be brought to these special rules for fishermen. An ad hoc committee of ministers had reviewed these regulations the previous week and agreed upon a number of amendments made by the Unemployment Insurance Commission. These amendments would not likely increase the burden on the Treasury to any degree.

(Copies of a submission to council and attached regulations had been circulated).

16. The Cabinet approved the amendments to the fishermen regulations under the Unemployment Insurance Act made by the Unemployment Insurance Commission and recommended by the Minister of Labour.

(An order in council was passed accordingly; P.C. 1958-1595, Nov. 26.)

Defence estimates; assumption re decision on Arrow aircraft

Start Here 11/25/58

17. The Minister of National Defence noted that there was a problem, in making up his main estimates for 1959-60, as to what assumption should be made about the decision to be taken before the end of March concerning future policy in regard to the Arrow aircraft and the Iroquois engine. He proposed to assume that the contract would be cancelled and to include only the cancellation costs. Should the decision go the other way, a supplementary estimate could be submitted to Parliament.

18. The Cabinet agreed to Mr. Pearkes' suggestions on treatment of Arrow aircraft costs in defence construction.

Strike at Sorel Industries

19. The Minister of Defence Production reported that he had received a telegram from the National Metallurgical Federation (Mr. Gérard Picard) saying that a strike had been declared at Sorel Industries Limited. The company and the syndicate had failed to reach agreement on salaries and other monetary advantages. Mr. Picard had stressed the importance of Sorel Industries for the defence of Canada. He had stated that, after serious study, the syndicate was requesting that the Canadian government, in the general interest of the country, either grant subsidies to Sorel Industries in order to retain the experts who would otherwise probably be lost to Canada, or nationalize Sorel Industries in view of the vital importance of this arsenal for the defence of Canada and the members of N.A.T.O.

SECRET — Dec 22/58

- 7 -

Start Here 12/22/58

Air defence requirements; Arrow aircraft
(Previous reference Dec. 2)

24. The Prime Minister said he had been shocked at the statement Air Marshal Slemon had made about the Arrow. It was not a question of whether Slemon's remarks had been misinterpreted or not but whether he should have made a statement of that kind at all. Avro had put on a tremendous publicity campaign and this played right into their hands. If the government decided to continue development it would be accused of giving in to a powerful lobby. Pressure was coming from other sources in Ontario too. Even if he thought the decision reached last September was wrong, he was determined, because of what had happened since, to adhere firmly to it. The future of the CF-105 would have to be discussed before Parliament opened.

25. The Minister of National Defence pointed out that it was still his understanding that development would be terminated by March 31st. In Paris, the U.S. Secretary of Defence had made it quite clear that the U.S. was not interested in the CF-105, even if it were equipped with the MA1 fire control system and the Falcon missile. The U.S. had now decided not to proceed with the development of any new interceptor aircraft except for the 108 which was years in the future. This was a long range aircraft of advanced design to be employed from bases in Alaska and Greenland. This U.S. decision would strengthen the government's position in deciding to abandon the CF-105.

26. The Cabinet noted the reports of the Prime Minister and the Minister of National Defence on the situation regarding the CF-105 and agreed that a decision be reached on the aircraft's future before Parliament re-opened.

Proposed request for withdrawal of Soviet Assistant Military Attache
(Previous reference Dec. 16)

27. The Secretary of State for External Affairs again reviewed briefly the activities of the Assistant Military Attache of the Soviet Union. He thought the government should ask to have the man withdrawn.

28. During the discussion the arguments for and against taking action were again considered. It seemed that whatever was done would not affect the current trade negotiations with the U.S.S.R. It might be advisable, however, to defer a decision until after Christmas.

29. The Cabinet agreed that unless new arguments were submitted by the following week against doing so, the Soviet authorities be requested to recall the Assistant Military Attache for engaging in activities not in keeping with his diplomatic status.

SECRET — Dec 31/58

- 3 -

Invitation to Soviet leaders to visit Canada

6. The Prime Minister, referring to the forthcoming visit of the U.S.S.R. First Deputy Premier to the United States, asked whether Mr. Mikoyan should be invited to come to Canada following his U.S. visit. He also wondered whether Mr. Khruschev should be invited.

7. During the brief discussion there was general opposition expressed to inviting either Mikoyan or Khruschev. The purpose of Mikoyan's visit to the U.S. was still not clear. There was some hope that he might be prepared to discuss the Berlin situation. During the recent Soviet-Canada trade discussions, the Soviet delegation had suggested that the resulting agreement, if this met with the this time, be signed in Moscow. If this met with the government's approval, Mikoyan might be invited here as a friendly gesture. However, unless the government had in mind achieving some real benefits from a Russian visit, invitations had better not be made. Opposition would certainly come from Quebec and groups of new Canadians, etc. It was recalled that when Khruschev had visited the United Kingdom, he had appealed directly to the British people over the head of the U.K. government.

8. The Cabinet agreed that no action be taken to invite Soviet leaders to visit Canada at this time.

Civil Service; time off for Roman Catholics on Epiphany

9. The Secretary of State said he had sent a letter to the Prime Minister that day about a request from the Civil Service Commission that Roman Catholic civil servants be given time off to attend church services on Epiphany. He explained that this request had always been granted in the past. It was a purely routine matter.

10. The Cabinet agreed that the Civil Service Commission be allowed to grant to Roman Catholics time off to attend church services on January 6th, Epiphany Day.

CF-105 (Arrow) programme; cancellation
(Previous reference Dec. 22)

Start Here 12/31/58

11. The Prime Minister asked whether any member of the Cabinet wished to change the decision which had been made on the Arrow programme.

12. The Minister of National Defence said that there was no change in the opinion of his advisers on the matter and he pointed out that, if the government decided to make an announcement before March 31st, the sum of $10 million could be saved from the following year's estimates. Only $50 million had been included in these estimates to cover cancellation charges or to enable the development to be carried on for a three-month period should the decision go the other way. He added that the latest cost figures provided by Avro (with the Falcon and Hughes fire control and missile system) indicated that the best cost possible per aircraft would be $5 million.

SECRET

- 4 -

13. During the discussion it was hoped that something could be done for the aircraft industry to soften the blow which would result from the cancellation of the Arrow programme. It was pointed out that, if the Convair-Canadair bid were accepted by the United States, the business would not go to Avro but to Canadair in Montreal.

14. The Cabinet noted the comments of the Minister of National Defence on the question of cancelling the Arrow programme.

R. B. Bryce,
Secretary to the Cabinet.

Start Here
1/10/59

SECRET

- 8 -

Jan 10/59

Report on Arrow (CF-105) aircraft programme
(Previous reference Dec. 31, 1958)

28. The Prime Minister asked that the statements which had appeared in the Globe and Mail of that day on the Arrow (CF-105) programme be analysed so that he could answer them in detail.

29. The Minister of National Defence said that, as far as the Chiefs of Staff were concerned, there were, as at December 31st, 1958, no new military factors, either in regard to the manned bomber threat or new developments to meet this threat, which they considered would have any bearing on the Arrow aircraft programme. He read from a report submitted to him the day before by the Chief of the Air Staff. It indicated that the MA1/Falcom/MB1 could be worked satisfactorily into the Arrow aircraft and would provide a suitable interceptor weapon capability. There were at present five Mark I Arrow aircraft, and their handling and performance characteristics were extremely reassuring. The adoption of the Falcon and Hughes systems had given additional fuel storage space so that, in a supersonic mission, the radius of action of the aircraft had been increased from 238 to 354 nautical miles, and in a subsonic mission from 347 to 506 nautical miles. Another effect of the adoption of the U.S. fire control system and weapon to the Arrow programme was that development could be speeded up. The Avro Company had now advised that the first operational aircraft could be delivered for squadron use by September 1960 and that after January 1st, 1961, aircraft would be delivered at the rate of four per month. If 100 aircraft were required, the last aircraft could be delivered some time in 1963.

As far as the costs were concerned, the original price for 100 aircraft, as from September 1st, 1958, was $12.86 million per aircraft. The revised figures under the new programme, as from April 1st, 1959, would be $7.02 million per aircraft. The price had, therefore, dropped from $12.86 million to $7.02 million per aircraft. (This did not include cancellation charges of the Astra/Sparrow systems).

He then referred to the relative contributions of the United States and Canada towards the deterrent forces in North America. Figures from the U.S. indicated 800 supersonic interceptors in service and sufficient funds to procure another 650. The United States had recently decided to cancel the F-106C and F-106D programme and to use the funds so saved to develop the long range reconnaissance aircraft, F-108, which was not dependent on SAGE and was now on the inventory of NORAD. An additional 100 interceptors from Canada would make a small contribution. Furthermore, the CF-105 could not cover all of Canada. Its range was limited from 300 to 500 miles.

SECRET

- 9 -

The Minister indicated that another reason for the decrease in the company's cost figures was that it had been found that only 20 pre-production types would be required instead of 37.

In answer to questions, he said that the Bomarc was now operational and that Canada would not be faced with the need to buy U.S. interceptors. He pointed out that when there would be no further requirement for the CF-100, a much cheaper means of defence would be found in the Bomarc. Reliance could be placed on the United States to provide whatever interceptor defence was necessary.

30. During the brief discussion it was pointed out that this would not be the appropriate time to make a decision on the Arrow programme in view of the fact that the government had said that they would not make this decision until March.

31. The Cabinet noted the report of the Minister of National Defence and agreed that no decision be taken that day on the Arrow programme.

R. B. Bryce,
Secretary to the Cabinet.

Arrow aircraft; alternative aircraft programme

- 6 · *Jan 28/59*

Start Here 1/28/59

17. The Minister of Finance said that almost as soon as he tabled the main estimates for 1959-60 it would become known that there was no provision for expenditures on the Arrow beyond April 1st, except cancellation costs.

18. The Prime Minister said he had received suggestions that Avro might be given a contract to produce, under licence, a Blackburn aircraft of United Kingdom design. It was his understanding that this aircraft might be suitable both as an interceptor and for ground attack purposes. Such a development would be helpful in furthering the government's Commonwealth policy.

19. The Minister of National Defence said the Blackburn aircraft was not in existence yet and could not be available for three years. It had been studied as a possible replacement for the F-86 in the R.C.A.F. Air Division in Europe. The N.A.T.O. military authorities had in mind two roles for the Air Division,- all weather reconnaissance and strike. These could be carried out as long as the CF-100 remained in operation. They had suggested, however, that the F 86, with which the Air Division was also equipped, be replaced by an aircraft with a strike capability. The most promising was a Grumman machine. This would have a large measure of Canadian content in it perhaps 70 per cent, and much of the work might be done at the Avro plant at Malton. It would be manufactured under licence from the U.S. company. It was just barely supersonic. At the moment he was inclined towards replacing the F-86's in the Air Division and doing nothing about the CF-100's.

20. The Cabinet noted the brief reports on the Arrow and possible future aircraft programmes and agreed that these matters be discussed again in the near future.

St. Lawrence Seaway tolls; Memorandum of Agreement with the United States
(Previous reference Jan. 14)

21. The Minister of Trade and Commerce said he had no objections of detail to the recommendations contained in the Tariff of Tolls on the St. Lawrence Seaway. He would naturally prefer no tolls on the Welland Canal at all, but he had no specific proposals to make at this time.

22. During the discussion the question of charging tolls on the Welland Canal was reviewed again at length. If it was decided not to levy tolls now it would be impossible to impose them when "twinning" of the locks was undertaken to increase capacity. This would cost approximately $100 million, and was a burden which the taxpayers generally should not reasonably be

Freight rates; subvention to alleviate recent increase
(Previous reference Jan. 28)

8. The Minister of Transport reported that one plan which had been developed for applying the $20 million freight rates subvention involved payments to all the carriers, including water carriers, associated with the application for the 17 per cent freight rate increase. This would only reduce the increase to 10 per cent, however, and was therefore not acceptable to several ministers.

9. During the discussion the following points emerged:

(a) If the subvention had to be paid to all carriers, then an additional $4.3 million would be required to reduce the increase by approximately 50 per cent. Several had argued that it was unnecessary to make payments to all the carriers involved, but this would be discriminatory and undoubtedly lead to difficulties with those companies whose wage rates had also risen.

(b) An alternative proposal that the subvention apply only to shipments into and out of the Western and Atlantic regions and within those regions themselves had been put forward, but a study of it showed that the Maritimes would not receive an adequate proportion of the $20 million. This was not satisfactory.

10. The Cabinet noted the report on possible methods of applying the $20 million freight rate subvention to alleviate the 17 per cent freight rate increase and agreed that the Cabinet committee on this subject continue its studies and submit a suitable proposal.

Bill to amend the St. Lawrence Seaway Authority Act

11. The Cabinet approved the resolution to precede the bill to amend the St. Lawrence Seaway Authority Act.

Feb 3/59

Estimates 1959-60; possible announcement on the CF-105 Arrow aircraft
(Previous reference Jan. 28)

Start Here 2/3/59

12. The Prime Minister said that, when the estimates for 1959-60 were tabled, questions would probably be asked about production of the Arrow aircraft. In the circumstances, it might be advisable to make a final decision now, and announce it when the estimates were tabled. He had discussed the Arrow and other defence matters with the Chiefs of Staff a few days ago, and they had said that no new military factors regarding either the manned bomber threat or developments to meet the threat had emerged since September which would have a

bearing on the Arrow decision. He had raised with the Chiefs the possibility of the United Kingdom "Blackburn" replacing existing equipment in the Air Division. If this were a suitable aircraft, then the work might be given to AVRO. However, they favoured U.S. equipment.

13. During the discussion the following points emerged:

(a) It was not vital to make a statement immediately. The wiser course would be for the Cabinet Defence Committee and the Cabinet to consider what steps might be taken to maintain employment at AVRO and then announce a programme at the time the final word was given on the Arrow.

(b) It was impracticable to think of providing other work for AVRO as soon as the Arrow programme was halted. It would take many months before any contracts could be awarded.

(c) The sooner the decision was made on the Arrow, the more money would be saved on cancellation charges and could be made available for other purposes. It was quite evident what the decision would be. Nothing would be gained by deferring it any longer.

14. The Cabinet deferred decision on the future of the CF-105 Arrow aircraft programme to the next meeting.

Administrator under British Columbia Coast Steamship Service Act; termination of appointment

15. The Cabinet approved the recommendation of the Minister of Labour that the appointment of Mr. R.K. Smith, as Administrator under the British Columbia Coast Steamship Service Act, be terminated with effect from February 3rd.

(An order in council was passed accordingly; P.C. 1959-118, Feb. 3).

Wheat export programme 1958-59; government assistance
(Previous reference Aug. 29, 1958)

16. The Minister of Trade and Commerce recalled that, last August, the Prime Minister had stated that the government intended to ask Parliament during the current session to continue to provide financial assistance for exports of wheat and flour. During the 1957-58 crop year, exports were 316 million bushels, of which 285 million were commercial sales and 31 million gifts or special loans. Commercial sales for the 1958-59 crop year might not exceed 260 million bushels and, to reach the target of 300 million, assistance would be needed either by a special sum in the estimates

- 3 -

Start Here 2/4/59

Feb 4/59

<u>CF-105 Arrow Programme</u>
(Previous reference Feb. 3)

6. The Minister of National Defence reported again on the present state of the CF-105 Arrow programme. In addition to the information he had given previously, he noted that, from the end of September 1958. until the end of January 1955, $60 million had been spent on the development of this aircraft and that, if development continued until March 31st, $45 million more would be expended. The average cost per weapons system for a programme of 100 operational aircraft was now estimated to be $7.81 million. This excluded termination charges for the Astra/Sparrow from September 1st, 1958, which were estimated to be $28 million. Although the cost had been reduced from $12.6 million to this figure, he still considered that the production of 100 such aircraft could not be justified at this price. The Chiefs of Staff were, as directed last September, urgently investigating requirements, if any, for additional air defence missile installations in Canada, and for interceptor aircraft of the nature of the CF-105 or alternative types.

He recommended that development of the CF-105 be discontinued and that the Chiefs of Staff present at an early date the recommendation they had been requested to make.

An explanatory memorandum was circulated, (Minister's memorandum, Jan. 30).

7. <u>Mr. Pearkes</u> added that, at the moment, there did not appear to be anything in the U.S. inventory of aircraft that would justify a decision to purchase. The Chiefs of Staff were considering the possibility of having some Bomarc squadrons moved from south of the border in the central U.S. to areas in western Canada. If it were felt that the manned bomber threat was decreasing, then it was obviously preferable to concentrate on defensive missiles rather than to continue with the production of interceptors.

8. <u>The Prime Minister</u> said it would be necessary to have a meeting of the Cabinet Defence Committee before making the final decision on the Arrow.

9. <u>During the discussion the following points emerged:</u>

(a) If a question on the future of the Arrow were raised when the estimates were tabled, it should be answered in a way which would show that a decision on the programme would be taken before March 31st. There was sufficient money in the estimates to pay for cancellation charges or to continue development for a while.

- 4 -

(b) If the Arrow development were cancelled and no alternative interceptors were produced in Canada or purchased elsewhere, then, in the event of a war, and when the CF-100 was no longer in service, Canada might have to rely on the U.S. to provide manned fighter defence. Under the terms of the NORAD agreement, U.S. squadrons could be stationed temporarily on Canadian airfields.

(c) The personnel in the R.C.A.F. which would have otherwise been employed in flying the CF-105 and servicing it would be absorbed in work in connection with S.A.G.E., additional radars and on other duties.

(d) The re-equipping of the Air Division in Europe was a separate problem. At the moment, the most urgent aspect of the situation was a replacement, if any, for the F-86 Sabre which was obsolete. The Cabinet Defence Committee would be considering this problem and would make recommendations in the near future to the Cabinet about it. Replacing the Sabres overseas would cost at least $350 million.

10. The Cabinet noted the report of the Minister of National Defence on the CF-105 Arrow programme and the ensuing discussion, and agreed that the matter be considered by the Cabinet Defence Committee the following day.

<u>Premium Iron Ores</u>
(Previous reference Dec. 16, 1957)

11. <u>The Minister of Justice</u> said representations had been made on behalf of Premium Iron Ores that the government should insist that the United States government bring to the attention of the U.S. court hearing the case, the view of the Canadian government that its position in the matter was not in accord with the stand taken by the U.S. administration. Premium Iron Ores said this should be done because the counsel for the U.S. government had stated, during the court hearings, that the Canadian government's position was the same as that of the U.S. He had raised this matter with the U.S. Attorney-General when he was in Washington recently, and Mr. Rogers had informed him that, in their briefs presented to the court, there had been no reference to the position of the Canadian government nor had counsel referred to it in his oral argument. However, counsel for the defendant had, but in doing so had stated that the Canadian government's views were at variance with those of the U.S. government. It was not at all appropriate to accede to the request of Premium Iron Ores.

SECRET

Feb. 10/59

Start Here 2/10/59

- 2 -

CF-105 Arrow programme; report of Cabinet Defence Committee (Previous reference Feb. 4)

1. The Minister of National Defence reported that the Cabinet Defence Committee had considered the recommendations he had made to the Cabinet that further development of the CF-105 be now discontinued and that the Chiefs of Staff be asked to present soon their recommendations on what requirements, if any, there were for additional air defence missile installations in Canada, and for interceptor aircraft of the nature of the CF-105 or alternate types. During the meeting, the Chairman of the Chiefs of Staff Committee reported that the Chiefs of Staff had reviewed the position concerning the production of the CF-105, and were still of the opinion that the changing threat and the rapid advances in technology, particularly in the missile field, along with the diminishing requirements for manned interceptors in Canada, created grave doubts as to whether a limited number of aircraft of such extremely high cost would provide defence returns commensurate with the expenditures.

The committee concurred in the recommendations and agreed that they be submitted to the Cabinet for consideration at an early meeting.

An explanatory memorandum was circulated, (Memorandum, Secretary, Cabinet Defence Committee, Feb. 6 - Cab. Doc. 46-59).

2. Mr. Pearkes added that it was impossible to give any assurance that manned interceptors for the defence of Canada would not be bought in the United States some time in the future, if the CF-105 programme was discontinued. It was his own opinion that the threat of an attack on North America by manned bombers was rapidly diminishing. He felt that Russia would not consider launching an attack until it had a large arsenal of intercontinental ballistic missiles. Against these, manned interceptors were useless. If, however, new evidence became available that the Soviet Union was developing more modern manned bombers, then interceptors might have to be bought. The question naturally arose as to why Canada was installing Bomarc when it was effective only against manned bombers. The answer was, that some insurance premium had to be paid against the possibility of bomber attack and this premium was cheaper by far than the CF-105. The U.S. had agreed to pay $91 million out of a total of $110.8 million for the installation of the two Bomarc squadrons in Northern Ontario and Quebec.

SECRET

- 3 -

3. During the discussion the following points emerged:

(a) At the meeting of the Cabinet Defence Committee, the Chief of the Air Staff had stated that the R.C.A.F. would need 100 to 115 interceptor aircraft for several years ahead. These would have to be bought in the U.S. or, failing that, presumably U.S. squadrons would provide interceptor defence for Canada. This would be particularly awkward when, at the same time, the 1st Canadian Air Division might be in the process of having its F-86 aircraft replaced by more modern machines at a cost of about $400 million to $500 million. In effect, Canada would be defending Europe, and the U.S. would be defending Canada.

(b) On the other hand, the role of the Air Division was different from that of the R.C.A.F. in Canada. Furthermore, if the F-86 were not replaced, the Air Division might just as well be withdrawn from Europe, and the implications of this for the N.A.T.O. alliance were very serious indeed. The proposal now being considered was to assign the Air Division a strike-attack role and equip it with aircraft suitable for the purpose.

(c) It was not true to say that the U.S. would be defending Canada if the CF-105 were discontinued. Canada would be manning the Bomarcs, the warning lines, S.A.G.E. and other installations. The U.S. would man the aircraft which, after all, was a steadily decreasing part of the defence, as the nature of the threat changed; this would mean that the presence of U.S. servicemen would be less apparent than if they were employed in different capacities.

(d) The U.S. intended now to develop the long range F-108 interceptor, which would operate from Greenland and Alaska. It was a large aeroplane, less dependent on ground environment, and very expensive. It would be defending Canada just as squadrons of the U.S.A.F. were doing today in complementing the R.C.A.F.

4. The Cabinet deferred decision on the recommendation of the Cabinet Defence Committee that the development of the CF-105 Arrow be discontinued.

SECRET

- 3 -

Feb.14/59

Various means were considered for resolving the apparent deadlock in the Cabinet on this issue. It was considered whether or not a majority of, say, two thirds should be required, either to sanction execution in any case, or at least to act contrary to the recommendation of the jury for mercy. It was believed that traditional practices of Cabinets in the past gave no guide in this matter.

It was finally considered that, in view of the serious division of opinion and the recommendation for commutation that had been made by the Solicitor General and the Minister of Justice, as the responsible law officers of the government, it would not be proper to decide upon execution.

4. The Cabinet, therefore, after most exhaustive discussion, decided that the sentence of death imposed upon J.J. Vollman, Jr., convicted of murder by the Supreme Court of New Brunswick in Fredericton in November, 1958, should be commuted to life imprisonment.

(An order in council was passed accordingly; P.C. 1959-184, Feb. 14).

Arrow (CF-105) aircraft; undertaking to pay development costs; decision to terminate development
(Previous reference Feb. 10)

5. Mr. Green, as Acting Minister of Defence Production, stated that it was necessary to reach a decision as to whether or not a clear undertaking should be given to the Avro Aircraft Company that the government would meet the expenses involved in continuing development until notice of termination of the contract was given. The company had noted that the costs of this development were, in fact, likely to exceed the financial limitations that had been previously set on the programme, and that, unless these financial limitations were increased, it would be necessary for them now to begin laying off personnel until such time as the contract was extended or terminated. The Minister proposed to reply saying that the company would be paid reasonable and proper costs incurred under the development contract until it was terminated.

6. The Minister of Finance said the Treasury Board had withheld approval of proposals of this kind in recent weeks and should not be over-ridden in this matter but should be allowed to consider it again. He noted that the board was confronted with too many such faits accomplis by ministers or departments in taking on commitments that exceeded the financial limitations that had been previously established.

SECRET

- 4 -

7. In the discussion of this proposal, the opinion was expressed that, if this undertaking were now given to Avro, it would increase the government's expenditure undesirably on this contract; no such undertaking should be given but, instead, a decision should be taken forthwith on the termination of the development contract. On this latter proposal it was noted that the Cabinet was clearly of one mind that work on the Arrow should be discontinued. A decision on the matter had practically been taken some weeks ago, but it had been thought that the Cabinet Defence Committee should meet and discuss it again with the military advisers of the government. This had now been done and the committee had recommended termination.

8. In further discussion the following points emerged:

(a) When a decision was announced it would be desirable to say as much as possible about arrangements with the United States on production sharing. It was not clear why the statement on that subject had been delayed. It should be recognized, however, that it was not possible to give Parliament any firm assurance as to the scale of the orders that the United States would, in fact place under the production sharing arrangements, even though the Secretary of Defence and others in the U.S. administration were well disposed to place such orders.

(b) No member of Cabinet present was opposed to the termination of the development of the Arrow, although it was recognized that the Minister of Labour, who was not present, was impressed with the employment problem that such action would create.

(c) In the statement on this matter in September, it had been said that development would be continued until March. It was noted, however, that the circumstances which had been spoken of in that statement had changed in the meantime, particularly in regard to the crisis over Quemoy, and the government, in the present circumstances, would be justified in deciding to terminate now the development programme.

SECRET

- 5 -

(d) It was pointed out that the government faced a serious decision in regard to the equipment of the Air Division of the R.C.A.F. in Europe. The replacement for the F-86 in the Air Division might cost over $500 million. In fact, no decision had yet been taken by the Chiefs of Staff or the Minister of National Defence to recommend replacement, and it might be that missiles would be used instead, or some other course followed.

(e) It was also pointed out that the government faced the possibility that the R.C.A.F. might be using interceptor aircraft to defend Europe but not to defend Canada itself, which would be defended by American interceptors. This would create quite a political issue. On the other hand, it was noted that the R.C.A.F. would be using Bomarcs to defend Canada, and no decision was being proposed now to use aircraft in Europe. This issue was not directly related to the decision on the Arrow.

(f) It was agreed that other ministers should be present for this major decision, particularly the Minister of Defence Production. The final decision should therefore be taken on Tuesday next and Mr. O'Hurley be asked to be present, even at the cost of having to cancel his appointment in Halifax that day.

(g) A statement should be made in the House of Commons at the same time that the company was notified of the termination, and that statement should be ready when the final decision was taken on Tuesday.

9. The Cabinet agreed that the final decision on discontinuing the development of the Arrow (CF-105) aircraft should be taken at a meeting of the Cabinet on Tuesday, February 17th, and the decision when made should be announced forthwith to Parliament at the same time that the company was informed of it.

Start Here
2/14/59

Start Here 2/17/59

Arrow (CF-105) aircraft; report of Cabinet Defence Committee; decision to terminate development
(Previous reference Feb. 14)

12. The Prime Minister said a draft announcement on the termination of the development contract for the Arrow had been prepared. It included a section on arrangements with the United States for production sharing and a section on the acquisition by Canada of nuclear weapons for defence. He had gone over the draft in great detail but it was not yet in the right form to be made that day.

13. The Minister without Portfolio (Mr. Macdonnell) reported that, the previous day in Toronto, the Premier of Ontario had spoken to him in strong terms about the effects of terminating the Arrow contract upon the municipalities in the vicinity of Malton.

14. The Minister of Finance said Mr. Frost had also spoken to him in pungent language about work on the Arrow being stopped. Mr. Frost had complained about so little notice being given to Avro, and had asked why other contracts could not be given to the company. He had replied that the matter had been exhaustively considered, that all possible alternatives had been reviewed, and that the decision would be taken in the light of the best military advice available. He had also told Mr. Frost that, right from the outset, it had never been said that actual production would proceed and that everyone understood that the matter was to be reviewed year by year.

15. During the discussion the following points emerged:

(a) The sooner the announcement could be made the better, because the decision to terminate was bound to leak out and the longer the announcement was delayed the more would be the cost.

(b) The most appropriate time for the announcement appeared to be the following Friday. This, as proposed, should refer not only to the Arrow termination but also to production sharing and to the acquisition of nuclear weapons. The Prime Minister's statement should be followed by one by the Minister of Defence Production, which would deal in greater detail with production sharing. In considering this question of timing, the possibility of a motion to adjourn the house to discuss a matter of urgent public importance should not be overlooked.

(c) It would be desirable that notes be exchanged with the U.S. to implement the agreed arrangements on sharing the costs of the new radars, gap fillers, S.A.G.E. and the two Bomarc stations in Ontario and Quebec.

- 5 -

16. The Cabinet,-

(a) agreed that the development of the Arrow aircraft and Iroquois engine be discontinued, effective as of the time of announcement;

(b) that an announcement concerning this decision, the production sharing with the United States, and the acquisition of atomic weapons be made in the House of Commons, probably on Friday;

(c) that the contractors be notified of the termination of their contracts at the same time; and,

(d) that an agreement be made with the United States, in the form of an exchange of notes, for the implementation of the agreed arrangements on the sharing of the costs of Bomarc and S.A.G.E. installations in Canada and the associated extension of radar coverage.

Wheat; interim payments on 1957-58 crop

17. The Minister of Trade and Commerce said that the interim payments on wheat which would be recommended would be the same as the previous year, that is, 10 cents a bushel. He noted, however, that the payment for durum wheat each year had been higher than ordinary wheat, being 25 cents instead of 10 cents. Durum wheat had for some years been in good demand, and the farmers had increased their production for export. The Wheat Board was a four year over-supply for export. By now there was recommending that, in order to provide less incentive for the production of durum, the interim payment should be dropped to 10 cents. He wondered, however, whether it would not be possible to proceed in two stages: provide an interim payment this year of 15 cents and the following year one of 10 cents.

18. During the discussion the following points emerged:

(a) Should an announcement about this interim payment be made far in advance of the proposed march of the western farmers on Ottawa? Some felt that many farmers were waiting for these payments and that there was really no reason to delay them. It would be good tactics to make the announcement during the first week of March.

SECRET

Feb. 19/59

- 2 -

Start Here 2/19/59

Statement on the Arrow
(Previous reference Feb. 17)

1. The Prime Minister said that he would make a statement announcing the termination of the Arrow contracts in the house the following day. The C.B.C. Television Service would present a programme on the following Sunday or Monday on the development of the Arrow. It would be well to make the statement before the broadcast.

He had gone over the draft statement several times but thought that it should be redrafted by a committee of ministers. The redraft could be considered by Cabinet before the statement was made in the house.

2. The Cabinet approved the suggestion of the Prime Minister that Messrs. Fleming, Pearkes, Fulton, Smith, and O'Hurley meet that afternoon to revise the draft statement on the Arrow aircraft and related matters.

Bond issue result; report
(Previous reference Feb. 12)

3. The Minister of Finance reported that the bond issue authorized the week before, made up of two maturities in the aggregate principal amount of $200 million, had been over-subscribed by approximately $142 million.

Response to the $200 million issue had been as follows:

(a) On the 13 month, 2-3/4 per cent bond, $189 million had been subscribed.

(b) On the 21½ month, 3 per cent bond, $153 million had been subscribed.

It was somewhat mystifying that some investment dealers had apparently stuck to their orders while others had subscribed much more than the orders on their books. This apparently meant that some firms had over-subscribed expecting that they would get only a fraction of the allotment.

The allocations would be $85 million on the short-term payments and $115 million on the longer-term bonds. In making allocations he had set a ceiling of $10 million on each subscription.

There was reason to consider the issue a success in the present circumstances.

4. The Cabinet noted the report of the Minister of Finance on the recent bond issue.

SECRET

Start Here 2/23/59

Feb 23/59

- 2 -

Arrow (CF-105); cancellation of development; parliamentary tactics
(Previous reference Feb. 19)

1. The Prime Minister said the opposition were sure to move to adjourn the house to discuss the cancellation of the Arrow development programme. He wondered whether it would be advisable to have the debate that day, or whether it would be helpful to attempt to postpone it for 24 hours by saying that the government would welcome a debate the following day.

2. **During the discussion the following points emerged:**

(a) It would be wiser to have the debate immediately. The Speaker was sure to rule a motion to adjourn in order. A government suggestion for postponement would be unusual and an indication of weakness. On the other hand, the latter course would provide more time for preparation and enable the government to make the first statement in the debate, which was always an advantage.

(b) During the debate, the history of the project should be outlined with an indication that production had never been approved, and that development had been reviewed year by year to see whether it should be continued.

(c) The two principal points of criticism on the decision to cancel the Arrow programme were, first, that no efforts had been made to provide alternative employment for the Avro workers and, second, that Canada would be still further dominated by the United States.

(d) The lay-offs had been particularly abrupt, the excuse given by Avro being that the company had received no advance notice of the Prime Minister's announcement. This was unfair and misleading. The company officers were well aware, or they should have been, that the contract might be cancelled and should have been making preparations accordingly.

(e) Avro claimed that, since the Prime Minister's announcement of last September, the company had proposed alternative programmes to the government but that the latter had not seen fit to discuss these matters or consult with Avro's officers in any way. This was not true. Avro's officers had spoken to ministers frequently in the past few months. In one instance, the Minister of Transport had informed Mr. Smye of Avro that, if the

- 3 -

SECRET

company had a reasonable proposal to make, say for production of aircraft for civilian use, the government would consider it most carefully. In fact, during this period no such proposals had been made by the company to the government.

(f) It might be worth making payments which would enable the company to pay employees more than the usual separation and holiday pay provided for by contract. This, however, would be a dangerous precedent and it would not help the sub-contractors. In any event, those being laid off would receive unemployment insurance.

(g) Another possibility was to provide assistance for employees moving away for new jobs. This too had difficulties in that it would require an order of the Governor in Council designating the areas as a surplus labour area. If such action were taken for that region to include greater Toronto as a whole, it would also have to be taken for other localities.

(h) There had been a prospect of Canadair obtaining a large U.S. contract for radar picket aircraft but, unfortunately, this seemed to be less and less hopeful in view of the pressure from the aircraft industry in the U.S.

(i) The President of Avro had referred to the company's development of a vertical take-off aircraft. Support for this had been provided mainly by the U.S. A small amount could be made available from National Defence appropriations but, until it could be seen if the project had any possibilities of success, it was not worth allotting much money to it.

(j) In defending the decision it could be said that it had been taken in the light of the best military advice available, and that the cost of the Bomarc, which was to perform the same role as the Arrow, was very much less than that of the Arrow. Emphasis should be placed on the fact that Avro had plenty of notice that the project might be cancelled and that it had made no alternative plans. There was no call to be delicate with the company.

- 4 -

SECRET

(k) Mr. Plant, one of the Vice-Presidents of Avro, had recently suggested to the Department of Transport that the company might undertake the development of a pure jet, short range aircraft to replace the Viscount in a few years time. Companies in the U.K. and the U.S. were working on bigger, longer-range aircraft, but no one seemed to be developing plans for a shorter-range type for use on inter-city routes in North America or Europe. Government assistance would be needed for such a project, perhaps to the extent of $15 million or $20 million. This would be a small amount compared with what would be saved by cancelling the Arrow.

(l) As regards the point that cancellation would mean that Canada would be still further "under the wing of the U.S.", it should be remembered that maintaining freedom from U.S. control was a continuous struggle. It might appear that the present decision was a retrograde step. But there would be other opportunities to assert Canadian sovereignty and independence. For example, it might be necessary in the near future to introduce legislation to ensure the independence of Canadian companies.

(m) It would be unwise to blame the U.S. for the outcome of the Arrow contract.

(n) The Prime Minister and the Minister of National Defence should participate in the afternoon's debate, and other ministers too if there were time. Prior to the debate, the Minister of Defence Production should make the proposed statement on production sharing with the U.S.

3. **The Cabinet noted the reports and discussion on the reaction to the cancellation of the CF-105 Arrow contract and on the manner in which the government would proceed in the debate expected to occur in the House of Commons that afternoon.**

Tolls on the Welland Canal
(Previous reference Jan. 28)

4. Mrs. Fairclough said the intention to levy tolls on the Welland Canal had aroused serious criticism in the Hamilton and Niagara districts.

Start Here 6/30/59

Choice of aircraft to replace F-86 for the Air Division in Europe
(Previous reference June 19)

1. The Minister of Defence Production reported on the studies he and his advisers had made of the problem of choosing between the Grumman F11F-1F and the Lockheed 104G aircraft for replacement of the F-86 presently in service in 8 of the 12 squadrons in the Air Division in Europe. For the Grumman the order of magnitude of cost for 214 aircraft was $445 million; the figure for the Lockheed was $420 million. These costs assumed that spares and support, engineering charges and engineering and tooling manpower levels would be restricted and controlled. The figures did not include allowances for missiles, nuclear warheads or other armament. In either case the aircraft would be manufactured largely in Canada. At the peak of production 3,500 persons would be added to present levels of employment in the case of the aircraft plant and 1,450 for the engine. Supporting facilities would, of course, also benefit.

Substantially the complete airframe of either aircraft could be built economically in Canada. Other than a possibility of free tooling which had not as yet been chosen by any other country, there was no indication of production sharing possibilities in regard to the Grumman. However, the Lockheed had been chosen by West Germany, who had ordered 66 and would build 200 under licence. If Canada chose the Lockheed, the company would place in Canada a substantial amount of the work involved in the 66 for Germany, provided the United States Air Force agreed and the Canadian government had approved the contract for the Air Division replacements by August. Any mutual aid offers would also be filled from the tooling placed in Canada for this purpose. The engine, which was the same for both aircraft, could also, in large part, be built economically in Canada. The bulk of the items for electronics and fire control were within the capabilities of the Canadian electronics industry and he recommended that they be produced in Canada. As regards production sharing generally, it was intended to offset what procurement had to be done in the United States by using every effort to have sub-contract work for common programmes or for American procurement placed in Canada.

There were three possible methods of choosing the contractor for the airframe: allocate to Canadair on a negotiated price basis; request proposals from Canadair, de Havilland and Avro with firm prices on as many elements of the programme as possible, in order to assess the competitive position of each company; or allocate to Avro on a negotiated price basis.

Canadair's manpower level was 9,300 now but by 1961 it would be reduced to 1,000. This level would be uneconomic, but the company had to be maintained in operation as it would be supporting most of the other aircraft used by the R.C.A.F. Canadair had a successful record of manufacturing under licence with several firms, including Lockheed; it had made successful inroads in the commercial field, and any serious drop in employment would adversely affect its ability to continue in this field.

- 3 -

The contract for items in the BOMARC programme would be seriously affected if employment were to decline drastically; and, finally, if Canadair received the airframe contract, the Department of Defence Production would ensure that a reasonable share of work would be given to Canadair's existing sub-contractors.

If de Havilland were the successful bidder, it would have to act as a programme manager, subcontracting the majority of the work because it did not have sufficient space for manufacturing.

If Avro received the contract, the company would have to build up a large labour force again and then reduce again to less than the present levels. If it, or Avro had no firm programme for the future. If it, or de Havilland, received the business, the Canadair problem would remain to be solved.

Ideally, requesting the three companies to bid on a fair price basis was the best approach. But firm price bidding was unrealistic in the present circumstances.

As for the engines, there were two possibilities for production: Canadian Pratt Whitney or Orenda Engines Limited. It would, however, be an incompatible situation if a subsidiary of Pratt Whitney were chosen to manufacture a General Electric engine, as the two firms were direct competitors in the United States.

The Minister recommended,-

(a) that the Lockheed F-104G be selected as the replacement for the Sabre squadrons in Europe;

(b) that the airframe contract be allocated to Canadair Limited on an incentive type contract; and,

(c) that the engine contract be allocated to Orenda Engines Limited, on a firm price basis.

An explanatory memorandum was circulated, (Minister's aide memoire, undated).

2. The Minister without Portfolio (Mr. Macdonnell) said that it was the Minister of Finance's understanding that this matter would not be considered in his absence.

3. The Minister of National Defence said it would be very embarrassing to him when his estimates were before the House on Thursday next to announce that the Air Division was being re-equipped but not to be able to say with what aircraft. The Minister of Finance was more concerned with the allocation of contracts and the details involved, not the choice as such.

- 4 -

4. Mr. Pearkes added that the Cabinet Defence Committee had had the report of the Minister of Defence Production before it at its last meeting. Since then the Chiefs of Staff had discussed the matter further with Defence Production officials, and had stated that they would be willing to go along with a decision to re-equip the Air Division with the Lockheed F-104G.

5. During the discussion the following points emerged:

(a) If it were decided to acquire the Lockheed, $14 million worth of work would be placed in Canada in respect of the 66 machines being purchased by Germany.

(b) It was undesirable for Canadair to be given most of the work, in view of the fact that it was fairly busy now and in the light of Avro's position following the cancellation of the Arrow. The Minister of National Defence, in his opening statement on his estimates, should make it quite clear that the Arrow could not have been used for the strike attack role in Europe.

(c) The implication of the views of the Chiefs of Staff was that they would prefer a better aircraft than the F-104G if more money were available. It would be highly embarrassing if, at some time in the future after the government had announced a decision to purchase the F-104G, it became known that the Chiefs of Staff were, on military grounds, in favour of a different and presumably more efficient type of aircraft. The Chiefs of Staff should be asked to submit a firm recommendation on the F-104G, taking into account all the factors involved, before the Cabinet reached a decision.

(d) Assuming a decision was taken now on the type of aircraft, the Air Division would not be completely re-equipped for five years. It would probably be another five years after that before the Lockheed or the Grumman would cease to be effective.

6. The Cabinet approved the choice of the Lockheed F-104G to re-equip 8 squadrons of the Air Division in Europe subject to receiving a firm recommendation from the Chiefs of Staff for it, and subject to discussion of the matter with the Minister of Finance before announcement.

Start Here 7/2/59

- 2 -   SECRET

Choice of aircraft to replace F-86 for the Air Division
in Europe
(Previous reference June 30)

1.   The Prime Minister said he and the Minister of National Defence had discussed this question further and had agreed on the words to be used in the opening statement on the debate on the National Defence estimates. The Minister of Finance had concurred. It would be said that the Lockheed F-104G would be selected as the replacement provided agreement could be reached with the Lockheed Aircraft Corporation on cost, production sharing and other contractual terms.

2.   The Minister of Defence Production said that discussions had been held with Lockheed concerning the licensing arrangements for manufacturing the F-104G. The cost of these would total $3 million for the basic licence, $20,000 per aircraft up to 200 aircraft and $15,000 for each aircraft over 200 aircraft and 5 per cent royalty on spares over the lifetime of the aircraft. This latter item would be 5 per cent on roughly $100 million worth of business.

He wished to have the approval of Cabinet to invite proposals from Canadair, Avro and de Havilland for the production of the airframe and the management contract. He proposed that manufacture of the engine be allocated to Orenda Engines Ltd. It was important to settle the contract by August 17th so that Canadian companies could share in the production of the 66 104's ordered by West Germany. When proposals were received, his department would scrutinize them carefully and then forward them to the Treasury Board.

3.   During the discussion it was said that, while a good case could be made for allocating the contract for the engine, it was risky to depart from the tender principle for the airframe and the management contract. The government should not allow itself to be charged with favouritism in such an important contract as this.

4.   The Cabinet,-

(a)   confirmed the decision that the Lockheed F-104G aircraft be selected to replace the F-86 in the Air Division in Europe;

(b)   agreed that the contract for the production of the engine for the F-104G be allocated to Orenda Engines Ltd; and,

(c)   authorized the Minister of Defence Production to invite proposals from Avro, Canadair and de Havilland for the production of the airframe and for the management contract for the production of the aircraft as a whole.

- 5 -   SECRET

(g)   In presenting the current proposal, emphasis should be placed on misleading advertising.

(h)   Merchants were pressing for government assistance by way of credit to small businesses. They were more interested in this than the bill to amend the Combines Act. In the circumstances, it would be wiser to drop the latter and introduce something more substantial for small business next year.

7.   The Cabinet agreed that the Minister of Justice request the unanimous consent of the House of Commons to withdraw the order for second reading of the bill to amend the Combines Investigation Act and the Criminal Code, in order that he could introduce a new bill containing only the provisions in the present bill for the protection of small business and a clause to deal with the fishing situation in British Columbia.

Start Here 7/7/59

Authorization to photograph Arrow aircraft
(Previous reference July 2)

8.   The Cabinet agreed that now that the classified equipment on the surplus Arrow (CF-105) aircraft had been removed, there would be no objection to authorizing photographs of the aircraft itself for publication.

Start Here 7/9/59

Cost of Lockheed F-104G programme

9.   The Cabinet agreed that the Minister of Defence Production should give to the House of Commons soon the government's estimate of $420 million for the cost of the new Lockheed F-104G programme, in order to offset the erroneous impression that the programme would cost approximately $250 million.

Gut Dam claims; alternative course of action
(Previous reference July 3)

10.   The Secretary of State for External Affairs reviewed the history of the claims arising out of the construction of the Gut Dam in the St. Lawrence River which had been built in 1903 and removed in 1953. He noted that the International Lake Ontario Board of Engineers, established by the International Joint Commission to consider the problem of regulation of water levels of Lake Ontario, had submitted reports on the subject, one of which dealt with the effects of the Gut Dam on the level of Lake Ontario. He reviewed a number of alternative courses of action which might be followed for disposing of the claims and made recommendations as to how the government might now proceed in this matter.

An explanatory memorandum had been circulated, (Memorandum, Secretary of State for External

---

- 5 -

boundary, in exchange for the transfer to British Columbia of that portion of the Northwest Territories lying west of a northerly prolongation of the Alberta-British Columbia boundary. The Minister had replied that greater detail would be needed for the consideration of such a proposal, and he believed the Premier would make fuller representations. He observed that the cost of maintaining the highway was about $17 millions per annum.

The Minister further commented that such a transfer of territory had far-reaching implications. It might lead to similar proposals from the three Prairie provinces affecting those portions of the Northwest Territories lying north of each of them.

13.   The Cabinet noted the report of the Minister of National Defence on his conversation with the Premier of British Columbia regarding possible arrangements for the maintenance and administration of the Alaska highway.

Start Here 8/10/59

Lockheed F-104G; allocation of contracts
(Previous reference July 7)

14.   The Minister of Finance said that, prior to the next meeting of the Cabinet, the Treasury Board expected to give consideration to the allocation of contracts for the production of the Lockheed F-104G.

15.   The Minister of Defence Production reported that Belgium had adopted this aircraft and hoped to arrange for its manufacture in Canada. Similar action was expected by the Netherlands and possibly Switzerland, and Australia and Japan were actively interested in this aircraft. He had also learned that the Lockheed F-104G, even before improvement of ejection seat arrangements, had experienced the second lowest mortality rate of the ten operational types used by the U.S. Air Force.

16.   The Cabinet noted the reports of the Ministers of Finance and Defence Production regarding progress in the allocation of contracts for the production of the Lockheed F-104G and regarding prospects for its manufacture in Canada for other countries.

Retirement; Auditor-General

17.   The Minister of Finance referred to the recent resignation of Mr. Watson Sellar as Auditor-General on attaining the age of sixty-five. The Minister explained that, as the Auditor-General was an officer of Parliament, the Cabinet had no authority to extend an incumbent's tenure beyond that age. Further, Mr. Sellar had not been prepared to continue in office because he believed another person should be appointed at this time. He had agreed to continue actively in office until his sixty-fifth birthday, instead of adopting the usual practice of proceeding on leave six months earlier. The Treasury Board was therefore giving consideration to the payment of a proposed allowance equal to six months' salary.

260

- 3 -

Start Here
8/13/59

Allocation of contract for Lockheed F-104G
(Previous reference Aug. 10)

3. **The Minister of Defence Production** reported that tenders for the manufacture of the Lockheed F-104G had been received from de Havilland, Canadair and Avro aircraft. The bid of de Havilland was almost 50 per cent higher than the other two who had provided almost identical tenders. De Havilland apparently did not have facilities to manufacture the plane itself and had to go to sub-contract for most of the work. The figure of Avro was slightly lower than that of Canadair but did not appear realistic.

4. **Mr. O'Hurle** pointed out that the time element was of essence and, of the three companies, Canadair, owing to the fact that it had past experience in producing Lockheed aircraft under licence, was in a more favourable position. A decision had to be reached on the allocation of the contract prior to the 17th of August if contracts in connection with the manufacture of 66 Lockheed aircraft for West Germany were to be obtained.

It was the view of the Department of Defence Production that it would not be possible to support three major aircraft firms in Canada. Canadair Ltd. had been markedly more successful in commercial sales than Avro which seemed to have made no effort in obtaining commercial contracts. If the contract were awarded to Canadair other government contracts would benefit as a result of lower overhead, which would mean a saving up to $12.5 million over a five-year period; furthermore, the company would be in a position to assign experienced workers to this programme as other contracts phased out. Avro, on the other hand, would have to build up a large labour force again for a short period of time and then reduce to probably less than its present manpower level. On the other hand, an award to Avro would be of benefit to the Canadian government in that the Crown would be relieved of the payment of $2 million under the terms of the Capital Equipment Agreement. On the overall basis award of the contract to Canadair would result in a saving of approximately $9,750,000.

5. **The Minister of Finance** said that allocation of this contract had been carefully examined by the Treasury Board. The Board had come to the conclusion that the proposal by Canadair was the most advantageous to the Crown in terms of cost, realism of the estimate and demonstrated ability to perform generally and to manufacture on a licence arrangement in particular. The Board has also noted that the manufacture of the engine, of almost equal dollar and employment size to the airframe manufacture was being allocated to Orenda Engines of Malton, Ontario. The Board had also agreed that the manufacture of the aircraft by Canadair would provide a more stable aircraft industry, while awarding it to Avro would require a rebuilding of that company's work force with a serious re-adjustment of employment being required once again in a relative short period of time.

- 4 -

He also pointed out that the Board had felt that the main terms of any contract with a successful company should be accepted before the choice was finally made. The firmest possible arrangement should be secured in order to place upon the company the responsibility for successful management of the contract in financial as well as technical terms. The Board had recommended that Canadair be offered the first opportunity to make its proposal a firm bid on the basis that its proposed cost be the actual cost ceiling price, the cost to the Crown to be the actual cost of manufacture up to that amount, with the manufacturer to receive a reasonable proportion of the savings which would arise if the actual cost fell below the ceiling. On such terms, the company would have to accept financial responsibility for completion of the contract on the basis of its own proposal.

6. **Mr. Fleming**, in addition, pointed out that, in order to limit the incidence of change in design (they had been frequent during the development contracts of the CF-105), the Board had suggested that in its approval of any contract that major changes would have to be approved by the Board or the Cabinet and that the course of the contract be monitored closely by a senior committee of officials from the Department of National Defence, the Department of Defence Production and the Treasury Board Secretariat.

Explanatory memoranda were circulated, (Aide Memoire, Aircraft Branch, Department of Defence Production. Aug. 11, 1959 and Memorandum, Chairman, the Treasury Board, Aug. 12 - Cab. Doc. 243-59).

7. **During the discussion** the following points were raised:

(a) It would not be profitable to obtain a new figure from de Havilland since they were obliged to sub-contract a very large part of the work. To some, this might have the advantage of spreading the work across the country. This advantage, however, was greatly offset by the fact that the de Havilland's figure was almost 50 per cent higher than its competitors.

(b) By awarding the contract to Canadair, the government would, of course, find itself in a position of having to defend the award to the second lowest bid. The Defence Production Department had added $3.3 million to the Canadair bid on the assumption that labour costs might rise. However, Canadair had given the assurance that there would be no escalation on labour or material. Therefore, by removing this amount of $3.3 million the difference between Avro and Canadair had been reduced to $1.3 million. Canadair had a series of contracts with the government which would cause a reduction in overhead over the life of the proposed contract. Avro on the other hand, had no prospects for future commercial work. This would, of course, cause an increase in overhead.

- 4 -

(c) If estates were authorized to purchase Canada Savings Bonds there would be some loss in the market for regular bond issues, since estates had been major investors in regular issues. Furthermore, as the savings bonds were redeemable at any time, even the initial net gain might shrink later through resale of savings bonds.

(d) On the other hand, the admission of estates as eligible purchasers would remove an unnecessary restriction which might have been an irritant in some quarters. Estates appeared less likely to redeem savings bonds quickly than most other kinds of purchasers. Moreover, their investment in savings bonds, though perhaps offset to a degree by reduced purchases of regular issues, would still leave a net gain in borrowings.

11. The Cabinet,-

(a) approved the recommendation of the Minister of Finance for the issue of Canada Savings Bonds, including an increase in individual salesmen's commissions from 3/4 per cent to 1 per cent; and,

(b) agreed that estate funds, but not other forms of trusts, be authorized to invest in Canada Savings Bonds.

(An order in council was passed accordingly; P.C. 1959-1043, Aug. 14).

Start Here 8/14/59

Allocation of contract for Lockheed F-104G airframe
(Previous reference Aug. 13)

12. The Prime Minister suggested that a final review of the considerations affecting the allocation of the contract for the production of the Lockheed F-104G would be useful.

13. During the discussion the following points were raised:

(a) Award to A.V. Roe would make certain the operation of the Malton plant for at least two or three years, and would offset the local disappointment about the abandonment of the Arrow programme.

(b) Disregarding secondary economies, the A.V. Roe proposal had quoted the lowest price. On the other hand, on an overall basis the proposal of Canadair was the lowest by a margin of $9,350,000. This net saving would be achieved through lower overhead charges on other government work if the award were made to Canadair.

- 5 -

(c) As a matter of policy, it was desirable to divide the work between the competitors in different areas. The contract for the engine had already been awarded to Orenda, a subsidiary of A.V. Roe. This would add some 3,600 workmen to the working force at Orenda. The engine represented 31 per cent of the cost of the aircraft, and the airframe 36 per cent. Therefore, if the airframe were allocated to Canadair the division of the work between the Toronto and the Montreal area would be approximately equal.

(d) If the award were not made to Canadair, up to 8,000 workmen would be laid off there in 1961 unless the plant meanwhile obtained additional orders.

(e) The fundamental question was whether Canada could afford to maintain three major aircraft plants. The industry was overexpanded, and it seemed unlikely that requirements for piloted aircraft or for missiles in the foreseeable future would be sufficient to keep all three plants in full operation.

(f) The Canadair plant, though owned by a U.S. parent company, could reasonably be regarded as a Canadian establishment. It received no orders from the parent company.

(g) Canadair had taken the initiative of seeking private orders, whereas A.V. Roe had failed to do so and had merely disintegrated.

(h) If given the contract, Canadair would give subcontracts on a widely decentralized basis, ranging from the Maritime provinces to Fort William.

(i) An award to A.V. Roe at this time, several months after the cessation of the Arrow programme, would be criticized.

(j) Even if A.V. Roe received the contract it would merely postpone the evil day. It would inflate the working force for a brief period, with a serious readjustment of employment being required once again in a relatively short time. An award to Canadair, on the other hand, would help to provide the basis for a stable aircraft industry.

- 6 -

14. The Cabinet agreed,-

(a) that the contract for the manufacture of the Lockheed F-104G airframe should be allocated to Canadair;

(b) that a public announcement should be prepared as quickly as possible by the Ministers directly affected, and submitted to the Prime Minister for approval. The release would be made by the Minister of Defence Production; and,

(c) that the announcement should refer to the general policy of spreading government contracts between different geographical areas wherever possible; to the fact that the engine contract had recently been awarded to Orenda, a subsidiary of A.V. Roe; and to the fact that the award of the airframe contract to Canadair would save the Treasury about $9,350,000.

Pan American Games 1963; request from City of Winnipeg for financial assistance

15. The Minister of Finance said that a request by the City of Winnipeg for financial assistance in connection with the 1963 Pan American Games had been considered by the Treasury Board. As the City had not yet been selected as the site of the Games, the Board had recommended that no commitment of assistance be made at this stage. A reply to this effect had been drafted.

The Minister recalled that no assurance of aid had been given to the City of Vancouver until after its official selection as the site of the British Empire and Commonwealth Games. Winnipeg had requested the sum of $600,000 each from the Federal and Provincial governments. The Premier of Manitoba had written stating that the Province would contribute $200,000 and recommending that a matching grant be made by the Federal government; he had further requested that up to $100,000 be made available to assist athletes from various parts of North and South America with their travelling expenses.

16. During the brief discussion it was noted that a non-committal response might make it impossible for the City to proceed with its application.

17. The Cabinet agreed that Mr. Churchill should speak informally to the Premier of Manitoba stating that, if the City of Winnipeg should be officially selected as the site of the 1963 Pan American Games, the Federal government would be prepared to make a matching grant of $200,000 to the City and also to make available a sum not exceeding $100,000 to assist athletes from various parts of North and South America with their travelling expenses.

- 2 -

Appointment to the Board of Trustees of the Queen
Elizabeth II Canadian Fund to Aid in Research on
the Diseases of Children
(Previous reference June 25)

1. The Prime Minister said that it would
be essential to have a woman on the Board of Trustees
of the Queen Elizabeth II Canadian Fund to Aid in
Research on the Diseases of Children. The name of
Dr. Norma Ford Walker, of Toronto, had been suggested.
It would be appropriate to find out who she was and
what were her qualifications.

2. During the brief discussion, the name
of Dr. Patterson, a Vancouver paediatrician, was
suggested. There was some feeling that a prominent
doctor with administrative ability such as Dr. Stuart
Finlayson, President of the Children's Memorial Hospital
in Montreal, should be on the Board.

3. The Cabinet agreed to give further
consideration at the next meeting to possible appointments
to the Board of Trustees of the Queen Elizabeth II
Canadian Fund to Aid in Research on the Diseases of Children.

Allocation of contract for Lockheed
F-104G
(Previous reference Aug. 14)

**Start Here
8/19/59**

4. The Cabinet agreed that the Department
of Defence Production be immediately informed that the
decision taken by Cabinet on August 14th with respect
to the awarding of the contract for the manufacture of
the Lockheed F-104G airframe did not include approval
of the suggested procedure for allocating a contract
to a selected contractor for the manufacture of the
fire control and associated electronic systems (para.
C of the aide-memoire dated August 11th, circulated
by the Minister of Defence Production), and that the
Department should take no action on this particular
contract until it had been considered by Cabinet on
the return of the Minister of Defence Production.

Exchange of Ambassadors with Poland

5. The Secretary of State for External
Affairs raised the question of a possible exchange of
Ambassadors with Poland. He thought it would be
appropriate to raise the status of the Canadian Mission
in Warsaw for the following reasons:-

(a) If Canada declined to exchange
Ambassadors as the Poles had proposed
and could not give a valid explanation,
the action might be interpreted by the
Polish government as a deliberate rebuff.
The Polish suggestion was in fact based
on an earlier Canadian proposal for an
exchange and, in fact, the Cabinet had
noted with approval in November of 1957,
that the Secretary of State for External

- 11 -

26. During the discussion it was pointed out
that the Governor in Council had to take a positive step
to extend the right; it did not follow merely as a
matter of course. Parliament had provided that the
right could be extended and had established the necessary
procedures for this to be done. The law and regulations
had been fully complied with and there was no reason
why the request of the bands should be denied. Liquor
privileges so far granted to Indians in the last little
while had not aroused interest or controversy. If
consumption on the reserves proved to be an unwise
policy, Parliament could be requested to amend the Act.

27. The Cabinet agreed that the right to
possess and consume liquor on Indian reserves be extended
in Ontario in accordance with the appropriate provisions
of the Indian Act.

Royal Commission on Energy;
Second Report
(Previous reference Oct. 25, 1958)

28. The Cabinet agreed that the Second
Report of the Royal Commission on Energy be formally
submitted to the Governor General.

(An order in council was passed accordingly;
P.C. 1959-1140, Sept. 2.)

Lockheed F-104G; allocation of contract for fire control
and electronic system
(Previous reference Aug. 19)

**Start Here
9/5/59**

29. The Minister of Defence Production said it
was proposed to build four-fifths of the F-104G(CF-111)
fire control system (NASARR) in Canada at an estimated
cost of $28 million. The system would have to undergo
several changes; its design was not complete and no
drawings or specifications existed at the moment.
Any delay in manufacturing would retard the F-104G
programme as a whole. The R.C.A.F. equipment was to be
largely the same as the German Air Force NASARR requirement
but the Germans wanted an air to air computer while
the R.C.A.F. wanted a missile launch computer and a GE
bombing computer. The development costs were estimated
at $6 million, to be shared evenly by West Germany
and Canada. The cost ($1 million) of developing the
GE bombing computer would be Canada's responsibility
alone. The Germans wanted to import 66 radars for the
aircraft being built by Lockheed Corporation.

The Electronics Branch of the Department of
Defence Production had conducted a comprehensive survey
of existing facilities in Canada capable of making
airborne electronics to determine which company was best
suited for the job. It was felt that competitive
tenders would not provide a solution to achieve lowest
cost and satisfactory delivery and technical performance.

SECRET

- 12 -

There was nothing on which to base a realistic estimate, to which a contractor could be held. Two teams, each member of which had made an individual estimate, one from the Department of Defence Production and the other from Autonetics Division, North American Aviation Corporation (sole owners of the NASARR system) had visited the following four companies who had requested consideration as possible prime contractors:

Canadian Aviation Electronics Ltd.
R.C.A. Victor Company Ltd.
Canadian General Electric Co. Ltd.
Canadian Westinghouse Company Ltd.

All members of the survey teams had come to the conclusion that Canadian Westinghouse Company led by a considerable margin in every important department as far as facilities were concerned. The company had gained extensive experience in advanced airborne electronics on the Velvet Glove programme, the Sparrow Seeker and the current "Bright Light" programme.

The Minister again stressed the fact that the fire control system was the pacing item for the aircraft and recommended that the Canadian Westinghouse Company, on the basis of having demonstrated the greatest technical competence to handle the job, be nominated as contractor for the manufacture of the NASARR fire control system.

Explanatory memoranda were circulated, (Minister's memorandum, undated, Cab. Doc. 262-59, Memorandum to the Minister from G.W. Hunter, Sept. 1, 1959 - Cab. Doc. 265-59).

30. During the discussion the following points were raised:

(a) Some felt that proposals should be called for from the companies which could make the system, as had been done recently for the manufacture of the airframe. This procedure had given the government the benefit of a target price, plus any savings achieved, in the proportion of two-thirds to the government and one-third to the manufacturer. Since four companies in Canada were interested in the contract, the government would find itself in an invidious position if it did not adhere to the general principle of calling for tenders as it were and, instead, placed itself in the hands of one contractor and that on a cost plus basis.

SECRET

- 13 -

On the other hand, for this particular type of contract, tendering by several companies, some of whom were not clearly competent to do the job, would really be a "liars' contest". How could the government protect itself against the possibility of a company not really able to do the job bidding lower than one which could?

(b) In fairness, and to avoid adverse political repercussions, there seemed to be no reason why representatives from the four manufacturers could not go to the U.S. to be briefed by Autonetics and to be given afterwards the same opportunity to put in proposals. The Department of Defence Production, it was true, was of the opinion that Canadian Westinghouse was the logical and proper choice to manufacture NASARR in Canada, because they were the one company at the present who had the basic facility, organization, personnel, experience and developed techniques to begin immediately on the programme. Timing was a vital consideration. If competitive tenders were called, companies would have to be security cleared and briefed in the U.S. In addition, time would have to be spent in preparing proposals, etc., and as much as three months might elapse. It was not clearly established what effect the three months might have.

(c) At the outset it would be necessary to purchase 49 units from U.S. sources (estimated cost per unit: $70,000). If delays made it necessary to purchase another 50 from the U.S. or perhaps more, then it would be most uneconomical to manufacture the remaining sets required in Canada. Here again timing was of the essence.

(d) It was not clear why the R.C.A.F. wanted to increase the power of the system from 75 to 250 kilowatts, nor whether they would not - as under previous contracts - press for other changes from time to time. The change in the role of the aircraft probably accounted for the required modifications. The 104 was an interceptor, while the 104G was for reconnaissance and strike.

SECRET

- 14 -

(e) It would appear desirable to have the matter referred to the Cabinet Defence Committee for further consideration in the presence of officials who would be called on to give technical explanations.

31. The Cabinet agreed that the question of selecting a contractor for the manufacture of the CF-111 fire control and electronic system be referred to the Cabinet Defence Committee for further consideration and report.

R.B. Bryce,
Secretary to the Cabinet.

With much appreciation...

Jozef H. VanVeenen

Incredible work in
record time.

Ken Barnes

Jim Macleod

Peter Brennan

Ed Patton

Dane Lanken

Smoothing the bumps.
Going with the flow
right to the end from
coop to cover.

Wilf Farrance

Les Wilkinson

Joan Leonardo

Jan Zurakowski

Encouragements

Barb Aubrey
Marvin Barber
Jeff Bird
Peter Bullman
Ed Burtt
June Callwood
Mark Chappell
Tom Dugelby
Ron Gould
Paul Hellyer
Sylvan Lanken
Larry Milberry
Greg Newell

Ron Page
Bob Pearson
Ross Richardson
Dave Thompson
Marc André Valiquette
Peter Wadell
Red Wilson
Christie Family
Holmes Family
Wilkinson Family

...and many more!

Lynn Macnab for continued support, suggestions and
the scrapbook idea.

Acknowledgements

Staff at NAM, NRC, DHIS/HER, National Archives, DSIS,
CWH, Parry Sound Museum, Camtec Photo, Various
Airshows, EAA, RAA and flying club organizations.
Many thanks for those who financially supported the
publishing of the scrapbook. Without your help the
real story of the Arrow could not have been revealed.

Video-stills provided for *The Arrow Scrapbook* by Jim Lloyd of Aviation Videos Limited

The Story Behind the Videos

My introduction to the Avro Arrow occurred back in 1969 while I was attending college. Up to that point I had little knowledge of the Arrow or its tragic demise 10 years earlier. I vividly remember that time when I first saw a film on the Arrow. Following the screening, a number of the college staff who worked at Avro spoke about their involvement with the Arrow program. The film was only 12 minutes long, but it sparked an interest in the Arrow that has lasted to this day.

Eighteen years later in the summer of 1987 I started thinking about the Arrow film that I had seen many years before. By that time I had a part-time audio-visual business and the possibility of making a video production on the Arrow seemed like an exciting project. Thus through the late summer of 1987 and into the winter I worked on my first video production, and this culminated in "Avro Arrow, CF-105...A short History" in February 1988. By coincidence I completed it in time for the 30th anniversary of the Arrow's first flight on March 25, 1959, which proved to be an excellent launch for the video.

Since that time I have completed three additional videos on the Arrow along with numerous other productions on Canadian aviation history. For the CBC mini-series "The Arrow" I provided some of the actual Arrow footage used throughout the docu-drama.

All of my productions are recognized as excellent quality documentaries and are sold in aviation museums, specially stores, and hobby stores across Canada and into the U.S.

James Lloyd
Aviation Videos Limited

Videos On The Avro Arrow

• Arrow From Dream To Destruction
• Avro Arrow Computer Animation
• Avro Arrow
  CF-105...A Short History
• Testing The Arrow Design
  CF-105 Avro Arrow Enthusiast Edition

• The Arrow...
  CBC-TV Mini-Series
• The Legend Of The Arrow
  The Making of "The Arrow"

To Order Videos contact:
Aviation Videos Limited, Toll Free 1-888-215-8290
Web Site: www.aviationvideos.com/avs/

Bibliography

Campagna, Palmiro, *Storms of Controversy*,
Stoddart Publishing Co. Ltd., Toronto, 1992
(first edition) and 1997 (second edition)

Carson, Don & Drendel, Lou, *F-106 DELTA DART in Action*,
Squadron/Signal Publications, 1974

Dorr, Robert F., *The Great Jet Fighters Inside*,
Motorbooks International Publishers, USA, 1996

Dow, James, *The Arrow*,
James Lorimer & Company, Toronto, 1997

Gunston, Bill, *Early Supersonic Fighters of the West*,
Ian Allan Limited, Shepperton, Surrey, 1976

Hellyer, Paul, *Surviving the Global Financial Crisis*,
Chemo Media Limited, Toronto, 1996

Kinsey, Beret F-4C, *F-4D & RF-4C PHANTOM II, Volume 43*,
Airlife Publishing, England 1994

Page, Ron, Ricard Organ, Don Watson, Les Wilkinson,
Avro Arrow, Boston Mills Press, Toronto, 1980,
Revised edition 1992

Peden, Murray, *Fall of an Arrow*,
Stoddart Publishing Co. Ltd., Toronto, 1987

Ragay, J.D., *F-102 Delta Dagger in Europe*,
Squadron/Signal Publications, Texas

Reithmaier, Larry, *MACH 1 and Beyond*,
TAB Books, McGraw-Hill Inc., USA, 1995

Shaw, E.K., *There Never Was an Arrow, 2nd edition*,
Steel Rail Education Publishing, Ottawa, 1982

Siuru, Bill, John D. Busick, *Future Flight, 2nd edition*,
TAB Aero, McGraw-Hill, Inc. Bule Ridge Summit,
PA, 1964

Smith, H.C. "Skip", *The Illustrated Guide to Aerodynamics,
2nd edition*, TAB Books, McGraw-Hill, Inc. USA 1992

Stewart, Greig, *The Life and Times of Crawford Gordon
and the Avro Arrow*, McGraw-Hill Ryerson Limited, Whitby,
Ontario, 1998

Stewart, Greig, *Shutting Down the National Dream*,
McGraw-Hill Ryerson Limited, Whitby, Ontario 1997

Wings of Fame, Aerospace Publishing Ltd.,
England, 1996

National Archives Of Canada

Call no. RG 2, series A5a, volume 1899, August '58 to December '58

Call no. RG2, series A5a, volumes 2744, 2745, 2749, 2752, January '59 to September '59

Call no. RG 24, series 83/84/167, volumes 6420-6439, file name 1038 CN 180

Call no. RG 24, ACC 1997-98/260, file name 1038 CN 179, 180, 183-6, 189

Call no. RG 24, series 110, 121, 61, C6772/3/4

Call no. RG 24, vol. 433, file 159-RA-17, 1957-1960

Call no. RG 49, vol. 423, file 159-29-6-1, 1955-1956

Call no. RG 49, vols. 781-782, file 207-6-3, pts. 1-5, 1959-1963

Call no. RG 49, vol. 5, file 159-RA-26, 1952-1965

Call no. RG 49, vol. 11, file 159-RO-18, 1959-1963

Call no. RG 49, vol. 12, file 159-RO-02-1, 1959-1962

Call no. RG 49, vol. 434, file 159-RO-5, pts 1-2, 1953-1959

Call no. RG 49, vol. 433, file 161-4-9, pts 1-2,

Call no. RG 98, vol. 68, p1-31, 80/81-2

Call no. RG 98, vol. 260, box 76/77, file name 1038 CN 179, 180, 183-6 189

Department of National Defence
Directorate of History and Heritage

Raymont Collection, file nos. 73/1223 series 1, file 15, 73/783, 72/550, 72/552, 77/619, 77/620, 77/506, 79/27, 79/333, RAC/72

Diaries for Hendriks, Air Vice Marshall, Air Member for Technical Service

National Aviation Museum Library,
Circa 100 files

National Research Council,
Parkin Library, circa 800 files

CRAD,
directorate of Scientific Information Service, circa 150 files

270

Become a member!

Inspiring a new generation by rebuilding the Avro Arrow

Complete static display model plus a full-scale flying replica

Contact Us

Phone/Fax: (613) 874-2838

E-mail: director@arrow-alliance.com

Website: www.arrow-alliance.com

Address: 21570, The Laggan Road

R.R. #1, Dalkeith, Ontario K0B 1E0

Initial Membership Includes

Individual member
- 1 Scrapbook
- 1 Arrow Pin
- Certificate
- Interactive www-newsletter

Individual Patron
As individual member plus:
- Framed Certificate
- Name engraved on both models for all time
- Arrow Model
- Scholarship Presentation

Corporate Member
- 5 Books/Pins
- Plaque
- Arrow Model
- Sponsor of 1 Arrow Scholarship
- Company Name on plane
- Annual List
- Choose participating school
- newsletter

Corporate Sponsor
- 20 Books/Pins
- Plaque
- Arrow Model
- Sponsor of 10 Arrow Scholarships
- Publicity Package
- Access to Scholars in all programs
- Corporate name and logo featured on plane and all literature
- Newsletter

☐ **Individual Member**

Intial membership $50.00
Annual Renewal $25.00

☐ **Individual Patron**

$1000.00
Life

☐ **Coporate Member**

$5000.00
$3000.00

☐ **Coporate Sponsor**

$100,000
$75,000

Name: _____

Address: _____

E-mail: _____

Date: _____

Tel: _____

Fax: _____

Signature: _____

Thank you for becoming a member of the new Arrow Alliance. Items are in production and will be available as soon as possible.

Please make cheques payable to the "Arrow Alliance."
The Arrow Alliance gratefully accepts any and all donations of an intermediate nature. Tax receipt status pending.